Suzanne Grouêt
2007 South 7th Str.
232-4742

J. Mason

10^{13} 1470

860

860

124044

Principles of
Learning and
Memory

Principles of *Learning* *and* *Memory*

B. R. Bugelski

PRAEGER PUBLISHERS
Praeger Special Studies

New York • London • Sydney • Toronto

PRAEGER PUBLISHERS,
PRAEGER SPECIAL STUDIES
383 Madison Avenue, New York, N.Y., 10017, U.S.A.

Published in the United States of America in 1979
by Praeger Publishers,
A Division of Holt, Rinehart and Winston, CBS Inc.

9 038 987654321

Library of Congress Catalog Card Number: 78-19760

Printed in the United States of America

for Ricky

Preface

This is a book about what I think are the central ideas and issues in the field of learning. It is intended for anyone concerned with the general area of the psychology of learning. It is not written "down" or "up" for any particular class of students, and enough background is presented for anyone to follow the argument. It is, essentially, an argument or essay, with some rather dogmatic positions presented as approximations of the truth. It should be obvious that students and scholars are not expected to merely accept or endorse the writer's proposals—they are expected to consider them and refute them if they can. In the exercise of refutation, the issues can become clarified and appreciated.

The field of learning has expanded beyond anyone's attempts at mastery, and a great number of specialties have attracted different investigators. No single book can present enough data and documentation to satisfy each specialist. What I have tried to do is to present the classical and current issues that demark the field, with the expectation that interested students will pursue special concerns in the many fine books now available on each of the issues. The amount of reading that is required to cover the area is beyond anyone's capability. I have tried to remedy the student's difficulties in a small way by preparing a volume of abstracts (Bugelski 1975), which represents over 100 journal articles that might be useful for supplementary reading. The bibliography for this book cites other references for those whose energies permit.

In the 20 years since my last book in this area, there has been a veritable revolution in the research in the psychology of learning. Old questions were dropped without being answered as investigators turned to new and perhaps more promising issues. I have tried to indicate the nature of these new interests without sacrificing consideration of the original questions, most of which were first considered by rather ancient philosophers. The psychology of learning is an extension of the philosopher's concern with the nature of man and the association of ideas. It behooves the concerned student to take occasion now, if he or she has not done so before, to go back to Plato and Socrates; to the British associationists, who were reacting to Descartes; to Darwin; to Sechenov and Pavlov; and to the modern ethologists and social biologists, all of whom were and are concerned with man and his nature and how it has changed.

In the past few years, many new texts have appeared whose titles promise a treatment of the psychology of learning. One can justifiably question the need for another. My reason for offering this book is my lack of satisfaction with present texts, which neither do justice to the thinkers of the past nor give appropriate consideration to new developments. In my judgment, new findings in the fields of imagery, incidental learning, and perceptual learning (observation and imitation) are either ignored or underappreciated. The topic of imagery is commonly treated as a mnemonic aid instead of being recognized as a central principle. The facts of incidental learning have burgeoned to the point where the concept of processing must be regarded as a major learning question and which must lead to a re-evaluation of the role of reinforcement. In this text, reinforcement is regarded as the major controlling operation for behavior change but as of no functional importance in learning itself. The importance of perceptual learning in observational or imitational settings is given central importance in this book because, in my opinion, most learning is accomplished in "show and tell" situations. It is not suggested that all of the issues involved are assessed appropriately and are effectively resolved. They are raised, however, with the hope that psychologists who study learning will turn to examining the learning operations of people who are acquiring facts from books, from other media, and from each other. We are only beginning to learn about "free learning" in connected discourse. Here, research is sparse, and the field is not even outlined.

The aim of this book is to help the liberal arts student evaluate issues that confront him or her, as well as the average citizen, on a daily basis—issues in education, personal identity, and delinquent or disturbed behavior. The controversies that abound in these areas are not solved here; at best, only some clarification is anticipated.

In preparing this book, I had the benefit of advice and argument from many students, both undergraduate and graduate, as well as that of my colleagues, W. Leslie Barnette, Edward Hovorka, Kenneth Kurtz, and Erwin Segal, none of whom agrees with everything I said. They are in no way responsible for what dogmatism remains in this book or for any errors of fact or fancy. I am most especially grateful and obliged to Terri Wrazen, whose patience and efficiency were more than adequate to cope with the problems involved in turning my frequent "new and improved" versions of manuscript copy into a book.

B. R. Bugelski

Contents

		Page
PREFACE		vii
LIST OF TABLES AND FIGURES		xvi

PART I: THE HISTORICAL SETTING

INTRODUCTION	3

Chapter

1 THE PROBLEM	5
Where Do We Start?	7
Reism	9
Learning as an Inference	10
Some Paradoxes	13
The Unloyal Opposition	16

2 MAPPING OUT THE TERRITORY	18
Nativism versus Empiricism	18
Nativism	19
The Domain of Learning	27
Experimental Epistemology	29

3 THE ASSOCIATION OF IDEAS: FROM ARISTOTLE TO EBBINGHAUS	30
Aristotle and Contiguity	31
Concept of Isolation	32
The British Associationists	33
Redintegration	35
Psychology and Associations	36
Appendix on Mnemonics or Memory Tricks	40

PART II: THE EXPERIMENTAL APPROACH TO LEARNING

INTRODUCTION   47

4 EBBINGHAUS AND NONSENSE SYLLABLES   49

  Serial Order   50
  Nonsense Syllable Findings   50
  Evaluation   54

5 OF MICE AND MEN, MACHINES, AND MODELS   56

  Using Animals in Research   57
  Philosophy and Evolution: Descartes and Darwin   60
  Darwin and Evolution   62
  Another Paradox: You Learn What You Know   64
  Early and Late Learning   65
  Problem of Subjects in Learning Research   66
  Summary and a Question   67

6 CLASSICAL CONDITIONING   69

  Pavlov and Thorndike   70
  The Psychic Reflex   70
  The Conditional Reflex   71
  Conditioned Inhibition   80
  Interference Interpretations   81
  Pavlov's Position and Contribution   83
  Critical Attacks on Pavlov   85
  Summary   99

7 LEARNING BY DOING   101

  Instrumental Learning   101
  Conditioning and Learning   102
  Operant-Respondent Distinction   104
  Reinforcement Theory   105
  Trial and Error and Chance Success   107
  Law of Effect   107
  Law of Exercise   108
  Law of Readiness   109
  Law of Associative Shifting   109
  Law of Belongingness   110

The Decline of Punishment   110
A Basic Problem   111
Importance of Action   111
Hull and Primary Reinforcement   113
Law of Primary Reinforcement   113
Secondary Rewards and Secondary Drives   114
Secondary Drive   116
Skinner and Reinforcement   117
Evaluation of the Thorndikian Position   118

8 CHARACTERISTICS OF INSTRUMENTAL BEHAVIOR   121

Partial Reinforcement: Schedules of Reinforcement   122
Explanations of the Partial Reinforcement Effect   126
Contributions of the Instrumental School   126

9 WHAT IS LEARNED?   144

The Behaviorists   144
What Is Learned in Verbal Learning?   160
What Is Learned? A Pause to Reflect on the Answers   161
Mediation and Mediated Associations   163
What Is Learned? The Need for Integration   166

10 ATTEMPTS AT INTEGRATING LEARNING THEORIES   167

The Mowrer Theory—An Integration   168
Evaluation of Mowrer's Theory   175
Cybernetics and Feedback   176

PART III: THE COGNITIVE APPROACH

INTRODUCTION   183

11 THE ROLE OF IMAGERY IN LEARNING   185

Historical Background   185
Imagery as a Response   188
Imagery Research   189
Experimental Approaches to Imagery   190
The Image as a Hypothetical Construct   191
The Image as an Associated Response   192
Voluntary Behavior—Ideomotor Action   194
Imagery and Instrumental Behavior   196

Imagery and Meaning   197
Semantic Differential   200
Paivio's View of Meaning   200
Noble and Meaningfulness   201
Propositional Models   201
Imagery and Concepts   203
Abstract and Concrete   203
Static and Dynamic Imagery   205
Learning without Action   206
Summary   207

12 PERCEPTUAL LEARNING   **208**

The Nativist Issue Again   208
Responses to Stimulation   210
An Appraisal of the Gestalt Contribution   218
Two-Stage Learning   219
The Observing Response   220
Learning How to Learn: Formation of Learning Sets   220
Generalization and Discrimination   221
Undirected First-Stage Learning   225
Acquired Distinctiveness and Acquired Equivalence of Cues   227
The Observing Response as a Habit   229
The Second Stage of Learning   230

13 LEARNING BY SHOW AND TELL   **231**

Unlearned Knowledge   232
Learning by Seeing—Imitation   233
Early Denials of Imitation   234
Later Studies of Imitation   236
Imitation as Modeling: The Mowrer Explanation   236
Imitation and Imagery   237
Superstitition   240
Superstition and Imitation   242
Propaganda   243
Summary   244

14 VERBAL LEARNING   **245**

Nonsense Syllables from the Time of Ebbinghaus   245
Time and Learning   246
Spaced versus Massed Learning   247
Time as a "Hidden" Variable   248

Attempts to Integrate Nonsense Syllable Learning with
    Conditioning Principles   249
Nonsense Syllables as Useful Stimulus Materials   250
The New Verbal Learning   251
The Analysis of Learnability   252
The Innovation of Free Recall   254
New Methods in Verbal Learning   255
Animals and Language   257
The Behavioral Orientation   259
Learning and Reading   261
Strategies in Verbal Learning   262
The Orienting Task   265
Incidental Learning   266
Kinds of Orienting Tasks in Incidental Learning Studies   267
Incidental Learning: An Example   267
Anti-intentional Learning   269

15 VERBAL LEARNING AND PROCESSING   274

What Is Orienting?   274
Attention and Learning   276
The Orienting Reflex   277
Consequence of the Orienting Task   278
Processing   279
Processing as Activity   280
The Work of Learning   280
Understanding   281
Learning and Meaning   282
Research Problems in Connected Discourse   288
Studies of Learning of Connected Discourse   289

16 TRANSFER, PROACTION, AND RETROACTION—OR THE INFLUENCE OF THE PAST   292

Transfer of Training: Formal Transfer   292
Past and Future Experience   293
Retroactive and Proactive Inhibition   294
Interference Hypothesis   296
The Osgood Analysis   297
Effects of Past Experience on New and Old Learning   298
Osgood's Transfer and Retroaction Hypothesis   299
Negative Transfer in Proactive Interference   301
Nonspecific Transfer   304

17 RETENTION AND FORGETTING 307

Memory versus Retention 307
Availability and Accessibility 308
Kinds of Memory 308
The Nature of Long-Term Retention 312
The Course of Forgetting: Forgetting Curves 312
Methods of Measuring Retention 315
Variables in Forgetting 317
Theories of Forgetting 320
Forgetting and Extinction 324
Retrieval 325

PART IV: APPLICATIONS

INTRODUCTION 331

18 A THEORETICAL RECAPITULATION 332

A Theory of Learning 332
Basic Postulates 333
The Question of Why Associations Occur 335
Processing 337
The What of Association 338
Learning and Performance 339
Mediational Responses 341
Summary Statement 342

19 THE NATURE AND FUNCTION OF PUNISHMENT 343

Some Philosophical Views 343
Law and the Rational Man 344
The Determinist View 344
Reasons for Punishment 345
Definitions of Punishment 346
Aversive Stimulation 347
A Definition of Punishment 348
The Role or Function of Punishment 349
Temptation 353
Misbehavior and Morality 353
The Mowrer Theory of Neurotic Conflict 354
Nonneurotic Crime 355

20 A LEARNING APPROACH TO BEHAVIOR DISORDERS 357

Structural and Functional Disorders   357
Treatment of Symptoms   358
Learning and Misbehavior   358
Learning and Psychotherapy   359
Biofeedback   366

21 EDUCATION AND HOW TO STUDY   370

Learning and Being Taught   371
The Function of Teachers   372
Conditions for Learning   374
Learning Strategies   375
Learning through Reading   377
Learning from Lectures   378
Discrimination   379
Examples and Teaching   380
Student as Teacher   380
Learning as Invention   380
Learning and Forgetting: The Need for Tags   381
The Procrastination Problem   382
Warm-up   383
The Tired Student   383

BIBLIOGRAPHY   385
NAME INDEX   410
SUBJECT INDEX   415
ABOUT THE AUTHOR   421

LIST OF TABLES AND FIGURES

Table		Page
9.1	The Components of Classically Conditioned Associations	158
9.2	The Components of Instrumentally Conditioned Associations	162
14.1	Mean Recall Scores for 20 Words in or out of Sequence (Total) with or without Imagery Instructions	268
14.2	Some Samples of Incidental Learning Studies	270

Figure		
4.1	Serial learning curves based on classroom data	52
5.1	The evolution of a learned response	63
6.1	Theoretical curves of generalization favored by Hull (a), Hovland (b), and Guthrie (c)	78
6.2	The form of the eyelid blink over a brief time span	86
6.3	The wrong r_gs have been generated in Little Dennis	90
6.4	Habit-family hierarchy	91
6.5	A T-maze	94
6.6	The T-maze with starting leg reversed	95
6.7	Serial responses in typing the word "and"	98
6.8	Stimulus trace conditioning in a serial response	99
8.1	Stylized cumulative records of responses in extinction	125
8.2	Skinner's chaining demonstration box	131
8.3	Bisecting an angle. Step 1	137
8.4	The bisection completed	137
8.5	Proof of the bisection	138
9.1	A cell assembly	156
9.2	A phase sequence	156
9.3	A phase sequence with a motor outlet	157
11.1	Images or propositions?	202
12.1	Negative and positive stimulus objects differing in size	213
12.2	A positive generalization curve	213
12.3	A negative generalization (extinction) curve	214

12.4 The algebraic summation of the positive and negative curves   214

12.5 Organized and unorganized figures   218

12.6 The formation of learning sets   222

12.7 Faces differing in hair and eyebrow features   223

12.8 Stimulus differentiation   224

12.9 Association differentiation   224

16.1 The Osgood transfer and retroaction surface   300

16.2 Effect of identical stimuli in learning successive lists of
      paired-associates   303

17.1 Retention of the name of the sixth-grade teacher by people of
      different ages   314

I

The
Historical
Setting

INTRODUCTION

This book is made up of four parts. The first part deals with the general problem of what learning might be, the historical foundations of the speculations of philosophers, and other, nonlaboratory orientations. Parts II and III deal with experimental approaches. Part II covers the behavioral approach, which dominated American psychological thinking in the first half of this century. Part III deals with more recent developments, which have come to be considered as a more cognitive approach. Part IV deals with applications to problems of interest to every student—education, delinquency, and personality disorders.

In Part I, I try to clarify scientific and philosophical problems that underlie much of the thinking about learning. The analyses of armchair spectator–observers and the presumably more controlled observations of laboratory investigators will be compared. There is something of value in both, and it will be recognized that the problems which concern the modern student concerned Socrates and his predecessors. In general, two views dominate the field: one, the rationalist view, tries to reason its way through the problem area; the other, the empiricist view, tries to follow the facts of controlled observation. Commonly enough, we will find some theorists who follow both lines, developing a theoretical approach based on some facts and trying to deduce new facts on the bases of postulates generated from the earlier observations.

In Part I, we will follow the speculations of a string of philosophers who contributed to the evolving story of association theory. The philosophers were not so much concerned with learning as they were with memory and how the mind worked. While modern psychologists use different language, the problems are still pretty much the same. Complications arose when biology began to make some strides and opening the skull revealed not a mind but a brain. Later, biological discoveries of chromosomes and genes and their bearing on heredity created new problems. How much of our behavior is acquired? How much of it is traceable to our ancestry? The older philosophers assumed that everyone was born with certain "faculties," among which were will, intellect, and memory, and that these faculties accounted for, or were in charge of, our behavior. Their interest in heredity was minimal or nonexistent as far as behavior was concerned.

Today, psychologists no longer talk in terms of faculties as independent agencies controlling behavior. Instead, they regard man as an organism, a body with physical structures determined by heredity but with much of the behavior of that organism determined by experience in the environment. Such experience is commonly confused with, identified with, or related to, learning. Many psychologists tend to denigrate the role of heredity and, perhaps, overemphasize the influence of the environment. As an example, most psychologists in the United States would support the position that intelligence is more a product of learning, experience, and environmental influence than of heredity. There are notable exceptions, but the large majority opinion sides with environmental or learning interpretations of individual differences.

The modern computer has influenced psychological theorizing in many ways. The essence of a computer operation, discounting "hardware," is the program fed into it. A computer at work is said to be programmed. It can do certain things and not others because of its construction and program. In the same sense, the human organism is considered to be programmed by its experience within limits set by its structure. Some psychologists describe behavior as including some hereditary programming, although very few venture into specifics. There are no hard answers to questions such as, Is man aggressive by nature?

In this text, the major effort will be to describe the nature of learning and to explore its range and limitations. It will not be possible to answer all questions about the totality of behavior—other factors besides learning have roles to play, and they are the subjects of other texts. There will be enough problems relating to the nature of learning to take up all of anyone's time.

1

The Problem

By the time you get around to holding this book in your hands with some intention of reading it, or at least getting some idea of what is said in it, you will have already learned a great deal in your life. You were brought up by individuals who were involved in some way in your learning to talk, among a lot of other things, and you went to school, where you learned something about reading, writing, and arithmetic, again, among other things. In all probability, you did not especially want to go to school or learn anything except "how to drive a car." While you were learning whatever you did learn, you never *felt* yourself learning and probably never learned how you learned anything. Again, probably, if someone asked, you would be likely to say that when you were learning, it involved "working" at something until you "got it" or that it came about through practicing. Somewhere along the line, you picked up the notion that "practice makes perfect" or, at least, is necessary. The work part of it possibly was related to homework. The work involved in learning to drive was alright, fun even, but the work in algebra might have been less exciting or less eagerly sought after. How you "got" something might be difficult to explain.

If you are now called upon to teach someone else some operation, for example, how to tie shoelaces or a bow tie or how to read or go to the bathroom on appropriate occasions, you might not know much about how to go about the teaching task. But if you become a parent, you will need to know something about how to handle such problems, and even if you know how to do these things yourself, you might have a lot of trouble teaching a youngster. In all probability, the youngster will learn to do such things, grow up, and have the same problems with his or her youngsters.

If you decide you want to teach a child to read, you might have even more trouble. In a literal sense, you probably do not know the first thing about the teaching of reading. Nobody else seems to, and why should you be an exception? What is the first thing to consider about teaching someone to read? Would you start with letters, words, or pictures? If you were to start with letters, with which letter would you start—*a*? Is *a* the easiest letter to learn? What would be the first word you would teach a child to read—*mama*? Would you teach writing at the same time? Children can read some words before they can control a pencil or crayon well enough to produce anything that looks like a letter. But they could form letters out of little plastic sticks and curves.

What about arithmetic? Where would one start—with number one or with addition? The simple fact is that no one knows where to start teaching anything—be it geography, history, foreign languages, psychology, or even cooking a rabbit. The old advice that "first you catch your rabbit" may be the only instance where we know the first step to take, but that does not really involve learning. No one knows the first thing about teaching anything. The reason for this situation is that we probably do not know the first thing about learning or teaching someone about learning. Happily, we do not have to know the first thing to get some teaching done; however, teaching, necessarily, becomes inefficient, and perhaps difficult and painful, if we do not follow some appropriate method in our efforts. A lot of people have learned a lot of things over the centuries that man has considered the need to teach and learn. We do not know the cost in time and trouble nor can we know what could have been learned if people had been taught properly. Incidentally, if we really do not know the first thing about teaching, then there are no great teachers around either. We all have some kinds of values by which we judge things—one book is better than another or one hot dog is better than another. There are the ten best movies of the year, and Miss America is the loveliest girl in the land (to some people). Our practice of rating things extends to talking about teachers in terms of one being better than another, but that kind of talk is mostly nonsense. If we do not know what makes a good teacher, how can we tell a better teacher from a worse one? We all know what we like, as the people in the art gallery say, but liking someone does not mean he or she is a good teacher. It appears reasonable that a teacher who teaches you more is better than one who teaches you less, but even this criterion is a little shaky—more about what? Sometimes, we learn more than we want to know. Maybe, the best teacher is one who does not teach you anything and somehow forces you to learn by yourself. Until we learn more about learning, we should stop giving prizes to teachers.

We can take another look at good and bad teachers after we find out more about the nature of learning, if that can be done. Note that we are not talking about how some specific operation is learned but about learning itself. This is perhaps a little ambitious, since we do not know the first thing about the first question, that is, how something specific is learned, and since we are asking a question that is far more abstract. However, it may be that we cannot answer the first question without knowing the answer to the second. How can we go about the business of finding out what learning is?

For about a century (since 1880 or so), psychologists have been looking into the question of what learning is or how it takes place. This is not to say that the subject did not receive attention before that. Many philosophers have looked into the problem during the course of our civilization. Education has been around for a long time, both formally and informally. Some people have been assigned to the jobs of teaching the young because they were believed to be able to do so or because no one else wanted to. Some people who are not teachers but like to feel superior have remarked that "those who can, do, and those who can't, teach," but that is probably an irresponsible canard. Those who "can" probably cannot teach. We have had teachers around for centuries, however, and presumably, they have taught something to someone, at least on occasion. But if so, what is it they have done? The psychologists investigating the problem have found out a lot, but a great deal of what they have discovered is not very helpful in answering the basic question of what is learning. If you look over a book about learning, you will learn a lot about what psychologists have been doing and discovering but you will not learn enough about learning to help you teach someone to wipe his or her nose.

The question that faces us is, Where do we start?

WHERE DO WE START?

The logical place to start in investigating any phenomenon is to ask ourselves if there is something to investigate, that is, Is the alleged phenomenon more than that, Is it real? Is there, in the present instance, such a thing as learning? While the question may be considered absurd by some, many serious people through the ages have considered it. One approach to a denial of the role, significance, or reality of learning is to assume that nobody actually learns anything, that is, that each person is born with certain capacities, innate connections in his or her nervous system, or innate knowledge that will emerge as a function of growth and development at the proper time—on schedule, as it were. Reflect on the point of *significance*. Maybe, learning is not as important as some make out, even if there is such a thing as learning. Other operations, such as understanding or insight, might be more important.

While people are not wasps or salmon, it may be that like wasps and salmon, they do the right thing at the right time in many circumstances with or without training, instructions, or, even, example. That last item, example, may be putting the case somewhat too strongly, but the whole area of invention must give us pause. When someone does something appropriate or effective for the first time, that is invents something that no one could have taught that person because no one knew what to teach, we have to be a bit careful about emphasizing learning.

When we consider such things as walking or talking as examples, we have to ask if anyone has ever taught anyone else to talk or walk? There are pundits around who argue that people are born with some kind of innate capacity to organize their speech in some grammatical form and that the emergence of grammatical speech is not something that is learned per se. The particular language may be learned, but the grammar or function of speech is not, so they say. With walking, they might have even a better case. Most babies go through a rather characteristic developmental sequence of leg movements, crawling, standing, and finally walking, and no amount of training seems to be effective in hurrying the process. Does the same kind of argument apply to *performance* in arithmetic? Teachers of arithmetic have good students, average students, and poor students. They take credit for teaching the good ones and blame the poor ones for various lacks and weaknesses. Do they actually teach anyone? Or do they provide environments where arithmetical capacity can manifest itself in varying degrees and which is dependent on something other than teaching or learning?

When teachers in a psychology class find a normal distribution of grades from a test, should they not ask themselves if they have taught anyone anything? They could argue that there would have been a lower distribution if the students had not taken the course, which is true, probably, but what does that tell us about the nature of the teaching or learning? Did the students learn, or did they, as Socrates might argue, react to the questions inherent in the course in a logical and rational manner and reach appropriate conclusions—conclusions that they were not in position to assert with confidence prior to the course, since up to that time, they had not put their minds to the problem involved? If the latter is the case, learning would amount to using some kind of rational capacities in examining facts or data and drawing proper deductions. There would be no need for practice or any of the operations that learning psychologists have been concerned with in the last century. Teaching would amount to providing problem situations that those people with logical minds would in due course solve. It might help with those who have not fully developed their logical capacities to arrange the problems in such a way that the logical steps (discovered by someone else earlier) would be more likely to be taken. We will look into this matter in the next chapter, where we will consider Socrates and his teaching.

The average psychologist in the twentieth century is not inclined to favor the Socratic method in its pure form. Because of many (probably social) influences, he or she is more prone to accept an approach that starts with denying that anyone has any innate knowledge or that learning is a logical, deductive, rational affair. Like Locke (1690), the modern psychologist favors the view that a person is born with a blank mind, if he or she has a mind at all, and that experience writes on this "tabula rasa," or clean slate, in such a way that the person is molded by his or her environment to react automatically in certain ways as a function of environmental influences on his or her biological, physical mechanism, that is, that a person's behavior is like the operation of a machine—a machine, delicate and complex, if you will, but still a machine, with a complicated neural system. The modern psychologist also favors the view that it works in the way it does, in part because of its nature and structure, but also, and perhaps for the most part, because it is modified by the kinds of experiences to which it is subjected. The psychologist is inclined to believe that experiences which favor survival, which are adaptive, and which are in some way good for the organism will modify the nervous system in ways that result in more effective behavior.

For the moment, let us reflect on a popular interpretation preferred by some psychologists in the past century. For a variety of reasons and in various ways and interpretations, they chose to assume that if an organism (a person or an animal) did something either through being forced to or more or less spontaneously or by chance and if that behavior (reaction, activity) resulted in some kind of benefit (pleasure, reward, satisfaction, drive reduction, or, generally, "reinforcement"), then the organism would tend to repeat such a response or behavior pattern because of some natural law, which says, in effect, that useful, adaptive, or pleasant behavior is strengthened by its consequences. This is the famous law of effect (see chapter 7). According to this law, the behavior of an individual is assumed to be a function of his or her experiences (positive and negative in the sense described) and that behavior changes (learning takes place) as the organism is modified by its experience. Some psychologists have argued that the nervous system is necessarily changed by such experiences, so that the *machine* involved could be described as a modifiable machine. Because every organism would have a different reinforcement history, every organism would then be different. Similar behaviors might reflect some common behavioral history or the action of different reinforcers at different times and places where or when appropriate reinforcement occurred.

There is no question that rewards (and punishments) affect and control behavior (within limits), but whether they actually affect learning is another matter, which we will look into in due time. For the moment, let us consider what Socrates would say about this. Obviously, one could decide or deduce that a behavior pattern that leads to a reward might be preferable to one that did not. On the other hand, and we may be sure that Socrates would consider the other hand, one might deduce that a preferred or available reward was undesirable at the moment (as many a child has demonstrated, by turning down bribes of one kind or another) and do something that would not be rewarded at the moment. The subject of rewards and punishments is an intriguing one. Whether it is related to learning is something we will reserve for later discussion.

REISM

To get back to our starting point, we want to ask if there is such a thing as learning. There is a philosophical point of view called reism (see

Kotarbinski 1966) that maintains that we should be careful about postulating the existence of things, especially when we imply the existence of things that are named by adding *ion*, *ing*, or *ence* to verbs. Thus, we speak of digestion, thinking (that ends up with a "thought"), circulation, perception, emotion, intelligence, and so forth. Sometimes, we drop a proper *ing* and create a noun (the name of an object, place, or thing), as, for example, "Let's take a swim" or "I'll have a smoke." Now, there is no such thing as *a* swim. We know what the speaker means, but he or she is abusing the language from a purist's, or reist's, viewpoint. We might know what somebody means when he or she says, "There was an explosion" or "There was an eruption of some volcano," but if you stop to think about it, you will probably agree that there is no such *thing* as an eruption. True, volcanoes erupt, but there is no such thing as an eruption. The word exists—it is in the dictionary ("act of breaking out or bursting forth"). The only trouble is that there is no such thing as "breaking out" or "bursting forth." If there is, show it to someone. To show it to someone, you will find that you have to get some thing, some object, and have it do something or have something done to it, that is, put some object in some kind of motion (there is some question, by the way, about whether there is such a thing as motion), and so we had better say "have some object move in some way." But that is the point, namely, that only objects exist, and all objects move in some ways, if only infinitesimally, and that is all there is in this world. To study something called learning, then, we would have to study some object moving in some way. So far, no one has figured out what objects and what "moves" to study in ways that would result in agreement among observers that they were studying learning.

LEARNING AS AN INFERENCE

When psychologists are asked to define learning, they usually wind up with some statement that does not satisfy everyone, not that we need universal agreement. A classic effort was that of McGeoch (1942), who said, "Learning is a change in performance as a result of practice." This definition looks good to some people, who do not care to ask what kind of change, how much change, in what kind of performance, what is meant by practice, how much practice, what kind of practice, and under what conditions? Sometimes, people do not change in some performance by practicing a lot, and sometimes, they change in one trial. Is one trial considered to be practice? Other psychologists (some of the most respected ones) say that learning is a change in behavior that cannot be attributed to fatigue, illness, drugs, or maturation but is related to some activity or training. This tells us something about what learning is not but not a great deal about what it is.

It is reasonably clear that we are not ever going to see anything called learning occurring before our eyes. We will, at best, see people or animals doing something, and after we have seen them do something under some conditions and then later under some other conditions, we might draw some inferences about them and their behavior under such conditions. These inferences we might then describe as reflecting the results of learning. Actually, there is no such thing as learning in the sense of a thing, and we will make more progress in our concern if we talk about the things we observe and the motions we witness in the presence of other things and motions (conditions). What all this amounts to is that we might find out what things to arrange in what ways (times, places, and motions) that are related to what people do or will do in the same (or other) times and places when those things (or other things) are arranged in some ways.

The First Question

This all sounds very cumbersome, but all it amounts to is saying: What are the conditions that must be established for someone who now does not behave in some way to do so in the future? It is necessary to include here the additional proviso that the someone who is not doing something does not know how to and wants to or would like to and that there is no physical reason (the person is not old enough or too old, too feeble, too sick, too tired, too perceptually incapacitated, and so forth) for the someone not to make the required movements. To take an example, suppose we ask someone to "give the date of George Washington's birth," and the person says, "I don't know." Our problem is to spell out the conditions under which he or she will later say February 22, 1732, when there is no physical reason that makes it impossible to do this and when we can be reasonably certain that he or she would be glad to oblige us with the correct answer.

Our problem in defining learning, then, becomes one of finding out the nature of the conditions, that is, what must be done in order that someone does something that he or she cannot do unless those conditions are met. In the case of the present example, all that needs be done with some people, for example, normal English-speaking adults, is to tell them, once. If they say, "I don't know," and we tell them, and then they give the right answer on being asked again, we say they have learned. If they have learned, what has happened? The latter question is the question we must answer if we are going to say something meaningful about learning. Some psychologists are only concerned with whether or not the answer is given. We might judge that they are not interested in learning at all. They are teaching technologists.

Our example opens other issues or problems. We might find some people who have to be told twice or more often, especially if we wait a while after giving the information. Children in a history class might not give the correct date in some final examination if the information was given some months before and not reviewed recently (or ever). They will then say they have forgotten. But forgetting is part of the learning question, as we have to say something about how long we expect the conditions that we set up for learning in the first place to have their effects or results. We must recognize that most people regard learning as some kind of relatively permanent operation. If something goes in one ear and out the other, we will not regard that as serious learning, even if someone can give the right answer before it goes out of the other ear. But, then, what is relative permanence besides a pair of self-contradicting words?

We recognize then that retaining some behavior in relation to some situation for a while, at least, is an important consideration in talking about learning. We cannot really talk about learning without some criterion of retention. Incidentally, for convenience, we can talk about such things as answers, reactions, behavior, and so forth as responses and symbolize then as R and the conditions or questions that lead to such Rs as stimuli, or Ss; in the future, we can save repetition by referring to the formula (S ⟶ R) in the typical situation we will find ourselves in when we want to have certain responses occur to certain stimuli.* When we talk about learning, then, we refer to the retention of some S ⟶ R combination for some period of time. Ordinarily, we expect some S ⟶ R patterns to last more or less indefinitely (but when they do, we also find that there are many occasions when there is the necessity for review or practice). Other S ⟶ R patterns, such as infrequently used telephone numbers, we do not normally expect to last longer than it takes to dial them (after we look them up). Some course-related material we hope will last up to the examination date, and then we do not care much if we forget it—that is usual, normal, we say. But some things we learn in about the same way stick with us without practice, and such retention calls for an explanation.

The Second Question

Learning is not a thing or some "process" because there are no processes

We have now considered the first question and answered it in a way. There is, to be sure, no such thing as learning in the sense of a thing, or even some "process," because there are no processes. When we talk about learning, we are referring to the results (revealed by certain tests) of certain still unspecified conditions. These results can be described as changes in behavior. The second question, naturally, is, What are these conditions? More precisely, under what conditions is it likely that some *S* that is not followed "naturally" by some *R* comes to do so. By naturally we mean that at some prior time, this *S* was not followed by this *R* and was not likely to do so even though desired. Because of some intervening experience (conditions), this *R* now has a higher probability of occurring, always assuming the learner wants to respond. We are talking, then, about a change of some kind that can be tied to, or related to, the intervening circumstances or operations. We could have asked about the nature of the change, that is, what

---

*The arrow ⟶ means followed by.

parts of the learner's body have been altered and in what way, but that becomes a physiological question, and we actually do not know much about such changes. We could speculate about such changes in the nervous system, for example, but we probably could not prove very much, and we might more profitably restrict ourselves to the changes in observable behavior that are consequences of the conditions which were imposed on the learner.

SOME PARADOXES

When a small child begins to talk, the new activity delights the parents—they begin to have hope that they can now (or soon) explain things, instruct the child, get him or her to do things without the parents getting up, and, in general, take advantage of the multiple applications of language to get things done at a distance. The parents soon discover that their hopes are not being met at a desirable rate. The child utters a word, or some semblance of it, and then does not repeat it for some time, perhaps for days. Slowly, other words are spoken. After months of strange vocalizations with private words, which parents learn to interpret, the child becomes more or less a talker. The process cannot be rushed; it amounts to a word or two at a time. In due course, the child picks up some strings of words that obviously mean nothing to him or her, for example, "one, two, three." The child looks bright and may be, but the language is acquired bit by bit and not in large chunks. The point is that with babies, we resign ourselves, or are more or less content, with the learning of one word per day or week. When a child enters school, we somehow lose this contentment and ask for the learning of more than one thing at a time (the *time* being a class hour, day, week, or other unit).

It is commonly the case that through the early years, the child is told stories or nursery rhymes, jingles, and other sequential assortments of words but is not asked to learn them—he or she is being, we hope, entertained. When, occasionally, the child shows signs of expecting what is to come, we notice that he or she is learning something, but we are by no means sure of what has been learned—whether it "means" anything or not.

Because the school-age child appears to be able to comprehend some things (learned slowly over many trials), we are tempted to expose him or her to equal-sized packages of material, with some great expectations about his or her learning and retention. For example, the child who can recite a four-line nursery jingle that he or she has heard 100 times might be asked to recite a four-line verse heard for the first time. Failure to do so may puzzle or frustrate the teacher; if the teacher is patient and experienced, a second or third repetition may be suggested. The problem of learning rears its head. Why is the child not able to repeat a new sequence of words when he or she is able to repeat old sequences? After some repetitions, the child does master the new sequence, but no one knows how he or she came to do so; the assignment having been learned, the teacher produces a new assignment and so on through the grades. Children learn, but no one knows how they learn or what happens. We now observe a curious paradox. The schoolchild, probably anyone over the age of four or five, can *say* just about anything he or she is asked to say as far as single words, brief phrases, or sentences are concerned. Thus, children can say "supercalaphragalisticexpialadocious" with relatively little difficulty. They can also say "1492" when they have previously been told that that is the answer to a question and the question is then put to them. In brief, given a particular stimulus and a particular response, as in a "Simon Says" game, children can perform adequately, but no one knows how. Nothing is learned about learning in a situation where a child is shown something and told what its name is, for example, a kumquat, and then asked, What is it? The child says "kumquat," having heard the word once in his or her life. Only when more than one new thing is shown and named will the child have trouble. The more things shown, the fewer will be named (in high probability). Only now do we become concerned over the nature of learning, that is, when it does not occur. As a result of this paradox, psychologists have rarely inquired into the single S→R situation because they can see no learning problem there. They have chosen, instead, to use situations where multiple or sequential responses were required and where it was unlikely that anyone could respond correctly to each of several stimuli. Here, where there was no learning, or where there was at least incomplete learning in one trial, the psychologists felt they had found their field. They could not get some facts, data, or observe some relationships. For example, they could count the number of trials it took to memorize (learn) a list of words, the number of words learned per trial, the relative difficulty of long and short lists, which items were easy or difficult, and a great variety of other features. The unfortunate fact was that nothing was discovered about how a single S→R combination was learned. That either happened or did not happen. In the context of numerous experiments, involving many combinations of conditions, confusions arose, giving rise to a variety of speculative interpretations (theories of learning) that could not win general acceptance.

One of the great preoccupations of psychologists in the first half of this century was that of running rats through complicated mazes; a great deal was learned about the behavior of rats in complicated mazes, but it is safe to say nothing much was learned about learning, at least directly, that was not known from other sources. After years of maze studies, Tolman (1938) decided that perhaps more (or something) could be learned if a rat was put into a simpler situation where it had to turn either to the left or to the right. Even this situation, which appeared promising in that it approached the simple and single S→R condition, did not prove to be too helpful; it gave rise to even more controversy.

What happened in the psychology of learning is that too many psychologists tried to explain too much too soon. There were investigators who had the correct orientation; two early in this century, one in the United States, the other in the Soviet Union. Both of these, Edward L. Thorndike and Ivan P. Pavlov, assumed that learning consisted of the formation of a connection between a stimulus and a response, and both were determined to discover how such bonds came into being. It is the work of these two researchers that we must examine, along with that of some of their students, if we are to learn about learning. Our problem would not be too difficult if we could retain our focus on the central issues, the development of S⟶R bonds. The trouble is that both Pavlov and Thorndike were too eager to get on with the story, as were their students, and the basic question was dropped too soon—Pavlov went off into psychotherapy and neurological speculation, while Thorndike went off into education; the basic question was dropped before they had found the answers they originally set out to discover.

Similarly, the students of both were too eager to apply their too limited understanding, so that John B. Watson, for example, proposed to solve all our social, child-rearing, ethical, and educational problems by use of Pavlovian conditioning. Through his advancement of behaviorism, Watson transformed the interest in learning into a concern with behavior. In this century, the leading psychologists who are identified with learning actually were more concerned with Behavior with a capital B. The titles of the most significant works of the first half-century give us a clue. We have Tolman's *Purposive Behavior*; Hull's *The Principles of Behavior, Essentials of Behavior*, and *A Behavior System*; and Skinner's *The Behavior of Organisms, Science and Human Behavior*, and *Verbal Behavior*. Even with D. O. Hebb, who was genuinely concerned with learning, his major work came out under the title, *The Organization of Behavior*. There are dozens of books with the word *learning* in their titles, but they too talk more about behavior than about learning, perhaps because not enough is known about learning to fill a book.

The reason that behavior assumed such an enormous role in learning psychology was, as we made clear earlier, because no one can see or study learning directly. What can be seen, studied, and measured is some sample of behavior, that is, some organism or part of some organism in motion. Such observations eventually came to be recognized for what they were, namely, some kind or type of performance. The nature of any learning factor could only be inferred from performance; thus, the authors listed above were being honest enough. They knew they were discussing behavior and not learning. Anything significant that could be said about learning had to be based on observations of performance either at the time of the alleged learning or at some later time. As if the crcumstances were not sufficiently confused, a rather difficult issue arose in the recognition (after much debate) of the fact that some learning can go on in the absence of any performance at the time of learning and, yet, must be admitted to have occurred because of some later type of test. What we are discussing here are the issues of latent learning and imitation, both of which will be dealt with at the proper time.

THE UNLOYAL OPPOSITION

By concentrating on behavior as a function of environmental experience, psychologists opened Pandora's box. For centuries, people had been observing behavior and had come to various conclusions as to its causes. For all kinds of reasons, some people found it difficult to accept experience as the cause or even an important contributor to behavior. Kings and queens and associated nobility found a hereditary account of their social status to be much more convenient. People in power anywhere liked to think they were especially selected because of their talents or inborn characteristics. Somehow, they were special. Even persecuted and downtrodden groups considered themselves "chosen" for better futures either in this world or some other. Racial differences were convenient "natural" indicators of superiority of whichever race was in position to exploit another. "Blood will tell" was a common explanation of much of behavior.

The notion that behavior could be a function of experience, of how one was brought up, had an egalitarian taint to it. The social implications were somewhat frightening, and criticism was not found wanting. Watson was attacked as a revolutionary atheist who would destroy society. Soviet "communistic" conditioning was flayed by Aldous Huxley in his *Brave New World*. Behavioristic psychology was regarded as a threat by all who, for whatever reasons, cherished an *individual difference* orientation concerning man. Such individual or class differences became the growing concern of critics who feared some kind of equalization prospects. The reaction to behaviorism led to renewed concerns over hereditary influences, and new sciences of ethology and behavior genetics were born. In the next chapter, we will review the efforts of nativists to account for behavior along other than learning lines.

We should note, in passing, such matters as "mental health" and criminal or delinquent behavior. These matters, which have always been with us, have always called for some kind of action. Is psychopathology a hereditary problem? Such a position is not attractive to parents of psychopaths, who would much rather believe that the "mental illness" was perhaps acquired through exposure to a virus, or, if necessary, to some environmental conflict. Perhaps, it could be cured by psychotherapy. But psychotherapy is often a form of retraining, with the implication of faulty *original training*.

When the juvenile delinquent is apprehended by the police, can the hereditary explanation be accepted by the parents? The mother frequently asks, "Where did I go wrong," indicating a belief in some form of environmental influence. The notion that environmental experience accounts for delinquency and crime has become widespread throughout the legal system, where reform and rehabilitation have been the proposed cures.

The question of what is learned and what is given has not been answered as yet. The answer may be a long time in coming, and we can only begin to make progress toward the answer by trying to determine what we mean by learning and where and how it takes place. As a starting step, we can look at what the nativists have to say.

2

Mapping Out the Territory

Before we even begin to consider the nature of learning, we have to restrict the area of discussion lest we become involved with an encyclopedic problem, namely, that of trying to account for all human behavior. Not all human behavior is learned; a problem arises because we do not know with certainty how or where to draw the lines between what might be called nature and nurture, heredity and environment, maturation, and learning.

NATIVISM VERSUS EMPIRICISM

Are we born to be what we are or are we made that way by our experiences? This is the classic question that has preceded and accompanied psychology throughout its history. From time to time, psychologists have adopted a strong environmentalist bias and have ignored the problem of heredity—this was especially true in the period between 1915 and 1965, when a behaviorist or neobehaviorist view was rather generally accepted.

Watson (1924), for instance, ignored ancestry, asking only for health, and promised to make any normal baby into anything anyone chose. His famous claim reads:

> Give me a dozen healthy infants, well-formed, and my own specified world to bring them up in and I'll guarantee to take anyone at random and train him to become any type of specialist I might select—doctor, lawyer, artist, merchant chief and, yes, even beggarman and thief, regardless of his talents, penchants, tendencies, abilities, vocations, and race of his ancestors.

What Watson was undertaking to do was based on the tabula rasa proposition of Locke, with the additional assumption, if not presumption, that an appreciation of the nature of the interaction of organisms and their environments would explain reasoning (thinking), insight, some alleged maturational effects, all wants or motivations, successes or failures to achieve, the functions of teachers, and the nature of invention. While the claim of Watson was extreme, no one ever took him up on it, and generations of psychologists followed his general orientation without glamorous successes, to be sure, but with enough self-rewarding experiences to convince them to carry on. In recent years, a strong revival of nativism has been mounted from several sources, and some psychologists have either retreated from a thoroughgoing behavioristic view or have even joined what used to be regarded as the enemy.

From the now-beleaguered environmentalist, or empiricist, view, psychologists favored Thomas Jefferson's axiom of the self-evident equality of all men. True, as George Orwell pointed out in his *Animal Farm*, some were more equal than others. No one ever closed his or her eyes completely to individual differences, except possibly for Watson, who believed he could adjust environments for exceptional cases, for example, make small pianos for small people; but hereditary differences were regarded by Watson as rather trivial—the color of eyes or hair or modest variations in height or weight are trivial and hardly worthy of notice. Differences due to disparities of environment, on the other hand, *seemed* obvious and open to attack. There is not much one can do about heredity, once the product is there. Rearing, training, and teaching, however, are at least feasible. How effective they are may be difficult to establish. That some failures have been observed or suspected must be the case in view of the current rise of hereditists in one form or another. They must be recognized and considered in any evaluation of the necessarily environmental operations of psychologists.

NATIVISM

Who are the nativists? They are not new on the scene and have been around since the days of Socrates. From Plato to Immanuel Kant to Noam Chomsky, the doctrine that man is "master of his fate and captain of his soul" and not just a creature of the environment has nourished poets and romanticists, as well as politicians and "movers of men." The Kantian (1781) list of categories of intuitive knowledge if not the most complete is perhaps the most formal proposal of what an individual brings into the world with himself or herself. It does cover a broad sphere—consider the list: man, by his nature, knows or intuits knowledge of space and time. He is similarly equipped to deal with unity, plurality, totality, reality, negation, limitation, substance and accident, cause and effect, reciprocity, possibility-impossibility, existence-nonexistence, and necessity. So equipped and prepared by nature, man is ready to reason his way to appropriate understandings and solutions of the problems that he encounters. These skills cannot and need not be taught.

Faculty Psychology

A long tradition, going back to the earliest recorded thinkers, has held that an individual behaves as he or she does because that is the way he or she is. The individual is the way he or she is because he or she was made that way (today, we say because of his or her heredity or chromosomes and genes) or because he or she was either blessed or punished by the gods. How the individual was made was answered in various ways by the earliest philosophers, but there was some general agreement that among the individual's features, possessions; structures, or functions, there were various faculties residing in a soul or mind which an individual used or which used the individual (such an issue was never resolved) and which would account for his or her behavior. The faculties included such functions as reason or intellect, will, and memory, which would bear on rational matters and judgments; less rational affairs would be functions of other faculties, which today might be called personality traits, such as courage, independence, virtue, and so on. Such a faculty psychology flourished up through the nineteenth century, and even today, we have phrenologists reading our personalities by feeling bumps on our skulls to discover which of our many faculties are more fully developed than others.

When phrenologists do not prosper, other kinds of "readers" take over and consult the stars or measure us by one test or another for abilities, talents, or traits. Faculty psychology is not dead. The man in the street is well prepared to explain anyone's behavior by referring to "a mean streak" or "pure cussedness." Even when the man in the street is puzzled by someone's behavior, he is puzzled in faculty terms—for example, "I never realized he was capable of such a thing" or "I didn't know he had it in him."

Our entire legal system rests on the postulate that a person is rational, endowed with God-given reason, which makes behavior an individual responsibility. A lawbreaker knows (reason) that an action is wrong and chooses (will) to do it. Usually, the law does not apply to children. Age limits differ in different states and countries; apparently, the age of reason is a territorial variable, but the age of reason is not specifically tied to any learning history. In some states, women can marry at 18 but men cannot prior to 21. Apparently, men attain the age of reason later than women. Whatever the age, reason is not expected of babies, but they do grow into it, or at least, some of them do—that is, reason is a maturational faculty. Once attained, reason allows the rational person to solve problems, possibly without any learning or educational background of any serious importance—at least, so it has been held since the time of Socrates. Even today, we tell our friends, "Use your head!" Socrates was one of the earlier proponents of what we will call rationalism.

Rationalism

In Plato's *Meno* (see Grube 1976), Socrates has a dialogue with Meno, one of his students. Meno wants to learn to be virtuous, but Socrates convinces him that virtue cannot be taught—it is a gift of the gods. In the course of the dialogue or argument, Socrates finds it desirable to suggest that nothing really needs to be taught. He demonstrates to Meno that one already knows such things, for example, as that virtue cannot be taught. There are some virtuous men and some of little if any virtue, but nowhere are there any teachers of virtue, and virtuous men often have unvirtuous sons, even though they would give anything to make their sons virtuous. Socrates says:

> As the soul is immortal, has been born often and has seen all things here and in the underworld, there is nothing which it has not learned; so it is in no way surprising that it can recollect the things it knew before, both about virtue and other things. As the whole of nature is akin, and the soul has learned everything, nothing prevents a man, after recalling one thing only—a process men call learning—discovering everything else for himself, if he is brave and does not tire of the search, for searching and learning are, as a whole, recollection.

While the passage quoted is somewhat confusing, the main point here is that one does not have to learn anything but merely recall from the soul's previously acquired knowledge. How the soul acquired its knowledge in the first place is not clarified by Socrates. Instead, Socrates proceeds to demonstrate that an untutored, uneducated attendant of Meno's already knows the Pythagorean theorem, even though he never heard of it before. Socrates asks questions each of which the slave can answer on the basis of logic or reason and, according to Socrates, arrives at the theorem through the process of careful, step-by-step reasoning. In a modern replication of this Socratic performance, Cohen (1962) demonstrated that the Socratic procedure was very much like modern programmed learning. Cohen also discovered that not all students could arrive at a successful statement of the proper conclusion, but then, we do not know that the slave actually knew the theorem. Socrates did not test him.

The notion that you do not necessarily learn everything you know or become able to do did not die with Socrates. Today, some psychologists and other pundits proclaim the same principle.

Piaget (1954), the Swiss biologist, suggests that certain "concepts" arrive in due course as the child develops through several "stages." The concept of unity, or conservation, for example, might take a little time, but when it comes, it comes. The same view is part of the working operation of those psychologists adopting the Gestalt approach. For them, observations of learning were fruitless and idle because one did not *learn* answers or solutions. One arrived at them. Sooner or later, as one faced a problem, one would acquire "insight," pieces of the problem would fall into place, and one would see the perspective—the "whole" would emerge. If it did not, should one teach the uninsightful? Would it be a waste of time? Undoubtedly, one could assist by pointing out unobserved features or through demonstration but basically, "understanding" came or did not come. The "aha" experience was imperative.

The Ethologists

The *nativists*, as we might classify them, propose a variety of nonlearning orientations. It is necessary to mention them here if we are to assign the learning field to its proper arena. The nativists, in one way or another, argue that some kinds of behavior are natural, native, inherited, or instinctive and will appear in due course or at proper periods in one's life. They might be correct in what they say; our problem is not to confuse what they say as having any bearing on learning. The burden of proof should always be upon the proponent, and if the nativists can prove their points, no one should deny their findings. We can look at a few samples of nativistic thinking to clarify the issues.

Instinct

Before the twentith century, many writers with or without scientific credentials tried to explain some of the behavior patterns of various kinds of animals, including man, as attributable to instinct. Instinct was supposed to be a matter of hereditary programming, such that certain creatures would behave in certain specific ways because they were unable to do otherwise. Their inheritance had provided them with certain structures and/or functions that operated more or less blindly and which were not, nor could they be, modified by individual experience. Certain birds built certain kinds of nests or sang certain songs because they had to and could not do otherwise. Instinctive behavior was said to be universal in a species, unlearned, and more or less perfect on the first occasion. Even where some animals appeared to teach their offspring how to hunt, for example, the teaching was done by instinct. The behavior of homing pigeons, salmon, wasps, bees, and much of that of mankind was thus explained. A prominent British, later American, psychologist, McDougall (1908), accounted for much of man's social behavior in terms of seven basic instincts. But instinct is just a word, not an explanation. It does refer to behavior where no satisfactory learning explanation is readily available, and there may well be such behaviors. But the evidence for instinct up to relatively recent times has not been based on much more than casual observation.

Some psychologists try to explain at least some "instincts" through the use of learning concepts. Skinner (1966), for example, offered a learning account of the African honey bird's alleged instinctive behavior of following natives who harvested the honey. Whether such efforts are worthwhile is debatable. The believers will not be convinced. There is enough learned behavior to account for without explaining away all instincts.

In more recent times, a number of "naturalists" of a much more professional level have taken to field observations and, in some limited ways, to laboratory or experimental investigations, where the basic or guiding influence is a desire to observe what certain species will do in their natural habitats. Thus, certain biologists have gone into areas where gorillas or chimpanzees live (sometimes, even attempting to live with them) and have made careful observations and photographed the characteristic "wild" behavior. As might be expected, their observations do not correspond to what one would see in a zoo, where the animals are placed in a restricted environment and fed by a keeper. Whether the observations will be of any significance for learning theory remains to be seen.

Other ethologists have observed barnyard animals, especially fowl, such as geese and ducks, and varieties of fish (in tanks) and have announced some strong conclusions about important kinds of behavior that are also displayed by man. For example, Lorenz (1965) has promoted the view that aggression or aggressiveness is an innate disposition across species and not a learned behavior pattern. According to Lorenz, aggressiveness can only be sidetracked or rechanneled in man via sports or other activities, and if it is not, it leads to one kind or another of pugnacious behavior. As part of hte aggression "release" mechanism, Lorenz advances the concept of territoriality, the notion that various creatures, in a sense, stake out areas that they consider their private domains and resent and resist intruders. Other writers, for example, Montague (1975), insist that aggressiveness is an acquired trait and has no innate basis for automatic release.

More recently, Wilson (1975) has reviewed the research on various kinds of social insects and animals and has suggested various hereditary and evolutionary mechanisms that operate to produce a natural "altruism" which accounts for social or group living. Other kinds of social behavior are explained by other biological mechanisms. We cannot become embroiled in controversies as to whether man is by nature aggressive or altruistic.

Our concern is not with the source of every kind of behavior that can be described but rather with whether some or any kind of learning can be demonstrated in relation to such behaviors. It is obvious that some people are aggressive in some situations and not others. We can be interested in the positive and negative instances from a learning viewpoint and try to determine, for example, whether certain stimulus situations, like TV violence, generate aggressive displays in observers. When we do find some relationship, the problem of learning is not solved; it is only opened and requires a different kind of study.

Imprinting

One of Lorenz's (1935) early observations was that certain behaviors are established in certain creatures at certain "critical" periods. Thus, baby goslings, a few hours after birth (17 hours is favored), start to follow any moving object in their vicinity. This is usually, but need not be, their mother; the "following" behavior is said to be "imprinted" more or less permanently, so that the goslings follow the chosen object wherever it goes. Ducks, turkeys, and geese show this striking pattern of behavior in their early months. It has been interpreted as a native filial reaction—in this case, initiated by a moving object as the natural, unlearned stimulus. In experimental settings, the imprinting can be elicited by any moving object, for example, a moving block of wood, a rubber ball, or anything that can be set in motion.

The early investigators emphasized the critical period of 17 hours, but Hoffman and De Paulo (1977) indicate that successful imprinting can be achieved with ducklings after five-day periods and possibly later. There is an initial period of distress or fear if the imprinting object is presented several days after hatching, but the ducklings gradually overcome this fear and become imprinted. The point of the imprinting studies is that certain stimuli are "natural" for certain responses in the sense that some specific behaviors are displayed in their presence very early in life. Baby monkeys, for example (see Harlow, Gluck, and Suomi 1972) appear to want to cling to soft furry objects, which usually turn out to be their mothers. Given a choice between a surrogate mother made of wire shaped to resemble a mother figure and one covered with terry cloth, the infant monkey clings to the terry cloth surrogate, even it is fed only on the wire one.

The fact that certain stimuli naturally bring out certain reactions cannot be denied. On the contrary, it must be asserted if we are to make any progress in analyzing learning. What is important, however, is that given these natural reactions to natural stimuli, it is also necessary to recognize that other, unnatural stimuli can also bring out these same reactions.

In their studies with ducklings, Hoffman and De Paulo found that if ducklings were exposed to two stimuli at the same time, they would, initially, be imprinted to respond to only one of them; however, if the second stimulus (nonimprinted) was then presented repeatedly, the ducklings would gradually become imprinted on this second stimulus as well. According to the investigators, learning had occurred in the transfer of the response pattern to a new stimulus. We will find this arrangement of pairing natural and unnatural stimuli to be the basic pattern followed by Pavlov in his studies of conditioning.

Nowadays, we have many authorities who emphasize the crucial early years in human childhood, but just what they are crucial for, we do not know. Some authorities (Kagan 1976) argue that the early years may be important but not critical for at least some kinds of test performances and that children might "catch up" in later years in areas where they show some initial weakness. Again, these people are not talking about learning directly, and we will not worry over such matters until they do.

The Heredity and I.Q. Issue

In the decade of the 1970s, a long-buried issue was disinterred. Some psychologists (Jensen 1969; Hernnstein 1971) and some sociologists (Jenks et al. 1972) began statistical studies of genetic and environmental influences that led them to believe that the strong emphasis on the importance of the environment in determining behavior, which characterized most American psychologists, was misplaced. They argued that correlations of I.Q. scores for identical twins reared apart, compared with those reared together, or of fraternal twins and siblings, for example, indicated that heredity was far more influential in determining I.Q. than the environment. Jensen, for example, suggested something like an 80 percent to 20 percent division of importance. Other psychologists quickly attacked Jensen. Kagan (1969) and Kamin (1974), for example, questioned the validity of the data relied on by Jensen, and a bitter controversy ensued. Kamin accused some psychologists of fraud and worse. Again, the issue does not concern us. In the first place, no I.Q.s are inherited as such. I.Q.s are numbers obtained from test scores and cannot be transmitted by genes. Whatever I.Q. scores mean, they have only a statistical relationship to learning, if that. I.Q.s are rarely compared with direct measures of learning. Usually, they are compared with school grades, which are the products of many variables. When I.Q. scores are compared directly with learning (Lester 1932), the correlation ratios are virtually zero. Even if the I.Q. and learning were highly correlated, we would not have any reason to infer a causal connection. We could only say that high-I.Q. people learned faster or that faster learners had higher I.Q.s—a conclusion of dubious value. The I.Q. would be an intervening variable,* not an independent one; its value would be to help predict a learning score, but it would not explain anything about learning. The good learners would still have to learn, and they could only learn in terms of *learning* principles; they might follow different methods, and if this were the case, the methods followed could be examined in terms of how they related to learning. We must leave the controversy to those who happen to be interested in it, as it has no bearing on our problems, whatever social implications are seen by others.

---

*An intervening variable is some measurable factor, for example, age, sex, strength, or whatever can be assigned a number, which might affect a prediction; it has no explanatory value. A horse race bookmaker works with intervening variables, such as number of races won by the horse and by the jockey. He does not always pick winners.

Linguistics

In the area of language behavior, we also see the influence of nativism. Some linguists (Chomsky 1957) entertain the idea that certain aspects of language are somehow innate. They recognize that different languages, that is, vocabularies, are learned by different cultural groups but argue that the *grammar* of any language is not itself learned but gradually unfolds as a natural human proclivity. This view intrigued many psychologists for a time but is gradually waning in influence. The interesting findings by Premack (1970) and Gardner and Gardner (1975) with chimpanzees who master some grammatical forms may have something to do with the decline in interest in innate human grammars. Again, we cannot be too concerned with the possibility that some kinds of behavior do not have to be learned. Our problem will be to explain learning where we do see it and not to try to explain something as learned when we do not see the learning occur. Nor do we have to accept something as unlearned just on somebody's say-so. The unlearned aspect should be established by some kind of evidence.

Species-Specific Factors

One more kind of attack on learning with a nativist implication comes from recent findings that suggest that some animals do or learn some things well and others poorly, while the reverse might be true of some other animals. The argument is usually related to species differences but is frequently extended to individual differences; many students, for example, avoid mathematics because it is not their "bag." By the time they reach the age of mathematics avoidance, they are likely to have trouble with mathematics and less trouble with the arts or literary or verbal tasks. We need not immediately accept a nativistic explanation, of course. Their histories with respect to handling numbers may have been unhappy for many unremembered reasons.

The problem just mentioned has been escalated to book size by Seligman (1975). Seligman argues strongly that psychologists must take account of not only individual but species differences. Some creatures simply will not learn some kinds of tasks or responses that other creatures seem to do or "pick up" naturally. What this means, of course, is that one cannot generalize freely from one species to another. Sometimes, it is a matter of stimuli to which some species is sensitive as far as some specific response-to-be-acquired is concerned. Thus, much is made of a study by Garcia and Ervin (1968), who found that if they paired bright lights and noisy water with electric shock, a rat would learn to avoid that water and would not drink it. If they paired water containing saccharine with electric shock, the rat would not learn to avoid it. On the other hand, if the rat were made sick by X rays or drugs after drinking saccharine tasting water, he would avoid the water. In short, a relationship between taste and sickness might be readily learned in an avoidance situation, while one between taste and electric shock would not. At the same time, avoidance could be acquired to bright lights and noise but not to taste with a shock as the aversive stimulus.

Seligman's position is that some creatures are ready and able (prepared for) to respond in certain ways to certain stimuli or can learn some stimulus-response pattern quickly while they are *contraprepared* for learning other kinds of relationships. To generalize from one creature's behavior in one situation to some other species' behavior in the same or different situations may be extremely unwise. But the argument is directed pretty largely at a straw opponent. Few psychologists go around generalizing directly from observations on some one simple species in one simple situation to the behavior of humans in complex settings. At worst, the observations made on rats or pigeons are used to generate ideas that can be tested with other organisms in different situations. Animal experimenters (Breland and Breland 1961) have always known that some species resist learning some kinds of behaviors. This problem will be explored again at a later time.

THE DOMAIN OF LEARNING

But what is the acceptable scope of learning psychology? What remains for learning to explain? We can now consider some examples.

When Rumpelstiltskin asked that he be named, no answer could come forth until he was overheard muttering his name to himself. No amount of instinct, intelligence, reasoning, guessing, or any other predisposition or talent could supply the name. No one can say something like Rumpelstiltskin to the question, What is my name? without a specific prior experience. A whole catalog of such "answers to questions" can be included in the learning camp's arsenal. Venturing further into the verbal arena, even the nativists admit that different languages are spoken in different environments and that the names of things and actions, that is, the whole vocabulary, must be learned, since words are arbitrary noises that bear no necessary or logical relation to the things they signify.

We turn now to the vast realm of stimulus and response connections that are basically unnatural or nonnatural. This is the real field of learning—we only learn what is unnatural. No dog, naturally, would salivate when a bell rang; as with any other reflex, there is a proper, natural stimulus for salivating, namely, food in the mouth. If by pairing food and bell, the bell can come to elicit salivation, can we, indeed must we not, speak of learning? Could not the dog reason that "every time the bell rings, food shows up. Ah, the bell is ringing, I think I'll salivate?" Besides endowing the dog with the capacity for deductive logic, such an explanation is a bit weak. Dogs, like people, cannot decide to salivate. While there may be people around who can initiate some kinds of reflexes, the resultant response does not have the characteristics of the reflex. If you try to fake a knee jerk, for example, the result will not be convincing to the trained observer. Some people, but not many, can cry "at will," and some people can stop their hearts, but, again, not many. Usually, reflexes occur only to restricted classes of stimuli and cannot be voluntarily initiated. If a new class of stimuli can be arranged to control reflexes, then we have more territory for learning to explore.

As an extension of the above, if we can "train" a learner to respond to one arbitrary stimulus but not to another, we have a case of discrimination. This kind of case may be a little tricky, but if it can be shown that other learners can be made to react in opposing fashions to the two different stimuli, the case for learning might be established. There is still room for doubt or controversy. The learner might have "reasoned" out the desirability of responding to one stimulus and not to the others.

We come now to a more dubious area. We want to teach a dog to "lie down and roll over." Saying the words to the dog results in nothing the first time. If we go through some appropriate routines (see Chapter 7), the dog lies down and rolls over upon command. Is this voluntary? Is it an act of will? Does reason enter—does the dog know that it pays to behave and then chooses to cooperate? Was it slow about it because it did not know what we wanted or because it did not understand, comprehend, or appreciate what we wanted? If we spoke to the dog in dog language could it have done the trick the first time, as a cooperative child might have done? One mother reported the case of a teen-ager who promptly fell to the floor in a collapsed state when she told him to "drop dead." No direct learning was called for— he had never done this before.

The language of dogs is not extensive and not too well appreciated by humans, but we can be sure it does not include any "lie down and roll over" units. It might be safe—but not too safe—for learning psychologists to venture a claim of teaching tricks to animals. Some animals, for example, porpoises, are asserted to be smarter than people by some porpoise lovers. Certainly, they do marvelous tricks with minimal training. Are we saying that some learners are better than others? But we have seen that this is not our problem. Our problem is to account for those behaviors that do not occur naturally, spontaneously, without some kinds of prior experience, where the natural response does not work or is socially disapproved. Among the latter, we will find that "I don't know" is a commonly unsatisfactory response, and when an "I don't know" response is changed to a more acceptable one, we might be dealing with learning. The rest of this book will be concerned with such changes in behavior, where sometimes we will find that something is being done in a situation in which it was not done before or where something new is being done in situations where something else used to be done. In these two situations, we will find the problems that learning psychologists have been concerned with for the past century. Even in these situations, however, we will have to allow the nativists to offer their suggestions: they might even be correct, sometimes. We can close this chapter with a statement of the position of most contemporary learning psychologists.

EXPERIMENTAL EPISTEMOLOGY

The empirical learning psychologists start by denying any role to heredity, instinct, or maturation unless such can be established by experimental methods. All behavior is considered learned or modified by learning unless proven otherwise. Both rational and empirical psychologists are addressing themselves to the same general problem: What is the nature of human nature? From time to time or person to person, the specific problems under investigation will differ, and each group will tend to view its own problems and concerns as more significant or important in making progress toward basic goals. If one group appears to have an edge in explaining some specific problem area, it is regarded as only a temporary advantage by the other side.

In attacking the question of human nature, both groups are concerned with the problem of the nature of knowledge—in philosophy, the problem of epistemology. What is knowledge? Of what does it consist? Where does it come from? How is it applied to affect behavior? The rationalists hope to solve this problem by thinking about it, by reasoning it through. The empiricists' hope is that experimental investigations under controlled conditions will bring the answer. For this reason, learning psychologists can be described as investigators engaged in "experimental epistemology," a label happily proposed by Hilgard and Bower (1975).

The solution to the problem of knowledge and its nature is obviously not at hand. The continuous criticism of educational systems suggests that there are weaknesses in our teaching efforts. Any successes that may have been attained may be ignored or underevaluated. It may be that advances have been made, but they are obviously not impressive enough to silence criticism. Even when the problem of learning is solved, it may prove that nothing much can be done to attain goals that appear desirable to some citizens, and the criticism will continue, perhaps increase. Not all solutions to problems satisfy all interested parties. Because no solutions to the questions of what knowledge is or how it is acquired have yet been of such power as to receive general acceptance, the question of application is moot. Our first problem is what is learning and how does it come about?

3

The Association of Ideas: From Aristotle to Ebbinghaus

You are asked to give the first word you think of when someone says a particular word to you. The stimulus word is *bread*. You say "butter" (probably). When asked why you said "butter," you have a ready answer— "Butter goes with bread." If pressed a little more, you might say that you "associate" butter with bread. You are not quite correct in such a statement; the first answer was better. You do not associate words with one another— you can associate with other people or camels or whatever, but as far as words are concerned, the situation seems to suggest a more impersonal approach. Actually, the words are not associated with each other; there is no place in the nervous system for words to exist as such—what must be associated is some neural activity generated by the first word and some neural activity generated by the second. We cannot discuss this problem at the moment, however, and will continue the present account of association as if words, objects, or experiences did become associated. Words, then, are associated with one another, but *in* you and not *by* you. You do not choose to associate or choose not to associate words with each other. They either become associated or not, depending to some extent on what you do, but only to some extent. Most of your associations to a list of 100 words, for examples, were formed without your intent or even awareness and will pop up automatically in a free association exercise. If I say "snow," you will probably think of "white" and say "white," unless you are trying to be uncooperative. The whiteness is just there, immediately, automatically; it does not call on you to do anything to have it occur. The association was there and only had to be called for. The really and only serious question is, How did it get there?

Before we try to answer that question, we want to consider the concept more carefully. It is an old and honorable concept in the histories of both philosophy and psychology, although in recent years, some psychologists have tried to denigrate it, possibly to their eventual regret.

ARISTOTLE AND CONTIGUITY

The concept of association goes back even to before Artistotle, who provided the key principle for most traditional theories of learning even though he was not concerned with learning as such; he was more occupied with the problem of reasoning. Aristotle (in *De Memoria et Reminiscentia*, see Beare 1931) was concerned with why you thought of something when you did. The answer for him was because what you thought of had been connected with, or associated with, something you were already thinking of. If you thought of some man, you might think of his wife. Plato, through Socrates, referred to much the same operation when Socrates (in *Phaedo*) asked his students if knowing a particular lyre did not make them think of the owner. In both these instances the principle, or law, of contiguity is being offered as an explanation of an association. One thing reminds you of another because they "go together," or, more properly, *went* together at some earlier time. When things are perceived at the same time or place or one as part of another (belonging together) (see chapter 7), Aristotle suggested that the principle of contiguity would account for the subsequent recall of one item, given the other.

Aristotle, like most of the philosophers to be mentioned, thought of associations as operating between Ideas which were largely *images* of former percepts, and while psychologists never did have a good idea of what an idea might be, it was clear to Aristotle that associations occurred within a person and not "out there" in the external world, where two or more things might be next to each other, that is, contiguous. This point is important to appreciate at the outset, because we shall see psychologists, much later, talking about associations between stimuli and responses or responses and consequent events or objects, that is, rewards or punishments, all of which are external events. Equally commonly, psychologists will be talking about the associations between words and words or nonsense syllables and other nonsense syllables. In all those cases, we must remember that any learning represented by such associations must take place within the learner, presumably, within his or her body—and, more specifically, as reactions within his or her nervous systems—not, as Artistotle was inclined to surmise, within his or her heart. You might want to learn this "by heart"!

Aristotle was clearly not satisfied that contiguity alone could account for all associations, although with a little stretching of the concept, it would cover a great many. He considered frequency and intensity of ideas but stressed more a second law, namely, that of similarity and contrast— something that occurs to you (either in the real world or in a thought sequence) activates the memory of something else because it is similar to, or opposite in nature to, the original image. A zebra reminds you of a horse or jackass not because they are now together or ever were in your experience but because when you see your first zebra (after having seen horses) the "thought" of a horse occurs because of similarity. The two thoughts occur together or in such close proximity as to allow us to continue to talk about contiguity. Later on, the mention of a zebra will arouse the association of horse because of that original contiguity. Or consider seeing something very large, say, an apple the size of a grapefruit or pumpkin; the only way the largeness of the apple can have an impact is in terms of a contiguous thought of small apples. The law of opposites or contrast turns into a special case of contiguity. We should note that Aristotle was quite clear on the automaticity of the associations in a thought process. The associations came up as a, b, c, . . . without any choice on the part of the associator. The individual could stop a series or start it but could not direct it.

Many writers throughout the history of literature and philosophy have described situations that reflect or illustrate association or conditioning. We are indebted to Mowrer (1960a) for a story from a play by Lope de Vega (1615). In this play, a boy is forced to compete with cats for his food. Pieces of food are thrown on the floor in the monastery where the boy lives. A group of cats rushes for each morsel, and the boy suffers in his diet. He may not fight the cats in the presence of monk dispensing food. One day, the boy captures the cats and puts them all into a bag and proceeds to beat the bag while emitting slight coughs. Every time he coughs, he pummels the bag. When the monk returns to feed the boy (and cats), the cats begin their usual forays. The boy coughs discreetly, and the cats disappear. This might be the first record of avoidance or escape conditioning, although we lack details on many experimental features that are the heart of learning theory.

CONCEPT OF ISOLATION

Benedict Spinoza (1632–77) also found the mind not to be free to think for itself; he believed that it thinks of one thing or another because of a cause that has a prior cause, and so on ad infinitum. In talking about memory, Spinoza proposed two factors that might be interpreted as laws of association or, perhaps more properly, of learning and memory. To remember something, he said, it helps if one understands the matter or material. He gave no help on the business of understanding beyond stating that the less intelligible something is, the less well it will be remembered. But his second point bears some consideration. In *The Ethics* (1677), he appears to have been quite aware of what modern psychologists call retroactive inhibition (see chapter 16). He talks of remembering a play better if one does not read more plays thereafter. Reading additional similar material, he says, will lead to a mutual confusion (proactive inhibition is hinted at here) and will result in faulty memory. We can label Spinoza's suggestions here as a *law of isolation*, or *law of uniqueness*, meaning that we can recall something better if the matter is separated out, differentiated, or is not like a lot of other events or experiences. Later on, some psychologists will offer laws of novelty or vividness; they are probably referring to the same principle.

THE BRITISH ASSOCIATIONISTS

CAUSATION as determiner of associations

Thomas Hobbes (1588–1679), the first of the British empiricists, suggested a principle of causation as a determiner of associations. Reducing causation to a matter of antecedents and consequences, Hobbes introduced another principle of association: when we see something that in our prior experience happened before or after some other event, we will think of that other event—for example, a dark cloud will make us think of rain or the sight of ashes might recall a fire. Here, we have contiguity again, but with an interactive relationship helping the contiguity along. Hobbes was a materialistic thinker; except for his method of speculation, he could be considered to have been a behaviorist or a physiological psychologist. External movements (stimuli) would create movements in the brain that might eventuate in some behavior. If one kind of movement in the brain activated another previously established movement, one would have the basis for an association. Brain movements continued more or less indefinitely, once started (law of inertia). We will meet such recurrent brain movements again when we look at Hebb's (1949) concept of neural cell assemblies. (See Hobbes's *Human Nature* 1650).

Through perception + reflection complex ideas are developed from more simple sensory experiences

John Locke (1632–1704), perhaps the most prominent of the British empiricists because of his writings on politics and government, is best known to psychologists for his position that man is born with no preconceived (in the literal sense) ideas. At birth, his mind is a blank—tabula rasa—a clean slate or white paper on which experience will write. Through perception and reflection (a kind of internal perception or examination, which includes such operations as "thinking, doubting, believing, reasoning, knowing, willing"), complex ideas are developed from more simple sensory experiences. Locke is of primary interest in the history of association theory because of his extension of the principle to include motor activities (not just ideas). He described the case of a young man who learned to dance in the privacy of his attic, which happened to have a large trunk on the floor. The young man followed instructions in a guidebook and learned to dance in that situation. When testing his skills at a ballroom, he found himself to be inadequate. The trunk in the attic was sorely missed. Locke was the first writer to use the word *association* to describe the connection between events or ideas.

(Bishop) George Berkeley (1685–1753), in developing his *ideal* system of knowledge, discussed such matters as the perception of distance or of objects in terms of contiguity. Talking about hearing a coach outside and leaving his house to enter it, he describes the ideas "intromitted" by each sense, which while distinct and different from each other "but having been observed constantly to go together, they are spoken of as one and the same thing." Here, we have contiguity, with a suggestion of frequency as a sublaw. We can pause to note that for Berkeley, there are no real objects in an out-there world—there are only ideas composed of experiences (sensations) that go

First to use the word "association" - connection between events or ideas

together. Thus, "a certain colour, taste, smell, figure, and consistence having been observed to go together are accounted one distinct thing, signified by the name apple; other collections of ideas constitute a stone, a tree, a book, and the like sensible things" (Berkeley, 1709).

David Hume (1711–76) was perhaps the first to draw a formal distinction between sensations and images. He called these "impressions" and "ideas," the latter being "faint images of" impressions, differing in "degrees of force and liveliness." Hume sought for some universal principle that would account for normal and common or usual successive and organized thought processes. One idea does not lead to another merely by chance. There are rules, and Hume suggested three: resemblance, contiguity in time and place, and cause and effect. These rules appeared to Hume to be self-evident, that is, requiring no proof.

David Hartley (1705–57) is often cited as the father of association theory. He, too (1749), espoused contiguity with a sublaw of frequency; thus, "Any sensations A, B, C &c. by being associated with one another a sufficient Number of times, get such a Power over the corresponding ideas a, b, c, &c. that anyone of the Sensations A, when impressed alone, shall be able to exite in the mind, b, c, &c. The Ideas of the rest." Hartley was aware of the facility of verbal associations and wrote of the circumstance of one word in a sentence leading to another. Hartley is famous for his efforts at a physiology of association through his postulation of neural vibrations. When a nerve is activated, vibrations are set up in its immediate vicinity so that other nerves that may also be functioning (and vibrating) will generate a mutual tendency to set off virbrations in one another. After thousands of joint functions, the vibrations in nerve A will set up vibrations in nerve B and vice versa, accounting for any associations that may be generated.

The British doctrine of association came to its fulfillment with the summarizing and categorizing efforts of Thomas Brown (1778–1820). Brown (1820) began by suggesting that Hume's causation principle was really only a case of rather intimate contiguity. Contiguity and resemblance he described as major principles, or primary laws. A number of secondary laws, however, proved necessary to account for the operation of the primary laws. Thus, the law of *duration* supplements the law of contiguity because many contiguous events do not enter into association. "The longer we dwell on objects, the more fully do we rely on our future remembrance of them." A second subsidiary law is that of liveliness (brilliance, vivacity). A third law, frequency, along with a fourth, recency, are the major secondary laws of association, or "suggestion," as Brown would have it. To these, he added some four other secondary laws, that is, laws modifying the primary principles. The first of these, number five, is a principle that reminds us of Spinoza's law of isolation. Brown describes a situation wherein a particular song is sung by only one person. Later, the song will remind us of that person and that person alone; in the case where many people might have sung that melody in one's hearing, no particular individual would be recalled. The sixth, seventh, eighth, and ninth principles, which deal with states of health and body temperament, emotion, and prior habits, never attained any prominence. The five important secondary laws listed above have played important roles in the subsequent psychology of learning.

Another philosopher of consequence in our brief history of association-ism is James Mill (1773–1836), whose work is currently of some interest to cognitive psychologists. Mill argued that all our ideas are derived from sensations. The sensations are either simultaneous or successive. If we have experiences that generate a number of simultaneous sensations (for example, eating an apple or watching a violin recital), our ideas will similarly be simultaneous or synchronous on some future occasion when only one or some of the sensory precursors is present. If the sensations are successive, so will, then, one idea lead to another in the (historical) order. "Our ideas spring up, or exist, in the order in which the sensations existed, of which they are the copies." "This is the general law of the 'Association of Ideas'." We might be somewhat cautious about the generality of these temporal restric-tions of Mill. In recalling a story, we may very well think of something that happened later in the story before we get to it in a recital of the tale.

Mill recognized his basic law as that of antecedents and consequences (Hume's causality). He also recognized a need to consider degrees of associative strength. Some associations are stronger than others. They last longer. The differential strength Mill assigned to the laws of vividness and frequency, with vividness closely related to pleasure and pain.

Mill's psychology was sometimes referred to as mental chemistry, because he tried to show how complex ideas were developed through association out of simpler, more elemental ideas. Thus, a number of synchronous ideas could fuse into a complex idea, which could only be broken down into its components with great difficulty, just as white light can be broken down (with difficulty) into its spectral components. You can then easily have an idea that looks novel, strange, and unaccountable because it is composed of unrecognized elements. Complex ideas are composed of sim-pler or of less complex ideas in combination. John Stuart Mill (1806–73) was to dispute his father in some of his mental chemistry speculations and sug-gested that complex ideas might be generated by simpler ones and not mere-ly consist of them. We will not argue this issue and turn instead to Sir Wil-liam Hamilton (1978–1856), famous for many contributions to psychology, and one of particular interest in this context, the principle of redintegration.

REDINTEGRATION

Sir William (1861), crediting St. Augustin with the original observation, argued for only one general law of association, that of redintegration, or totality, which he expressed as "those thoughts suggest each other which had previously constituted parts of the same entire total act of cognition." He thought of this law as a higher order integration of the previously suggested laws of contiguity or affinity (similarity). Thus, the supreme law of association is that "activities, excite each other in proportion as they have previously belonged as parts, to one whole activity." A favorite illustration of this law for many psychologists is the revival of a terror reaction in some ex-soldier when he hears the sound of an airplane in peacetime. Some terrifying episode of his wartime experience is recreated by what had to be only a part of a larger situation.

Many other writers, French as well as British, contributed to the evolution of the concept of association. We have seen enough to recognize that many problems central to a great deal of research in the psychology of learning had been considered by many thinkers over a long period of time. The passage of time has not proved especially helpful. We are still concerned with problems of contiguity and similarity (much of our behavior consists of *not* responding in some specific way to a similar stimulus but behaving in a discriminated fashion). The problem of frequency is still with us in connection with one-trial learning, as well as with short-term (STM) and long-term memory (LTM). Redintegration and isolation are currently of interest in studies of grouping, clustering, and subjective organization. Recency and primacy (a new term for vividness?) are obviously still alive and living in the learning laboratories of many universities. Uniqueness (the Von Restorff effect) is still unanalyzed.* The role of emotion and pleasure and pain that James Mill emphasized are obvious current concerns. Whether we have improved much over the associationists remains to be seen. What cannot be denied is that learning theory has taken as its major question the problem of how associations are formed, even though the language has been changed to such terms as *learning* or *conditioning*, and the components of associations have been changed from such terms as *sensations* and *ideas* to *stimuli* and *responses*.

PSYCHOLOGY AND ASSOCIATIONS

It is customary to date the birth of psychology with the opening of Wilhelm Wundt's laboratory in 1879 in Leipzig, Germany. Also, in 1879, in London, Sir Francis Galton was beginning a whole series of psychological measurements and researches; however, this work requires us to classify him as an experimenter rather than an armchair philosopher, as those thinkers we have just considered must be labeled. Among many other interests, Sir

---

*The Von Restorff (1933) effect refers to the relative ease of learning some item in a group where the item is distinctly different, for example, a word printed in red in a list of words, a numeral in a list of words, and so forth. See Hilgard and Bower (1975) for a discussion.

Francis was interested in association. He performed the first known experiment (in 1879) in what we might call memory or learning by translating a casual walk along London's Pall Mall into an experimental exercise. In the course of his walk, he observed that many items which he saw (a squirrel, a stone, a tree, a carriage) would remind him of something else, some prior experience. To formalize and regularize this observation, Galton wrote down the names of 75 objects, and looking at one term at a time, he allowed himself to "think" of two separate "thoughts" to each term, timing himself with a stopwatch. He repeated the study four times and found a considerable consistency in his responses. He described his reactions as basically the arousal of imagery from various periods of his life, finding some to be somewhat revealing and rather intimate and not suitable for publication. Galton did not draw any profound conclusions from his study, but he did demonstrate something about the speed of thought, its relative automaticity and stability over a period of time, and its relation to past experience. The primary finding Galton reported was the occurrence of various kinds of images when a word was viewed.

Galton's technique was expanded by Jung (1910) and the psychiatrists Kent and Rosanoff (1910), who prepared a standard list of common terms (100 words) and attempted to locate sources of "complexes" within subjects, who were asked not for their thoughts, as was the case with Galton, but for the first word that came to mind given a particular stimulus word. Long delays in reaction time, different responses on repetition of the list, or unusual responses were alleged to point to hidden problem areas. Jung was able to pinpoint a thief out of a group of three suspects by analyzing each suspect's responses. Kent and Rosanoff standardized norms on 1,000 subjects.

The work of Galton, Jung, and Kent and Rosanoff led to a whole host of studies and modifications of procedure in using word lists in psychological research (for a great many different purposes). The nature of words themselves became a separate area of inquiry. Words were analyzed for their frequency of usage, their pronounceability, their meanings, "association value," concreteness, abstractness, and imagery-provoking capacity, as well as probability of occurrence in sentences. We will have occasion to look at some of this work later.

Almost simultaneously with Galton, a German investigator, Ebbinghaus (1885), hoping to improve on the rote-learning practices in German schools, embarked on a study of how lists of words could be learned most efficiently. Almost immediately, he recognized that words had their associates from past experience and that these associates varied in strength, making it impossible to compare one technique of memorizing with another, because the lists could not be prepared to have the same order of difficulty. To solve his problem, he invented new words, consisting of a consonant-vowel-consonant (or CVC) but having no meaning for him; accordingly, he called these "nonsense syllables." Equipped with some 2,000 such manufactured items, he proceeded to arrange them in lists of convenient size and began memorizing one list after another, varying his procedure as he devised new arrangements.

Ebbinghaus thought of his operation as one of assocation. One syllable was associated with another syllable, that with the next, and so on. Whatever the virtues of his work, psychologists were quick to seize upon the new kind of "verbal" materials, and the nonsense syllables became the basic tool of psychologists for almost a century. Later on, many psychologists turned to another kind of serial learning, the maze, using rats as their learners; to a degree, psychologists became identified as people who ran rats through mazes or students through nonsense syllables.

At the present time, neither nonsense syllables nor rats are very popular with learning psychologists, and identifying psychologists with such operations is no longer meaningful; however, both rats and nonsense syllables served a purpose in their time and will have to be looked at.

For the moment, we can look back at the concept of association and what philosophers and psychologists tried to do with it. The armchair pundits recognized a number of vital points that cannot be denied:

1. Associations (however described) do represent something that occurs in learning. Something is connected with something else, and in the future (memory), one of the items in association can (sometimes) generate the other.

2. Associations are formed only *under certain conditions* (that, by the way, is a good point to recognize when we talk about conditioning); certain conditions must prevail, or "things" will not be associated. The basic problem of learning will be to account for the conditions that are both necessary and sufficient for learning to occur. The philosophers we have mentioned, from Aristotle on, had uniformly agreed upon at least one condition, that of contiguity, as a primary and necessary law of association. This condition seems reasonable enough, but we will find some psychologists questioning its role and significance. It may, in some views, be only an apparent condition, which obscures the operation of more important operations, where the contiguity may very well exist but not be operative in any functional way. Thus, for example, there is no way for *snow* to be noncontiguous with *whiteness*, yet the relationship of snow and white might be the important factor in the learning and retention of snow-white. Similarly, a door and a house have a contiguous existence, but it might be the part-whole relationship that is functional. We will consider this problem later (see chapter 12).

3. Associations are formed *in* the learner and not *by* the learner. This point is crucial. Either learning takes place or it does not. The learner has quite literally nothing to say about it. The student should not say, "I associated this with that"—he or she should say, "This was associated with that in

me." In other words, learning occurs, presumably in our brains as a function of the circumstances that prevail or the operating conditions. It is automatic and quite unconscious. These points will be made again, but for the moment, it should be appreciated that you as a person, a "self," are quite helpless about what you have learned or will learn. In the process of trying to form an assocation in which, to be sure, anyone can indulge, what occurs to you cannot be controlled. Suppose you try to associate some word or throught representing an orange with some other word or throught representing a swimming pool. In the process, you might have various thoughts occur; you can reject them or accept them in the sense of allowing new or additional thoughts to occur, but you cannot dictate what you will think of next. Try it.

The statement (above) that you do not actively engage in the formation of associations does not mean that you and your nature are not involved. Different people retain different associations from what might appear to be the same experience. Certainly, different animals learn different things with varying efficiencies. You as a human being respond to situations in terms of your structure and nature. You notice some things and not others; you may react to parts and not to the whole or vice versa. Some people see the trees and not the woods, while others do not react to the trees as such. In later sections, we will try to take account of some of the personal or organismic functions that determine what we learn or remember or do not learn or remember.

At the present time, the concept of association is not as popular as it was over the past centuries. Some psychologists hope to account for learning without talking about it. They can be encouraged and may have some kinds of success, but the great tradition in learning psychology is that learning itself amounts to association, however it is labeled and however it comes into being. It may be that many other operations or activities will have to be recognized and appreciated before we can discover how an association is formed, but the end product will still be an association.

In the 1930s, the interest of psychologists in the laws of association enjoyed a brief revival with the publication of Robinson's *Association Theory Today* (1932). Robinson represented the then active functional school of American psychology, which had broken with Wundtian structuralists but could not quite join the ultraobjective behaviorists. Robinson's work should be examined for a more detailed appreciation of the meaning and role of the various laws of association he considered.

In recent decades, the term *association* has come to be used rather casually, not technically. Other terms, such as *conditioning*, or *a function of*, or *relationship* have come to assume more technical status. There may be a restoration of revival in the making, as demonstrated in a 1975 symposium on Operant–Pavlovian interactions (see Weisman 1977), where the term *association* was frequently employed to describe the essence of the learning operation.

APPENDIX ON MNEMONICS OR MEMORY TRICKS

The discussion of the laws of association in this chapter might appear to be somewhat ethereal to some students. It might surprise such students that philosophers have been concerned with practical problems all through our historical past. One of the persistent problems of all time has been that of how to improve "the memory." It was a topic that concerned Cicero and other writers on rhetoric, and some of what they said has not been improved upon. It might be useful at this early stage in our investigation of learning to look at mnemonics.

We all forget many things that other people remember, and as we grow older, the situation grows worse. When others remember things we think we should have remembered, we tend to envy their better memories. But as we have argued, there are no such things as memories, good or bad; there are only people who remember more or less for a lot of different reasons. Yet, the delusion persists, and we would all like to remember better. Such a state of affairs has been going on for a long time, starting before Socrates, who urged his students to develop their memories. Socrates frowned on the new art of writing as leading inevitably to the deterioration of mental powers.

The ancients regarded memory as a basic skill, to be practiced as part of the general art of rhetoric. If you were to appear in public and make speeches, you would not be impressive and convincing if you had to refer to notes. Modern college professors and politicians do not seem to support the ancient view. Today, a president not only reads an address on the state of the nation but has it written for him. The only real memorizers left appear to be concert violinists and pianists, who apparently feel some pressure to play a Beethoven concerto without benefit of notes. Even in music, some rebels are appearing who use notes at the piano, arguing that they have better things to do than memorizing something that could easily be forgotten and which, if forgotten, would result in an artistic disaster.

Still, some people would like to remember more or better, and the felt demand has always generated suppliers. The suppliers offer a variety of mnemonic aids or procedures that have a rather limited virtue. The techniques that have been developed apply primarily to sets of rather unrelated or random items. It is possible, for example, to use some procedures to remember a long grocery list, the names of a great many people in some gathering, the telephone numbers on any number of pages of a telephone book, or what article appears on what page of a given issue of *Time* magazine. The question one should raise is, Why bother? It is much easier to write down a grocery list, for example, or to use the telephone book when you want all those numbers (you would have to have the book available to prove to anyone that you had such ridiculous information memorized), and about the most useless information one could have is the page number of an article in *Time*. After all, there is a table of contents. What would be far better in the last example would be to know what the article said. Its location is quite irrelevant.

Suppose someone could recall a set of ten three-digit numbers after hearing them once—a rather remarkable performance to be sure. Luria (1968) wrote a book about a Russian gentleman who was able to remember such trivia more or less indefinitely. In this country, Lorayne and Lucas (1974) wrote a bestseller, *The Memory Book*, describing a variety of procedures that might help one remember a great many unrelated items if one planned to be an entertainer demonstrating such capacities. Before we describe the procedures of such memory experts, we might recall that successful and important people are too busy to spend time memorizing what does not need memorizing. Remember, presidents read speeches written for them. A staff of experts should be able to write a better speech than the president, and a president who spends time memorizing a speech is probably not attending to his responsibilities.

Loci et Res: The Method of Pegs

What do the masters of mental wizardry do to be able to recall a large number of items? The basic trick goes back to ancient Greece, where a poet-entertainer named Simonides hit upon a method for remembering unrelated items in what was thought to be a sequence. In a fascinating and scholarly work, *The Art of Memory*, Yates (1966) describes the origin of mnemonics by introducing Simonides, who is improvising a poem honoring the host at a banquet. Halfway through the poem, Simonides began to lavish praise on the gods Castor and Pollux. When he finished the poem, he requested his fee, but the host offered only half the agreed upon sum with the suggestion that Castor and Pollux be billed for the rest. At that moment, a servant called the entertainer to the door, saying there were two young men asking for him. Simonides went outside but found no one. Just then, the roof of the banquet hall fell in, killing everyone inside. Simonides was called upon to help identify the bodies, as they were mangled beyond recognition. It occurred to Simonides that he could identify the guests by their positions at the table, and he proceeded to do so. With the success he enjoyed from the recall of the people by their places, Simonides decided that any thing (*res*) could be recalled if one had first noted its place (*locus*). The memory method of loci et res was born.

To implement the method of loci et res all you have to do is to place things to be remembered in some already known sequence of places. The most convenient known place might be your home. Consider a floor plan of your own home with a front door, front hall, living room, kitchen, bath, bedrooms, and so forth. Think of them in some orderly way, for example, the front door is Number 1, the front hall is Number 2, and so on. Now if you want to remember a number of things in order simply think of each thing (form images of them) and place them mentally at the numbered places. If the problem is a grocery list and the first thing you want to buy is bananas, imagine a bunch of bananas on your front door as a kind of decoration. If the next item is eggs, picture the front hall floor covered with broken eggs. The next item might be coffee. If so, imagine serving coffee to guests in your living room, and so on. The number of things you can remember in order is limited only by the number of places you can recall in order. Some Australian psychologists, Ross and Lawrence (1968), used their university campus and its various buildings as a suitable frame of reference, or sequence of "pegs." There were 50 buildings in a known sequence, and they were able to remember 50 different randomly selected items by picturing the first item in one building, the next item in the next building, and so on.

Imaging

Instead of using actual places, you can use a substitute arrangement, where you first learn some kind of cue word, or peg, or "hook," for each number and then imagine the to-be-remembered items in relation to each of the previously learned words. Thus, if you want to remember ten things in order, you can first learn a simple childhood jingle (one-bun, two-shoe, three-tree, four-door, five-hive, six-sticks, seven-heaven, eight-gate, nine-wine, ten-hen). This should be easy enough. Now, to remember any ten things in order, picture the first with a bun, the second with a shoe, and so on. Give yourself a little time for each bit of imaging (five to eight seconds should do; see Bugelski, Kidd, and Segmen 1968). When you finish, you will find that thinking of one-bun will automatically bring up the first item, and the same for the rest. One warning is in order: think of each pair, the peg and the item, as interacting in some way and not as just sitting there side by side. If item nine (wine) happens to be a horse, picture the horse in a huge tub trampling grapes or sitting around in the barn with the other horses having a wine-tasting party. The more active and *interactive* the imagery, the better.

Note that while you can report the items in sequence or backwards or forwards, you can also report them at random. You do not actually learn a sequence—you learn some "paired associates," which you happen to be able to report in sequence.

If you want to remember more than ten items, you can extend your original base by first learning a cue word for 20, 50, or 1,000 numbers. There is actually no limit on what you can recall in this way. Actually, you do not even need to have a prepared set of real or substitute loci. If you want to remember 20 words in a row, all you have to do is image the first word in some interaction with the second word, the second word in an interaction with the third, and so on. With a little practice 20, 30, or even 50 words will come back quite easily (Bugelski 1974); mnemonists call this procedure linking.

Atkinson (1975) extended this method to learning foreign language vocabulary and demonstrated some superiority for the method over the normal operations. To learn the meaning of a French word, for example, *fenêtre*, you would look for an English-sounding word in the French one. Fenêtre has the English-sounding word *net* included within it. The word means "window." To remember the translation, you would picture a window with a net over it, as a curtain, perhaps, and whenever you hear the "net" sound, you would automatically think of a window. The method works for any foreign word that has an English sound in it, and that happens to be true for most French words, for example, *poisson* ("fish") has the word *son*; *aprés midi* includes the sound "pray" or "prey." Such a procedure is, of course, quite artificial, but it does work and might be used if one is having trouble remembering any particular word.

What has just been stated is that almost any word can serve as a peg for any other word if the items named by the words are imaged in an interaction. Presumably, you should be able to remember hundreds of pairs of words in the sense of being able to report which word of a pair went with the other if you imaged them together. Experimental data gathered on unselected military personnel indicated that soldiers would remember up to 95 percent of 500 word pairs if they were given a few seconds to consider the separate pairs. Note that simply listening to 500 pairs of words at five seconds a pair would take about 40 minutes. A detailed recall of 40 minutes of study is truly a remarkable performance, yet most college students should do quite well in such a task (Miller, Gallanter, and Pribram 1960). All you have to do is to let an appropriate set of images occur.

For remembering what name goes with what face, the same procedure is employed, except that now some feature of the face is selected which "makes you think" of the name or some part of it. This obviously calls for some study, perhaps more than is ordinarily necessary, but the experts who remember dozens if not hundreds of names find that it pays. To remember the name of Vice-President Mondale, for example, you might think of mountains and valleys and look for some feature that might also make you think of mountains and valleys. You can do a lot of things if you are determined to remember a person's name, such as saying it over several times or writing it out in the air or on your palm with a finger. Most of us care only for our own names and want to be remembered by others. Good recall calls for work, usually an unattractive operation.

There are many other little tricks to recall certain items. Little rhymes can be used to recall the cranial nerves in order. There is little or no point to remembering them in order. What is important is to be able to trace the nerves from their origins to their terminations. For such recall, there are no easy tricks. "I before e except after c" is useful for *receive* but not for *seize*.

In general, the mnemonic tricks that can assist in recall are of no great benefit to mankind. They illustrate a point that needs appreciation, however, and that is something everyone should learn, namely, it usually takes some effort to remember something. Instead of complaining about a poor memory, the forgetful person should admit that he or she did not take the trouble to learn something. The ability to recall is not a gift. It is the result of good learning and, often, of frequent rehearsal.

Associations:
1) something is connected with something else and in the future, one of the items in the association can generate the other
2) associations are formed only under certain conditions (certain things must prevail or "things" will not be associated
3) associations are formed "in" the learner

II

The Experimental Approach to Learning

INTRODUCTION

As long as philosophers continued to speculate about learning and memory, they could only be honored for their efforts. They could even be quite correct, but no one had to take them seriously in the practical world. They had no evidence. The successes in the sciences of physics and chemistry resulted in many practical applications in the real world, and the interests of some philosophically minded investigators were drawn to the prospects for advances in understanding human nature through empirical studies. Before there were any formally designated psychologists, some laboratory or laboratory–like investigations were initiated into the nature of the mind by such people as Ernst Heinrich Weber, Gustav Theodor Fechner, Sir William Hamilton, and many others. Most important for us, among these others, were Herman von Ebbinghaus, Ivan Pavlov, and Edward L. Thorndike. These three investigators opened the field of learning to experimental attack. All three began their work before the nineteenth century came to a close, and each still has followers working along lines they initiated; thus, we can now consider the psychology of learning to be about 100 years old. What have learning researchers discovered in the last 100 years? Have they made any marked progress beyond the original discoveries of Ebbinghaus, Pavlov, and Thorndike?

In the remainder of this volume, we will examine the original contributions of the pioneer investigators, as well as those of their followers. We will also recognize that the rationalist approach did not die. Because the laboratory trappings of the experimentalists added a certain charisma to their findings, the experimentalists almost preempted the field, but some rationalists also donned laboratory coats and continued to expound their views of human nature (supported by some experimental findings). Most prominent among these are proponents of the Gestalt school—Max Wertheimer, Kurt Koffka, and Wolfgang Köhler, and their followers. The Gestaltists emphasized the apparent creativity of man in problem-solving situations. Their chief stock in trade was the concept of insight, which was based on their more fundamental views of innate perception principles. For the Gestaltists, perception was the basic human operation or function, and it, in turn, was based on primary organizing principles that were natural human proclivities. When an individual is exposed to his or her environment, that person organizes what he or she sees; the parts become organized into a whole as they fall into place, and the relationships of the parts to each other then determine the perception. When a problem situation is properly perceived, its solution becomes obvious, automatically. An insight is developed. Without insight, learning is inadequate, dull, rote, and easily forgotten.

The views of the Gestaltists will receive some attention in subsequent chapters, although their contribution cannot be taken too seriously. If one must await the arrival of insight, there is not much that can be done about learning; either you get your insight or you do not. Such a view is not too enticing to those charged with a responsibility for teaching others, and the lack of convincing experimental findings has not endeared the Gestalt approach to many modern learning psychologists. Their emphasis on insight might be translated into a concern over "meaning." The latter topic will receive our concerned attention. For the present, we will turn that attention to an earlier German investigator who was concerned primarily with nonmeaning, or nonsense.

4

Ebbinghaus and Nonsense Syllables

By the middle of the nineteenth century, the laws of association had enjoyed enough discussion by philosophers to allow for the conclusions of Brown and the Mills to appear to settle the matter. But the philosophers had never found or bothered with proof for their laws. They had worked backwards. Taking any selected association as a sample, they would explain how it happened to occur. They had never bothered to produce associations "from scratch," or "de novo," if you prefer.

Around 1875, Ebbinghaus (1850–1909), at that time a nonacademic scholar, became interested in the possibilities of applying experimental methods to the study of memory. He is said to have been inspired in this direction by the success of Fechner in the field of psychophysics. Ebbinghaus had studied in England and was impressed by the British associationists' emphasis on frequency or repetition as a major factor in association formation, and he undertook to apply scientific methods to isolate the role of this variable.

Using only himself as a subject, Ebbinghaus embarked on a rigid daily routine of memorizing, using the process of repetition; he began with poetry but discovered almost at once that no comparisons could be made because poems of comparable difficulty were not available. In what might be regarded as a stroke of genius, he hit upon the notion of manufacturing his own verbal material by making up combinations of consonants and vowels in the form consonant-vowel-consonant (CVC), thereby producing a reasonably unlimited supply of new and (assumed) equally difficult materials. Ebbinghaus developed some 2,300 nonsense syllables by using all the possible CVC combinations that did not result in meaningful words. In English, the procedure followed by Ebbinghaus will produce only about 1,200 nonsense syllables for most literate people. Many nonsense syllables, such as *bac*, sound exactly like meaningful words and should not qualify.

With a supply of learning materials at hand, it was now possible to prepare a list of any desired length and to start memorizing by repeatedly reading the list over and trying to recite it without looking at the syllables unless he had to. Ebbinghaus kept a strict time limit by using a metronome to control the exposure or recitation time. Ebbinghaus invented what is called the anticipation method, because after an initial reading of a list, he would try to think of the first syllable without looking at it, then the next, and so on, always trying to anticipate what the next syllable would be before looking at it. Later investigators would invent the memory drum, a revolving cylinder on which a list of syllables could be mounted and exposed one at a time in a viewing window at a fixed interval (usually, one, two, or three seconds).

SERIAL ORDER

The method followed by Ebbinghaus can be called that of learning in serial order. What Ebbinghaus was trying to do was to approximate something like learning passages of words in sequence, as in sentences, paragraphs, or verses of poetry. He did not choose to study any single association, and for this, we can fault him, as his conclusions would only apply to lists of nonsense syllables and not necessarily to anything else.

It may be that the educational practices of the time dictated his choice. Schoolchildren learned by rote memorization, repeating lists of rules, lines of poetry, or even whole compositions, and it was the role of repetition that intrigued this investigator.

As an early experimental comparison, Ebbinghaus learned an 80-syllable verse of poetry and then learned 80 nonsense syllables. The poetry took nine trials and the nonsense syllables 80 trials; Ebbinghaus concluded that nonsense syllables were about nine times as difficult to learn as poetry. Here we at once recognize that the difficulty of the poetry must be evaluated—a 30-syllable limerick can be learned in one or two trials by the limerick fancier, and 30 nonsense syllables will keep one busy for a long time.

NONSENSE SYLLABLE FINDINGS

Ebbinghaus discovered a large number of findings, which he reported in his famous book, *Über das Gedächtnis* [*On Memory*] in 1885. These findings have been replicated thousands of times in learning laboratories, and we will list some here.

Amount learned. To learn a list of eight nonsense syllables often takes the average college student about eight trials. This correspondence might suggest something like a syllable per trial, but if you increase the list to ten, 12, or 16, many more than ten, 12, or 16 trials will be required.

Intertrial forgetting. If you try to repeat a list in proper order, you will normally find a steady gain in number of syllables, but from trial to trial, you may forget some that were previously learned while you gain new syllables, showing no net gain. Even after a perfect recitation, you cannot be sure that another test will be successful.

Serial order effects. Normally, the first few syllables in a list are learned first, the last syllables next, and the ones in the middle last. This finding is so common and so well-established that it has acquired the name of *the serial learning effect.* Figure 4.1 shows the serial learning curve of three different classes of students who were given five trials to learn the eight nonsense syllables shown on the baseline. The classes differed in the learning time allowed per syllable (three, four, or five seconds). Note that with longer times, there were fewer errors, but in every instance, the curves followed the same form. This phenomenon is so striking that many investigators have tried to account for it, but there is no universally accepted explanation.

We will not try to explain the serial order pattern here. An early attempt by the author (Bugelski 1950) did not enjoy acclaim. Instead, we can point to some other features. Note that the first syllable has a decided edge over the others and that the most difficult syllable stands just past the middle of the list. This is not due to any special difficulty of that syllable—it would be true for any ordinary nonsense syllable. Perhaps, the ease of the first syllable has something to do with displacing the error difficulty to just past the middle.

Kinds of errors. When someone learns nonsense syllables, he or she can err by announcing a syllable before its proper turn. This is called an intralist error or intralist intrusion. The person can report a syllable that is not in the list (an extralist intrusion) or can recombine letters of syllables (*mof* and *gex* can become *mex* or *fog*); such errors show that the individual is learning something but also suggest that other factors are at work. Of course, the subject may say nothing at all when some syllable should be reported. Technically, this is an omission error, but frequently, it is interpreted to mean that the subject did not have anything to say or that nothing occurred to him or her. Such is not always or even commonly the case. The subject often thinks of a syllable, knows that it is wrong, and refrains from overtly committing an error. Failure to discover what the subject did think of might lead to an erroneous interpretation of what is going on.

Remote associations. Ebbinghaus believed that anticipating intralist intrusions represented some possible learning between list items that appeared early with later items. Thus, Syllable 1 could be associated with Syllable 2, but it might also last long enough in terms of its stimulus value (as a trace) to become associated with syllables 3, 4, 5, and so on. Similarly, each syllable

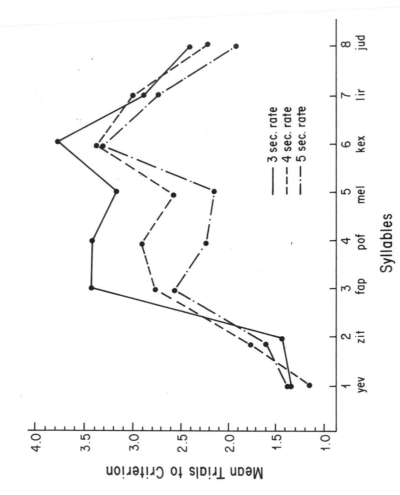

FIGURE 4.1: Serial learning curves based on classroom data. The traditional picture emerges despite the lack of laboratory refinements.

could have such forward or backward associations with every other syllable in a relatively short list.

Ebbinghaus tried to prove this hypothesis by using what he called the "method of derived lists." Suppose that after a list is learned, a new list is made up from that now old list, with the syllables 1, 3, 5, 7, and 9 appearing as 1, 2, 3, 4, and 5 and syllables 2, 4, 6, and 8 appearing as 6, 7, 8, and 9. If there is a prior *remote* association between syllables 1 and 3 from the first learning and if similar remote associations have been partially formed between the other items, such a new list should be learned quickly, compared with a random rearrangement of the syllables, where the remote associations would be weaker, backwards, or otherwise inappropriate for the new order. Ebbinghaus reported that such derived lists are indeed more easily learned. His explanation, however, is still not accepted by some critics, for example, Slamecka (1964).

The notion of remote associations was to find a role in later theoretical developments in the concept of the stimulus trace (Hull 1943), and such traces or aftereffects of stimulation are widely accepted as necessary for accounting for any kind of retention or even for learning (Hebb 1949).

The forgetting curve. Ebbinghaus mastered and forgot many hundreds of lists of nonsense syllables, and the course of forgetting so interested him that he embarked on a very exacting experimental investigation. He would learn a list at a fixed time of day, wait for a period, and then test his retention. With a prolonged waiting period, such as a week or 30 days, he would not recall many, if any, syllables, and he devised the *relearning* method to measure retention. If it took ten trials to learn a list the first time and only five trials to relearn the same list on a later occasion, Ebbinghaus assumed that he had actually retained 50 percent of the learning, even though he could not demonstrate this by a recall test. By using the relearning method and the savings score, computed by the formula

$$\frac{\text{trials to learn—trials to relearn}}{\text{trials to learn}} \times 100,$$

Ebbinghaus was able to compute the amount remembered (or forgotten) after any period of time. He learned and relearned lists after half an hour, two hours, eight hours, two days, six days, and 30 days and plotted his famous forgetting curve, which is reproduced in many general psychology and psychology of learning texts. It is not reproduced here because it is misleading and might confuse the student. It is misleading because it is not a general forgetting curve. It is the curve for one man, in mature years, learning lists of nonsense material in serial order to a particular criterion (one perfect recitation). Further, the learner is an experienced operator with nonsense syllables and highly practiced in a particular method. Ebbinghaus found, for example, that after half an hour, he had "saved" only 58 percent of the list. Such a figure may have nothing to do with what anyone else will remember after learning something other than a nonsense syllable list.

EVALUATION

Ebbinghaus' great contribution was not the invention of nonsense syllables. That might have been his big mistake. His great contribution was to demonstrate that experimental methods could be applied to learning and retention. We could now begin to see how an association might be formed (not that Ebbinghaus did so) and need not rely on philosophical speculation. The publication of *Über das Gedächtnis* in 1885 marked the beginning of an experimental attack on problems of learning. The demonstration that learning, a "higher mental process," could be studied by laboratory procedures stimulated what turned out to be thousands of experimental investigations, especially in the United States, where the nonsense syllables were quickly adopted, and systematic research began. Difficulties with nonsense syllables soon were identified. It became clear that one syllable was not equal to another in learnability or "association value," and new techniques were devised for assessing syllables, presenting them, and determining causes of forgetting. We will have ample occasion for examining these developments later. For the moment, we salute the genius of Ebbinghaus.

What Ebbinghaus had done was to point to frequency or repetition as the basic operation in learning. To learn something, all you had to do was to repeat it or be exposed to it often enough. Such a position appealed to many American psychologists. It was *objective* and did not call for much consideration, if any, of what the learner himself might be doing as a *subjective* contribution to learning.

Soon after Ebbinghaus' book appeared, George Müller, the inventor of the memory drum, in Germany, replicated many of Ebbinghaus's findings, but he asked his subjects what they were doing while learning the lists. His learners reported that among other things, they were trying to make sense out of the syllables and trying to organize them in some ways. Müller's pioneer efforts at studying "subjective organization" were forgotten and did not get further consideration until some 60 years later. We will look into such matters later (chapter 15). For the moment, we can conclude with the observation that Müller opened another larger area of research by his observation (with Pilzecker 1900) that retention seemed to improve if after learning something, the learner would rest for a while. During the period of rest, the learning would "consolidate," because of the perseveration of activity of the recently aroused traces. Any activity following the learning might interrupt this perseveration and prevent the consolidation.

One immediate inference students drew from this hypothesis is that you should go to sleep after learning something. This interpretation has been followed up in several American experiments, the classical one being that of Jenkins and Dallenbach (1924), who found that a period of sleep following learning resulted in less forgetting than an equal time period of normal daily activity. The finding is not of great value in a practical world and is open to other interpretations, as we shall see.

Later on we will find that while the perseveration theory was never accepted seriously, a great many investigations into what came to be called retroactive inhibition (chapter 16) were initiated by this view. Other theoretical developments of a more physiological flavor were also generated from the hypothesis of perseveration. Hull's (1943) stimulus trace and Hebb's (1949) perseveration of firing of neural circuits could be considered to be descendants of Müller's brainchild.

Müller
subjective organization - trying to make sense out of the syllables + organize them in some way
Perservation - period of rest or consolidate to improve retention of learning

5

Of Mice and Men,
Machines, and Models

This chapter does not really deal with mice but rather with the question of what is the value, if any, of psychologists' long preoccupation with animals, especially the rat. Of all the species of life around (over 1 million), why did psychologists devote so many years to the study of the albino rat? This particular kind of rat has been bred in captivity for so long that it shows little behavioral resemblance to its Norwegian ancestor. Beach (1951) raised this question many years ago, but he was interested in comparative psychology and wanted psychologists to study other creatures. Some did. We will deal with cats, dogs, and pigeons to some extent. But pigeons have bird brains and are closer to reptiles than to people, and if Alexander Pope was correct in declaring that "the proper study of mankind is man," why should psychologists study any other kind of creature than man if they are, as most would declare, interested in the nature of man?

From any evolutionary argument, the closest creatures to man are the great apes. Why not study them as the species of choice? Well, they are a bit dangerous for one thing, as well as being expensive to obtain and care for. You can talk to them, but it does not help too much, even though they seem to be able to master some language, as current studies by Premack (1970) and Gardner and Gardner (1969) have shown. College students are far less expensive (for psychologists) and much more tractable; they can talk back very easily, and so they have been and still are the favorite species for psychological study. There are some difficulties about using students as subjects, however, which should be recognized. They are not typical human beings in the sense of representing the average man or woman. First, they are restricted in age (17 to 21 or so); they have more education than the average human on this globe; they have, in general, higher I.Q.s; and they are at a point in the development of almost being at the peak of their capacities. Champions in various sports seem to peak at about 25 or 26. Of course, there are exceptions.

What you learn about learning by observations on the learning of college students may not apply to babies, grammar school children, people who never went to school, or older people. Furthermore, being a college student does not in any sense eliminate differences in heredity and prior experience, two powerful variables in any kind of situation. It will be well to keep these points in mind as we go along.

USING ANIMALS IN RESEARCH

But back to the rat. The rat was introduced into psychology back around 1899 by W. S. Small, who first put rats into mazes. We might raise some questions about mazes, too, as people rarely if ever get involved with mazes—although some strange or new buildings might be analogs. Still, getting around in buildings does not appear to be much of a problem for mankind, while mazes do represent problems for rats. Some critics argue that mazes put rats at a disadvantage because they are unnatural to rats, and consequently, what we observe in mazes are the reactions of a frustrated animal in an abnormal situation. Such a criticism might not really be serious. Maybe, human learning only occurs when humans are frustrated, albeit mildly, in an abnormal situation. Is there anything "normal" (in the sense of natural) about what people learn? What is so normal about eating with a fork or blowing your nose gently into a square of cotton or silk or paper? What is normal about driving a car, typing, or even speaking English? Most people do not. What is normal about calling an apple *apple* when every Frenchman knows it is a *pomme*? As far as the frustration goes, imagine yourself dropped into a Russian village and trying to find your way to the nearest airport. Learning consists of doing the unnatural. If it did not, there would be no need to learn.

But again, back to the rat. Why were rats so popular? (They are not so much used in these days—only a handful of old stalwarts still use rats in learning studies.) The usual answers offered by students when asked this question are the following: (1) rats are cheap—the statement is true but the reason is not; (2) they are easy to house, handle, and breed, so that their environments can be controlled and their heredity can be, to some degree, appreciated—again true, but incorrect as a reason; (3) they are animals, and humans are animals, too, and there should, therefore, be some relationship between rat behavior and human behavior. True, and getting warm, but there are other animals that meet reasons (1), (2), and (3), so why the rat? We can throw in another reason of a negative nature here and get it out of the way: people do not like rats and do not care what you do to them, whereas cats and dogs are to some extent loved and honored by people who, through various organizations, might give psychologists trouble. True, but these are not really reasons. We go back to (3).

The A/S Ratio

The real reason was made clear by Hebb (1949), when he pointed out that rats are docile, that is, teachable, in situations that psychologists happened to devise for them. The rats behaved the way psychologists wanted them to and, what is more, expected them to. But the wants and expectations were based on an assumption, not always clearly verbalized, that the rat's brain worked in the way all animal brains work (including the human brain); the human brain was commonly assumed by psychologists to operate like a telephone exchange that just sat there in the head, making connections between incoming signals or impulses from the sense organs and outgoing impulses to the muscles and glands. Most psychologists held such a view up to about 1950.

Now it is true that the brain does do these things, that is, receive, connect, and send out neural impulses, but that is about all the rat's brain does, whereas the human brain does a great deal more besides just sitting there, waiting for a call.

In making his point, Hebb described brains as comprised of, among other parts, sensory areas, motor areas, and association areas. Ignoring the motor areas for the moment, we can assess the amount of brain tissue concerned with sensory inputs and the rest of the brain, assuming that to be concerned with associations or learning, and calculate a ratio, A/S, or amount of association area to amount of sensory area. Such a computation, for the rat, would be of a relatively low decimal order, as the sensory area accounts for most of the rat's brain, which consists primarily of an olfactory sensory area, with comparatively small areas serving vision and other senses. Rats, especially albino rats, do not see well. Hooded or black rats see much better, but they still primarily operate on a sense of smell. Giving a rat visual problems is not an efficient way to spend your time, as many psychologists were to learn.

The human brain, in contrast to that of the rat, has an enormous association area, or at least areas whose function is not too well known, and relatively less of the brain is concerned with sensory functions. Human olfactory lobes, while not negligible, are far less important. In view of the low A/S ratio of the rat, Hebb called the rat a sensory-bound creature, responding to virtually any and all sensory stimuli. In contrast, the human can and does ignore or dismiss the thousands of casual intrusions on his or her more associative activity. We ignore unimportant creaks and noises, shadows, flickers, brushes against our arms or elbows; we avoid olfactory stimuli from our "deodorized" neighbors and frequently even eat our dinners without tasting them. We have ignored smells and tastes to the point where we cannot describe a wine in meaningful terms and have to learn to appreciate a fine wine or even recognize a good one.

As long as psychologists held to the telephone switchboard analogy

or interpretation of the brain, the rat was a superb subject. It fulfilled the
S→R formula as closely as any creature would. Other creatures were not as
tractable, either because their A/S ratios were different or because of other
kinds of biases their species membership imposed on them.

Hebb's book, *The Organization of Behavior* (1949), marked a revolution in psychology. Psychologists began to learn about the reticular formation and its controlling operations; they began to appreciate the constant activity of the brain with or without external stimulus inputs; they were forced to recognize what Hebb described as "spontaneous neural firing" in his description of the nature of neuronal activity. It became possible for psychologists to entertain the notion that someone might do something or think of something without an external energy activating a chain of neural discharges. Psychologists, at least some of them, took a "new look" at the nervous system. What they saw was that there was not only a switchboard but an exchange center, where operators took time off on occasion, went "on strike," made wrong connections, frequently had busy lines, overloaded lines, or no lines at all for some calls, and where, on occasion, calls went out that nobody made.

We are not going to go into the nature of actual neural structures or activity in this text. What is important to observe is that the assumptions one makes (and everybody makes some kinds of assumptions) about the nervous system will determine one's theoretical and practical operations in regard to learning. We will find Skinner (1938, 1953), for instance, considering the nervous system as virtually irrelevant to psychology. Such a position is quite tenable. We cannot go around tinkering with people's nervous systems directly, at least not as psychologists. We have to work from the outside, manipulating stimuli, environments, and conditions. But if we make erroneous assumptions about the nervous system, we can get into trouble. We should, at a minimum, be aware of our assumptions and check them occasionally.

Values of Animal Research

With the "new look" at the brain and with a more respectful appreciation of the nature of the human brain, psychologists began to turn away from the rat as a subject, but some turned too far. There is no reason *not* to use rats as experimental subjects if you know what you are doing. Suppose your basic orientation toward rats is, as was the case with Hull (1943), to get some ideas about behavior that you can then test out on people if the ideas seem to have some merit. Why put people through all sorts of time-wasting operations and perhaps awkward or painful situations if you can get a lead on some broad, general principle from observing rats. Of course, rats are not men or vice versa, but their behavior can be a *source* of speculations that can be tested or checked later on if it seems fruitful to move onto the human level. The same argument, of course, applies to flies, horses, pigs, or gorillas. There is no reason to avoid observations on any creature, and following such observations, one can consider the likelihood of some principle of behavior applying to other creatures. Sir Isaac Newton observed the falling apple and eventually applied his speculations to the sun and the planets. If observations are valid and principles can be derived, one can subsequently test the applicability of the principles whenever one chooses. The only danger is from over-hasty generalization without prior testing.

In this book, we will feel free to talk about cats and dogs and monkeys or rats or human babies or grandfathers if there appears to be a reason for doing so. To dismiss a priori any observations because they were made on goslings or sticklebacks is the real folly. There is a potential danger of getting out of sight of the goal, namely, an appreciation of human learning, if we get bogged down with tadpoles, flatworms, or porpoises, but if we keep in mind that we are looking for principles and not for facts about animals, there should be no problem.

As a matter of fact, the two main sources of our speculations about learning will come from observations made not on rats at all but on cats and dogs. American learning psychology began with the observations of Thorndike on cats. He did use other creatures, including chickens, monkeys, goldfish, and college students, but his basic views were determined by his studies of cats. A different orientation imported into the United States by Watson was based on observations made in Russia by Pavlov on dogs. Pavlov, too, looked at leopards and gorillas, among other creatures, but spent most of his life working with dogs.

Hilgard (1956) asserted that learning psychology amounts to agreeing or disagreeing with Thorndike. What is implied here is that Thorndike said so much about learning that if one could sift out the valid statements made by Thorndike and his critics from the invalid ones, one would have a respectable theory of learning. The same could probably be said about Pavlov and his critics. Because the views of Thorndike and Pavlov appeared to be in such strong opposition and because one used cats while the other used dogs, one could describe the body of learning theory as the remains of the biggest and longest international cat and dog fight ever. We will watch this cat and dog fight over many rounds in pursuit of our goal. When rats and pigeons enter as substitutes for a round or two, do not be put off too quickly.

PHILOSOPHY AND EVOLUTION: DESCARTES AND DARWIN

The use of animals in psychological research can be traced back to two important sources of influence. One was the speculative philosophy of René

(margin note: "dualism" — mind & body)

Descartes (1596–1650), and the other was the evolutionary theory of Charles Darwin (1809–82).

Descartes is largely responsible for the view held by most people today that a human being consists of two parts, a mind and a body. This view is called dualism. Prior to Descartes, no clear distinction was made by philosophers between mental and physical activities. Man was somehow a unity—his mind, or soul, was indistinguishable from his body; the two were intimately intertwined as form and substance. To illustrate in terms of illness, when someone was sick, all of the person was sick, and all of the person was to be treated. Today, we recognize this as the concept of psychosomatic illness. But Descartes proposed a division of two functions, structures, or agencies. The mind was one structure, the body another, and their interaction, via the pineal gland, was minimal or not important. Bodies were somewhat less important as contraptions or machines that housed the mind. Without a mind, the body was merely a machine working along hydraulic principles, with fluids or "animal spirits" coursing along nerves, swelling now this muscle or that to bring about movement. All physical movements were of a reflex nature, and behavior consisted of a collection of reflexes.

According to Jaynes (1973), Descartes may have derived his views about bodily action from observations made in his youth, when as a somewhat sickly adolescent, he wandered about the gardens of St. Germain, designed by the brothers Francini, along the banks of the Seine. The gardens contained statues that moved and danced, as well as mechanical birds that moved and sang. If a visitor stepped on a hidden plate, a statue would move toward him or her or turn away as if to hide. The marvelous mechanically articulated and hydraulically driven statues appeared to do everything but think. But only the mind can think. Everything else in the world moves by one thing pushing another thing—the world is a machine along with everything in it except for the mind of man.

For Descartes, animals had no minds and were, therefore, strictly machines (water statues). Kick or beat a dog, and it will yelp and howl because the various parts move each other about so as to produce the noises (hydraulic hisses) you hear. The dog feels nothing and knows nothing. It reacts reflexively. Vivisection was perfectly reasonable. You could not hurt a dog by cutting it apart anymore than you could hurt a mechanical statue by removing or changing its parts. "The Francini brothers from Florence had built more than they knew; they had created the essential image behind modern psychology" (Jaynes 1973, p. 171).

For Descartes, any motion was the result of some kind of pressure, which caused "animal spirits" to move through the nerves. The pressure usually arose from external energies and was followed by movement. Here, we have the essence of the S $\longrightarrow$ R formula: an external energy (S) is transformed into movement (R). Descartes clearly had the concept of the reflex, although he spoke only of "reflection." The term *reflex* was contributed by Marshall Hall in 1833.

As Descartes' inadequate physiological speculations were exposed and refuted, his distinctions between man and animal became less attractive to scientific thinkers. Descartes, for example, proposed the pineal gland as a locus for the interaction of mind and body on the grounds that animals had no such organ. He should have (and may have) known better. Because animals do have such a gland, the distinction between man and animal suffered, and animals could be considered suitable experimental resources for questions about the nature of man. The doctrine of animal spirits making muscles larger was found to be untenable in experimental studies, where it was discovered that the total volume of a muscle system was not altered in movement. Animals became closer to, rather than more distant from, man.

Descartes was as responsible as anyone for the structure of modern scientific psychology, and at the same time, he created a psychology for the man in the street. For the man in the street, Descartes provided a mind. For the scientist, Descartes provided a mechanical model—man as a machine. No matter how psychologists talk or behave in public or at home, in their laboratories, they deal with living organisms as if they were machines, however complicated. It is, of course, recognized that the hydraulic mechanics of Descartes were inadequate—that chemical and electrical activities are the basis for functions of living organisms and that living organisms develop, grow, and decline in structure and function, quite unlike other machines. It is also recognized—and this is most important for us—that living organisms are modified in some ways by their experiences. The problem for the learning psychologist is how, that is, under what conditions, the living organism is modified for better or worse.

DARWIN AND EVOLUTION

The publication in 1859 of Darwin's *On the Origin of Species by Means of Natural Selection* revived and reinvigorated the question of man and animal relationships. Was man only a different kind of animal operating on the same principles, or were animals some kinds of inferior men? (The superiority of man was rarely questioned, possibly because men, in general, controlled, subdued, or used animals for their own benefit). Many writers rose to the occasion (Hobhouse 1901; Romanes 1882), proving by anecdote that animals were intelligent, had memories and other human faculties, used reason, had insight, and, in general, were like people in their inner lives. The opposing view, which came to prevail in psychology, was to deny or diminish the operation of mental faculties not only in animals (the Cartesian view) but to deny them as well to man. Thorndike's (1898) Ph.D. dissertation was designed to refute the "romantic" notions of Romanes. There were no mental faculties, no such "things" as Intelligence, Memory, or Reason (with initial capital letters). These were just terms to describe the results of behavior, itself quite mechanical and determined by circumstances, by individual histories rather than species evolution, although the principles of evolution might apply. Thus, Thorndike pointed out that just as species survive through chance modifications which permit some members to live long enough to procreate (the survival of the fittest), so it is in an animal's (or human's learning history, where some chance response is more adaptive (more fit) than another. The chance response survives if it fosters the adaptation of the performer of that response.

The formula proposed by Thorndike, and later embraced by learning psychologists generally, is illustrated in Figure 5.1.

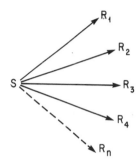

FIGURE 5.1: The evolution of a learned response. To any stimulus (S) an organism responds in some natural manner (R_1). If the stimulus or problem persists, other responses occur until some response eliminates the S. The successful response "survives."

The formula pictured in Figure 5.1 is basic to the behaviorist position. In the diagram, S is some energy change in the body or outside it. This energy generates a response (R_1) as a necessary consequence. It is, so to speak, "wired in," natural. So far, we have the Cartesian view. But suppose R_1 is of no value, that is, the S persists (the problem remains). Here, the evolutionary hypothesis enters. The organism responds in a new fashion (R_2). This is not a "chance" response. It may be thought of as also wired in but less directly or less effectively, for whatever reason. If this response does not work either (does not promote survival), it gives way to R_3, a still lower level of directness or effective correction. Eventually, the organism reacts with some response that does work, perhaps R_n. The S is eliminated, and the organism is ready to respond to the next stimulus that comes along.

Note that what is proposed here is a built-in, innate *hierarchy* of possible responses to any possible stimulus. Note also that if R_1 is adequate, we accept the behavior as natural, innate, unlearned. In fact, we never speak of learning if R_1 works and is acceptable to "society." But R_2, R_3, and so on are equally natural, just less likely to occur. If R_3 or R_n replaces R_1, we do speak of learning. What has happened? All that we can witness is that the probability of some response has been altered. R_1 drops in probability; R_2 or R_n rises in probability. From such changes in probability, we draw inferences about learning. Various theorists have drawn various inferences about why the probabilities alter. The grounds for the inferences may be observable or hypothetical conditions that might be influential. To explain why R_1 dwindles in likelihood, we might postulate, for example, that the organism gets tired of performing it. Hull (1943) will say that reactive inhibition (a state analogous to fatigue) develops as a response to repeated (see chapter 6). Others will speak of frustration or some other inhibitory influence. Why does some other R increase in probability? Some will say the connection between S and R_2 or some other R grows in strength because the new response results in "a satisfying state of affairs" (Thorndike), or because it reduces a drive (Hull), or because it gets rid of the stimulus (Guthrie), or because it confirms an "expectancy" (Tolman), or because it is followed by reinforcement (Skinner), or because it just does (if some other conditions are met). We shall examine all of these views. For now, we can pause to reflect on the essential point.

ANOTHER PARADOX: YOU LEARN WHAT YOU KNOW

According to the views just mentioned, learning amounts to changing the strength of connections (presumably, in the nervous system) that are already there in varying degrees of strength. This view is a modified form of nativism—a nativism with something added—you already know anything and everything you will ever "learn." Put another way, you cannot learn anything you cannot already do. Such a view might be quite correct for some kinds of "learning" but may be restricted to simple physical movements of a restricted range. You cannot learn to type if you cannot move appropriate fingers in appropriate directions, for example. But is that all that is involved in learning to type? Is there an inborn connection between the visual stimulus of the *A* key and the motor pattern involved in pressing it at an appropriate time, as, for instance, after pressing the *C* key in typing *cat*? Consider a baseball player at bat. Is there an inborn connection to swing the bat at an approaching ball, assuming that the ball "looks good" to the batter? He or she may not swing at a good offering if the other factors in the situation dictate taking a strike.

Is there an innate connection between saying "1492" when asked for the date of the discovery of America? The view that learning amounts to strengthening existing connections does not appear to apply when new connections are called for. If someone is asked to say "Rumpelstiltskin" when the name of some evil dwarf is at issue, there presumably can be no innate connection. Such an "association" must be created or established de novo. A connection must be built; a new association must be established. How new connections are established must be determined if we are to learn about most kinds of learning that interest us.

Yet another kind of behavior must be considered besides the skills and knowledge types that have been mentioned so far. People fear, hate, distrust, or love things, animals, and other people. Emotional responses abound. Are they innate or learned? A baby does not have to learn *how* to cry. The baby might learn when to cry and for how long and/or what to cry about. Watson told us that fear, anger, and love are innate, that is, inborn reactions to a limited and restricted class of stimuli. But we sometimes fear things Watson did not list as innate provokers of fear—snakes or cats, for example—and some people love shoes or horseshoes, and we assume they were not born that way. Certainly, learning is involved in some way in relation to emotional behavior, and this, too, must be examined.

EARLY AND LATE LEARNING

Genetic influences over behavior have come to be recognized, in a scientific sense, only recently through the development of a new research area, that of behavioral genetics. We can hope that someday we will know what a given individual member of some species would do "naturally" in a given situation. With such knowledge, we would have an ideal subject for a learning experiment if we could keep it from learning anything until we were ready to use it. Such creatures do not exist. We cannot ordinarily start with a newborn creature and expect to make learning observations until the creature is old enough and strong enough to begin to do something.

There have been some unusual attempts to study the behavior of creatures even before they are born or shortly thereafter. Carmichael (1926), for example, arranged for salamander (Ambystoma) eggs to hatch in a solution that contained a movement prevention drug. When other salamanders of the same age were swimming about, the drug was washed out, and the now drug-free salamanders also began to swim. Swimming was thus shown to be a normal or natural reaction pattern for this species—a pattern that came about through maturation, not through learning.

Spelt (1948) succeeded in demonstrating that as yet unborn human infants could be "conditioned" to respond to a vibrator placed on the mother-to-be's abdomen in the same way that they reacted to a loud noise which was strong enough to evoke a "startle reaction" in the embryo. (See next chapter.) According to Spelt, we can learn something even before we are born. Other experiments (with ten-day-old babies, for example—see Wickens 1940) were not so successful and raised some questions as to the feasibility of learning (in this case, leg withdrawal to a buzzer) in young infants.

How much learning goes on in humans or other species before the learning psychologists begins his or her observations? We can suspect that some learning goes on in a baby's crib as it looks about its environment and hears various noises. Hebb made a great point of such "early" learning in infants, who seemed to be doing nothing much more than eating, sleeping, and crying occasionally. Infants do move their eyes about. They see things, and they probably learn. So do young rats. But rats are rarely used in learning research before they are three months old. By that time, they might have learned a great deal, which might affect their reactions to the learning situations that are imposed upon them. To assume that college students come to learning laboratories with no learning history would be a patent absurdity. The psychologist for the purposes of the experiment only assumes that the subjects are "naive" with respect to the problems that will be assigned to them.

When animals are reared in what are called impoverished environments, they are very different from their age mates that are brought up in normal or enriched environments. Scottie dogs raised in boxes that precluded their seeing anyone or anything except the inside of the box for a year or a year and a half would, upon release, appear to be quite retarded. They learned slowly compared with normal dogs (see Thompson and Heron 1954). Were they handicapped by their previous solitary and unstimulated existence, or were they learning "from scratch"?

As one grows older, all prior learning experiences become "early" or earlier learning and present learning becomes "late" learning. How one responds at any given time becomes a function of one's prior history. Different people with different histories will acquit themselves differently in any given late learning situation. Some may learn in one trial what others take many more trials to learn. Your history can help or handicap your capacity to learn. Young children are supposed to learn to speak foreign languages more easily than adults. There may be many reasons for this, assuming its truth. We presume in such a case that practice with one's own native language somehow develops patterns of talking behavior that are inhibitory of other kinds of articulation. Late learning is not always better; it depends on what was learned early. We will return to this topic when we discuss transfer (see chapter 16).

PROBLEM OF SUBJECTS IN LEARNING RESEARCH

From our review thus far, we appreciate that what we are going to learn about learning depends considerably on what learners we are going to observe and what tasks we are going to put to them. We know now that the species and age and early background of each creature will matter greatly. To add to our problems, we must note two kinds of biases that enter into much research despite careful efforts to avoid such.

Subject Bias

With human subjects, we face problems of motivation (interest or apathy) to begin with, but in addition to these, we find subjects speculating about the experimenter's purpose and trying to help or hinder him or her in reaching his or her goals whether or not they truly appreciate the experimental design. Such efforts on the part of subjects are called subject bias and can be very confounding and misleading when the experimenter wants the subjects to behave in one way or respond to certain stimuli while the subjects are working at some kind of cross purpose, perhaps looking at or looking for something else.

Experimenter Bias

We like to pretend that scientists are objective and accept all results they obtain whether these support or deny their experimental hypotheses. However, scientists are just people, with their own aspirations, expectancies, and fond predictions. They like to see results come out "the way they should." We are not talking about the relatively rare frauds that are publicized from time to time. We are concerned about little things that can affect research, such as how gently a rat might be placed in a maze, for example. Little variations in procedure over a number of instances can mount up to produce an effect. The common practice of using assistants who know what results would please the researcher might be responsible for approvable findings. Such biases need not be intentional. The famous case of Clever Hans, the counting horse, baffled many astute observers before it became evident that the trainer was, presumably unwittingly, providing cues to the horse that told the horse when to stop tapping its hoof.

The problems in research outlined above should suggest to us that we do not accept every report of someone's observations as the final proof about any statement concerning learning. Because a fly does this or an elephant does that does not mean that beavers or people do the same thing when they learn something. Besides, someone else may turn up with different observations. The history of learning psychology has been replete with conflicting theories and contradictory experimental results. We are well warned to view all conclusions about learning with a quiet skepticism.

SUMMARY AND A QUESTION

We can see how psychologists came to use animals in their attacks on learning problems. We can see how observations on animals may be useful as sources for suggesting principles about some kinds of human learning, especially physical skills or simple motoric activities and emotional responses. When factual knowledge, or information, is involved, animals may not be of much help. We recognize that there are different kinds of learned activities, and our problem is that of accounting for how the learning takes place in each kind of activity. Can we account for learning with one principle, or do we need different principles for different kinds of learning? Some theorists would prefer to think that learning is learning and that only one principle is required. They are guided by a law of parsimony. But, parsimony may not prove to be the wisest course. Other theorists propose or accept different principles for different kinds of learned behavior. We can try to determine who might be correct.

6

Classical Conditioning

The concept of conditioning described by Pavlov (1849–1936) is probably the most widely known psychological principle in the world today. By now, it has trickled down to the point where the Sunday supplement reader knows about Pavlov and his dogs. Not so many appear to be aware of Thorndike and his cats, but even with Pavlov, the average citizen can only say something about bells and saliva. Actually, Pavlov did not use bells frequently. He tried out all sorts of stimuli (tuning forks, electric fans, bubbling water, automobile hooters, circular and ovoid discs, and lights, flickering and otherwise). One of his favorite stimuli was the old-fashioned metronome, which included the feature of an easy measurement—so many beats per minute.

What Pavlov discovered with his bells and dogs is of far more importance than that a bell could arouse a salivary discharge or that any of the other stimuli mentioned above could also do so. Pavlov's discovery was nothing less than a revolutionary approach to appreciating behavior, an approach that in Watson's hands, changed the entire course of psychology in the United States, with a new emphasis on the role of learning and environment, a rejection of virtually all nativistic approaches, and a denial of all mentalistic orientations. To dismiss Pavlov as a cantankerous old Russian who rang bells for dogs is fatuous if not dangerous.

In one of the great coincidences of scientific history, the problem of learning was attacked by two investigative geniuses at about the same time. As mentioned in the last chapter, Thorndike and Pavlov, unaware of each other's existence at the time, began to work in the animal laboratory with different approaches and biases, different animals, and different procedures at the close of the nineteenth century.

PAVLOV AND THORNDIKE

Historically, there is some question about who came first. Pavlov (1927) mentions that he was familiar with Thorndike's work but says (p. 6) that he was already engaged upon his own conditioning studies before he read Thorndike's 1898 dissertation on *Animal Intelligence*. We shall begin with Pavlov's work, even though this work came to have its impact in the United States only after 1918. In the late 1890s, Pavlov was engaged in the analysis of digestive secretions, a work that brought him the Nobel Prize. To collect digestive juices, Pavlov had to surgically separate a dog's stomach into two parts, so that pure secretions uncontaminated with food could be collected from one part through a fistula to the outside of the dog's body. Normally, such secretions accumulate in the stomach when food is physically present, and Pavlov could accept such glandular reactions as ordinary reflexes. In Pavlov's thinking, a reflex was an automatic reaction to proper physical stimulus and required no explanation. But Pavlov observed the obvious everyday event that the digestive acids began to flow *before* food had entered the stomach and even before it was in the dog's mouth—the simple arrival of the food with its accompanying sounds, appearance of feeders, and so on was enough to set off the reflex. Here, no physical stimulus, such as food, was in the stomach, and without such a stimulus, the reflex had no business occurring. At first, Pavlov described such an event as a "psychic" reflex, but then, driven by recollections of Sechenov's *Reflexes of the Brain* (1863), he determined to discover how such reflexes could occur. He turned away from his chemical studies and became a psychologist, studying behavior, even though he always regarded himself as a physiologist studying the higher cerebral centers of the nervous system.

THE PSYCHIC REFLEX

In ruminating over his problem, Pavlov reflected on ordinary human reactions to sights and sounds of food or even to the mention of such viands as sour pickles and lemons. Most people will agree that the expression "mouth-watering" is an appropriate description of what happens when one sees a succulent morsel. On the human level, we might say, "Thinking of sucking a lemon makes my mouth water." If it would turn out that we can make a dog's mouth water by our manipulations of the dog's world, it might be possible to explain what we mean when we say "thinking." Maybe thinking is only another kind of brain reflex, where the necessary stimuli have to be identified. We know the stimulus for a knee jerk and for normal salivation. These are obvious physical events. What is the modus operandi of a "psychic" reflex? What do we mean by saying a thought made us salivate? Maybe it was not a thought at all but some so far unidentified neural action brought about by some perfectly proper *physical* stimulus.

Pavlov's rationale for attacking psychic reflexes was adopted from his earlier observations. There was no reason to suspect that a dog's salivary glands would not operate in the same way as do those of humans, and Pavlov chose to study salivary secretions as an easier and safer procedure (less dangerous operation) to get at these psychic reflexes. The previously observed watering of the stomach at the approach of a feeder or the sound of a food dish obviously meant that these stimuli had acquired control or power over the response. But these stimuli seem to be naturally involved. Every pet owner has seen his pet come to some regular feeding station at the sounds of food preparation. What if some other kinds of sounds that had nothing to do with food could be arranged to have a similar power or control? Would it not suggest that the normal sounds had also acquired their power (been learned) through some prior experiences when the sounds and food had appeared together or in quick succession? It need only be shown that a metronome or trumpet call or flashing light could be just as effective as the sight or sound of food in bringing about salivation in the dog. If this could be arranged, there would be no mystery, no need for an appeal to thoughts or psychic phenomena.

THE CONDITIONAL REFLEX

Taking his lead from such observations, Pavlov proceeded to present some arbitrary, irrelevant, or novel stimulus the dog had never before seen or heard just before the dog was fed. The dog had been prepared by surgery so that saliva could flow through a fistula in the cheek to a collecting tube. At first nothing meaningful happened—the dog would respond to the novel stimulus by what Pavlov called a "curiousity reflex"—what we would call an orienting reflex (OR). Typically, according to Sokolov (1963), a novel stimulus, such as a buzzer, might make a dog tense up and look about for the source of the sound, as well as cause pupil dilation, an increase in heart rate, an electroencephalogram (EEG) change in the brain, some breathing changes, and, in general, an "alert" reaction. As soon as the food arrived, the dog would busy himself with the more important matter of eating. After a few trials, perhaps as many as ten, Pavlov observed that the dog would begin to salivate as soon as the novel, previously irrelevant stimulus was presented. He had solved his initial problem—some stimulus that did not originally or naturally produce a particular response could come to do so by the simple process of pairing it with one that did. To handle the problem of standardized communication, Pavlov invented some terminology. The original or natural stimulus for a reflex was labeled the *unconditional stimulus*, or US, meaning that it ordinarily or normally would be followed by the response; it might not always do so (sometimes dogs are sick or frightened or not hungry and will not salivate when food is offered), but it can normally be depended upon to evoke or elicit the response. The better reason for calling it

US – that it ordinarily or normally would be followed by the response unconditional was to distinguish the other stimulus, the unnatural, novel, irrelevant stimulus, as a conditional stimulus (CS). (In this book, the Americanized terms, *conditioned stimulus* and *unconditioned stimulus*, will be used hereafter.) Note the spelling, which emphasizes that the CS will come to evoke the response only under certain conditions. The basic condition has already been mentioned, namely, that it be presented a number of times *in contiguity* with the US, that is, at about the same time. There are some details to consider here, but they will be discussed later (see Temporal Factors: The Concept of Antedating below). Another condition, studied intensively somewhat later by Sokolov (1963), was that the OR to the CS must occur at first—what this means is that the dog must respond to the CS as such. If there is no OR, the stimulus (CS) might not be having any impact on the dog (this does not mean that the dog must "notice" the CS—it merely needs to react to it). American psychologists with their penchant for symbolic diagrams would portray what happens when a CS becomes effective as

Early trials	Later trials
CS $\longrightarrow$ OR	CS$\searrow$ *take this*
US $\longrightarrow$ UR	CR *as evidence of learning*

where OR is the orienting response or original response to the CS. Unconditional response (UR) is the response to the US. The dashed line arrow respresents a new, learned, or acquired connection, and the CR is the conditional response, which is like (similar to, but not exactly identical to) the original response to the US. (In this book, the Americanized terms, *unconditioned response* and *conditioned response*, will be used hereafter.)

The diagram suggests that an association or connection has been developed between the CS and the CR. The actual connection could be between the CS and the US [see below] or between the CS and some other functional locus, some pool of neurons serving as an association center (AC), which has connections with both CS and US inputs, as shown below in (b):

CS
│
↓
US $\longrightarrow$ CR

(a)

CS$\searrow$
     $\searrow$ (AC) $\searrow$
US$\nearrow$ $\searrow$ CR

(b)

No one actually knows what happens in the nervous system, either how or where, but behaviorally, it is clear that one stimulus has come to do the work of another, at least in part. For this reason, the operation that has taken place can be described as stimulus substitution, or the association of one stimulus with another (S—→S), or, American style, as conditioning. In American usage, the CS is commonly described as the condition*ed* stimulus, and the dog is said to have been condition*ed*. The usage is not quite precise, although it is acceptable, because the CS may not work in the sense of evoking a CR but still be a CS in the sense of its procedural manipulation. "Conditioning" may not take place, although a conditioning procedure is followed. It is best to regard the CS as a novel stimulus that is presented along with a US. Whether conditioning occurs may depend on still other conditions. All that Pavlov meant to imply by his usage is that under certain *conditions*, a new connection may be formed. The study of learning or of acquired behavior thus becomes the study of the conditions under which new connections or associations are formed. Contiguity of CS and US is only one of these conditions. Some *frequency* of contiguous pairings appears to be another condition (although some CRs may be formed in one trial—see Voeks 1954).

Pavlov's Physiological Speculations

Pavlov always referred to his work as amounting to cerebral physiology. He believed the cerebral hemispheres were involved in conditioning and did not regard spinal conditioning as possible. What happened, the hypothesized, was that any stimulus (CS) affecting the central nervous system would first travel to some area he considered to be sensory analyzer—the neural activity was described as a wave of excitation. If a second stimulus (US) now affected the organism, it too would create a wave of excitation in another sensory analyzer area. The two waves of excitation (like Hobbes's motions or Hartley's vibrations) now interact and under appropriate *conditions*, come, in some way, to initiate one another. Because each excitation might have a motor or glandular outlet, the temporal order would be important in determining which response would become a CR. (If food was followed by a severe shock, the food should come to function as a CS.) Pavlov invented a variety of physiological operations to account for his behavioral observations. Because none of these has been supported by independent anatomical or physiological evidence, we can dismiss them and will not discuss his physiology further, except to note that according to Pavlov, waves of neural *inhibition* could also be generated by the failure of a US to appear at its proper time and account for extinction, a feature of conditioning that now calls for examination.

Extinction

Pavlov was the first scientist to study systematically what might be considered the elimination of previously acquired habits. He found that if an established CS was not followed by the US over a number of trials, the CS would gradually lose its capacity for evoking the CR. The *procedure* of omitting the US is all that is meant by Pavlov's usage of the term "experimental extinction." Sometimes, the animal would continue to respond more or less indefinitely—the term does not then refer to any outcome of the procedure but only to the procedure itself. The outcome is usually a gradual diminution in the frequency and amount of response, with a gradual increase in latency or reaction time.

No "typical" graph showing the course of extinction is shown here because the course is frequently erratic, varying with the stimulus conditions, prior extinctions, drive, type of response, kind of organism, and so forth. Some responses, for example, emotional reactions, are sometimes highly resistant to extinction. Like Ebbinghaus' forgetting curve, the extinction curve is an individual affair, and any single sample would be misleading. In research efforts, the average *number* of extinction responses under one condition can be compared with the average number under another condition. The courses of extinction might well vary. (See the stylized extinction curves in Chapter 8.)

Why should a CR cease if the US does not arrive on time? Pavlov thought of a latter a US as a *strengthener* or *reinforcer* (he is the first to have used the latter term) of the new association. But why would its absence lead to a decrease? Pavlov accounted for the decrease in responding by postulating a wave of inhibition being generated when the unconditioned stimulus failed to occur. What should initiate such a wave Pavlov could not explain very well, except in situations such as those described in a further development of his studies, situations labeled as *conditioned inhibition*. Before we continue with the negative aspects, however, there are a number of features of a positive nature we should consider.

Spontaneous Recovery

After an extinction session during which a CS has been rendered inoperational, that is, no longer evokes the CR, there may be a revival of some strength of CR activity, depending, in part, on the amount of rest. If a whole day passes since the last stimulation, a presentation of the CS may evoke a rather adequate CR, for example, 50% of the normal CR. Pavlov called this "spontaneous recovery." If the US is still omitted, the revived CR will diminish more rapidly and recover less on a second test later on. If the original extinction procedure is continued in a first extinction run long after the animal has ceased responding, there will be less spontaneous recovery. Pavlov referred to this as "extinction below zero." The facts of spontaneous recovery remind us that we cannot depend on having gotten rid of some response merely because one extinction session had resulted in no further CRs. Later on, we will find an interesting application of the spontaneous recovery finding (Chapter 14).

Higher-Order Conditioning

In contrast with the findings to be described later in connection with conditioned inhibition, Pavlov found that once a CS had been established effectively, another stimulus could be paired with it as a new CS with the old CS now functioning as an unconditional stimulus, and a higher order of conditioning could be established. Thus, once a bell regularly evoked salivation, a light could be paired with the bell and a new CR (light→ salivation) could be developed even though the light was never paired with the original food US. Once the light was effective a third CS, for example, a metronome, could be paired with it, and a third-order CR would be established. Pavlov described the procedure as sensitive and one that called for great care (not to establish conditioned inhibitions), with frequent repairings of the original CS and US mandatory. For higher-order CRs the new CS would precede the old one. For conditioned inhibition, the two stimuli would occur together.

Temporal Factors: The Concept of Antedating

While we have been speaking of contiguity between CS and US. Pavlov favored presenting the CS a little earlier than the US. An interval of five seconds would be considered suitable, with the CS coming first. Under such conditions, it would be possible to observe the UR occurring more and more rapidly, until it would occur before the US. Here, we have convincing evidence that the CS is effective. We also have a cardinal principle of conditioning before us, namely, the tendency for a CR to occur sooner and sooner to the CS, a circumstance that can be labeled *antedating*. Antedating can be considered the hallmark of conditioning. It, in fact, defines learning for us. It is only when an organism responds before the US, that is, in effect, before it must, that we know that it is able to and will respond to the CS. In human terms, if you cannot give an answer *before* you are prompted, you do not know the answer very well or perhaps at all. The only way we ever know that someone knows something is to have him or her perform in the absence of some direct (unconditioned) situation or stimulus. If you have to be told someone's name, you do not know it. Later, calling out the person's name when you see the person indicates that you have, in fact, learned.

Note that if the CS came after the US we could never know if conditioning had occurred. Pavlov referred to such an arrangement as "backward conditioning" and declared it to be impossible. Because some responses have longer latencies than others, it might be possible, physiologically speaking, to present some US with a long latency and then quickly introduce a CS, which technically could be interpreted as following the US, and still get conditioning because the CS might become effective in the time period passing before the UR occurs. Demonstrations of backward conditioning have been rare and questionable, and Pavlov may have been correct in his adamant stance. For practical purposes, it appears best to present the CS before the US. The actual time intervals will vary with the kind of response. The eyelid blink with a reflex latency of about 0.45 of a second is conditioned best with a CS occurring about 0.5 of a second before the US. In an avoidance situation with rats responding to shocks, two-second or five-second interval between CS and US is commonly effective.

Delayed and Trace Conditioned Responses

After some preliminary training at appropriate time intervals a CS can be introduced with a longer delay between CS and US. If the usual interval is five seconds, the experimenter can extend this to seven seconds, then to ten, later to 20 seconds, and so on. The dogs in Pavlov's laboratory would at first respond quickly after the CS but with extensions of the interval, they would tend to delay the CR. If a dog had been trained to salivate to a metronome about four seconds after the metronome was started, it might now not respond for ten or 20 seconds, while the metronome ticked away. At about the appropriate time for the US to occur, the dog would salivate. Pavlov assumed that the delay in salivating was due to some kind of inhibition and consequently dubbed such situations as illustrating "inhibition of delay."

The same kind of procedure could be followed without allowing the metronome to continue ticking, that is, the metronome would be started, then stopped immediately, but the US would not be presented for 20 seconds. The animal would still respond at the appropriate time, say, 16 seconds after the metronome ceased ticking. Pavlov thought of this as also illustrating inhibition of delay, but because there was no stimulus in the interval, he assumed the response was made to the *trace* of the conditioned stimulus. The concept of a stimulus trace became very important in subsequent work, and it should be understood as a continuing neural activity initiated by a stimulus that is no longer physically present.

One other temporal feature should be noted. No actual sensory CS need be provided to develop a conditioned response if a US is introduced at some regular and systematic interval. Thus, if a dog is fed precisely on the hour (some small amount), it will begin to salivate just before the hour is up. In a variation of this arrangement, a rat might be shocked every 15 seconds unless it jumps over a hurdle in a two-chamber box (divided by the hurdle). After a number of shocks, the rat would begin to cross the hurdle at about 13 to 14 seconds after the last crossing. In one instance, a rat given 96 trials a day (24 minutes) got to the 100 percent level of responding for a full hour—never missing a jump and always jumping between 13 to 15 seconds since the last jump (Bugelski 1950). Pavlov would call this "temporal conditioning."

Temporal variables relating to the occurrence of the CS and US have been investigated extensively (see Gormezano and Moore 1969), with many provocative findings. In laboratory studies, the time between CS and US, that is, the interstimulus interval, or ISI, can be varied over a wide range, including forward and backward arrangements of the CS and US as well as simultaneous presentations. Some overlap of the CS and US appears to be most effective in developing CRs. The intertrial interval, or ITI, can also be varied from seconds to days. The usual conclusion favors longer intertrial intervals for faster development of CRs but the intervals studied may not justify any practical conclusion. Among the temporal variables, we should include such items as the duration of both CS and US. A long unavoidable shock, for example, can prove to be much more potent than a short shock (Boe and Church 1967). In general, we might note with Gormezano and Moore that subjects in conditioning studies might learn *when* to respond.

There are two more features of conditioning first reported by Pavlov that (beside the original principle of association by contiguity) are the great psychological contributions of Pavlov. These are generalization and discrimination. They require more extensive treatment.

Generalization

Common experience demonstrates for us all that we frequently make mistakes in what might be called judgment situations. The little child refers to any man as "daddy." Or, when a little older, the child will mistake strangers for friends. He or she will ask, "Was that the phone?" when some nonphone sound occurs or head for the phone when the doorbell rings. In school, a child may attack an arithmetic problem confidently and incorrectly, using an inappropriate technique. In a geography lesson, a child may mistakenly call a state "Colorado" instead of "Wyoming" if he or she glances at the outline of the state on a map. In all these cases, an individual is responding to signals or cues, but the responses are considered wrong because only certain specific cues are to be responded to in certain specific ways. It can be said that one has generalized.

Pavlov found that once conditioning was established or well under way, it was not necessary to present exactly the same stimulus to evoke the CR. A dog might respond postively to any stimulus within a *range* of stimuli on some dimension. Thus, if the original CS was a metronome beating 60 times per minute, a change to 70 or 50 beats would not disturb the animal; it would still respond, although the amount of response might be slightly decreased— and similarly for other kinds of stimuli. If a tone of 1,000 Hz was the original CS, the dog would salivate to tones of 2,000 or 500 Hz among others. Dogs trained to lights of medium brightness would respond to brighter or dimmer lights. According to Pavlov, such generalization would diminish if the conditioning procedure was extended. Gradually, with continued training, the dog would come to respond only to a narrow range of stimulation, and "errors" would decrease. The nature of the pattern of generalization became a controversial issue for a time. Thus, Hull (Bass and Hull 1934) originally believed the "curve" of generalization followed a convex course, falling off gradually from the point of original conditioning, as in (a) in Figure 6.1. Hull's student, Hovland (1937), believed the curve was concave in pattern, as in (b) in Figure 6.1. Others, like Guthrie (1935), argued that it was essentially a straight line, parallel to the base, an all-or-nothing kind of interpretation, as in (c) in Figure 6.1.

The issue is difficult to decide because the shape of the curve depends on the psychological equivalence of the steps on the abscissa, or horizontal axis. The curves provided by Guttman and Kalish (1956), working with pigeons, appear to be like those found by Hovland and may represent the best available answer. The subject if of some technical importance, but the empirical facts of generalization are apparently quite sound. Subjects will respond to variations of the conditioned stimulus within some limits.

Generalization has been described in terms of erroneous responses. Actually, the errors are social or definitional matters. Commonly, a response to some nonprecise stimulus is prefectly appropriate. If you learn to avoid a parent's automobile in your own driveway, you can avoid any other kind of model of car in other situations. Stimuli do not have to be duplicated exactly for us to respond effectively. A dish is still a dish, even though we see it from different angles; a person remains the same, though he or she turns around or away from us. If conditioning is learning, it would be impossible for us to learn all that we "know," in the sense that by generalization, we become prepared for a host of stimuli we never encountered before. Every time we meet a new person, we can respond with, "Hello, glad to meet you."

Discrimination

Despite the virtues of generalization for everyday encounters with common stimuli, some generalized responses will be classed as errors and, if important for any reason, must be eliminated. Pavlov found an easy remedy.

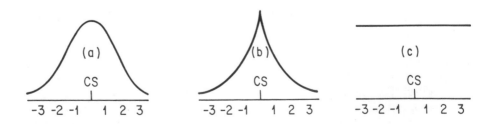

FIGURE 6.1: Theoretical curves of generalization favored by Hull (a), Hovland (b), and Guthrie (c).

Simply extinguish any response given to any variation of the original CS by withholding the US. Keep reinforcing the original CS. Slowly the subject will begin to respond more and more efficiently, giving fewer positive responses to stimuli at a distance on the similarity continuum. Thus, Pavlov's students trained dogs to salivate to a circle but not to an ellipse. Slowly, the axes of the ellipse were altered from two to one to make the ellipse more circular. After suitable training, the dog responded to the circle but not to the ellipse, even when the ratio of the axes of the ellipse approached nine to eight. At this point, the animal began to show signs of disturbance. Pavlov regarded the disturbance serious enough to warrant being called "experimental neuroses" and thought he had discovered a causative factor in human neurotic disturbances. It is unlikely that humans ever "break down" because they are faced with the need to respond differently to closely similar stimuli. Such cases do not seem to be included in neurotic case studies, and we will not pursue the matter. The point to be made, however, is that dogs and other creatures can be trained (or learn from experience of positive and negative instances) to respond positively to one stimulus and negatively (that is, not respond in the same way) to variations on that stimulus if the variation is of some minimal degree. The parents of identical twins can learn to refer to each by the correct name, even though a stranger may be confused for a long time. Such differential responding has been called discrimination.

Before we leave the topic, the student should be warned that the term *discrimination* must be used only to refer to the *result* of a reinforcement-extinction training program. There is no justification for postulating some aptitude, capacity, or function that might be called discriminating. We are not entitled, because of the research, to say that the dog (or anyone else) "discriminates." Such usage suggests that the individual involved is doing something on his own (judging, evaluating, or deciding) that we have no evidence about. All we know is that he or she does something in the presence of one stimulus and that he or she does not do the same thing in the presence of another (presumably similar) stimulus. To endow someone with discriminating powers is to go beyond the evidence. A color-blind person who cannot see red or green, for example, and cannot respond appropriately to red or green stimuli might be said to represent a failure of discrimination. The fact that the normal color-seeing person does not make such mistakes does not justify any conclusion other than that certain wavelengths of light affect the normal person differently and that he or she responds differently after appropriate training. In short, we do not *make* discriminations or *discriminate*. Discrimination, if anything, is something that happens as a consequence of differential training. It is a result, not a process. The topic of discrimination will occupy us further in later chapters when we deal with more "human" learning. For some psychologists, it is *the* topic, the basis for all learning.

NEGATIVE ASPECTS OF CONDITIONING

CONDITIONED INHIBITION

We return now to the more negative aspects of conditioning, which are as important as are the positive ones. We have had a hint of their importance in the brief discussion of discrimination. It is time to consider them in a little more detail.

When Pavlov found that his dogs would not salivate if the US no longer followed the CS, he was not content to leave it at that. Why did the dogs no longer salivate? Why did the shepherds in the fable stop coming to the rescue when the boy shouted "Wolf!" for the third time? Had Pavlov asked himself this question, he might have come up with a different answer from the one he did propose.

Why did the shepherds stop coming? Because the story is a fable, we cannot answer this question on the basis of any facts. We can only assume that the shepherds no longer believed the boy and considered the trip a waste of time. We can also assume they were somewhat annoyed with childish pranks. But can we assume a dog no longer believes that food will come and chooses not to salivate? How can an animal choose not to salivate? Here, again, we might assume that whatever the explanation, it is probably not a matter of choice.

For Pavlov, the explanation that appeared more reasonable was to assume that the failure of the US to appear would come to initiate or generate some kind of inhibitory process. He spoke of a wave of inhibition spreading over the cerebral cortex of the dog. Where it came from or why, he could not say, but there certainly had to be some kind of negative operation if the saliva was not to flow. It is this negative operation that we must now consider.

For Pavlov, simple extinction, then, was due to the development of inhibition, which now came to be the response to the CS. Suppose the original CS is a metronome tick; it has now become inhibitory, and it results in inhibition instead of a conditioned response.

External Inhibition

If during the presentation of a CS some other stimulus, for example, a shadow, some unexpected noise, the opening of a door, or so forth, should occur, the CR is likely to be disturbed or fail to occur. Pavlov ascribed such failures to external inhibition, with no detailed account beyond the statement.

Disinhibition

Should such an external disturbance occur during an extinction trial series, the conditioned response, which had been declining in amount or frequency, might return to full strength. Such an inhibition of an inhibition was termed *disinhibition*. In both external inhibition and disinhibition, we have hints of some kind of interference operation.

③ Conditioned Inhibition

If the original CS is occasionally accompanied by some new stimulus (CS$_2$) but no US is presented, this new stimulus (CS$_2$) will serve as an external inhibition generator and its occurrence will come to prevent the CR. If the original CS is a tone and is always followed by food and the tone is now accompanied by a light but the combination is not followed by food, the light will become a conditioned inhibitor. Presenting the light at any time will prevent CRs to other established stimuli. Such conditioned inhibitory stimuli have been studied in a variety of situations by Rescorla (1969) and are readily and reliably reproduced in modern conditioning laboratories.

INTERFERENCE INTERPRETATIONS

The vague status of the concept of inhibition has not been satisfactory to many American psychologists. What might be termed *the American way* is to postulate some kind of interference process that prevents the conditioned response from occurring or replaces it. Thus, Guthrie (1935) argued that the explanation for extinction is simple: the dog is frustrated when it salivates in a preparatory manner for ingesting food and no food arrives. The dog can be regarded as becoming angry or emotional, and it is commonly agreed that when animals (and people) are angry or frightened, the salivary response will not occur. The mouth dries up. Anger, then, for Guthrie, is all the explanation we need. The anger is a competitive or interfering response.

Wendt (1936) similarly argued that interference is the basis for extinction. One response replaces another. The only way to inhibit one response is to perform another, and Wendt demonstrated in an eye movement–conditioning situation that the original conditioned response must, in the first place, *replace* a primary or usual response to the CS. As conditioning proceeds, this primary response recedes or subsides, giving way to the conditioned response. When the US is no longer provided the original response begins to recur and eventually replaces the CR. Hilgard and Marquis (1935) similarly demonstrated the fact that in dogs, conditioned eye blinks replace an original binocular reaction, and this returns when the US is no longer presented. Such demonstrations have been described as supporting an interference theory of extinction, which has some evidential support, in contrast with Pavlov's hypothetical waves of inhibition or inhibitory processes.

Reactive Inhibition

Hull (1943) was also interested in accounting for the failure of the conditioned response to continue. He was interested in some observations by Hovland (1936) that even without an extinction process, that is, even if the US was continued, animals would tend to slow down or stop responding. Hovland had termed this observation "inhibition of reinforcement." Hull looked at it as a kind of fatigue reaction. Since *fatigue* itself is a vague term (see Robinson 1934), Hull argued for a state he called "reactive inhibition" (I_R), which refers to a gradually developing tendency to cease any frequently repeated reaction whether or not some reward or reinforcement follows. In broad general terms, it covers even such situations as getting tired of voting for the same candidate, hearing the same joke again, eating the same food, wearing the same clothes, and so forth.

Assuming that such a condition as reactive inhibition (I_R) follows a response (and building up with repetition), Hull could account for extinction by postulating a different kind of interference. Thus, we can diagram the conditioning operation as

$$CS \dashrightarrow CR \rightarrow I_R$$

As the I_R develops, the organism seeks some kind of relief or rest, because the I_R is regarded as a negative drive state, which leads to rest, refusal to respond, or a nonresponse or "nothing reaction," as

$$CS \dashrightarrow CR \rightarrow I_R \rightarrow Rest$$

Now, if the traces of the CS are still functional as the organism is engaging in the rest or nonresponse behavior, the CS will become conditioned to that behavior, as

$$CS \dashrightarrow Resting\ Behavior$$

and the CR will steadily decrease and eventually fail to occur because the resting response will tend to antedate and interfere with or prevent the CR. This is conditioned inhibition (CIR).

The student might draw a personal application from this analysis: Never study when you are tired or sleepy; never study too long, that is, to the point where you are getting tired. What might happen is that you will be "conditioned" to relax, rest, sleep at the sight of books, paper, typewriters, and so forth. In any event, it is very likely that any kind of work will decrease in efficiency as it is continued and might become distasteful, disagreeable, and even repulsive.//

Conditioned Emotional Response

Whatever the true explanation of extinction, we can recognize that American psychologists favor one form or another of interference theory. Later, we will discover that in other forms of behavior, a response can be at least temporarily stopped (inhibited?) by some painful stimulation. Thus, if a rat is trained to press a bar that releases a food pellet, it can be forced to stop pressing by shocking the animal whenever it presses the bar. The animal will then, at least for some time, stop pressing. Such a cessation is attributed to a conditioned emotional response (CER); this might be a sophisticated way of saying the animal now fears the bar. The CER can, of course, be acquired in response to some other stimulus or signal, for example, a buzzer, and the animal will cease responding whenever the buzzer sounds. As time passes and nothing happens, the fear may dissipate, and the animal may return to the activity. If it now does not receive any food, the bar pressing too will be extinguished. The CER was only a temporary condition and explains only temporary cessation of responding. Any more permanent extinction must now be explained, presumably, in interference terms—the animal learns to do something else.

PAVLOV'S POSITION AND CONTRIBUTION

Pavlov saw his animals as being transformed or changed by being subjected to certain conditions. Any given animal at any behavioral stage of its existence would remain at that stage (barring physiological changes) unless certain environmental manipulations were imposed on it. Such environmental manipulations amount to the *conditions* of stimulation that are provided by the environment, which, of course, includes the activities of other organisms. In the real world, the conditions are not controlled or governed by any systematic circumstances; rather, they are chancy and capricious. In the laboratory, a systematic manipulation of conditions can be introduced, and behavioral changes can be generated, controlled, and directed, presumably in any desired direction. By manipulating the temporal order, frequency, strength, and quality of various stimuli, any of an original (native) repertoire of reflexes can be systematically associated, through stimulus substitution, so that the organism can behave differently, its behavior being modified to suit the desires or needs of the trainer.

Note that Pavlov believed that any stimulus can be "conditioned" to any reaction of any creature. We have already noted there are some exceptions to this generality (Garcia) and that many reflexes resist easy conditioning. It might be necessary to modify the rule to read: some responses to some stimuli can be conditioned in some creatures. If these turn out to be the important responses to relatively common stimuli for most creatures, then the significance of the principle cannot be overstated.

We take note of the fact that while Pavlov did not hesitate to generalize his views, he himself had worked primarily with gastric secretions and glandular responses. Other Russian investigators did succeed in conditioning a great variety of other responses in both animals and humans. Soldiers with war wounds, which made various internal organs available for study and some kinds of manipulations, made ideal subjects for the study of the heart, lungs, kidneys, bladder, stomach, intestines, and glands in the visceral cavity (Bykov 1957). Some organs would be inflated with warm or cold water as unconditioned stimuli, while various external stimuli (colored lights, flickering lights, tones, buzzers, and so forth) were presented in the typical conditioning paradigm. Many such organic reactions were readily conditioned in the soldiers. In the United States, a great many studies of conditioning made use of the so-called psychogalvanic reflex (PGR) or galvanic skin response (GSR), a decrease in skin resistance to the passage of an electrical current, which is usually attributed to sweating (again, a glandular reaction). Gradually, the opinion developed that Pavlovian conditioning, if not restricted to organic reflexes, at least was most readily observable with such visceral or glandular reactions. Because such reactions are normally under the control of the autonomic nervous system, the judgment was made by many psychologists, notably Hilgard and Marquis (1940), Schlosberg (1937), and Skinner (1938), that Pavlovian (now called classical) conditioning was really (with modest exceptions like the eyelid blink) an autonomic nervous system operation or at least confined to reflexes controlled by the A.N.S. This view would have been a shocking blow to Pavlov, with his conviction that he was studying the higher cerebral processes, and he might have argued that although the responses in question may have autonomic aspects, the conditioning itself was a matter of cerebral changes. This interpretation could be correct enough. Certainly, the sensory stimuli involved as CSs could hardly be autonomic nervous system concerns. Conditioning of the cessation of alpha waves in the cortex itself might also be cited in Pavlov's support (Putney, Erwin, and Smith 1972).

Assuming, however, that most conditioning is related to autonomic functions does not denigrate the operations of conditioning. Indeed, it may even enhance its importance. The opposing view that nonvisceral reactions, that is, responses of striate muscles or skeletal muscle movements, are learned through some other agency, the central nervous system, does not make the learning of such responses any more important. We shall see Skinner and others suggesting just such an invidious comparison. Suppose, however, that all skeletal responses are themselves controlled by organic, that is, visceral, responses in a motivational sense, as proposed by Mowrer (1960a) and that they are not so much learned as directed by emotional (visceral) states (for example, fear, relief, hope, despair, or disappointment). If that is the case, Pavlov emerges as the theorist with the more correct view. Before we dismiss Pavlov as someone who rang bells to make dogs salivate, we must examine the alternate views and see how far they can take us.

We might take note of the fact that much of the criticism of Pavlov has come from novelists (Huxley in *Brave New World*) and nativists with views about the special distinction of man among the world's creatures. If one believes that man is different in various ways from "lower" animals, that man is "higher," more noble, possessed of special gifts or agencies, that man is equipped with mind, soul, reason, or intellect, that he is free to choose what he wills, then, in truth, Pavlov becomes anathema, an evil and dangerous threat to man's freedom and dignity. If Pavlov is correct, we cannot choose but continue whatever it is we are doing. In this case, we continue to examine what people have said about learning.

CRITICAL ATTACKS ON PAVLOV

Response Equivalence

A major problem for Pavlovian theorists is the size and range of the unconditioned response pool from which to develop the wide variety of responses in which the human adult engages.

The basic behaviorist position is that one is born equipped with a certain number (fixed by nature or heredity) of responses to rather specific stimuli. Such responses have to consist of the contractions or relaxations of specific muscles and the secretions (or inhibitions of secretions) of glands. Such response patterns are normally described as reflexes, and because some reflexes are observed as on-off, rapid, yes-no operations, for example, the knee jerk, they have been described (by those with somewhat negative views) as typically jerky or twitchy. Watson was derided for espousing a "muscle-twitch psychology" and for allegedly describing behavior as a bundle of "twitches."

When reflexes are observed carefully and their characteristics recorded faithfully, they appear to be rather complex operations, which, if anything, are smooth, with an onset, a recruitment period or buildup, and a return to the normal resting state all following a relatively unbroken course. (See Figure 6.2.) While an eye blink might look like a twitch, a photographic record over time looks like that shown in Figure 6.2 where some adequate stimulus, for example, an air puff, is shown as Δ . It can be seen that the eyelid closes and opens with a smooth onset and offset. Similar records are obtainable for knee jerks and other simple response units.

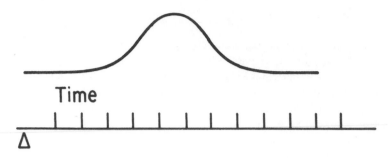

FIGURE 6.2: The form of the eyelid blink over a brief time span.

Leaving propaganda about muscle twitches aside, we can catalog the reflexes of the newborn child and the growing, maturing human into a rather extensive list of responses. Besides the eyelid blink, which can be elicited by an air puff, bright light, loud noise, electric shock, blow to the cheek, or even a threatening approach of some object (all innate responses), we can add such reflexes as the grasping reflex, sucking, swallowing, breathing, coughing, sneezing, crying, the Achilles and plantar reflexes, the Babinski reflex, the abdominal (skin reaction), the knee jerk, various reflexes of the eyes, for example, following a light, the crossed-extensor reflex, and reflex withdrawal of limbs from painful stimulation. The catalog of natural responses, some of which do not appear until some months or years after birth, for example, grasping small objects with thumb and finger, babbling and other vocalizations, tumescence, and so forth, is rather extensive. Add to these muscular reactions, such responses as alpha rhythm disappearance when eyes open, the galvanic skin response, (GSR or PGR), and the secretions of the glands of both duct and ductless glands, along with the presumably reflexlike reactions of various neural centers as responses to nutritive supply or deprivation, and we begin to have a rather extensive repertoire of behavior units.

In the field of emotion, Watson (1924) proposed that we are born with at least three distinguishable patterns of response to specific stimuli. He wanted to call them x, y, and z, but offered the names of fear, anger, and love to represent reactions to loss of support or loud sounds (x); holding arms and legs to the sides of the body, thwarting movement (y); and stroking erogenous zones (z). Later investigators saw a broader variety of emotional reactions maturing out of a preliminary or basic "excitement" stage.

Bridges (1932), for example, saw "distress" at about three months and, at about the same time, "delight." Out of distress came anger and disgust and at seven months, fear. At about a year, delight seems to break up into elation and affection. These emotions seem to be innately determined and to develop in the course of growth and development. How much substantial reality there may be to other emotional state labels can be ignored for the moment. Mowrer (1960a), for example, needed such labels as *hope, fear, disappointment, and relief,* each of which he assumed to be natural responses to the appearance or disappearance of certain kinds of stimuli.

There appears to be no shortage of native responses to stimuli to serve as the supply of reactions that can be conditioned to new stimuli or situations. The body comes suitably equipped with a stock of reactions to cover a wide array of demands. The organization of reflex reactions in what Sherrington (1906) called the "integrated nervous system" even provides for certain automatic adjustments to situations. For example, in some experiments, a subject might be asked to lay his or her middle finger (palmar side down) on a plate or surface through which he or she will be shocked. A conditioned stimulus might precede the shock. As soon as the shock occurs, the finger is *extended* in a reflex escape from the US. If conditioning is established and the subject is now told to reverse his or her hand so that the back of the finger is on the plate, the response to the same CS will be a flexion of the finger. Some psychologists chose to make a problem of such a reversal or substitution of flexion for extension and looked for "cognitive" factors, while pointing to the alleged impossibility of a conditioning explanation. According to Thompson (1976), there is no problem calling for an explanation. The nervous system is prepared by its own organization to respond with extension or flexion, depending upon the postural adjustments of the rest of the body. The response is still a reflex, governed by the direct action of the nervous system. According to Thompson, what an organism does in connection with a given stimulus depends on its posture and general distribution of its limbs, body surfaces, and so forth. A wide generality of reactions is thus provided for, many of which can be perceived as adjustive, adaptive, or problem-solving and quite without any cognitive intervention.

What we have just described is the matter of *motor equivalence.* In many situations, we perform by habit (learning) or naturally some specific kind of response. As an example, most people open doors by grasping a knob with their right hands. If their right hands are temporarily otherwise engaged, the left hand is extended, grasps the knob, and opens the door. This may not appear to be a very important issue, but a problem of some moment appears to exist for some critics of a behavior-oriented learning approach. How can someone perform competently or at least adequately by using some nontrained body member in a problem situation? When a romantic person writes, "I love you" in the sand on a beach with his or her toe without having used his or her foot or toes as writing implements ever before in his or her life, the problem might appear to have a broader scope. Here, toes are being equated in function with fingers and pencil-moving responses. Now, it is asserted, the learning explanation cannot apply; something else has to be introduced to explain this capacity, and the something else is usually presumed to be some cognitive operation, which is never detailed but implies some information or knowledge-processing activity—some intelligent, insightful, astute implementation of abstractive activity.

The motor equivalence involved in such adjustments can be viewed as a matter of transfer of training (see chapter 16) based on considerable prior history. Handedness may be a hereditary feature, and we may learn to do things in particular ways with a particular set of movements as ordinary routines. A man may learn to shave with a razor in the right hand. If his right hand is injured, he uses his left, usually not very efficiently but passably. He can do this because throughout his life he has had to, on occasion, do the same thing with his left hand that he normally does with his right—move a chair, pick up a book, open doors, and so forth. From time to time, the usual, preferred operation cannot be performed, and a different response is substituted, which has the equivalent outcome.

Fractional Antedating Goal Response: The r_g

Before we continue with the problem of response equivalence, we need to recognize one of the most potent constructs devised by Hull (1943) in his efforts to account for response equivalence among many other problems. While the principles at work are not always strictly Pavlovian, the applications made by Hull are regularly described in Pavlovian conditioning terms, and we can best introduce the student to this construct in the present context. The construct is that of the r_g (pronounced "little argie"), or fractional antedating goal response. According to Hull, this construct is necessary to explain any kind of purposive behavior, that is, any sequence of actions that terminate at a later goal—any "expectancies," incentives, or even thinking behavior. Such a construct deserves more than casual treatment.

The construct of the r_g is based on the original observations by Hull that when a rat runs down an alley where there is food at the end, it will, in the early trials, run faster and faster as it nears the goal end. This observation was described as the goal gradient and was used extensively in Hull's theoretical speculations. But why should the rat increase its speed as it approaches the goal? What new sources of energy or stimulation are being generated in the uniform environment of the alley? Hull's reflections followed something like the following line of reasoning.

Whenever we attain any goal or experience some negative consequence to one or another kind of emotional response may develop. The hungry rat finding food at the end of an alley will begin to eat. We can describe his behavior as the attainment of a goal, and the response of eating can be called a goal response, or R_G. But the eating is occurring in the presence of stimuli from the external surroundings, and inner conditions (the hunger, the exertion from the just prior running) and some conditioning of the eating behavior will occur. We can presume that eating is a satisfying, positive kind of behavior, meaning that the rat is also emotional (happy?, feeling better?) at the time. Presumably, the emotional response is also conditioned to external and internal stimuli.

As with any other conditioning, the CR of eating and of the emotional response (CR_E) will tend to advance in time, that is, to antedate the US. We might expect then that the rat on the next occasion of approaching the goal box will begin to eat and feel better before it actually gets to the food. But eating cannot actually occur in the absence of food. The above remark about eating before arrival at the goal can then refer only to those *parts* of an eating behavior pattern that can occur in the absence of food. Such parts include opening the mouth, chewing, swallowing, and salivating (at least), and the feeling better can occur readily enough without food in the mouth. Such partial or fractional responses that antedate the actual goal response, Hull called "fractional antedating goal responses," symbolized as r_g (pronounced "little argie"). In an alley situation, such r_gs could occur sooner and sooner and eventually occur even before a starting gate was opened, perhaps even while the rat was being placed in the alley. It would be only a matter of seconds before it was actually eating.

Hull described such preliminary (perhaps preparatory) responses as quite specific to the various patterns of goal behavior that we perform. Thus, there might be a different set of r_gs for eating chicken from those for chicken soup or a chocolate soda. Hull suggested that sexual tumescence is a readily observable r_g. Puckering up to be kissed is another obvious illustration.

Such r_gs came to play an important role in the systems of Hull and Spence (1956), Hull's most prominent successor. They were identified as the mechanism by which an incentive could work. In effect, they perform the role of bringing the future into the present and explain the philosopher's problem of "action at a distance."

For both Guthrie and Hull (although Guthrie did not use the term), r_gs played the role of maintaining a chain or a continuity of behavior. The r_g, like any other response, would generate stimuli, or s_{r_g}s, and these would become conditioned to a variety of responses, depending upon situation features, and would provide additional cues and even energy (motivational effects) for persisting in some line of activity.

Hull thought of the r_g as a pure stimulus act, that is, as one that had no virtue in itself but which could be useful in preparing for a goal response or for getting to a goal. Thus, there is nothing less useful than a pucker if one is not about to be kissed or a particular kind of salivation if the particular food does not arrive. By generating stimuli, an r_g could initiate a subsequent step in a sequence and keep behavior going. In Hull's analysis, an r_g could account for what we normally describe as a desire, a wish, or a thought. If one is not making r_gs, he probably does not want anything or is probably not planning to do anything.

DENNIS THE MENACE   By Hank Ketcham

"You'd be disappointed, too, if you had your mouth all
set for hot dogs an' potato chips an' root beer!"

FIGURE 6.3: The wrong r_g's have been generated in Little Dennis.

We observe that if an r_g, by definition, is a part of a goal response, then
one can only make such responses if he has previously attained such a goal.
Putting it in another way, one cannot want something he never had before.
This may appear absurd or paradoxical, but consider the first olive, oyster,
or glass of beer, cigarette, or sexual adventure. What one wants and what
one gets may be quite different. One may, by generalization, think he wants
something and be quite disappointed when one gets it or finds that it is not
quite what he wanted.

With the construct of r_g available to us, we are ready to see how Hull
handled the problem of response equivalence. We can now become acquainted with the habit-family hierarchy.

The Habit-Family Hierarchy

Hull accounted for motor equivalence or response substitution on the
basis of a learning history involving situations (S) that called for different
ways of arriving at some goal (R_G), that is, satisfying some goal that had

been stimulated into being. (See Figure 6.4.) As a simple illustration, he suggested that if we have some need to arrive at some destination, we may, in the course of our history, take many routes from the same starting point. Thus, a rat in a maze with two paths (one short and one long) to a food location can be forced to take one route on one trial and the other on the next. There may be many twists and turns (S) and (R_G) in each path. After some trials, the animal has two paths to the goal in its behavioral repertoire. We can assume a preference for the short path and test for this by free trials. If either path is blocked, the animal takes the other, demonstrating some equivalence for the pathways. If we wish, we can introduce more pathways and impose a training program that leads to familiarity with all of the routes. If the paths differ in length or labor, we can observe the development of a preferential ranking. Such a package of S⟶Rs, where the stimulus is identical and the goal is the same with different ways of getting there was called by Hull a "habit-family hierarchy." There would be a common (family) feature to each potential sequence of responses in that with the same goal responses involved, for example, eating, there would be common r_gs associated with each path. Because stimuli from the r_gs would be conditioned to each and every response, the rat could readily switch from one path to another if the first were blocked.

On the human level, we can illustrate the same kind of habit-family analysis in many ways. A child first crawls across a floor to some destination; later, it walks; with growth and maturity, it finds it can hop, skip, and jump;

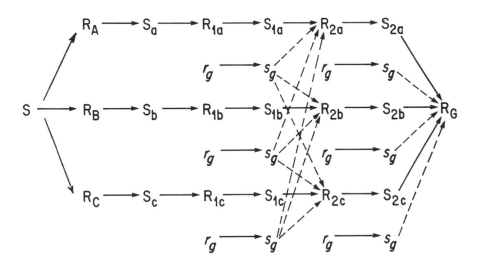

FIGURE 6.4: The Habit-family hierarchy. This family has three members. Note that r_g's start occurring soon after S and the stimuli they generate can be conditioned to all of the responses in any of the sequences leading from S to R. (After Hull 1943)

one-legged hops can be added, and even rolling or somersaulting can get into the act along with cartwheels, and so forth. Any one of the modes of locomotion can be employed if others are blocked, forbidden, or otherwise counterindicated. The human can, in fact, employ each of the above-listed modes of locomotion in one trip as the needs of the situation demand, and the stimuli from r_g s can dictate the relatively smooth transition from one mode to another without marked hesitation. But as Hull points out, each mode must in its history have been previously employed in attaining goals that could generate the r_g s involved. It is still a matter of transfer of training.

Suppose you wish to drink some coffee, and there is none around. You have a stove, various utensils, water, and ground coffee. The percolator is out of order, and the dripolator has a hole in it. Do you give up? If you have boiled coffee in a pot before, you need not surrender. You can have your coffee. Or you need an aspirin but have no glass at hand. What is wrong with your hand? You can make a cup of it if you ever did before this need arose.

There are many ways to skin a cat, but each has to be learned in its turn. As Dewey (1910) remarked, if you have enough habits, you do not need to think. Thinking without habits is not going to be very fruitful. Even methods of attacking problems where there are no prior habits can be learned and be habits in themselves, which can also be substituted in turn for one another as the occasion requires.

We return to the problem of motor equivalence and find it is not so formidable as it is made to appear by critics of Pavlov. There appear to be enough human response capabilities to provide for all the learnings in which we will engage, as new stimuli become associated to "old" or available responses. As different responses become associated with the same or similar stimuli, they can substitute for each other. In a famous short story, a prisoner manages to make ink out of shoe polish and uses the tip of a shoelace as a pen in order to write a note to an outside confederate, whom he reaches by tying the note to a thread made by unraveling a stocking. Such creative ingenuity poses no problem for Hull. Each component of the enterprise had to have been a member of a previously acquired hierarchy of habits. It would not be every man's set of hierarchies, but then, not every man escapes from a prison cell. Writing love messages in the sand dissolves as a problem for anyone who has used his or her feet to move objects, pick up small objects with curled toes, or otherwise used his or her feet as extra hands. There are armless painters who wield brushes clamped in their teeth. The mouth, as any cat knows, can be used to carry things, and many children saw their mothers holding pins in their mouths in the diapering process.

More Complex Behavior

The attacks on conditioning generated by those who rejected the Pavlovian approach in one way or another concentrated on the nature of the responses involved. The polemical nature of the attacks sometimes suggests an aversion to the basic deterministic, physicalistic approach. There must be something more to an appreciation of man's behavior; man cannot be an S——▶R machine. Such appears to be the underlying belief of the critics in search of new paradigms. They appear to seize upon any apparent weakness in the conditioning model and propose alternates in endless successions as they fail to work. It is necessary to examine some of the attacks on conditioning in this context of motor equivalence.

Differences between Conditioned and Unconditioned Response

The conditioned response (CR) is not the same as the unconditioned response (UR). This was an early (and still common) criticism of Pavlovian research. A search through the Pavlovian literature reveals no statement on the part of Pavlov to the effect that the CR and UR are identical. The CR, when salivation is the subject, is usually described as definitely less in quantity, for example. To duplicate the UR, one must present the US. It would be a rather remarkable adjustment for the nervous system to initiate a UR to a completely different stimulus, which would, of necessity, have to activate a different set of neurons to arouse anything like the US neuron pool.

Place versus Response Learning

Animals can find their way to a goal in a maze using completely different modes of locomotion from those in which they were trained. This is the classic attack initiated by Lashley (1924), who destroyed various motor nuclei in rats, which incapacitated them for walking and forced them to tumble their way through a maze. Other experimenters would flood a maze that animals originally learned to walk through so that now the animals had to swim to the goal instead of walk. Clearly, such animals could not be employing learned movements, as the movements were, in fact, quite obviously different. Such demonstrations do pose a problem for the conditioning theorist. The habit-family explanation does not adapt itself easily if an animal has never before swum to a goal. Without a swimming history, swimming could have no appropriate r_g s or stimuli therefrom. The tumbling rats might be a little easier to deal with. After all, rats do get about their cages in ways other than walking, for example, by rolling over. To handle the Lashley criticism, it is necessary to take a hypothetical leap and propose that behavior can be described in somewhat more molar terms than heretofore used. It can be assumed (without any direct and precise formulation) that organisms have some general (including emotional) response patterns that can be loosely described as approach behavior and escape or avoidance behavior repertoires. Perhaps, a repertoire of attack behaviors might be considered a desirable addition. After all, fighting and fleeing are commonly observed with a rather wide variety of components as far as specific movements are concerned.

If we can postulate some general pattern of behavior that merits the label *approach*, we can eliminate Lashley's criticism at once. The animals did not necessarily learn to walk or run through the maze—certainly, they paid no attention to their feet nor did they ponder which foot to move—they learned to *approach* the goal. Later, we will consider some details of this general behavior pattern we are calling approach—for example, we might learn to approach quickly or slowly, with caution or recklessly. For the present, we can stay with the general term.

In the context of a T-maze setup (see Figure 6.5), a rat can be trained (Tolman, Ritchie, and Kalish 1946) to make a left turn or a right turn, and if it turns appropriately, we might be beguiled into thinking that it had learned a specific movement, namely, that of turning at the choice point. Under some restricted conditions of learning, such as a room with no distinctive cues, a rat might learn just that, namely, to turn left at a certain point. Guthrie (1935) would be pleased to point out that the rat had learned a specific movement. But such learning is difficult and will only occur under such impoverished conditions as a bare room would provide. Tolman argued that "place" learning was easier, that the rat had a destination ("in mind"?), a "cognitive map," that it knew where it was going and how to get there. It is easy to fall into this cognitive trap by demonstrating that where there are cues, the rat learns "to go to a certain place," especially when such learning is easier than learning to make a specific turn (which necessarily depends on perhaps not too powerful stimulation from kinesthesis).

It is just as easy, and perhaps more correct, to assert that the rat does not learn to go to a particular place but rather that it learns to *approach*

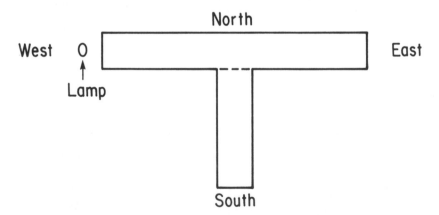

FIGURE 6.5: A T-maze consisting of two 2″ by 4″ pieces of wood at right angles. The pieces are elevated above the floor to prevent jumping. The rats starts at the point marked South.

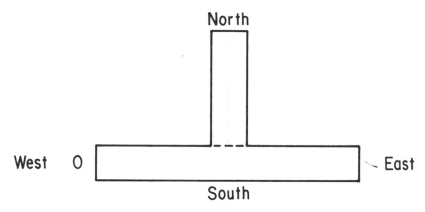

FIGURE 6.6: The starting leg has been reversed so that the rat now starts from North.

certain stimuli. This point was illustrated by the author in the following way. In an otherwise dark room, rats were trained to run a T-maze where one end had a low illumination (seven-watt) bulb one foot from the end of the runway. When ten animals had learned to turn left or to go to the lighted place, the starting leg was reversed, so that the animals now had to violate any left turn habit if they were to obtain food. (See Figure 6.6.) None of the animals failed to perform correctly; they all turned right. Tolman would easily accept this demonstration as one of place learning, since there clearly was a place, a lighted place, as opposed to a dark region.

In the course of the testing, an assistant, going to the north end, or the new starting leg, with a rat moved the stand holding the bulb a foot away from its original position and failed to replace it. The rat ran down the starting leg, made the right turn, and raced down the alley all the way to the end and, failing to stop, promptly fell to the floor. In a deliberate repetition of this study, with the light moved two feet away (after training with the light one foot away), ten rats out of ten fell off the alley in the first test trial from the north end. Such bizarre behavior cannot be accounted for by saying that the rats learned to go to a certain place. That place was presumably the end of the alley, and the rats ignored it, plainly preferring a place in outer space. A more parsimonious account might hold that the rats had learned *to approach* a lighted area to some point of light intensity and to stop as they neared that point. Because of the inverse-square law of illumination intensity, we can presume that a gradient of illumination was generated by the bulb so that the intensity or brightness of the light was of some specific value at the end of the maze. The light value fell off rapidly toward the choice point; when the rat had been trained originally, it had learned to turn toward the source of illumination and to move along until the light was of a certain intensity. At that point, it had learned to stop. Its behavior was a clear case of approach behavior. It had learned to approach (we could say that its behavior was guided by) the light. The fact that the light was in a certain place was of no importance. It could have been at the other end of the alley, but that would not permit an explanation in terms of approach, as a left turn would also be involved. Because the rats tried to continue their approach when they ran out of and off the alley, we can argue that they had learned an approach response and not a place response.

Assuming some merit to the argument above, it can be argued further that not only approach but avoidance or attack responses can similarly be accepted without regard to the specific movements, which might be rather different from one occasion to the next. The erratic and ungoverned fighting behavior of children bears little resemblance to the skillful and even artful behavior patterns of a professional boxer, who has indeed learned some movements.

What has been suggested, then, is that a general class of responses, which can be described as approach, avoidance, and attack, might be basic. Such class responses would be rather unorganized and undifferentiated patterns of responses, which can be conditioned as such. With specific training, some particular components of one of these patterns can be conditioned with some specialization—thus, we can learn to talk slowly or rapidly or softly or loudly; to walk, crawl, or swim; to walk on crutches or with a cane; to use a wheel chair or golf cart; and to attain a specific goal that might or might not be in a specific place. We can, after all, follow moving objects whose place is continually changing. We can also learn which objects to follow. Long before Tolman, rats had been trained to go to a lighted end in an alley regardless of which end was illuminated. Here, they were going to a movable place, which is no place at all.

In "avoidance training" of rats, where shocks are used to force rats to jump over a hurdle from one part of a box to another, we again face the problem of what does the rat learn. Again, we find that the CR is not like the UR in the sense that if the rat jumps to a buzzer CS it does not jump in the same way as it does when the shock is present. But after all, the shock is not present, and that should make a great difference in how the rat jumps. As a matter of fact, the rat does not jump in the same way twice when the shock is present. After a few shocks, the rat jumps quickly and efficiently, but by being quick about it, the rat also gets less of a shock. Does the rat learn to jump the fence, or does it learn to escape or avoid the shock? An easy answer is available if we remove the fence—the rat does not jump a nonexistent fence—it *runs* to the other side. Should we raise the fence to the ceiling of the box, then the rat starts climbing the fence, which it cannot jump. It will continue to attack the fence, climb, scramble, and, in every way possible to rats, to try to "get out of here." The fence is incidental and *requires* a specific movement or set of movements when it is there. In its absence, the rat avoids or escapes the shock in any of a variety of ways. The rat learns something. It learns that the area is unsafe or dangerous or painful and that it is unwise to remain there. *Avoidance* appears to qualify as a suitable response term, even though it is applied to a collection or repertoire of unspecified movements.

We must be careful in the use of such class labels as *approach* or *avoidance*, especially if we allow ourselves too many liberties in the direction of using class terms where they are not appropriate. Guthrie's emphasis on specific movements must be recognized when appropriate. Skinner (1938) chose to be somewhat free in his discussion of lever pressing. Any movement at all that resulted in the discharge of a pellet from the food dispenser was considered a bar press, even if it amounted to the rat's sitting on the bar (and possibly learning nothing). Logan (1956) suggests that behavior, that is, responses, be carefully examined for whatever features can be observed and measured, as we may not be too sure of what is actually being learned. In the bar press situation, for example, Logan is concerned with such details as how strongly does a rat press (the bar can be counterweighted, so that little or no work is required, or a load can be imposed, calling for an energetic reaction). Rats can learn to work hard or take it easy. In Skinner's schedules of reinforcement demonstrations, he showed that rats can work rapidly or slowly, in bursts or steadily, or in a wide variety of combinations. In an alley runway, Capaldi (1970) demonstrated that rats can run quickly or slowly, depending upon whether or not they receive large rewards or small ones or some reward or none at all. It is not enough, in all cases, to call a response a response and be done with it. Responses have latencies, amplitudes, directions, frequencies, durations, and other characteristics, depending on situations. A response may be correct or incorrect, random or controlled, and so on. The words "stop it" can be whispered or roared or merely spoken in a usual tone. Each manner of speech, that is, each response pattern, must be learned. The response to the "stop it" will also vary, depending upon how it is said and, also, when, where, and by whom. If it is an actor on a stage, we may do nothing but look and listen further. Other actors will behave in ways the audience might or might not anticipate, depending on the playwright's purposes.

no accounting for the performance in associated stimuli

Rapid Serial Response Criticism

A final objection to the motor or response level to conditioning again was emphasized by Lashley (1951). Lashley had some skill with the violin and was perplexed by the fact that musicians can play such instruments, particularly the piano and violin, so rapidly in terms of the fingering required that there appeared to be no accounting for the performance in terms of associated stimuli. James (1890) had proposed that serial acts can be accounted for by the fact that one movement will generate kinesthetic stimuli for the next. In such an activity as touch-typing, for example, one does not look at the keys because pressing one key provides stimulation for pressing the next key required. With practice, all possible combinations of

one movement will generate kinesthetic stimuli for the next letters get associated to such kinesthetic cues, and depending on what we want to type, the first finger response sets off the next.

Such an explanation might do for slow typists, but Lashley argued, the violinsts' fingers and those of fast typists move too rapidly for the nervous system to conduct the necessary kinesthetic impulses. Nervous impulses do have a limited speed, and according to Lashley's computations, there is no possibility that a second response could be initiated by aftereffects of a first.

No one denies the fact that violinists and pianists do perform and that they learn to do so. Learning is involved, but the conditioning or association explanation of James simply will not do. Such a failure of a simple conditioning explanation motivated Lashley to search for other approaches, and he became somewhat positively attached to Gestalt orientations, which would account for such learning in broad principles about integration or learning something as a whole, integrated unit—an explanation that may say much but serves no serious purpose and tells nothing.

Hebb (1972) was not especially distressed by Lashley's puzzle. Because Hebb's view was an associationistic one, if not directly Pavlovian, he felt constrained to account for such rapid serial learning or sequential responding. Suppose we take an example from touch-typing, where we can talk more easily about the possible cues and responses than we might with musical notation and violin fingering. If we wish to type the word *and*, we can picture the operation as shown in Figure 6.7.

Figure 6.7 suggests that we see the copy, read the word, and proceed to type by looking at the keys—finding *a* and pressing with the little finger of the left hand, as our instructor tells us to do. We will look for the *n* and press with the appropriate finger, going on then to *d*. Meanwhile, the pressing of *a* generates kinesthetic stimulation in the little finger of the left hand (S_1), and this stimulation is present when we press the *n* key to the visual cue; similarly, when we are about to press the *d* key, we have a kinesthetic feedback stimulus (S_2). Thus, S_1 can be conditioned to the visual or verbal cue of *n* and substitute for it. In the same way, S_2 can come to substitute for the visual/verbal cue of *d*. After a few trials, once *a* is typed, we need no longer look at *n* or *d* in order to type them by touch.

Typists who have to type Minneapolis, Minnesota, or Philadelphia,

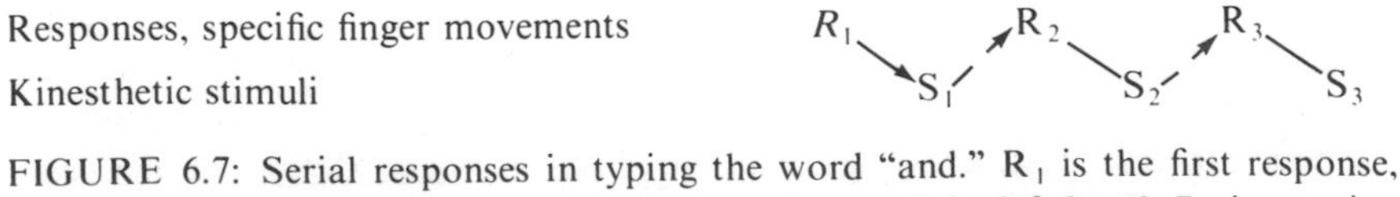

External world cues: the copy, the word *and*,   *and*
   typewriter keys, letters   *a*   *n*   *d*

Responses, specific finger movements R_1 R_2 R_3

Kinesthetic stimuli S_1 S_2 S_3

FIGURE 6.7: Serial responses in typing the word "and." R_1 is the first response, pressing the key with the little finger of the left hand; R_2 is pressing the *n* key with the right forefinger, and R_3 is pressing the d key with the left hand middle finger. S_1, S_2, and S_3 are the corresponding kinesthetic feedback stimuli.

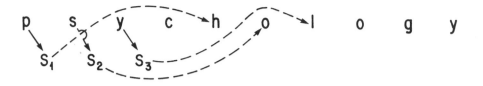

FIGURE 6.8: Stimulus trace conditioning in a serial response.

Pennsylvania, many times a day because they work in these cities come to type off the letters about as fast as their typewriters can accept the input. They are like Lashley's violinists and are typing too fast for the nervous system to cooperate by feeding in the appropriate kinesthetic stimulation. But according to Hebb, the nervous system does not have to follow the simple pattern we have just pictured. Because the kinesthetic stimulus trace can survive for some time, there is no reason to prevent the conditioning of S_1 to R_3, for example, and with longer words, such as *psychology*, the typist might find that typing the *p* is providing the stimulation for some letter later in the word, for example, *h*, and the second letter is providing the stimulation for the *o*, as shown in Figure 6.8.

In this account, some source must be found for the typing of the first four letters. They, however, might be learned to other cues, for example, to vocalizations.

In playing the violin or piano, the musician sometimes makes an error—if this occurs, the musician may find that he or she cannot continue effectively even if he or she goes on as if no error were made. The musician finds he or she must go back to some earlier point if he or she is going to continue successfully. The reason appears to be clear: an error on one note will not supply the appropriate stimulation for some note further on in the composition, and the errors will then multiply, resulting in total disruption. If one is playing for an unsophisticated audience and is also competent, one can "cover" the error by skipping to another secure point in the music and continuing with aplomb. If the audience is critical, the first error will not stand alone.

SUMMARY

We have looked at a number of criticisms of conditioning. The first one is that there are not enough responses to provide a satisfactory account of complex behavior. There seems to be an adequate repertoire to justify the conclusion that we do and we do not have to learn all the various responses in which we engage. Nature seems to have supplied us with the capacity to do, physically, whatever one is called upon to do, granted some exceptionally gifted or talented individuals. Some people have big hands and can span

12 piano keys. The concert pianist Van Cliburn is one such. The second is that there are variations in the response, depending upon postural arrangements. This is true, but it is also apparently provided for in integrated neural action, which allows either extension or flexion of limbs, depending upon how the rest of the body is disposed. The third is that conditioned responses do not duplicate unconditioned responses in such behaviors as escape and avoidance reactions. This is true, but explicable in terms of a class interpretation of avoidance or escape behavior. Similarly, an approach category of responses can account for changes in locomotion mode or so-called place learning. Finally, we considered the speed of skilled sequential movements in terms of kinesthetic conditioning. By proposing that kinesthetic feedback is conditioned to responses later in the sequence instead of to the immediately succeeding response, a satisfactory account appears to be available in conditioning terms.

The basic and generally accepted facts about conditioning have been described briefly above. Work on conditioning continues in many laboratories, and new findings continue to be reported. The interested student will pursue these reports in journals, books, and collections, for example, Estes (1975), Hall (1976), and Marx (1969). Some researchers continue to mine the original Pavlovian claim with new technologies and sophisticated elaborations. Rescorla (1975), for example, likes to combine two or more conditioning stimuli, either in acquisition or extinction sessions. The stimuli may be positive, negative, or neutral with respect to each other and to the unconditioned and conditioned responses. Among other interesting hypotheses, Rescorla suggests that higher-order conditioning can be extremely potent and autonomous and, once established, rather independent of its original reinforcing stimulus. Rescorla also suggests that conditioned stimuli, to be effective, might have to be informative. Thus, a neutral stimulus added to an already effective CS might not acquire any associative strength because it is redundant. A CS that does not predict the US will not result in any effective conditioning. Whether one must accept the notion that a CS must carry "information" may be questioned. It might be enough for it to arouse some preparatory neural action for the about-to-come US. Introducing abstractions such as information processing is not quite in keeping with the Pavlovian tradition.

The student should appreciate that conditioning has been the concern of thousands of investigators, and no single chapter or book can offer more than an introduction to the area. The present chapter has merely presented some highlights of an increasingly complex experimental preoccupation.

There are some unresolved issues that we can take up at a later point. We are now ready to look at the major counterapproach to learning, which started with the animal investigations of Thorndike at Columbia University in 1898.

7

Learning by Doing

INSTRUMENTAL LEARNING

At the time that Pavlov was working with salivating dogs, another Russian investigator, Vladimir Bekhterev, arranged for a different kind of response to be associated with a signal. Bekhterev did not bother to operate on his dogs. He would shock a dog's hind paw, forcing a withdrawal of the leg, which could be easily observed. Pairing a buzzer or any other stimulus with the shock would result in fairly rapid acquisition of an avoidance response. After a few trials, as soon as the buzzer sounded, the leg would be withdrawn, prior to the shock. The original escape reaction would become an avoidance reaction as a matter of the antedating characteristic of conditioning. It was Bekhterev's book, *General Principles of Human Reflexology* (1933), which Watson studied in a French translation, which brought conditioning to the United States.

Pavlov and Bekhterev were and remained rivals, although there were no apparent differences in the kinds of phenomena that were observed in either the salivary or leg withdrawal experiments. Later on, the Bekhterev situation was to be analyzed quite differently by American psychologists. Konorski and Miller (1937), a pair of Polish investigators working in Pavlov's laboratory in Leningrad, introduced a novel technique with respect to a dog's leg reaction. They attached a cord to the front paw of a dog strapped to the Pavlov frame and proceeded to raise the dog's leg by pulling on the cord. Just before the pull began, a bell would be sounded, as a conditioned stimulus. When the leg reached a certain elevation, they presented food to the dog, considering that the US for salivation. They found a rather interesting set of developments as trials continued. Not only would the dog begin to salivate to the CS—an involuntary reaction—but it would also begin to raise its paw. By not presenting the food unless the dog raised its paw to some specific height, the paw raising could be controlled by the experimenters so that the specific level was reached on each trial. Because the paw flexion, originally a passive response to the pull, had now become a self-initiated or apparently voluntary response, Konorski and Miller decided that they had hit upon a new kind or type of conditioning—the conditioning of a voluntary response. They believed that they had solved the problem of how habits are learned. They called their new kind of conditioning "Type II." Pavlov rejected their claims to anything new, as he had all along assumed that his conclusions about conditioning applied to all responses, whether these were of striated musculature or of glands.

By using a food reward or reinforcement following the lifting of the paw, Konorski and Miller had demonstrated the same kind of learning operation that Thorndike, in a much looser situation, had demonstrated long before. In the early 1930s, Skinner would demonstrate the same kind of behavior by having rats depress a small bar in a small compartment, where the bar press would be followed by a food reward. Neither Thorndike nor Skinner, however, would regard the behavior as learned through conditioning. Thorndike would emphasize the reward aspect, as we shall see. Skinner would regard the CS of Konorski and Miller to be a special kind of discriminated stimulus, which would leave it up to the rat as to whether or not it would press.

Konorski and Miller, however, insisted on the conditioning language. They believed that the conditioned stimulus in the situation would become associated with the proprioceptive stimulation generated by the raising of the leg and that, somehow, this proprioceptive stimulation would then result in the lifting of the leg. Later (1970), Konorski demonstrated that the proprioceptive stimulation was indeed involved, as dogs with the sensory feedback stimulation eliminated by surgery could not acquire the paw-raising habit. What we are left with is a recognition of the importance of kinesthetic stimulation in the acquisition of a voluntary response. We will examine this importance later (chapter 11). For the present, we turn to the importance of Konorski's US (or food) and its interpretation in the United States as a reward. Our question is, What does rewarding someone for a response accomplish?

CONDITIONING AND LEARNING

Conditioning and Learning is the title of a most influential book by Hilgard and Marquis (1940), and the period in which it was published was a time of great activity in American learning laboratories. The very title suggests a difference between conditioning and learning, and the suggestion was widely (if not too wisely) and quickly accepted. A number of papers and books appeared in which a convenient division of the learning area into two fields was declared. Hilgard and Marquis had proposed that Pavlovian conditioning could be assigned to autonomic nervous system functions (glandular discharges, visceral responses) while what Konorski had called "Type II conditioning" really amounted to what Thorndike had described as learning by the law of effect or learning by reward and punishment, where the learning would somehow be a function of the consequences of behavior.

Hilgard and Marquis (1940) summarized a great many studies of learning that had appeared up to that time and found it possible, and perhaps desirable, to distinguish four types or classes of learning where the consequences of some response were decisive; these four categories were the following:

onsidered instrumental learning)

1. Simple reward learning: here some response is followed by a reinforcer or desirable consequence.

2. Escape learning: here some noxious stimulation, for example, electric shock, is presented and the subject has to do something to get rid of the painful or undesirable stimulation.

3. Avoidance learning: here the subject, after some escape trials, begins to respond in some way that eliminates the noxious stimulus or prevents its occurrence. A signal that the noxious stimulus is about to occur is necessary for avoidance behavior. There must also be sufficient time for the subject to respond prior to the undesirable stimulus.

4. Secondary reward learning: here the subject is rewarded by the presentation of some stimulus that does not directly reduce any drive or need. The reinforcing stimulus has acquired reward properties by association with some "primary" reinforcer and now comes to act like one. A word such as *right* or *good* could be a secondary reinforcer.

All four of these categories of learning situations are characterized by one feature, namely, that the organism has to do something that the experimenter can observe and then reward. In short, the behavior must be *emitted* by the learner; the experimenter merely sits around and waits. When the response that the experimenter wants occurs, he or she then provides a reward. In the escape and avoidance situations, the experimenter does present stimuli, but it is up to the organism to do something desired by the experimenter before the reward (cessation of shock would have to be considered a reward in a negative sense—a negative reinforcer) is presented. Hilgard and Marquis conceived of such emitted behavior as "instrumental" in changing the organism's environment, and the responses in the four categories listed all came to be considered as examples of instrumental learning. In contrast, Hilgard and Marquis chose to describe the Pavlovian paradigm as classical conditioning. What was classical about it was not explained, but the label stuck.

According to Hilgard and Marquis, then, there were at least five kinds of learned behavior, or, at least, experimental learning procedures or paradigms and at least two kinds of principles that were required to account for the five classes. Pavlovian conditioning principles could account for one class (reflex responses and responses controlled by the autonomic nervous system, that is, involuntary responses). The other four classes, the instrumental group, called for some kinds of reward or "reinforcement" operation. The two major classes could be relatively easily distinguished by noting whether the behavior in question was *elicited* or *evoked* or forced out of the animal (Pavlov's conditioning) or whether the behavior was *emitted*, that is, was initiated by the animal, somehow, on its own.

OPERANT-RESPONDENT DISTINCTION

During the period when Hilgard and Marquis were preparing their book, Skinner (1938), working at Harvard, also chose to emphasize a distinction between the Pavlovian experimental situation with its conditioning principles and the kind of learning he was observing. While giving credit to Pavlov for his careful work on reflex behavior, Skinner believed that most behavior of any interest to people did not follow the reflex laws. Really important human interactions with other people or with their environments were not under direct stimulus control. Most behavior of any consequence was not involuntary. In most situations, we can respond but do not have to. To take a simple example, if a person picks up a pencil, such a response cannot be regarded as reflexive because he or she does not have to pick it up even if told to do so or threatened with severe consequences. The pencil is just there and does not control the picking-up behavior. If the pencil is picked up, it is because the response emerged from, was emitted by, the picker. Such behavior is ordinarily considered to be voluntary, and so we might consider the distinction Skinner was drawing as one between voluntary and involuntary behavior. Skinner, however, regarded the issue from a strictly behavioristic, deterministic view. If a person does pick up a pencil, he or she had to do it and had no choice in the matter. If the person did not pick it up, he or she had no choice in that case either. Whether one picks up a pencil or not thus becomes a question of how strong the tendency, habit, or response of picking up pencils might be, and this strength is presumed to be a function of one's history or background with pencils in the situation that prevails. Such a history would consist of how often one had been rewarded (reinforced) for picking up pencils or how often one had been punished.

The pattern of previous positive and negative reinforcements in any situation was described by Skinner as one's behavioral history. Kantor (1947) referred to such a history as one's reactional biography.

Emitted behavior, as Skinner viewed it, amounted to operating on one's environment and changing it in some way. Whatever one does alters the relationships between objects or brings about some consequence. Skinner chose to regard such behavior as consisting of "operant" responses in contrast with Pavlovian reflexes, which he called "respondent." Thus, a sneeze would be an instance of respondent behavior. Using a handkerchief to muffle the sneeze would be an operant response. The term *operant* came to be a special kind of identification label for Skinner and his followers. Those psychologists who did not identify with Skinner came to prefer the later Hilgard and Marquis label of *instrumental* responses for the same behavior. In any case, we recognize the distinction that Skinner was emphasizing as the same as that of Konorski and Miller's (1937) division of Type I and Type II conditioning.

For years afterwards, other psychologists would review the varieties of learning situations in which stimuli and rewards and punishments could be arranged in different patterns or compositions and suggest more and different categories of learning. Tolman (1949) was to propose six kinds of learning. Grant (1964) proposed eight subclasses, and Woods (1974) proposed 16. All of these efforts to categorize learning types are helpful in clarifying issues but do not address themselves to the basic question of what learning is. The implication of such classifications is that not only do organisms learn in different kinds of situations or arrangements of stimulus components or circumstances but that there are just as many different kinds of learning principles. The more conservative scientific philosophy would suggest a faith in fewer principles, perhaps only one, namely, that learning is learning and takes place in the same way regardless of situational differences. This is the question we shall try to explore. It is time to take a look at instrumental learning in more detail, and it is proper to start with the originator of the concept, Edward Lee Thorndike.

REINFORCEMENT THEORY

At the time Pavlov was busy substituting one stimulus for another, Thorndike became absorbed in the problem of substitution of one response for another. He equated the nature of learning with the operations in the solving of problems. In any given stimulus situation, one responds in some way. If the response made does not alter the situation (remove the stimulus), a problem exists and another response is *emitted*, which does, or again does not solve the problem. The emission of one response after another goes on until the stimulus disappears, that is, it is no longer present either because the actions of the learner removed it or removed the learner from the situation. The circumstances just described represent the essence of the Thorndikian paradigm.

To take a concrete example, consider the classical Thorndike (1898) investigation. A cat is placed inside a box large enough to allow some freedom of movement. The sides of the box consist of bars, making the box, in reality, a cage. The cat is hungry, and food is placed outside the box, where it can be seen. The cat usually appears to have no desire to remain in the box and appears to be attempting to get out. There is only one way to get out—through a door that can be opened in only one way, determined by Thorndike. In a given instance, the door can be opened by pulling a string that hangs inside the box. The other end of the string is attached to the door, which will rise if the string is pulled.

The cat can be seen to respond to the situation at first in what seems to be a natural way, that is, attempting to squeeze through the bars. If this worked, there would be no problem. Because there is insufficient space between the bars, the response does not alter the situation. We now have the situation described above. The cat can continue to try to squeeze through the bars (Response 1), but sooner or later this will cease, and some other response (Response 2) will be made. It could be one of surrender—curling up and going to sleep. In such a case, the problem will not go away, and nothing has been learned according to Thorndike. We might pause to consider that something has been learned, namely, that pushing through the bars does not work—but Thorndike never showed much interest in extinction. Should the cat respond in some other way (Response 3), for example, stretching to the ceiling and pushing thereat, this too would fail, and Response 4 would emerge—this could be any of a large number of responses but might be that of clawing at the string. Should a claw get caught in the string and the cat attempt to withdraw the claw by pulling away, the door will open. At this point, the cat might disentangle itself from the string and leave the box.

All that has been reported above is that one response followed another and that the last in a series met an experimenter's needs, as well as those of the cat. From Thorndike's point of view, the responses that occurred prior to the "successful" one were random or chance variations (like chance variations in bodily structure that Darwin used to account for evolution). Some chance responses were useless (of no survival value). One (still chance) response was useful. It solved the problem of the "survival" of the cat in the situation. We have not seen any sign of learning as yet, only behavior.

If the cat is now replaced in the box, one can wonder what will happen. If the cat immediately approached the string and pulled it, there would be grounds for talking about intelligence, reasoning, insight, understanding, and what not, but according to Thorndike, such behavior is never observed, and if it were, it would only be by chance that Response 4 would occur first.* Typically, the cat will go through responses 1, 2, and 3 but spend less time at them. It may then return to Response 1 or 2 or make new responses (5, 6 . . .n) before Response 4 reoccurs. Usually, but not always, the second trial ends in fewer minutes than the first. Additional trials take less and less time; the cat refrains from responses 1, 2, and 3 and so on and responds with

---

*The chance aspect refers only to the relationship between the solution and the general stimulus situation. In this sense, the responses are random. Actually, the responses would have some hierarchical order, in that there would be a higher probability of one response occurring sooner than another, then a second higher probability, and so forth.

Response 4 more and more quickly. Now, says Thorndike, we can talk about learning.

TRIAL AND ERROR AND CHANCE SUCCESS

The antics of a cat in a puzzle box were described by Thorndike as amounting to "trial and error and chance success." Some descriptions by other writers reduced this statement to "trial and error," but Thorndike usually insisted on the fuller phrase. The chance success was the critical or crucial feature. The emphasis on chance made the learning of anything a mechanical, nonrational affair. Hypothetically, in a situation where some one action can solve a problem, anyone could solve the problem if one was lucky. Another way of stating Thorndike's position is that we all learn anything we do learn by dumb luck. Intelligence has nothing to do with learning—quite the contrary: we become intelligent by learning. The more we learn, the smarter or more competent we are.

One important caveat must be introduced. No one is going to learn without trying. There must be trials and, probably, errors. Luck can only operate when someone is trying. Some people are luckier than others, and others try harder. A happy combination of a lot of luck and a few trials results in fast learning. Little luck and many trials make for slow learning. The approach of Thorndike is something like a story by Horatio Alger. Some people work hard and get no place; others work hard and, with luck, rise to the top.

Learning occurs, in the Thorndike situation, when a response, originally occurring by chance, comes to occur as the first reaction to a situation that originally was met with some other response. One response replaces another. But why does the new (successful) response become a more-likely-to-occur-sooner response? Simply recognizing it as successful does not answer this question. Here Thorndike fell back onto age-old hedonism in a modified form. It was commonly appreciated that we do things because they please us and refrain from doing things that might displease us. Hedonism proclaims that pleasure and pain guide behavior. Thorndike recognized that such language, which might satisfy citizens and philosophers, would not be acceptable to scientists. Yet, the "facts" were obvious. The cat wanted to get out, it got out, and perhaps ate the food just outside the box. Some way had to be found to relate these desirable consequences to the prior activity. Thorndike felt he could safely describe the operation in terms of what he called the "law of effect."

LAW OF EFFECT

Avoiding any hint of subjectivity, Thorndike described what he felt had to be the case in this fashion: between any situation (S) and any response

(R), there had to be a connection (presumably some neural arrangement), which Thorndike called a *bond*. If a response occurs at all, by chance or otherwise, there has to be such a connection or S→R bond. Because the behavior Thorndike witnessed indicated that such responses were occurring more and more readily, it could only be because the bond was becoming stronger. The only factor that could add this increment of strength had to be the consequence, result, or effect of the response. If the effect was negative, the tendency (bond) to perform the response weakened; if positive, the bond was strengthened, and the tendency to respond in that way would become greater. Casting about for suitable language, Thorndike chose these words: "If a response is followed by a satisfying state of affairs the bond between the stimulus and the response is strengthened; if the response is followed by an annoying state of affairs, the bond is weakened." All that remained was to define these states of affairs in objective language. Thorndike proceeded thus: "A satisfying state of affairs is one the animal does nothing to avoid, and frequently strives to attain. An annoying state of affairs is one the animal does nothing to attain and frequently strives to avoid." With these definitions, which might leave some questions about frequency and striving unanswered, Thorndike felt he had arrived at a general law describing the learning process. Learning became a function of the effects of chance variation among responses, just as evolution had been, for Darwin, a matter of chance variations in physical traits.

The average citizen could still operate in terms of pleasure and pain, rewards and punishments, and old proverbs. "You catch more flies with sugar." "The burnt child dreads the fire." "Spare the rod and spoil the child." Thorndike's language was operational and had the virtue of seeming to work.

LAW OF EXERCISE

Because improvement in performance was usually slow but progressive, Thorndike added another law, that of exercise, to account for the effects of practice: the more often an S→R bond was exercised successfully, the stronger it would become. Simple practice (without effect) was of no merit. It was the number of recurrences of satisfying states of affairs that mattered.

Thorndike performed many experiments that demonstrated the futility of practice without effect. The experiments have an aura of unreality about them, but Thorndike felt they had to be done to prove the point. He would ask people to draw four-inch lines when they could not see how well they were doing, that is, the subject, wearing a blindfold, would start a pencil moving along a rule and stop when he or she thought he or she had produced a four-inch line. If the subject were told "right" he or she would soon settle down to a close approximation (plus or minus $\frac{1}{8}$ of an inch), but if nothing was said, the subject would show no improvement over hundreds of trials, although he or she would settle down to some common length of line outside the limits. Practice, or exercise, Thorndike concluded, is of value only if the responses are correct.

LAW OF READINESS

Before a bond could be exercised, the organism had to be in a state of readiness for the activity involved to perceive or receive the stimuli and emit the response. With this consideration, Thorndike added a third law, the law of readiness.

This law is a form of an *attention* statement. It does not refer to some chronological or physiological maturation but to a preparatory set for some activity. The sense organs, muscles, and nervous system must be prepared for some specific stimulus and response if the learning is to occur.

LAW OF ASSOCIATIVE SHIFTING

Among other laws Thorndike proposed, we should mention one of his less frequently cited laws, namely that of associative shifting (Thorndike 1913). This law can be considered as equivalent to the principles of conditioning, although Thorndike believed it to be broader than, and inclusive of, conditioning, in which he showed little interest. According to this law, a formerly ineffective stimulus, for example, a command to a child, can come to *initiate* behavior that previously could only occur to some more direct stimulation, if the at-first-ineffective stimulus frequently accompanies the response. We will later see Skinner describing the same operation in other terms, such as *discriminated response*, when some stimulus of no direct bearing on an activity comes to develop control over the behavior. By underplaying the law of associative shifting and emphasizing the law of effect, Thorndike kept alive a controversy over the nature of learning, which persists to this day. Attaching more importance to the law of associative shifting would have been a concession of the field to Pavlov.

An illustration of associative shifting might bring out the controversial points. Suppose you wish to train a dog to lie down and roll over. Assuming that it is your dog, reasonably friendly, and fond of some kind of food, for example, candy, all you have to do is show the dog the candy, and when the dog tries to get it, you lower the candy to the floor. The dog will normally follow the candy down to the floor level while you say "lie down" and assist this command by some pressure on the dog's back. Now with the dog still eager but lying down on the floor, slowly rotate the candy over the dog's head while it follows the candy, and the dog's body flips onto its side. During this phase, you say "roll over," repeatedly. In a few trials, the dog will lie down and roll over more and more quickly while you repeat the instruction.

You could, of course, repeat the instruction in any language or say anything else you like, for example, "Go jump in the lake." You now have an educated dog, to a degree.

Where does the law of associative shifting come into the picture? You now no longer need the candy. The dog will respond to the command. The response pattern is no longer tied to the candy and the pressures on the dog's back. It has been shifted to the vocal stimulation. The words could easily be considered as a CS by Pavlov, with the candy and pressures as the US. Note that the dog was forced to lie down either by following the candy or the pressures. Was there anything voluntary about the whole act? Does a cat pull a string voluntarily? Do not all cats pull at dangling strings? If a response to a stimulus is natural, that stimulus is a US. We can see now why Thorndike was not eager to push his law of associative shifting. Pavlov had already "discovered" it.

LAW OF BELONGINGNESS

We will consider only briefly another of Thorndike's laws, that of belongingness. Thorndike was fond of this law and had great educational hopes for it, but it was never actually implemented in instructional situations, possibly because no one was ingenious enough to actually put it to work. According to this law, some stimuli and some responses have some more or less natural affinity—they go together or belong with each other. Thus, hypothetically, first names go with last names, and a set of first and last names might be learned more easily than a set of pairs of first names or pairs of last names. In a sentence such as "John is a butcher; Henry is a carpenter," John is readily linked with butcher even though the name Henry is closer to it in physical space. What Thorndike hoped to accomplish with this law was to arrange lessons so that the to-be-learned materials could benefit from any possible belongingness. State capitals, for example, would be learned with the state names because they go together. Perhaps Thorndike was anticipating the later development of interest in the phenomenon of "clustering" in free recall (see chapter 16), where learners tend to report words that belong to certain categories or classes or have some other kind of associative relationship.

THE DECLINE OF PUNISHMENT

From time to time, Thorndike, in a long career, added other laws and dropped some. After a series of attacks upon him and after some research of his own, Thorndike dropped the negative half of the law of effect. In some studies (Thorndike 1932), where he found that saying "wrong" to subjects responding in chance situations did not lessen the tendency to respond in ways that were followed by "wrong," Thorndike concluded that annoying states of affairs (punishment?) did not weaken bonds. At best, such states would force the learner to attempt some other response, if possible, where a satisfying state of affairs might result. We will look at such research and some other laws later. In any event, by 1933, the law of effect was only a positive statement, which could be interpreted as reading: responses that are followed by satisfiers (reinforcement, rewards) become more probable or more likely to recur in a given situation or circumstance.

A BASIC PROBLEM

Thorndike never explained how something that happened after a response could have any influence on what went on before. This simple question was raised by Guthrie and never answered, although many followers of Thorndike looked at the question and attempted answers, none of which appears to be satisfactory. Hilgard and Bower (1975), for example, state: "The criticism . . . is a faulty one. The effect is revealed in the probability of recurrence of the response when the situation next occurs; whether or not such an effect occurs is a matter of observation and experiment, not something to be denied on *a priori* grounds." Such a defense is not relevant to the issue. The issue is one of how can the effect strengthen a bond and not whether or not the behavior becomes more probable. The behavior could be more probable for many reasons, for example, the cat engaged in some reasoning, had insight, chose to repeat the behavior because it preferred the consequences, and so forth. What Hilgard and Bower are asserting is an empirical law of effect, a position taken earlier by McGeoch (1942) and by Skinner (1938), which amounts to saying rewards work (regardless of how). This does not help us understand learning, even though we are able to make better predictions of behavior.

IMPORTANCE OF ACTION

We come to a rather crucial issue. According to Thorndike, learning comes about when a satisfier follows a response. This means, in practice, that the teacher, trainer, or someone else in whatever capacity cannot reward a potential learner unless the learner does something the rewarder can observe. Learning becomes a matter of doing, of activity, of performance. Can anyone learn by just sitting and looking and/or listening? Can anyone learn by observation? Is there a possibility of learning through imitation? Thorndike did not comment on these issues except on the matter of imitation. Like Watson before him, Thorndike denied the possibility of learning by imitation, after some rather modest efforts to see if cats would imitate one another. But the question of learning by listening or looking remains. One could argue that looking and listening are responses and that the looker is doing something, but then the next question necessarily arises: Who is ever rewarded for looking? Certainly, teachers do not reward lookers and listeners, at least not in any overt manner. Perhaps the looker rewards himself or herself. The individual finds his or her looking or listening followed by a satisfying state of affairs. This could be admitted, perhaps, but it begins to get tenuous and perhaps dangerous to the theory. Can you not see something you do not like and consider it annoying or worse? Can you not hear bad news? Do you not learn what you have seen or heard?

If the response plus reward theory has to be stretched out of proportion to accommodate observations of nonaction learning instances, it may not find much justification. An escape into self-satisfaction is not much help, as in many learning situations, the learner feels nothing much more than anxiety and insecurity. For example, if one is asked to learn 20 words that are about to be read to him, one's first reaction is likely to be one of dismay if one perceives the task as important. We read the list and observe the learner? Does the person show signs of being rewarded, of relaxation, or of satisfaction? Would the person report such feelings if asked? On the contrary, if we ask the person at the conclusion of the reading if he or she knows the list, the person's only correct answer can be, "I don't know." We can ask, "How many do you know?" The person can say, "Some." We ask which ones? Again, the person cannot answer until he or she attempts to recall the words. The person actually does not know if he or she knows any, or which, and the only feelings the person can report are of uncertainty. Yet, if the person reports any words, he or she must have learned them. In some studies, a subject may be asked to guess what number from one to ten goes with each word of a list of, say, 40 words. The subject can be asked to try to remember his or her guesses. The experimenter pronounces "right" or "wrong" as he or she goes through the list, and the subject guesses. In a second trial, the subject can be asked if he or she remembers what number he or she guessed on the first trial and, further, if he or she remembers what the experimenter's remark ("right" or "wrong") was. Here, we have a curious mixture of reactions. The learner may remember what number he or she chose but may not remember whether it was called "right" or "wrong." Or the learner may remember that his or her response was called "right" but may not remember what his or her response was. The subject may remember a response and that it was called "wrong." In the latter case, we can wonder about how the subject learned (remembered) this, as he or she was not rewarded. The possibility that finding out that a response was called "wrong" is self-rewarding in some way (you acquire information) is somewhat farfetched, as most answers will be called "wrong" in such a situation. But the critical circumstance is the one where the subject learns what the experimenter said about a given word—for example, the word is *book*, the subject says "six," and the experimenter says "right." Now the subject remembers "book"—"right" but does not remember his or her response. In short, the subject learns what the experimenter says or did but not what he or she did. How is the law of effect working?

It is probably true that many instances of learning are accompanied by some kind of emotional reaction and that such reactions should be attributed to the outcomes of a learner's efforts. The presence of the emotion may be of great importance in controlling future activities or responses of the learner and have little to do with strengthening or weakening bonds between stimuli and responses. This aspect of learning will be examined more critically later. For the moment, we turn to some modifications of the law of effect as it was treated by followers of Thorndike.

HULL AND PRIMARY REINFORCEMENT

Clark L. Hull (1884–1952) was strongly influenced by Thorndike and even chose to use Thorndike's name to describe any kind of behavior that did not appear to be of a reflex nature, that is, where no specific stimulus would automatically elicit some reaction. Like Skinner (1938), Hull chose to classify behavior into responses that were *evoked* by stimuli (reflexes), like a knee jerk or eyelid blink, and responses that were emitted, like pressing a lever or running down an alley or maze. The latter kind of behavior Hull labeled *Thorndikian*. Skinner made the same distinction, using the terms *respondent* and *operant* for reflexive (evoked) and emitted bhevaior.

In Hull's opinion, Thorndike's law of effect was the basic operational principle for learning, but with his penchant for building bridges to physiology, Hull thought it could be phrased in terms that might lead to investigations which might reveal the mechanism of effect more intimately. Hull had also recognized that rewards or "reinforcements" could not be defined in absolute terms; rewards are always relative to desires or needs. A millionaire might not be affected by a ten-cent tip or bribe and would almost certainly refuse a dime reward. Hull, then, chose to relate the operation of a reward to needs or their presumed physiological expression in terms of *drive*. A drive (D) would be a tissue need generating drive stimuli (S_D). A reward, or, in Hull's phrasing, a "reinforcer," would be something that diminished a drive or a drive stimulus. Food for a hungry dog is an obvious example. Food for a satiated dog would not qualify.

LAW OF PRIMARY REINFORCEMENT

Hull also recognized that the effects of a reward are not always obvious; the response in question might not occur on the next trial or opportunity because its strength had not been increased *enough* by a prior reward. Maybe several, even many, rewards would have to be provided before some bond was strong enough for its existence to be demonstrated by a response. Hull called this the "principle of continuity," that is, every time a response is reinforced, there is an addition to the strength of the underlying connection. With a sufficient number of reinforcements, the response will reach and surpass threshold strength. He was now ready to restate Thorndike's law of effect thusly: whenever a stimulus is followed by some response and this is followed by a diminution in the strength of some drive or drive stimulus, there will be an increment in the strength of the connection (s⟶r) between that stimulus and that response—the s⟶r refers to the neural activity initiated by a stimulus and the motor impulses (r) that generate the response. Reduction of the drive is the reinforcement.

Note that Hull uses the term *diminution* to describe the decrease in drive. The term suggests that *any*, even a tiny, drop in drive would add some increment (and note that term, which also suggests, perhaps, a tiny amount) to the learning or habit strength. Later, Hull was to concern himself greatly over such matters as strengths of stimuli, both CS and US, amounts of reinforcement, delays of reinforcement, and quality of the reinforcement. In the end, however, Hull came to regard habit strength (S_HR) or learning as a function of, that is, dependent upon, the number of correct trials. A correct trial, by inference, is one that is followed by a reinforcer. For convenience, then, Hull assumed that the amount of learning could be expressed as a function of number of reinforced trials, or $S_HR = fN$, where N refers to correct or successful trials.

Note that what Hull has done is to propose that no learning can occur without a drive being present along with a reduction of said drive at least in some degree. This might appear to be solving one problem (defining a reward) by creating another, that is, requiring a drive to be present for any kind of learning to occur. Because psychologists had by this time cataloged a variety of drives (hunger, thirst, sex, fatigue, and exercise, among others), it might be thought that there might be one kind of drive or another in some active state to account for any learning that does take place. The problem, however, is to find the drive and the drive reducer when humans learn something like the Pythagorean theorem. What is the drive, and what is the drive reducer?

SECONDARY REWARDS AND SECONDARY DRIVES

At about the time that Hull was beginning to develop his behavior theory (1935), Skinner, then a young psychologist at Harvard, had developed a piece of apparatus that was to become more famous than the Thorndike box. Skinner created a situation where a rat could be placed in a box (about a one-foot cube), where it could cause little food pellets to drop into the box by pressing down on a lever at one end of the box. This was a nice variation on the Thorndike box, as the experimenter did not have to capture the animal after every response, and a great many responses could be observed in a fairly brief interval. Skinner called his equipment "the lever-press box," but the psychological world quickly renamed it "the Skinner box."

In 1938, Skinner reported a curious finding. In his normal training procedure, Skinner would first habituate rats to his box (with no lever present) and drop little pellets of food into the box, one at a time, by manipulating an automatic feeder from the outside. As each pellet dropped, the feeding magazine would sound out a series of noises, clicks, or rattles. Such sounds (call them "clicks") would precede the arrival of the food pellet in the food dish. In the study referred to, Skinner inserted the lever into the box *after* a rat had been presented some 60 "reinforcements" in the presence of the click. The rat now proceeded to press the bar, but there was no food in the magazine. Every press was followed by only a click and no food. The rat continued to press the bar, producing an ordinary or normal extinction curve, just as if it had been fed for every bar press. Skinner ascribed the behavior to the "secondary reinforcement." According to Skinner, the previous pairing of the click with food had resulted in the click acquiring the characteristics of a reinforcer, although the animal had done nothing except eat shortly after the signal.

About the same time, the author (Bugelski 1938) trained rats in Skinner boxes in the standard fashion. These rats received 40 reinforcements in the usual manner, that is, after pressing the bar. Just as in the Skinner experiment, clicks preceded the arrival of food. After training, the rats went through an extinction routine, with half the rats receiving a click and half no click in the now foodless situation. The rats that heard the click gave 30 percent more responses in extinction than the no-click rats. Here again, a simple noise that had at one time accompanied food appeared to have acquired the characteristics of a reinforcer.

Hull took such results to mean that any stimulus that accompanied a real or primary reinforcer would acquire reinforcing properties. Thus, to make a jump to the human level, any word heard in the presence of some other desirable, drive-reducing situation could become a reinforcer, secondary to be sure, but nevertheless, a reinforcer. When a baby is being nursed, and the mother murmurs "that's fine," "good," "wonderful," and so forth, such words, heard probably thousands of times while a drive is being reduced, could, conceivably, acquired enormous reinforcing power and last one all one's life. What 20-year-old college student does not like to hear, "That's fine" or, for that matter, what 65-year old president of the United States does not like to hear, "That's terrific, Mr. President." When Thorndike said "right" or "wrong," he could, with some justification believe he was rewarding or punishing college students. The "some" might be quite negligible in his number or word-guessing studies, but to the extent that such words have an effect, it would be ascribable to secondary reinforcement. Actually, Thorndike was quite empirical about his interpretations of reward and did not distinguish between cats' consuming food or students' consuming "right."

SECONDARY DRIVE

Hull could not be satisfied with secondary rewards available to him. His principle required that a drive be present to be reduced by whatever means. Experiments with rats had been performed wherein the rats appeared to have acquired fear states through the pairing of some signal, for example, a buzzer and a shock. The sound of the buzzer would be followed by some behavior, initially generated by the shock.

A study by May (1948) can serve as the prototype of a host of similar studies. May used a piece of apparatus known as the Miller-Mowrer demonstration box. This consisted of a 30-inch long box divided into two compartments by a low fence. The floor on either side could be electrified. When a rat was shocked on one side, it would more or less promptly "escape" to the other side. May trained rats in this box until they were good escapers. He then placed the rats (one at a time) in a small box with the same kind of floor but with no room to move and proceeded to shock them. Everytime they were shocked, a buzzer, mounted on the box, would be sounded. After five buzzer-shock pairs, the animals were put back into the demonstration box. When the buzzer sounded (with no shock), the animals now jumped the barrier, just as they did when they were actually shocked. May interpreted his findings as demonstrating that the buzzer-shock experiences in the confinement box had resulted in a conditioned response to the buzzer. Because there was no preselected response and not much the animal could do when shocked, it was possible that the response conditioned could be that of fear, generated by the shock. Probably few critics would deny that the rats were disturbed by the shock and could be described as fearful. When the rats were now back in the escape box, the sound of the buzzer could excite the same fear, and the animal would do what it had previously done when shocked (and fearful) in the original training trials.

May's findings were generally interpreted as demonstrating an acquired fear. We should note in passing that Watson and Raynor (1920) had demonstrated the acquisition of fear long before this. What May had done was to relate fear to drives.

If fear can be considered a drive, then May had demonstrated the learning or acquisition of a drive. The drive in such cases came to be labeled *anxiety*. The operation could be described in the following manner: a signal generates anxiety; anxiety is a tissue or organic condition with the characteristics of drive and generates stimuli; these stimuli either initiate or heighten activity of the type generated by the original stimulus for the anxiety, namely, the shock, and the animal executes some behavior that results in a reduction of anxiety. Thus, Hull has provided for the possibility that a variety of drives can be learned and come to function on human levels to provide the basic condition he postulated in his law of primary reinforcement, namely, the presence of a drive.

Because Hull was committed to a reinforcement position, he did not approve of a conditioning explanation for the acquisition of drives any more than he would of other responses. He chose to explain the acquisition of fear or anxiety by arguing that a connection between the stimulus (for example, buzzer) and the drive was strengthened by the relatively sudden decrease in the drive by the escape behavior or shock cessation. As soon as the rat left the shocked side of the box, there would be no more pain, and, therefore, no need for fear—the fear was reduced, and being a drive, its reduction would strengthen any neural bonds just exercised. Such an explanation never received any strong support where the fact of the acquisition of fear was generally accepted.

No one has reported any plausible evidence for the acquisition of any drives other than anxiety, and so we may be forced to assume, on the human level, that any learning occurring in humans is based on some generated anxiety. An argument to this effect is not too difficult to make if one cites such philosophers as Thoreau (1854), who left us the frequently quoted statement: "The mass of men lead lives of quiet desperation." How strongly we should push the argument might be debatable, especially if it might be possible to account for learning without postulating either drives or reinforcements as basic requirements for learning and assign them more proper roles as motivators of behavior.

SKINNER AND REINFORCEMENT

Skinner preferred to avoid any physiological entanglements, and in his approach to the problem of defining reinforcements, he took a stand that was more similar to the original Thorndike position. He believed, with Thorndike, that learning occurs only if there is a reinforcement following on the heels of some response, but he chose to define his reinforcements in terms of what happened to the behavior. If a piece of food followed a response and that response now increased in its rate of occurrence, the food would be labeled a *reinforcer*. If the rate was unchanged, the food was not a reinforcer, no matter if the rat liked it, ate it, and strove to obtain more. Should a child increase its rate of emission of some behavior after a spanking, the spanking would be a reinforcer, not a punishment, because Skinner also defined punishment in rate-of-response terms only in a negative way, that is, a stimulus object or situation that was presented after a response and which was followed by a reduction in the response would be a punishment. If the rate did not decrease, there would have been no punishment regardless of the nature of the stimulus. Thus, if a rat continues

Skinner – learning occurs only if there is a reinforcement following on the heels of some response to behave in some fashion even though severely shocked after each response, the shock is not a punisher. It is a shock.

Skinner insisted on this empirical test. Reinforcers are things (stimuli) that result in a change in the rate at which an operant is emitted. If the operant rate does not change, there has been no reinforcement, regardless of consequences. Thus, no change equals no reinforcement. This leaves Skinner with the need to find the kinds of things that will change the rate of response in any individual organism whose behavior he would like to alter. In general, this is not difficult. Animals, in general, can be reinforced by food or water or sex mates. People can be reinforced with "right," "good," money, and prizes. When a presumed reinforcer fails, we may have a problem. Some people will not work for money or praise, but they may for some other kind of reinforcers if we are clever enough to discover such. Sometimes, animals will not work for food—we would normally assume they are not hungry enough—Skinner, eschewing such wording, would say they had not been sufficiently deprived. If we withhold a cat's food for a few days, it will work for food. There is no need for a psychologist to infer hunger; he needs only to know how to make a reinforcer work, in this case, the "how" is simple. Deprive the cat.

Sometimes, animals and people will work where there is no need to. People, wealthy beyond their possible needs, may continue to work even longer and harder than their employees. Rats that have learned to press bars where the pressing is followed by food will sometimes continue to press even if there is a large supply of food in the vicinity of the bar and food tray. Neuringer (1969), for instance, found that rats and pigeons pressed bars or pecked at targets even though food and water were constantly available, with and without pretraining. Such work without ostensible gain is difficult to explain. James (1890) tried to explain it as based on the powerful force of well-established habits, which he called "the fly-wheel of society." The continuation of energy expenditure in these cases might be based on more subtle sources of reinforcement, and we mention the activity only to recognize that "man does not live by bread alone," without suggesting substitutes.

EVALUATION OF THE THORNDIKIAN POSITION

Hull was sympathetic enough with Thorndike to be included in the Thorndike picture. Skinner is not sufficiently different to be excluded. What we are concerned with here is reinforcement theory, and in this, there is no substantial difference among the three. The superficial difference between Thorndike and the others is that he made his cats get out of the box to get to the food via some response. The others arranged to keep the animals confined and provided access to the food inside the box (or alley), again, via some response. Hull and Skinner were more efficient and could get many more responses because their subjects were trapped, whereas Thorndike had to recapture his cats for every trial.

Although in some circumstances and problem areas, Hull was concerned with the stimuli in a situation, he was, like Skinner and Thorndike, primarily involved with responses or behavior. For Hull, stimuli were largely theoretical problems. Both Thorndike and Skinner tended to treat stimuli with rather general references to their experimental situations. All three were concerned with emitted behavior and the reinforcement thereof. Skinner did concern himself with discriminated stimuli (S^D), which will receive separate treatment, but his central concern was the rate of responding.

The preoccupation with behavior, with the prediction and control thereof, made *performance* the important operation, and in this preoccupation, *learning* was pretty much lost sight of. One can seriously question whether Thorndike, Hull, and Skinner, the outstanding learning psychologists of the century, were really dealing with learning. In one way or another, of course, they discussed the topic, but their major work was devoted to the concept of control over behavior, with motivation or deprivation variables and with the use of reinforcers to encourage animals to do what they already knew how to do. Before we go on, we should pause to note that Skinner did consider some activities that called for somewhat extended chains of behavior— response patterns that no animal would go through or emit on its own on a first occasion. Skinner described such training as shaping, and this will require our attention, but primarily all three theorists were demonstrating repeatedly what every good hedonist knew: animals (or people) will do what brings them pleasure and avoid what does them harm, and the only learning involved in Thorndike-Hull-Skinner studies may have been that certain responses are followed by good or bad consequences. The responses were already there to begin with, in fact, had to be performed before the reward was provided. It can then be asserted that the animals were not learning *how* to do anything. They were merely doing what they felt like doing. They could be described as having learned *when* to do something or how to feel about doing something, but the something was already in the repertoire.

All three Thorndikian theorists can be described as developing a psychology of behavior, not of learning. They each assumed that one does what pays off and will continue doing what pays off until it ceases to do so. Each of the three was concerned primarily with positive predictions and while interested in extinction (as a measure of response strength), none of them was concerned with such topics as forgetting, learning without activity, unintentional or incidental learning, learning by imitation, or by the age-old tradition of show-and-tell. It is highly probable that most people learn most of what they know by looking and listening, by show-and-tell, and that the actual movements or responses are more or less readily applied. When the movements themselves are refined or rapid, as in playing the piano or typing, the theorists are not of much help. In general, they confined themselves to rather restricted simple movements, like bar pressing or alley running, which no one had to learn in the first place, excluding the point of when to do something. When one comes to such learning exercises as learning a multiplication table, a list of words, a principle of physics, or a fact in chemistry, we get little help from reinforcement theory.

That the reinforcement psychologists were interested in performance and not learning can be demonstrated from their preoccupation with predicting (Hull) or controlling (Skinner) behavior. In Hull's case, the major emphasis was on what will some organism do. After years of theorizing, Hull settled for a formula that reads (in a simplified form)

$$S_ER = S_HR \times D \times K \times V$$

where S_ER refers to reaction potential or probability of a response and D is drive, K is the incentive, V is stimulus intensity, and S_HR, the only learning feature, is habit. Various additional features, such as inhibition and oscillation, have been omitted from the formula, but what is included indicates the range of Hull's interest. Habit was only one item to be included in a behavioral prediction.

8

Characteristics of
Instrumental Behavior

In describing Pavlovian conditioning, we listed some features or characteristics of conditional responses that were either discovered by Pavlov and his students or integrated with the Pavlovian theory. Among those, we noted extinction, spontaneous recovery, inhibition, disinhibition, generalization, discrimination, higher-order conditioning, and conditioned inhibition. We did not pay attention to the effects of changes in the unconditioned stimulus, which Pavlov called a "reinforcer," except to note that one gets stronger conditioning with a stronger US. It is time to look at some features of instrumental learning. Interestingly enough, many of the very same characteristics and features that Pavlov described have been noted by Hull and Skinner and their students in connection with instrumentally acquired responses. Both Hull and Skinner did show much more interest in manipulating the reinforcing stimulus than did Pavlov.

Kimble (1961) revised the influential Hilgard and Marquis book, *Conditioning and Learning*; in reviewing the features of both classical conditioning and instrumentally acquired responses, Kimble found that both learning paradigms displayed the same general characteristics and followed the same courses. Thus, when Pavlov withheld the US, extinction normally followed; when Skinner withheld his reinforcers, extinction would also be the consequence. Spontaneous recovery would then follow in either situation, and so with the rest of the phenomena Pavlov described. Both paradigms could be arranged to show generalization and discrimination and so on through a list of 15 comparisons offered by Kimble.

In his summary of the review of the similarities of the findings in the classical and instrumental paradigms, Kimble (1961, p. 107) stated:

The fact that the two forms of learning are similar in so many respects means one of two things: Either the inescapable classical conditioning

121

component of all learning is responsible for these effects, or classical and instrumental conditioning really are different forms of the same basic process.

By "inescapable classical conditioning component," Kimble was referring to the fact that a reward stimulus would necessarily have to occur in the context of some stimuli and, therefore, conditioning of an S⟶S nature was possible.

Kimble went on to say that he knew of no psychologists who had actually taken this position, although it is quite clear that Pavlov, Watson, Guthrie, and Tolman might assert or accept it as the correct stance. Certainly, Mowrer (1960a) did take this view. Kimble himself found a problem with accepting conditioning as the sole learning principle for two reasons. The first reason was based on the apparent restriction of Pavlovian conditioning to autonomic nervous system reactions and the relatively few demonstrations of Pavlovian conditioning of striate muscles (for example, eye blinks and knee jerks). The failure of instrumental procedures to incorporate autonomic conditioning suggests that instrumental procedures cannot be all powerful, but that does not then justify Pavlovian claims to instrumental territory. The second reason for Kimble's doubts was a difference in success between Pavlovian and Skinnerian procedures where partial or periodic reinforcement seemed to produce different results. We will examine the efforts of reinforcement-minded psychologists to teach subjects to control their organic processes later (see chapter 20). For the moment, we will look at partial reinforcement phenomena.

PARTIAL REINFORCEMENT: SCHEDULES OF REINFORCEMENT

Pavlov (1927) introduced a variation in conditioning known as partial reinforcement. In this procedure, a CS and US would be paired only occasionally, not regularly. If the US were presented on 75 percent of the trials, the conditioning would proceed, but slowly and not too effectively. If the US was provided only 20 percent of 25 percent of the time, the conditioning would not ordinarily occur. It should be noted that Pavlov did not begin with 100 percent reinforcement and that he would try omitting the US in the very early trials. Such trials would necessarily be "extinction" trials.

In contrast to Pavlov, Skinner (1938) would arrange for a rat to receive reinforcements after every bar press for a continuing series of trials (a 100 percent reinforcement schedule) for some time. After the rat was pressing regularly, Skinner would begin to omit reinforcements on occasion and noted that the rat would continue to press even more frequently. After the bar press habit was well established, Skinner could reduce the number of reinforcements step by step, for example, omitting every tenth reinforcement, then every ninth, eighth, and so on, until a rat would be reinforced only after every fifth, tenth, or twentieth, response. Once Skinner observed a rat pressing 192 times per reinforcement.

Fixed Ratio Schedules *= rat reinforced only after every fifth, tenth, or twentieth, response*

The procedure just described is called a fixed ratio schedule. The rat gets a pellet of food for so many presses, that is one for ten. Skinner compared this to piecework wages for factory workers who are paid by the number of items they produce. *A pellet of food for so many presses.*

Variable Ratio Schedules

If a rat receives ten pellets for 100 responses, it is on a one to ten schedule, but the pellets need not be provided after every tenth press. The pellets can be delivered at any time, for example, after the fifth press, the eighteenth, the twenty second, and so forth. The ratio overall, remains the same; the reinforcement comes at varying points in any ten presses.

reinforcement comes in any ten presses

Fixed Interval Schedules *Time*

Once the rat is working effectively, the trainer can decide to provide reinforcement after some period of time elapses between one reinforced bar press and the next to-be-rewarded press. Thus, if a rat has just been provided with a pellet, the trainer decides not to "pay off" until 30 seconds elapse. Any bar press in this period will not be rewarded. The first bar press after 30 seconds pass will be rewarded. Such a schedule is called a fixed interval schedule. The intervals can be long or short, for example, 15 seconds, or two minutes, or anything in between. Skinner compared such schedules to working for a weekly paycheck. *Every 5 minutes or 20 seconds*

Variable Interval Schedules

If a rat is on a fixed interval schedule, say, of 30 seconds, the trainer can decide to reinforce the rat after 15 seconds on one occasion and one minute on the next, then at 45 seconds or at ten, keeping an *average* interval of 30 seconds, so that in a period of ten minutes, the rat, if very precise, could receive as many as 20 reinforcements. *average interval remains the same.*

Partial Reinforcement Effect

Skinner discovered that if animals were trained on the various schedules, they would show rather gross differences in performance in extinction. Typically, an animal trained on continuous reinforcement would continue to press for some time after reinforcement was no longer provided. A plot of its output of responses would be called an extinction curve. After 40 continuous reinforcements, a rat might respond 100 or so times before its output fell back to an operant rate, that is, the rate of pressing a rat might demonstrate without ever having been reinforced.

If, on the other hand, the rat had received the 40 reinforcements on either a ratio or interval schedule, it would be very likely to press many more than 100 times. This excess of responding during extinction over the rate shown under continuous reinforcement training conditions came to be called the partial refinforcement effect or (PRE). It appears to be a paradoxical phenomenon, because a habit seems to get stronger the less often it is reinforced.

The strongest PRE is found with variable ratio schedules, then fixed ratio schedules, variable interval schedules, and, finally, fixed interval schedules. In the latter case, rats (and other creatures) appear to stop working after a reinforcement and slowly resume working, building up speed of responding as the interval is about to end. When plotted on a "cumulative curve," the curve shows a series of "scallops" between the intervals.* (See Figure 8.1.)

The findings from different schedules of reinforcement enabled Skinner to obtain records of large numbers of responses and to demonstrate how easily behavior could be sustained and/or varied by controlling the distribution of reinforcements. Once a habit or response has been established, it can be manipulated in a variety of ways. A rat, for example, could be switched from one schedule to another and, after a brief period of adjustment, would begin to work at different rates as a previously experienced schedule dictated. One of Skinner's conclusions was that if you want behavior to persist, do not reinforce it continuously. For best results, use preferably, a variable ratio schedule.

The rather striking results of partial reinforcement had bothered Kimble, because they seemed to differentiate instrumental learning from Pavlovian conditioning. We have noted Pavlov's own findings, where he did not use the basic 100 percent reinforcement procedure to begin with. Humphreys (1939) found equally striking results with the Pavlovian procedure when he conditioned human eye blinks with a partial reinforcement

---

*Cumulative curves are graphs in which each response is recorded above the previous response. If the plot is made on moving paper, a gradually rising graph appears wherein the total number of responses made up to a given time can be read off on the ordinate.

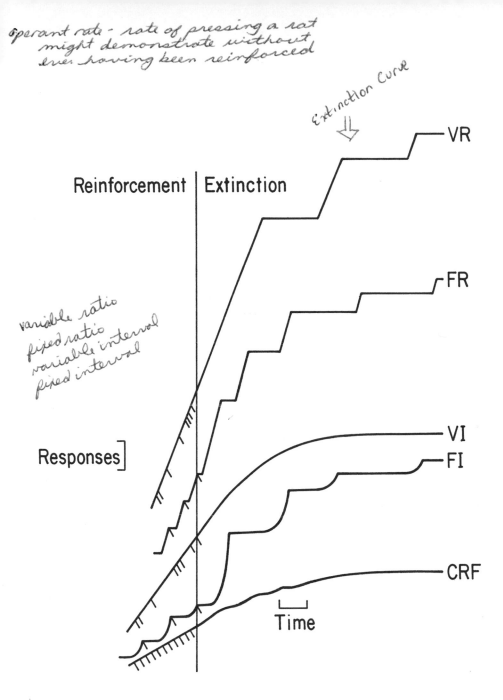

operant rate - rate of pressing a rat might demonstrate without ever having been reinforced

variable ratio
fixed ratio
variable interval
fixed interval

FIGURE 8.1: Stylized <u>cumulative records</u> of responses in extinction following reinforcement on each of five simple schedules of reinforcement. Reprinted from *Operant Learning: Procedures for Changing Behavior* by Jon L. Williams, copyright 1973. Brooks/Cole Publishing Co.

procedure, and Fitzgerald (1963) found a distinct PRE in conditioning dogs in a Pavlovian situation where acid was used to evoke a defensive salivary response. The findings of Humphreys and Fitzgerald might reduce Kimble's concern about the universality of Pavlovian conditioning. It may be a matter of what responses are being manipulated.

EXPLANATIONS OF THE PARTIAL REINFORCEMENT EFFECT

The PRE has been observed in other situations than bar pressing or eyelid blinks. Rats can be trained to run down an alley for food at the end, but the food need not be there on every trial. Capaldi (1966), for example, would provide food on every other trial or different amounts of food on successive trials. Capaldi found that rats would adjust their running rates in accordance with the conditions. Failure to find food on one trial might result in a slower run on the next trial, which would have a small reward. Capaldi argued that the consequences at the goal were serving as cues for later behavior.

In the bar press situation, failure to obtain reinforcements could be viewed in a similar way, namely, that food would come next time or soon. Such explanatory accounts suggest some kind of expectancy learning. Other explanations follow the earlier speculations of Guthrie, namely, that failure of reinforcement results in an emotional response, a frustration. Amsel and Roussel (1952) suggested that frustration could serve as the basis for extinction or come to add strength or vigor to the activity, thus prolonging a response sequence. The frustration, as in Capaldi's situation, could even serve as a cue or stimulus for the next response. When something works only occasionally but not all the time, for example, a cigarette lighter, we might come to accept a few failures before the eventual flare. When rats are working on a schedule, they are not counting; they learn to keep working until the food comes, that is, they have learned to *keep working* and not just to press once. It is a different "response" in that it consists of a group of responses.

CONTRIBUTIONS OF THE INSTRUMENTAL SCHOOL

Besides the partial reinforcement and scheduling findings, the followers of the instrumental learning paradigm added a number of important developments in learning theory, which we must now review. We will look at three developments: discriminated stimuli, shaping of chains of responses, and the concept of continuity. Each of these developments has important practical applications.

Discriminated Stimulus

Although Skinner recognized that all instrumental behavior must occur in the presence of stimuli, he also knew that the precise stimulus which might be related to some response could not always be specified. Why someone gets up out of a chair or sits down in one might be difficult to describe in stimulus-response terms. The getting up or sitting down is obvious—it can be seen, recorded, and even measured in some ways, but the stimulus in such situations may be very obscure or complex. If someone is sitting at a dinner table, he or she does not pick up all the silverware just because it is there. At some moment, the individual may pick up a spoon (if soup is presented); he or she is unlikely to pick up a fork. At some point, the individual will dip the spoon in the soup. He or she may have been watching his hostess and saw her pick up her spoon. Because everyone else at the table also picks up his or her spoon after the hostess does, there is an obvious relationship here. But the fact that someone else picks up a spoon cannot be a direct stimulus for a response like a reflex eyeblink to a puff of air. No one, in fact, *has* to pick up a spoon. In just such a situation, Skinner saw that stimuli could play different roles at different times. Some stimuli *evoke* responses; the response has to follow. Such stimuli would correspond to Pavlov's unconditioned stimuli. On other occasions, the stimuli might serve as signals, cues, or suggestions, which may be, but need not be, followed by some specific response.

Skinner was facing the problem of the initiation of behavior, the problem of why does anyone do anything that he or she literally does not have to do. Instead of pursuing this age-old question, Skinner chose to bypass it. He chose to *describe* what happens on an observational level in a practical or empirical way. Thus, he suggests, some responses that are observable just seem to occur, and we can observe, measure, or record these. Other responses only occur when some stimulus is present; these responses do not always occur when the stimulus is present, and so there is no direct causative relationship. When an organism does emit a specific response in the presence of such a stimulus, that stimulus can be regarded as "permissive," as setting the stage for the response, which then will or will not occur, depending on its history of reinforcement. Such a stimulus Skinner chose to call an S^D, a "discriminated stimulus."

How does a stimulus come to be a discriminated stimulus? Skinner illustrated the operation with a rat in a lever press box, where the rat has pressed the lever a number of times and been reinforced for doing so. In the box, there is a light bulb, which can now be illuminated by the experimenter. The light is turned on and stays on for a while. Any press made by the rat is reinforced. Now the light is turned off, and any presses are not reinforced. The procedure is repeated a number of times, and eventually, the rat starts pressing when the light comes on and stops when it goes off. With rats, the

S^D permissive, setting the stage for the response

operation is not always too precise. Sometimes, the rat does not press with any great regularity when the light is on, and sometimes it presses when the light is off, but in general, there is a difference in the rat's behavior in light-on, light-off periods. The light has become an S^D.

When the phone rings and you rise from a chair to answer it, the ring is an S^D. You do not have to answer. According to Skinner, you answer because answering has been reinforced often enough in your history to have that response be sufficiently probable or likely to occur. This reasoning is not especially powerful or convincing. It is easy to understand *not* answering when there is no ring. Why you do answer remains a mystery that Skinner did not probe.

Coming back to the rat in the box, we have the same question. Why does the rat press in the first place? It is already in a discriminated stimulus situation in the box. The pedal is an S^D in its own right. Any lights or tones that might be added are extra S^Ds. But why does the rat press the pedal? Here, Skinner leaves us with his first answer: some responses just happen, and we cannot spell out the stimuli that generate them.

The S^D has left us with a problem. Skinner denies that it is anything like a Pavlovian CS although many theorists have noted the similarity of operation. For the moment (but see chapter 11), we shall leave the question at Skinner's empirical level: some stimuli (S^D s) will predispose organisms to respond in specific ways.

Shaping and Chaining

In previous sections, we have not been too critical in citing illustrations of learned behavior and have thrown loosely together such items as eyelid blinks, lists of nonsense syllables, maze patterns, salivation, avoidance and escape responses, pulling strings, and pressing levers. Some of these are instances of simple reflexes, others of chains of behavioral units or steps; some are rather limited in number and, on the whole, not very impressive. Watching a cat pull a string and getting a door open might be dismissed as no more serious or important than getting a dog to lie down and roll over upon command. At best, such behaviors can be passed off as tricks. What about real learning, for example, learning to solve equations or learning to read? Skinner faced the problem of what we might classify as more serious learning by recognizing that even some simple behaviors, such as that of a rat pressing a bar, consists of a series of steps and, further, that one step leads to another, like links in a chain. When a chain of behavioral steps is run off in the presence of someone who has not seen how the chain was constructed, the behavior might be described as something more than "cute." The observer is likely to describe a lengthy chain as reflecting intelligence or at least ponder the question of, "How did he learn to do that?"

Shaping

In the above subsection, we have suggested that some behaviors consist of a series of steps that are unlikely to be undertaken if we merely sit and wait for them to happen. It does happen that a cat or dog will lie down and roll over on occasion. We do not know why and may not know how to initiate such behavior. Asking a cat or dog to do it is of no value and waiting for it to happen (be emitted) might be unrewarding. In such cases, we need not wait; we can instead shape-up the desired behavior. The term *shaping* was introduced by Skinner to describe a procedure where some desired behavior is unlikely to occur.

Shaping can only be practiced if the behavior shaper knows exactly what he or she wants to have happen and can recognize and define a sequence of steps in an ordinal arrangement, that is, the shaper must know what has to happen first, second, third, and so on, and most important, last. If our problem is to get a rat to press a lever in a small box and the rat shows no signs of doing so, it is obvious that we must first get the rat to approach the bar. If the rat is sitting quietly in a corner, there is nothing we can do but wait for the first sign of an approach. If the rat moves his head in the direction of the bar, we should reinforce this action. But reinforcement is difficult under such conditions—to put our hands into the box and offer food might frighten the rat. A preliminary stage of training is indicated. This stage would involve developing some stimulus that could be applied directly and immediately when the rat moved his head. Such a stage can be developed by associating a sound with eating. If the rat is hungry and will eat food (near the bar area), we can drop pieces of food to the rat from the outside, accompanying each piece of food with a preceding sound. If the food is being dropped by a mechanical dispenser, the sound of the dispenser (a click) will serve nicely. After a few click-food pairings, we find the rat approaching the cup as soon as the click is heard. For present and practical purposes, we can call this click a secondary reinforcer or learned reinforcer without committing ourselves to any theoretical position. All we know, for sure, is that when the click occurs, the rat moves to the food cup. Are we ready to start shaping? Actually, the click-food association cannot be established easily if the rat is fearful when first placed in the box—the rat will normally tend to huddle, wash itself, groom a bit, and then explore the entire box, at first favoring the sides and otherwise showing some concern over its whereabouts. Some bodily eliminations are strong possibilities (usually interpreted as signs of fear). Before starting click-food pairings, then, it is necessary to "habituate" the rat to the box in order to extinguish the fearful behavior. One way of doing this is to fill the food dish with bits of food, which (we hope) the rat will eat.

While with some rats the whole process can be speeded up, success can be virtually guaranteed if we follow a schedule running over several days.

Shaping - a procedure where some desired behavior is unlikely to occur

The schedule might be like this:

1. First week—put rat on feeding schedule so that it loses weight (down to about 80 percent of its normal weight).
2. After a 24-hour hunger or food deprivation period, insert the rat in the box with food in the food dish and leave it there for half an hour.
3. Next day, insert the hungry (24-hour deprivation) rat in the box without food. When the rat approaches the food dish, drop one piece of food into the dish by manipulating the mechanical dispenser. The click preceding the food may frighten the rat, but repeat about 40 to 60 times over half an hour to one hour.
4. Next day, insert the hungry rat, insert lever for the first time, and wait for the rat to press the lever

We are now back at the point where the question of shaping the bar press was brought up; we can now use the click as a reinforcer to get the rat to come to the vicinity of the food—the lever is usually mounted just over the food cup. We have "engineered" the rat into one that is likely to make investigative movements in the vicinity of the bar; such movements are likely to result in an accidental tripping of the bar. If the rat still manages to avoid contact with the bar, we can add some more shaping by putting food on the bar itself or smearing it with food paste. If the rat tries to eat the food, it will depress the lightly mounted bar and initiate the click-food operation.

The shaping of the bar press was described in such detail to make it quite clear that to modify behavior, one must know what one wants to have happen and to analyze the components in the action. Every complex action beyond simple reflexes is likely to have a series of steps or actions involved, each in its proper sequence. Each step must be prepared for by the prior step. If the behavior shaper does not know what he or she should do at each step, he or she is likely to refer to the rat as a dumb animal. Skinner was inclined to remark that there are no dumb students, only dumb teachers.
✳ The operation of shaping consists of introducing a reinforcer at the first sign of a movement in the right direction (the first step of any sequence) and building on this by requiring the second step (after the first is strongly established). The second step is then reinforced until it is strong enough to occur without immediate reinforcement, and the third step is then required (waited for) before reinforcement.

If you wished to train a dog to "shake hands" with this procedure, you would reinforce any approach response first. When the dog sits near you, you could extend your hand (a discriminated stimulus) or S^D and say, "Shake hands," another S^D. You would remain in that position until the dog moved its right forepaw at least slightly in the direction of your hand. At this point, you would reinforce the dog by feeding it candy or saying, "Good dog" or patting it, if "good dog" and a pat had previously been established as

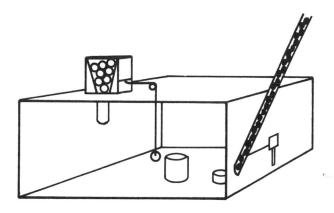

FIGURE 8.2: Skinner's chaining demonstration box. See text.

secondary reinforcers. You would then repeat the operation but wait for a more definite movement. As the dog began to get his paw closer and closer to your hand, you would reinforce each "improvement" until the dog placed his paw in your hand.

The procedure just described is obviously unnecessary. Any five-year-old can teach a dog to shake hands by grabbing the appropriate paw and shouting, "Shake hands." This procedure is referred to technically as putting through. You will recall that Konorski and Miller trained their dogs to raise paws when a bell rang. When the little boy grabs a paw, he is also "putting" the dog "through." The dog will learn quickly enough, perhaps as an avoidance response in disguise—the dog will find it more reinforcing to shake hands than to just sit there and be upended.

When more complex behavior patterns than shaking hands are involved, we get into the problem of chaining. In chaining, the behavior we wish to shape up may consist of a variety of responses that are quite different but which also have to be performed in a specific sequence. Here, we are calling for different behaviors, not just more of the same, as in a hand shake program.

We can begin our appreciation of "complex" learning by taking an illustration from Skinner. At one time, Skinner trained a rat (named Pliny) to pull a chain that dislodged marbles (one for every pull) from a dispenser. Pliny would pick up a marble and drop it into a cylinder that was two inches high at another part of the experimental box. When the marble was dropped into the cylinder, it tripped a switch, which activated a food dispenser, and Pliny would run to another part of the box to eat a pellet of food. (See Figure 8.2.)

Suppose you were given the assignment of teaching a rat to perform for an audience in the manner described. What would you do? What would be your first step? What would be the next step? And then what? We might warn you that taking the apparatus as shown and putting the rat into it would probably be of no value whatever. Your rat would starve.

How Did Skinner Do It?

To train Pliny, Skinner followed the old adage, "You have to know more than the dog" if you wish to teach dogs, or in the present instance, you have to know more than the rat. You have to know something about rats, to begin with. One thing you do know is that they eat when hungry. Because part of what the rat does is to eat, you might start there. But before the rat will eat, it must be inclined to eat, and so the training might follow Skinner's procedure. Skinner took two months to train Pliny. He thought he could possibly do it in two weeks. We will lay out a three-week program that might work.

Day 1. Starve the rat. Skinner uses the more genteel expression, deprive the rat. Feed the rat only small amounts of food daily for about a week, forcing it to lose up to a third of its starting weight.

Week 1. During the week, introduce food of the kind that will be dropped from the dispenser (small, hard pellets) so that the rat will recognize the food as such when it arrives.

Day 8. After a week on the deprivation schedule, place the rat in the box with only the food dish with some food in it. Allow the rat to wander about and get used to the box for about an hour. The rat will probably explore the box quite thoroughly.

Day 9. Replace the rat in the box with no food in the dish. Drop a piece of food by activating the mechanical dispenser, operating the switch from the outside. The mechanism will make some noises (clicks) and frighten the rat, but it will eventually come to the dish and eat. Do this about 40 times. The rat will tend to remain in the vicinity of the dish. After dropping the first few pellets, wait till it leaves the dish before dropping more pellets.

Day 10. Prepare a hole in the box large enough to receive a marble that can drop through, and close the switch activating the feeder. Tilt the floor in such a way as to direct the marble into the hole if it is in motion. Now, place the rat in the box and drop one marble into the box by operating an external switch on the marble dispenser. Wait for the rat to start playing with the marble—any motion it provides will send the marble rolling into the hole. As soon as the marble drops, the food mechanism will discharge a pellet, along with its click, and the rat will run to the food dish. Keep dropping marbles, and repeat this exercise about 40 times.

Day 12. Put a small ring around the hold so that the marble cannot roll in by itself. The rat must nudge the marble over the ring if it is to disappear. Repeat 40 times.

Day 13. Add another ring, raising the height of the rim around the hole. Repeat 40 times. ,

Days 14 to 20. Keep adding rings until you have built a sizable cylinder and your rat now must hoist the marble about two inches to have it drop into the hole. Repeat the operation as before, that is, 40 times per day.

Day 21. Insert the chain in the box and connect it with the marble dispenser mechanism so that if the chain is pulled, a marble will drop. Have the chain rather long, almost touching the floor, and jiggle it about if the rat ignores it. If necessary, smear some cheese on it. As soon as the rat is near the chain, drop a marble. After the first few marbles, wait until the rat touches the chain; then wait until the rat tugs the chain enough to close the switch. Repeat this part about 40 times. You now have a rat that pulls a chain and plays with marbles until they disappear.

We now have a performing rat. Has it learned something? Perhaps, we can learn something from the rat. For one thing, we can see that the whole training program operated backwards. The last thing done (eating) was the first step in the program, and the first thing that the rat does (pull the chain) was the last step or link in the chain of behavior. Is that the way people learn—last things first? Perhaps it would be a good way to go about some learnings. At least it would help teachers to have an orderly series of steps where they knew what was to be done first and last and sequentially in between. The whole point of programmed learning is illustrated in the above exercise. The teacher has to know where he or she is going to wind up and, working backwards, finds out where he or she must start.

But did the rat learn anything? And if so, what? Let us take another look at the steps.*

1. The rat eats. It already knows how to do that. Perhaps it learns where to eat—perhaps at the cup's location. Is there some place learning here? Tolman might take care of that for us. The rat acquires an expectancy through Pavlovian (S $\longrightarrow$ S) conditioning. Hull would talk about goal responses being conditioned to the surrounding stimuli.

2. The rat comes to the food cup when the dispenser clicks. Because it would not do so at first, we must recognize some learning here. Later, we will see that Mowrer (1960a) will argue that the click is a CS for an emotional response of "hope," which directs the rat to approach an area that previously

---

*The following discussion makes reference to principles advanced by Mowrer, Hebb, Guthrie, and Tolman. These are discussed in the next chapter. The student is advised to return to this section after study of the next chapter.

provided some positive emotional reaction. Note that the rat can already approach; it only learns to want to approach or when (when the click sounds). Such emotional conditioning would be of the Pavlovian stamp. The Skinner-Hull-Thorndike view that the response is strengthened may be only an empirical (probabilistic) description and not an explanation. The reinforcement theorists cannot use the click as an instigator of the activity. For Skinner, it would only be a discriminated stimulus (S^D), with no initiative power. Interpreting it as a secondary reinforcer in Skinnerian or Hullian terms does not help here, as it precedes the action. Skinner would like to have the click work in both ways, but it is probably neither an discriminated stimulus nor a secondary reinforcer in the technical sense favored by Skinner; it fits the Pavlov (Mowrer) view much better, at least in its role of an instigating stimulus for some response (the positive emotion).

3. Until the click sounds, the rat "fools around" with the marble until it disappears. Is this learning or killing time? The marble's disappearance and the immediately following click can result in an S→S connection of the Pavlov-Tolman variety: sign – (disappearing ball)→significate (click).* There could be other S→BR→S bits of learning—if the marble is pushed, it will roll. When the rings are placed around the hole, making a barrier, the rat must now pick up the marble and drop it. When the barrier gets higher, the task becomes more and more difficult. Still the rat does it (it knows how to), but this behavior raises some question as to the identity of the reinforcer for reinforcement theorists. Again, it has to be the click of the food dispenser, but this could just as easily be described as the stimulus for feeling better (Mowrer's hope).

4. The introduction of the chain presents a new feature. Its relation to the marbles is unknown to the rat. It is a new link to be established between the click of the marble dispenser and the sound of the dropping marble in connection with chain pulling. Does the rat learn how to pull chains? Obviously, it does not. We might have to make the chain attractive in some way for example, jiggling it or smearing it with food) so that with nothing else to do, the rat will grasp the chain, get to like it and acquire a new expectancy: if the chain is pulled, a marble will drop. The reinforcement theorists have to find a source of secondary reward for chain pulling. The marble could function in that role, to be sure, but it would have to acquire its secondary reward value from the secondary reward of the food dispenser click. Such acquisition of secondary rewards based on prior secondary rewards was proposed by Spence (1956) in his account of runway behavior, and it cannot be dismissed by simple denial. Empirical demonstrations of secondary-reward acquisition by one cue based on secondary rewards from

---

*S – BR – S is Tolman's (1937) formula for sign – behavior route – significate. It refers to learning where on stimulus (S) is followed by another S if some action (BR) is undertaken. See chapter 9 for a fuller discussion.

another are rare, however, and such an explanation has no greater plausibility than a Mowrer account in terms of positive emotional conditioning attached to the marble as a stimulus, with kinesthetic feedback from the approach to the chain and the pull as the higher-order CS. Besides, the Spence account dealt with merely maintaining a repetitive running response in a constant environment and not doing different kinds of things at different times with distinct stimuli. If the appearance of a marble were operating as a secondary reinforcer, one might expect the rat to stay in the vicinity of the chain and keep pulling it, thus, getting more marbles. It will do that if the balls do not go into the hole because the hole is blocked, but it will do so only after the sequence of behavior is interrupted by such failures. Normally, as soon as the marble drops, the rat would approach the hole.

In Skinner's own account of such a behavior chain, he, like Spence, must depend on the action of a series of secondary reinforcers as the response steps unfold. From Skinner's analysis, we have the following schema:*

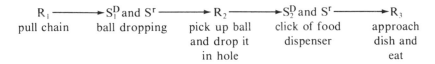

$$R_1 \longrightarrow S_1^D \text{ and } S^r \longrightarrow R_2 \longrightarrow S_2^D \text{ and } S^r \longrightarrow R_3$$

| pull chain | ball dropping | pick up ball and drop it in hole | click of food dispenser | approach dish and eat |

First, we have no good reason to suggest to explain R_1. It just is emitted. S_1^D could be a discriminated stimulus for R_2 and a secondary reinforcer (S^r) for R_1 (a dual burden). R_2 is a complex response (a *pure stimulus act* in Hull's terms), as it is a self-negating response, where the disappearance of a sought-after object is presumed to be reinforcing, but because the click follows immediately, we might accept this response as reinforced by the click, which also has to play the role of a discriminated stimulus for the next response of approaching the food dish.

The Skinner analysis depends on assuming that a particular event, the click, can serve as both a discriminated stimulus and a secondary reinforcer. This dual role for discriminated stimuli is clearly asserted by Skinner's followers, and they are rather concerned about pointing out (Shoenfeldd, Antonitis, and Bersh 1950; Williams 1973) that unless a stimulus is first established as an S^D it will not operate as an S^r (reinforcing stimulus).

In explaining any chaining of behavior, then, it is argued that as each step in the chain of events occurs, it is reinforced by stimuli generated by the preceding step. If any link in the chain is weakened by extinction, it will not reinforce the behavioral steps that occur earlier, and these will then diminish in probability of occurrence. Long chains are difficult to develop or

---

*The arrow $\longrightarrow$ means followed by.

maintain, because the secondary reinforcers are so far distant (in time) from primary reinforcement that they may not operate effectively. But rats have been trained to climb a staircase, pull a string that brings in a little "car," get in, walk on a treadmill to propel the car along a track, get to a new location, step into an elevator, ride to a new "floor," and, finally, press a lever for a food pellet. While it may tax credibility to accept that each step in such a chain is controlled by a secondary reinforcement from the stimuli associated with the next step, the Skinnerians are forced to such an assumption.

If we look more closely at what the rat actually does in such a setup, we see that nothing has been required of it that it cannot normally and, more or less, readily do. It can climb stairs when stairs are present. Guthrie (1935) would note with satisfaction that once the stairs are climbed, they are no longer there, the stair stimuli disappear, and the rat is in a new situation, where something else has to be done. The string is there to be pulled, and when the car arrives, the string is, in effect, disposed of. For Guthrie, the whole chain could be accounted for without mention of reinforcement. Tolman would equally have an easy time of accounting for the rat's learning of what leads to what, and with a "demand" (Tolman's substitute for drives or needs) for food, proceeding to perform. Mowrer would propose an emotional reaction of feeling better and better as each new stimulus stituation excited more hope and less fear (of not eating).

We can probably consider any sequence of behavior from the view-points of Guthrie, Tolman, and Mowrer with some benefit in appreciating what goes on. From the Thorndike-Hull-Skinner viewpoint, we can learn much about changing the program or schedule of events so that some performance will occur. They show us how some learner must be prepared (starved in the case of the rat) and how a reinforcer (incentive?) can be employed to initiate steps in a sequence. They also show us the importance of the sequence and how it is developed from last step to first. The role of reward, however, must be rather carefully analyzed and evaluated. On the animal level, with hungry rats and food rewards, we might be influenced to ascribe a learning value to the food intake. On a human level, with a sequential task like baking a cake or producing a geometric proof or even reciting a set of nonsense syllables, we might have to be less charitable to a reward function in the learning operation. It might pay to look at a human level learning sequence to see what problems might arise.

Suppose you wish to divide an angle into two equal parts with only a compass and straightedge. Someone tells you to swing an arc from the apex of the angle A, creating arc BC, as in Figure 8.3, (you might not think of doing so yourself immediately).

You may or may not know what to do next, although the arc might suggest something. The proper suggestion your teacher might make is to swing the compass, in turn, from B and C, creating a point in space D at the intersection of the two new arcs.

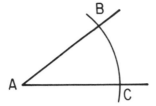

FIGURE 8.3: Bisecting an angle. Step. 1.

Now you draw a straight line from A through D, as in Figure 8.4, and the angle is bisected. You can probably follow the series of steps and bisect any new angles. The question of the moment, however, is, Where was there any reward, primary or secondary? You do not even know if you have actually bisected the angle. How do you know the two angles at A are equal? To determine the truth of the construction, you must now go through a proof. You may not know the proof, and your instructor suggests that you connect points B and D and C and D with straight lines. (See Figure 8.5.)

You do this because you are told, and you know what you have done, but the only new events are two more lines, and still there is no answer. Your instructor might point out, if you do not see for yourself, that you now have two triangles, ABD and ACD, before you. If you know about proving triangles to be congruent by demonstrating that the sides are equal, you might now recognize that you have such a case here with AD the common side and the other sides equal (same compass radius). You can now rejoice or feel good or get a gold star. The question is, Where was any reward of any kind applied in your learning of the proof?

The proof is only a sequence of steps. As each step is performed, new stimulus situations are created. Each new stimulus calls for a new response. To postulate reinforcements after each response is difficult to support in that the new stimulus creates only more mystery. It may appear that you are

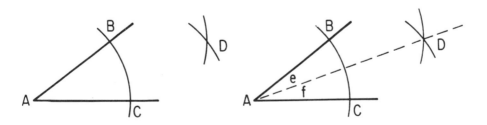

FIGURE 8.4: The bisection completed.

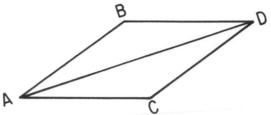

FIGURE 8.5: Proof of the bisection.

making progress, but if you do not know where you are going, the progress may not be very satisfying.

Consider now Battig and Brackett's (1961) demonstration of the study-test method compared with the anticipation method of learning paired associates. In the study-test method, you may be shown a dozen pairs of items; each pair is shown together for five seconds. You are asked to pronounce the response item. After all have been shown, only the stimulus items are presented, one at a time, and you are asked to recall the response items. In this case, responses were double digit numbers, and stimuli were nonsense forms. In the anticipation method, you first see the stimulus for five seconds, and then the response is shown while you pronounce it. In this case, after the first trial, you have immediate confirmation of your guess if you are correct or are informed of what is correct if you were wrong. Such immediate knowledge of results is supposed to be reinforcing. In the Battig and Brackett study, however, the students who did not get immediate knowledge (the study-test group) were significantly better at learning than those with immediate information. In the study-test method, the students never did find out (for sure) if they were giving the right answers until they were told they had finished. The applicability of any reward or reinforcement theory to such a situation is obviously in serious question. In this instance, the study-test group could not even tell it was making progress, except in some vague personal and unconfirmed way.

In preparing a batter for pancakes, one can get one's reward from the compliments that might come to the chef after the proof of the pancakes, but the step-by-step procedure involved again raises serious questions as to the possible role of any reinforcers. You do not know at any point how the pancakes will taste. All you see is a new visual display as each ingredient is added, and they disappear into the homogenous mixture almost as soon as they are added.

Our excursion into shaping and chaining has demonstrated that behavior can be altered, directed, and controlled by arranging the environment (chaining) or manipulating reinforcers, in the sense of requiring more and more effort or some changes in direction or activity. The shaping operation consists of insisting on a particular move before we provide a payoff. The move itself is not learned. If the move is simple, such as getting a dog to sit, we merely have to wait until it sits, when we tell it to do so. Because it may not be interested in sitting and we may not be interested in waiting, we can push the dog down while saying "sit." A reward at this juncture will be helpful (we can apply Guthrie's or Mowrer's explanation; Skinner is not helpful here for explaining much, as he merely says that it works).

Autoshaping

Brown and Jenkins (1968) reported a curious phenomenon they chose to call "autoshaping." How well-deserved the name is may be debated, as no shaping procedure is undertaken or undergone. What Brown and Jenkins did was to place a pigeon in a Skinner box equipped with a disc in one wall and a food tray that could be inserted into the chamber for a brief interval. Pigeons will quickly come to peck at the food until it is withdrawn. In the typical Skinner procedure, the experimenter waits until the pigeon pecks at or near the target and then presents food contingent upon there having been a peck—no peck, no food. Brown and Jenkins, however, chose to present food at certain intervals regardless of what the pigeon might be doing. Just before the food came into the box, the disc in the wall was illuminated and stayed on until the pigeon ate. The illumination would be cut off and the food tray removed until the next joint presentation of light and food. The Brown and Jenkins operation, then, is typically Pavlovian; that is, CS (light) and US (food) are presented together without imposing any obligation on the subject to act in any way.

The result of this procedure is that the pigeon quickly begins to peck at the illuminated disc even though this has no bearing on whether or not food is to appear. What is more, the pecking will continue even if there is no food presented or if the pecking delays the appearance of food (Williams and Williams 1969). If one wishes to get a pigeon to peck a disc, it is easier to meet this objective by using the Pavlovian procedure than the Skinnerian one. Hintzman (1978) calls this state of affairs an embarrassment for Skinner and suggests that all the time Skinnerians have been training thousands of pigeons to peck at discs, they have really been taking advantage of Pavlovian conditioning without knowing it.

In subsequent studies (Jenkins and Moore 1973), it has been demonstrated that if the US (reinforcer) is water, the pigeons will peck at the disc with a typical drinking posture (beak open) and will lick the disc. When the US is food, they will peck in the manner in which they peck at grain. The drive does not determine the manner of pecking; the US does. Thus, using two discs, if one disc is associated with water and the other with food, the pigeons will peck appropriately at the separate discs as they are illuminated.

Autoshaping is a problem for Skinner, as well as for everyone else.

When Pavlov observed his dogs, his interest was in saliva, but he also observed that when food was not delivered, the dogs would push at the dispensing tubes with their heads, and if light bulbs were used as CSs, the dogs would lick the light bulbs. Now, obviously, licking light bulbs or pecking discs is not the response to the US. The US, in the case of pigeons, calls for pecking at grain at the floor level of the box. Pecking at a disc calls for an upright posture and pecking at something that is not food. The CR is thus not the same as the UR unless one makes an easy identification of pecking as pecking, regardless of the target.

Gormezano and Kehoe (1975) argue that the autoshaped pecking is not actually a CR in strict Pavlovian terms as the original pecking response is not a UR to any known US. Because the response is not an instrumental one either, Gormezano and Kehoe suggest that autoshaping may be a new kind of learning "arising only from the *stimulus* presentation." (italics theirs).

A problem still remains, namely, that of accounting for the switch from pecking at grain to pecking at a plastic disc. If one were to judge from the behaviors, the pigeon is acting as if it were eating (or drinking) the disc. It appears to have identified the signal (CS) with the referent (the US). We can speculate that the pigeon has come to like the disc (Mowrer 1960a) or that it is not clever enough to discriminate between the disc and the food, but such speculation is idle. In a later chapter (Chapter 11), we will return to the problem of accounting for Skinnerian or operant behavior in classical conditioning terms. For the present, we will note that autoshaping is neither *auto* nor *shaping*, and although it is the result of a Pavlovian procedure, it is neither instrumental nor Pavlovian conditioning.

Continuity

Some things are learned more quickly than others. This appears to be an acceptable statement, but a moment's pause for thought, and we find it not quite so acceptable as it seemed at first reading. Learned by whom? That might be a good question. Certainly, different people or different animals learn some kinds of response patterns with different efficiencies. A new gambit in chess can be learned almost at once by a grand master. It could never be learned by an elephant or an otter. Even a chess amateur might have a great deal of trouble.

We have allowed for some species differences (chapter 5), and some individual differences among people and rats are obvious enough. Allowing for variations in health, strength, general vitality, and efficiency of sensory and motor structures, as well as temporary dispositions (drives, interests, and so forth), we might suspect differential learning histories with different backgrounds and degrees of experience or familiarity with the tasks. Later, we will look at Harlow's (1949) demonstration of the importance of learning sets or learning-how-to-learn as explanations of one-trial learning by educated monkeys (see chapter 21).

It appears then that past experience is certainly a variable of importance, and when learning appears to be going slowly, we may be observing the accumulation of what will become past experience when some assignment is mastered.

The Role of Practice

We usually associate learning with practice, and we normally observe improvement with practice. As we have seen, however Hull (1943) pointed out that it is not any old practice that counts but only practice of the correct response. But here, we encounter a new problem. Some tasks are easy and some difficult. In some cases, you need only one trial to learn something. If someone asks you to repeat c-w-j, you can repeat it, and we might speak of one-trial learning. But if we wait awhile, during which you are otherwise occupied, and we then ask you for the letters, you might not repeat them all, or any, or in correct order. Then, perhaps, you did not learn them or did not learn them very well. With more repetitions, you will be able to report the letters after longer and longer periods between tests. You will have increased the habit strength. How good can you get?

According to Hull, you can never get perfect at any learned habit, because Hull assumes that each repetition adds less and less strength to the habit as a proportional mathematical function of the potential remaining habit strength. Thus, if the first correct response adds 50 percent to the habit strength, which has 100 percent as a limit, there is only 50 percent left to learn. The next response, according to Hull, then adds 50 percent of the remainder, or 25 percent. The learned habit is now at 75 percent of its potential, with 25 percent left to be learned, but the next correct response will only add 50 percent of this 25 percent, or 12.5 percent, and so on. There will always be room for improvement. Such an arrangement of decreasing benefits from practice would account for the commonly reported negatively accelerated learning curves. Although you gain less and less, every correct trial does add to the habit strength. You get better and better. This is known as the continuity principle.

The point made above is that just because you do something right, once, you have not really learned it as well as it could be learned if we consider retention over time as one criterion. You could also improve by other criteria—reaction time, for example. Many things that we learn are of no great importance, and there is no great need to get better and better at them. One does not gain great dividends by remembering the names of one's grammar school classmates once one gets to college. Similarly, retaining a list of nonsense syllables for more than a few trials verges on nonsensical behavior. We could probably become superb at reciting the names of the states of the United States, but we would not get many requests to display our prowess.

The continuity principle, however, is not designed to account for rapid or one-trial learning, some forms of which can, indeed, occur when the task is brief, exciting, and easy, requiring only some modest exertion and having relatively few components. A 3-digit number is easy to learn; a 20-digit number would give anyone pause. Whenever there is a task where a good performance does take a lot of practice, we might be forced to reckon with the continutiy principle. We can take the example of a child learning to say "thank you" when receiving a gift or favor. It is probably a rare child that learns such a pattern in one trial. Parents, hovering about, tell the child: "Say, 'Thank you'" or, "What do you say?" The child, more concerned with unwrapping a gift, may ignore the directions or questions. With repeated gifts and repeated demands that "thank you" be said, the child gets to the point where he or she says "thank you" before the gift is in his or her hands; adults will frequently thank people for anticipated favors.

In the laboratory, it is difficult for a rat to learn to jump across a gap to a platform that can be reached only by knocking down a door marked with a cross when there are two doors, and the other is marked with a circle. The apparatus involved is called the Lashley jumping stand. A discrimination problem of this kind is rarely learned in fewer than several hundred trials. On difficulty is that in such situations, rats tend to favor one side or the other, a "position habit", and the experimenter moves the markers at random from one side to the other. The cross will appear on the right, for example, half the time, and a rat with a 100 percent right position habit will find food 50 percent of the time. Such partial reinforcement we have learned is extremely potent, and the position habit is difficult to break. To get ten correct jumps in a row might require 400 or so trials. At one time, a considerable controversy arose in attempting to account for such learning and its difficulties. It was argued, for example, that if the rat could be made to pay attention to the signals instead of the sides, it would learn more quickly. As an experimental demonstration that some rats were not attending to the signs, the signs would be switched in value after some 200 trials, and it would be argued that such a switch would make no difference in the total number of trials required to learn (to the ten in a row correct criterion). Such a test was assumed to demonstrate that learning would occur only if the animal began to discriminate between the signs (Kretchevsky 1946). The continuity theory (Spence 1936) holds that every successful jump (to the cross, regardless of side) would add to the habit strength and that, eventually, the rat would learn. It would, of course, make a difference if the proper cues could be brought to bear on the rat. Ehrenfreund (1948) was able to demonstrate that changing the cues before the rat showed any signs of learning did make a difference and did delay the acquisition. What this amounts to is to say that every correct performance does pay off even though the learning is slow and imperceptible. The mother who despairs of her child's ever learning to say "thank you" should persist. Eventually, the child will learn.

The question that is posed by the continuity principle is that of the criterion of learning. If we set a high standard and refuse to recognize approximations, then we can say that no learning has occurred until there is a perfect performance. In that case, learning will always be a one-trial affair, as no other trials count except the correct one. In the Rock (1957) experiment, a nonsense syllable was called learned only if it was pronounced in full. No partial credit was given for one or two letters or some other approximation. To conclude from this experiment that nothing had been learned before the perfect performance is not correct. Subjects in such experiments can recognize syllables they have been shown before, even if they cannot recall them. Tulving (1974) has shown that given the proper stimulation, a great deal can be recalled that is otherwise apparently lost.

However we regard the continuity principle, we cannot expect learning to occur by itself and always to full-blown perfection in one trial. Some *patterns* or sequences of response require many trials, where separate components may be learned in one-trial but many trials are required before the total "package" can be accepted as meeting some standard. An applicant for a driver's license may be good at parking but poor at turning around in the street. He or she can be denied a license. That person has not learned to drive.

In this context, we should consider Guthrie's view (see next chapter) that any act amounts to a great many different possible responses to a wide variety of stimulus patterns or combinations and that each combination must be learned separately, perhaps on one trial per combination, before the act is learned. We can conclude, then, that practice is necessary for many kinds of response patterns, but even practice cannot result in perfection. We cannot get better than 99 percent plus.

9

What Is Learned?

We have now looked at the major efforts of the early learning psychologists and found that they led to profound disagreements as to how learning took place. One view, that of Pavlov, stated that learning was the conditioning or association of one stimulus with another, a substitution of stimuli, such that one stimulus could now initiate a response formerly evokable only by the other. The other view, that of Thorndike, Hull, and Skinner, stated that learning consisted of substituting one response for another when and because the new response was followed by a reward. In one way or another, the learning psychology of the first half of the twentieth century amounted to attempts to support or clarify these two conflicting views. As the conflict developed, it became quite clear that the question of what is learning was being transformed into the question, What is learned?," that is, What is associated with what? Everyone assumed that learning consisted of associating one thing with another. The question that was raised in Chapter 3 is, What are the "things"? If this question could be answered, perhaps the question of what is learning would also be answered.

In this chapter, we will trace the development of some of the efforts to answer the question of what are the components of an association. We will find that those psychologists who pondered the matter added greatly to the general body of learning lore through their own individual observations of learners in action. We have already noted the contributions of Hull and Skinner, the followers of Thorndike. We turn now to some Pavlovian followers.

THE BEHAVIORISTS

Watson

It will be recalled that Watson (1878–1958), the founder of behaviorism, had based his psychology on the S⟶R formula, which states, in essence, that for every stimulus, there is a response, and every response must have a stimulus. If there is no response, the stimulus has to be considered as not meeting the circular definition of "a stimulus is some energy change in the environment or in the organism that activates a receptor." The simple S→R formula does not go very far in accounting for behavior, as different organisms might respond differently to the same stimulus. Such differences must be learned (Watson took a dim view of individual differences, instinct, or any other source of innate factors that could result in differences in behavior). But Watson had no learning theory until he came across Bekhterev's book on conditioning, whereupon he espoused conditioning immediately, following the Bekhterev model, which, it will be recalled, required only the pairing of a CS and US for conditioning to occur. There was no mention of rewards. The learning was mechanical, based on frequency of pairings. Although Watson had a background in physiology, he did not concern himself with any detailed neural accounts of conditioning, as had Pavlov. Watson took Bekhterev's views over directly and dealt only with observables. Stimuli were observable, and so were responses. When conditioning occurred, the association amounted to a new connection between some stimulus and some response. Besides S→R, Watson now proposed CS→R as an additional formula, with the components of an association being the CS and the R. Watson was not very rigid about describing his responses, referring to them generally as reflexes, reactions, or responses and including among them rather gross emotional states. For Watson, the question of what is learned was answered thus: a motor or glandular response is associated with a stimulus. *ANSWER*

Movement versus Act Distinction

Edwin R. Guthrie (1886–1959), originally a philosopher, took up a strong behaviorist position and turned into a most provocative psychologist. Throughout a long career, Guthrie maintained the original Watson dogma that in learning, stimuli were associated with responses; but he was extremely careful to insist that the responses consisted of movements that had to be observed as such and not in terms of their consequences. Too many psychologists, Guthrie felt, had confused the issue by observing not behavior but the consequences of behavior. Thorndike spoke of a cat opening a door. This was a statement about the psychology of doors, not of cats. The cat did not open a door. The cat pulled a string or pressed a paw against a pedal or latch. The fact that a door opened was Thorndike's doing, not the cat's. Thorndike could just as easily have untied the string from the door, and no amount of pulling would open the door.

Everything we do consists of movements of our bodies or appendages. And everything we do consists of a specific set of muscular contractions and relaxations. We do not open a car door, for example; we may grasp the handle in some specific way and turn our wrists left or right. Normally, the door opens. If we turn left when the door lock calls for right, the door will not open. Every door calls for its own special set of movements. Slowly, as we grow up, we get to open one door after another, some easily and some with difficulty. When we have opened enough doors, we can talk about the class of movements that we have gone through (and learned, in each case) as the "act" of opening doors. We do not learn *acts*, however. The word *act* is a class term, an abstraction. A rat in a maze does not learn to go through the maze or "know" the maze. It learns to turn left here, right there, run so far here, stop sooner there, and so forth. We loosely refer to the rat having learned the maze; actually, the rat has learned specific movements to specific cues.

Guthrie's position was adamant. If there is more than one way to do anything, it has to be learned as a movement to a stimulus. You even have to learn to eat with fork and spoon. Certain foods call for movements of their own—artichokes, for example. Watching people eat corn on the cob at a picnic should demonstrate Guthrie's point. You will see the "around and around," the "left to right," "the butter-it-all-at-once," and other varieties of movements learned by different people, each of whom will say, "Of course, I know how to eat corn on the cob." We have used some casual examples to imitate some of Guthrie's casual style of writing, but Guthrie was serious about laboratory observations. Unless you watched what the subject did, you would learn nothing about learning. Too many psychologists were concerned about the outcome of some behavior and not its components.

As long as we pay attention to the consequences of the movement, we will learn nothing about behavior, argued Guthrie. We will be misguided into thinking that rewards or other consequences have something to do with learning, when obviously, the learned response had to occur before a reward could arrive or be approached. Guthrie generalized his attack on the psychology of acts into a broad rejection of all abstract terms that we characteristically use in our shorthand descriptions of behavior. We say, for example, "Yes, I had dinner," but no one knows much about what or how you ate; perhaps, no one cares, but in other cases, the what and how become important.

We can illustrate Guthrie's major concern from two important kinds of events—crime and accidents. How can we stop or reduce either? There is no way that anyone can attack crime. Crime is a legal term covering a broad class of behavior, with each member of the class itself a broad category. Guthrie would propose that you consider one kind of crime at a time and break that down to very minute and specific descriptions of what comprises an instance of the crime. Thus, if we consider purse snatching a crime, we try to discover who snatches purses and how a purse may be snatched. We note at once that for a purse to be snatched, someone must be carrying it. How it is being carried may be important. If it is carried under a coat, it is more difficult to snatch than if carried loosely over the arm. If there is no purse at all, it cannot be snatched. Once attention is directed to specifics, some kinds of solutions emerge; they may not always be acceptable, but at least some alternatives of a meaningful nature may develop. Since men get along without purses, pants-wearing women might also. Is it a matter of pockets? Eliminating purse snatching might increase pocket picking, but the latter at least calls for a skill that might be in rarer supply. Similarly, one can deal with accidents. If an accident is properly described as a specific and particular kind of event, measures can be taken to prevent the occurrence. Thus, if people slip in tubs because they have nothing to hold onto, some kinds of handrails could be built into tub enclosures to assist stability. Auto accidents involving left turns could be prevented by outlawing left turns, and so forth. No accident will be prevented by a general attack on accidents. Telling people to be careful is a waste of breath. The basic trouble, as with crime, is that accident is a class term, an abstraction, and one cannot do anything about an abstraction but talk about it.

Operant researchers had always favored automating their equipment so that every depression of a lever in the Skinner box would be recorded in a cumulative graph. To ensure quiet and freedom from distractions, they would on some occasions place the box containing the rat into another box. Now, the researcher could watch his graph develop and never even see his rat at work. What the rat did was unimportant, so long as the marking pens did their job. What a rat does, however, seems rather more important than what a pen does or so it would seem to someone interested in behavior. Guthrie and Horton (1946) were able to report some rather fascinating observations when they put cats into boxes with glass walls, where the cats could not only be observed but also photographed at critical moments in a problem situation. They reported that each cat had its own way (or several ways) of moving a lever that opened the door and allowed the cat to exit. The highly specific movements engaged in by the cats convinced Guthrie, if he needed further convincing, that movements were the essence of behavior and that one ignored such movements at his peril.

Stimulus Complex

From such careful and sometimes casual observation of the behavior of cats, horses, children, and adults, Guthrie arrived at the conclusion that what is learned, when learning occurs, is an association between some stimulus and some specific movement. While insisting on specificity in describing responses, Guthrie was very loose about describing stimuli. Thus, he spoke of many components in any situation in which someone might refer to one item as a stimulus, when that item might or might not be important. Guthrie tended to emphasize kinesthetic or movement-produced stimuli (mps), which could not ordinarily be observed. By emphasizing such stimuli, Guthrie made his position almost unassailable.

Many energy changes might be occurring at the same time, and Guthrie preferred to talk about a "stimulus complex," which could include such things as whether someone was sitting or standing or was cold, tired, hungry, wet, or relaxed. No one exists in a vacuum, and the environment around us is always changing in illumination, temperature, activity, and so on. When one reacts, it is always to a relatively complex situation. Whatever movement is made will be associated with that stimulus complex, and if that stimulus complex ever recurs, the same movement will also recur. This is Guthrie's basic principle of learning—a law of contiguity in terms of stimuli and responses, spelled out in terms of a stimulus complex and a specific movement.

Law of Recency or Postremity

Guthrie placed great emphasis on basing predictions of what might happen on what did happen before. Thus, he argued, you always do what you did the last time you were in the same situation. He took this position in order to explain away the alleged importance of rewards. In any learning situation where a number of responses are possible but only one works, it is clear that whenever the correct response is made, it will be the one that is rewarded by an experimenter who is using a reward procedure. In the simple case of a T-maze with food on the left, a turn to the right will not be rewarded but a turn to the left will. Because the animal will come to turn left more frequently, the connection between the left turn and reward will seem obvious. But, says Guthrie, the relationship is more apparent than real. What is also the case is that turning left is the last movement performed in the choice situation, and it is this *lastness* that is the important variable. The fact that a reward followed is irrelevant.

What a reward does, in Guthrie's opinion, is to introduce a new stimulus into the situation that distracts the learner from making any other response to the stimulus to which it had just responded. The reward is an effective device for ending an S——▶R sequence and starting a new one. The original stimulus for the learned response, in effect, disappears, and the response made to it will be retained if no new response is made, and because the response eliminated the stimulus, no such new response can occur.

Guthrie based his views about the potency of the last response on casual observations of how children (and adults) can be seen to repeat patterns of behavior where any reward value seems unlikely. People will tend to sit in the same place at a dinner table, for example, and resent intrusions, where some "reasonable" person might argue that it makes no difference where you sit. A child will insist on drinking from "the red glass" and refuse any other kind if he or she drank from the red glass on the last occasion. Sometimes,

valance - either positive or negative mag. of quality of stimulus

only drastic measures can alter a behavior pattern of no ostensible value, because of our tendencies to behave as we did the last time we were in the situation. Voeks (1948) tried to provide some experimental data using punchboard mazes, where a subject would insert a pencil in one of a row of holes, which represented a set of choices. With a series of such rows, a learner would forget which holes he or she entered on the previous trials. Voeks was able to predict more effectively which holes would be entered by assuming that the subject would choose the same hole he or she did the last time than if she based her predictions on which holes were chosen most frequently. The experiment could not be conclusive, as no predictions were made that were based on the correctness of the choices. Later, Voeks (1950) chose the term *postremity* in order to emphasize the lastness of the response rather than its relative recency. We will look into this feature again in another context (chapter 16). For the moment, we recognize that Guthrie's answer to the question of what do we learn is: movements are associated with stimuli. *ANSWER*

It is important to recognize that Guthrie could cover a lot of psychological territory with his "movements"—movements make words, if the tongue is the moving musculature, and words make at least some kinds of thinking possible. We can, therefore, learn what we think (not how to think); in effect, we learn what we say to ourselves in a given stimulus context. We learn whatever we do, always recognizing that it is the specific movements in which we engage that we learn. We do not learn how to knit or cook or play bridge or golf. Each of these is a class term that covers a multitude of separate S⟶R units. In learning to play bridge, we may learn how to bid by certain sequential steps (movements), such as counting up the points in a hand. We might become fairly good bidders and fail to "play" the cards to the greatest advantage because we did not learn other movements, such as noting the cards that were played by opponents, and so forth. In any complex activity, such as basketball, we may learn to make certain kinds of throws and not others, to make certain passes and not others, and so on. Until we have mastered each unit, there is always something left to learn. Some people learn more units than others, and if the units are of equal importance, they can be described as "better at" something than others.

A student of Guthrie, Sheffield (1961), proposed that Guthrie's restriction of responses to motor activity or glandular secretions was too restrictive. There are such reactions as sensory responses to be considered. When one sees or hears something, one is also reacting, and the sensory responses can also be associated with other stimuli. Thus, a sensory reaction, such as seeing a person, could occur at the time his or her name was spoken by someone, including the viewer. Later, hearing the name could arouse some reasonable facsimile of the sensory reaction involved in seeing the person. Such a conditioned reaction would be called an image (as suggested by Leuba in 1940).

Extending the Guthrian view of S⟶R learning to include imagery greatly expands the scope of the Guthrian theory and begins to cover much of what "cognitive" psychologists think of as the proper realm of psychology. At the same time, adding imagery to the domain of what is learned raises some problems for the objectively oriented investigator. Movements of organisms are observable; images are not. Any investigation of imagery involves at least one additional inferential step in the S⟶R approach. Not only do we have to make inferences about learning, but we also must draw inferences about how imagery functions in learning. Inferences about inner behavior will be considered later in this chapter (section on Mediation). At the moment, we will return to the business at hand, namely, the consideration of what is learned.

Tolman's S⟶S Theory: Signs and Significates

Edward C. Tolman (1886–1959) considered himself to be a behaviorist, although he considered his behaviorism seriously different from that of Watson. For Tolman, psychology had to account for the purposive nature of behavior, and in this regard, Tolman felt Watson had failed. He agreed with Watson and Guthrie that rewards were of no importance for learning and that frequency of contiguous experiences was a sufficient principle, and he criticized Thorndike and Hull for their insistence on a reinforcement principle. Tolman (1932) demonstrated that whether rats or people were rewarded or punished, they would learn in either case.

We have already learned of Tolman's view that learning must be separated from performance. Performance can result from many sources or bases. Learning might dictate something about the kind of performance we might observe, its relative skill or refinement based on earlier experiences, but even in this regard, the performance would also depend on various physical factors related to sensory acuities and motor capacities. Tolman insisted on divorcing learning from performance and, as we shall see, offered the evidence of latent learning experiments in strong support of this position. Although Tolman was interested in predicting performance, he could see that performance was not essential to learning. Thus, Tolman (1932) argued that the basic association involved in learning was one between succeeding stimuli. One learns, for example, that thunder follows lightning. Here, one stimulus, lightning, precedes another, thunder, with the consequence that when one sees lightning again, an anticipation or expectation is aroused in some preliminary way and occurrence of the second stimulus "confirms" this "expectancy." Tolman chose to refer to the first stimulus in such a sequence as a Sign and the second as a Significate and the learning of such a Sign-Significate relationship as the learning of an expectancy. According to Tolman, then, we learn expectancies. Note that if

Thorndike } reinforcement
Hull } theory

we learn to expect thunder after lightning, we have, in effect, acquired information or knowledge. Knowledge consists of expectancies. Consider the sign 2 × 2. Immediately, in an educated adult, the significate "4" is aroused or initiated in some form. Note that the person who hears "four times four" does not have to do anything about it, even if asked. Responding is behavior, and behavior is performed, and as far as Tolman was concerned, learning and performance should be kept apart as separate concepts, as different operations, subject to the influence of different variables. Ask an irritated adult, "What is two times two," and he may not give a civil reply, even though the Significate of 4 quite probably was aroused.

Sometimes, a significate will not turn up naturally, as in the case of thunder. One might have to respond in some way to uncover, reveal, or develop the significate. Thus, if a doorbell rings (sign), the Significate that is aroused in experienced people is of someone at the door. The someone remains a mystery until one goes to the door and looks out. Such activity, which generates the "real life" embodiment of a significate, Tolman called a "behavioral route." The behavioral route might consist of merely standing and waiting, as with Pavlov's dogs. The bell (sign) will be followed in due course by the food (significate); the dog does not have to do anything. On the other hand, for Thorndike's cat, the string (sign) will, if pulled (behavior route) be followed by the opening of the door (significate). According to Tolman, then, associations are formed between signs and significates, with a behavioral route intervening between the two. We can depict the relationship as sign $\longrightarrow$ behavioral route $\longrightarrow$ significate, or $S \longrightarrow BR \longrightarrow S$, or even more briefly as $S \longrightarrow S$. Tolman's is an $S \longrightarrow S$ doctrine but not one of substitution of stimuli; rather, it is the association of stimuli. With Pavlov, Tolman attributed the formation of expectancies to contiguity, with frequency as the supporting principle. Note that the knowledge of a consequence (significate) given an antecedent (sign) can be of a positive or negative nature. One learns to dread the fire or be careful with knives. Rewards and punishments have nothing to do with association formation. One learns, instead, what is likely to be rewarded and what punished.

Tolman's analysis can be expressed as: you learn what leads to what. If the situation is spatial, for example, you learn where one path will take you and where you will end up if you take some other path. You may learn two or more ways to get to the same place. Given the opportunity to go to the place, you may decide not to. The knowledge does not call for performance. In a temporal situation, you learn what follows what. Again, you may choose not to stand around and wait. You do not have to answer the telephone bell even though you know someone is calling. You may even know who is calling and may be glad the call is by phone and not in person.

Tolman's theory has been described as a cognitive one because of Tolman's cognitive-sounding terminology. Tolman, however, styled himself a behaviorist, and while he wrote of expectancies, cognitions, knowledge, hypotheses, biases, and so on, he was careful to define his terms operationally and objectively. In the present concern, he simply took issue with other behaviorists, who chose to assume that associations were formed between stimuli and responses. For Tolman, this would mean that performance was being dictated directly by a learning operation, where he chose to attribute behavior or performance to other variables, such as needs, drives, or other predispositions he called "demand."

Tolman's arguments were directed primarily at Thorndike and Hull, as well as at Watson and Guthrie, all of whom espoused the S⟶R association assumption. But in the cases of Thorndike and Hull, Tolman was primarily opposed to their dedication to the importance of rewards or reinforcements. Eventually, Hull came over to Tolman's views on performance and recognized the distinction Tolman had been urging between learning and performance, but Hull continued to assume the S⟶R relationship as basic to learning. The power of Tolman's demonstrations of the apparent operation of expectancies bothered Hull. Tolman and Gleitman (1949) demonstrated, for example, that when rats were fed in both sides of a T-maze with quite different goal boxes and later shocked in one of the boxes (detached from the maze and in another room), the rats would not choose the path that led to that box even though they were never shocked for entering it after a run. Eventually, Hull felt he could account for such behavior on the basis of r_g s and suggested that expectancies and r_g s were really different names for the same kind of operation. Whether this was or was not a capitulation by Hull, it opened the door for supporters of each to deal with the concept of expectancy, something the old behaviorists would not tolerate.

Latent Learning: Learning versus Performance

In drawing a distinction between learning and performance, Tolman called attention to a very important feature of learning. In educational circles and in normal child rearing, there has always been an emphasis on proper action, on doing. Thorndike and Skinner had made action—responding—the key operation in learning. "You learn what you do" was the watchword. Now, it is obvious that if you do not perform or do not answer questions, no one can know that you can perform or that you do know the answers. Yet, you may not perform, and Tolman insisted that just because you knew something that was not sufficient reason to go around demonstrating it. He took advantage of some rather striking and unusual experiments by Blodgett (1929) to prove his point.

Blodgett trained some rats to find their way to a food goal in a six-choice points maze. They learned in the usual way over a period of seven days, at which time they were making few if any errors. Another group of rats was put into the same maze with no food at the end. As these rats moved about in the maze, doors would close after them every time they turned in the correct direction (the same procedure had been followed with the routine control group). Eventually, each rat would arrive at the foodless goal box. These rats showed no sign of learning, and it would appear that food was important, that is, that reinforcement or reward was necessary for learning. On the seventh day, Blodgett put food into the goal box, and the rats were rewarded for the first time. On the eighth day, these rats performed as well as the control rats, making no more errors than the regularly rewarded rats.

Tolman took Blodgett's findings to mean that just because there had been no signs of learning in the first seven days, one could not conclude that there was no learning. The unfed rats had learned as much as the fed rats but had no reason to display their knowledge. There was no point to go to an empty food box; in fact, knowing that it was empty might encourage a rat to go elsewhere whenever possible.

Tolman regarded such undisplayed learning as hidden or latent, ready to manifest itself when it might be worthwhile. It is, of course, obvious that we know more than we say or perform. We even lie about our knowledge when it seems appropriate to do so. It should be clear that failure to speak up or answer a question is not proof of ignorance; it might only be proof of unwillingness. In any event, we cannot insist on some overt action to be sure that someone learns something. Blodgett's experiment does not bear on this point because his rats did move about, but we will find later, when we consider *imitation* (chapter 13) that we can, indeed, learn without doing, at least overtly. We can learn, as Tolman insisted, what leads to what by merely observing a sequence or being told about it. The behavioral route may merely amount to watching, listening, or waiting.

Latent learning became a hotly disputed issue in the 1940s. After hundreds of experiments that tried to demonstrate or deny the reality of latent learning, the controversy slowly expired, with the general acceptance of latent learning as, indeed, a real operation.

Sensory-Sensory Conditioning

Tolman's assumption that conditioning was primarily a matter of the association of signs with significates was purely theoretical. He did not personally conduct any research that would support the assumption. It was simply an inference from his latent-learning and place-learning experiments. He did not at any time present two stimuli together and observe the formation of an association. Only a moment's thought should suggest the difficulties involved in trying to make such an observation. Suppose you sound a tone and flash a light together many times and you are reasonably sure that some subject hears and sees the stimuli. Now, you sound your tone alone. What do you expect your subject to do—see a light?

Sensory preconditioning

Brogden (1939) did just exactly what has been described above. He used dogs as subjects. The dog was strapped in a harness, which insured a stable posture and head position. He then paired a light and a tone for 200 trials over a ten-day period, making sure the dog's eyes were open at stimulation times. After the 200 pairings, he introduced a change in procedure. Only the tone would now be presented for two seconds, followed by a shock to the foreleg. The dog would raise its paw to the shock and after ten to 18 sessions, 20 trials per day, the dog would respond in that way to the tone alone. Now, Brogden tested the dog with the light stimulus. He was not surprised to see most of the dogs give a large number of avoidance responses to the test stimulus, which had never been paired with a shock. Brogden, of course, used the light as the CS for shock with some animals, who were then tested with a tone, and had control animals, who were given 200 lights and 200 tones separately. Control animals gave no responses to the test stimulus.

Brogden called his procedure "sensory preconditioning." His research was supported by other investigators using other kinds of subjects and responses. Wickens and Briggs (1951) used humans in a reaction time experiment. Silver and Meyer (1954) used rats with tones, lights, and shocks in a parallel experiment to that of Brogden. See, also, the studies of Wickens and Cross (1963), Prewitt (1967), and Tait and Suboski (1972). Apparently, in such S⟶S experiments, either the two stimuli become associated with each other and can substitute for each other or they come to be conditioned to some common response, which then generates additional stimuli. We will consider the explanation later when we review the concept of mediation.

Hallucinations and Synesthesia

Let us return to the question raised at the beginning of this section, when we asked what would happen if a tone and light were paired for a subject. Ellson (1941) asked human subjects to press a key when they heard a faint tone, which would rise in loudness from nothing to well above threshold over a 15-second period. When the tone was at about threshold level, a dim light would appear. After a number of such pairings, the tone would not be presented but the light would. Some subjects would press the key; the tone would then be sounded, confirming the subjects' judgment, although if he or she had heard a tone, it would have to be considered to be a hallucination or an image. Ellson demonstrated what has sometimes been claimed by people, namely, that they see lights, colors, and so forth when they hear tones or music. Other people talk about "dark brown tastes." Some music teachers ask students to learn to identify pitches on the piano by thinking of different notes as red, green, and so forth. Such cross-sensory modes experiences are called synesthesia. In a careful experiment using an adequate number of subjects, Kelly (1934) was unable to train people to "see" colors when scale notes were sounded, even after 1,000 trials, but his procedure might have been ineffective for a number of reasons, as Ellson pointed out.

Conditioned Sensations

images - "conditioned sensations"

We have mentioned Sheffield's theoretical extension of Guthrie's S→R psychology to include sensory reactions. His view was based on Leuba's (1940) demonstration that subjects, under hypnosis, could be conditioned to respond to a stimulus with a response appropriate to another stimulus. What Leuba did was to, for example, pass an odorous substance under a subject's nose and, at the same time, prick his or her hand with a pin. The pin prick would initiate withdrawal. After four or five trials, the subject would be "awakened," and when the odorous substance was passed under his or her nose, the subject would jerk his or her hand away, as if it had been pricked. The subject would explain his or her behavior by lame excuses, such as, "I thought a bee stung me." Leuba described his findings as the conditioning of a sensation. He went on to assert that the imaginary pain was just that, an image, and he, therefore, defined images as "conditioned sensations." Sheffield translated the "sensations" into "sensory reactions," a phrasing more in keeping with Guthrie's behaviorist orientation.

Leuba (1951) repeated his earlier work, but in this new study, in the training situation, he would simply ask his subjects to imagine two stimuli as paired together, for example, an odor and a pinprick; he would then ask the subjects to imagine the odor and to report if anything else was thought of. The subjects would report that they felt something like a bee sting on the hand. Here, Leuba felt he had evidence that one image could elicit another, and because of the history of the case, one could speak of the conditioning of one image to another.

We will return to the subject of imagery in greater detail later (see chapter 11). For the moment, we note that the Tolmanic position on conditioning as an S→S association is not without some kinds of support.

Thus far, we have considered only the Pavlovian approach, which is complicated enough when we recognize what different theorists thought was happening. While all of the theorists were obliged to postulate that the learning involved some activities or changes in the nervous system, they still differed about what such neural action might represent in behavioral terms.

Hebb's Neural Theory of What Is Learned

At this point, it is necessary to recall the neurological proposals made by Hebb. Hebb (1949) was convinced that learning could be appreciated best

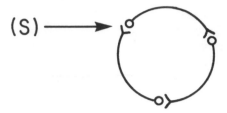

FIGURE 9.1: A cell assembly. Once a neuron is discharged it can fire other neurons and, in turn be refired in a recurrent cycle. (After Hebb 1949.)

by considering it in neural terms. Because our knowledge of the physiology of learning is limited, Hebb was constrained to theorize about how the nervous system might work—in short, he invented a nervous system, the conceptual nervous system, that would support what we know about learning from behavioral data. In describing the conceptual nervous system, Hebb was careful to assume nothing that was in any way contradicted by what was known of the real nervous system. By proposing certain kinds of hypothetical operations, Hebb hoped to help guide interested physiologists to look for appropriate mechanisms and/or functions.

Hebb began by postulating that when a neuron is fired, it will stimulate a discharge in adjacent or otherwise compatible neurons. In any real neural setting, there would, of course, be hundreds, if not thousands, of neurons involved. The neurons activated by the first neurons could then refire the original neurons and maintain a cyclical kind of repetitive firing of each other. Figure 9.1 shows three neurons (or sets of neurons) firing each other in repetitive succession after some stimulus (S).

Such successive refirings Hebb called a "reverberatory circuit" and he named any such chain of reverberative firing a "cell assembly." Such cell assemblies, on repeated activation, could be described as the neural activity related to some particular stimulus. The actual components might change from time to time, adding new neurons and dropping old ones, but the more or less constant components would represent the neural activity corresponding to, say, the consequences of a particular auditory or visual stimulus. With repeated reverberatory firing, the various neurons would develop

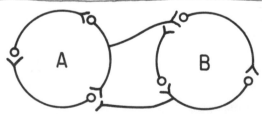

FIGURE 9.2: A phase sequence. One cell assembly comes to activate another assembly. (After Hebb 1949.)

reverberatory circuit - successive firings
chain of reverberative firing - cell assembly

physical or chemical attributes (changes at synapses) that would make them more and more likely to discharge as a circuit. If two such assemblies were fired in contiguity or close succession, then neurons from one assembly might begin to form functional or structural connections with each other, as shown in Figure 9.2.

The cell assembly, A, could come to fire cell assembly, B, and vice versa, depending on where some stimulation might occur first. Such a connection between two or more assemblies would amount to an association or learning. The successive firings of one assembly by another Hebb called a "phase sequence." The phase sequence could involve an indefinite number of cell assemblies, and one phase sequence could become associated in the same fashion with any or many other phase sequences. If we think of a cell assembly or a phase sequence as in some sense representing a thought or an idea, we have here a hypothetical physiological foundation for the association of ideas. Hebb wished particularly to point out that given a particular phase sequence, the firing of one assembly by another could precede the actual external stimulation that would normally fire the second or later assemblies. These later assemblies would then already be active when their normal stimulus occurred. Such prestimulus firing would amount to what is normally called an expectancy. According to Hebb, learning consists of the association of cell assemblies, each of which has to be developed (learned) in its own right by a prior (early learning) stage before it can enter into association with other cell assemblies. Some assemblies have motor components and thereby lead to some motor or overt activity, but learning could still occur in the sense of an association between assemblies, which did not necessarily result in overt responses unless some assembly with a motor component were to become activated. Thus, as in Figure 9.3, Assembly a and Assembly b could enter into an association and keep each other activated. Until Assembly c with a motor component (m) was fired, there might not be any observable behavior.

Whether or not any behavior will be observed, then, depends on whether motor activity is initiated by some discharging assemblies. Learning could very well occur as the association of one assembly with another where these assemblies underlay primarily sensory activity. Hebb is thus not committed to an S→R position, in fact, he (Hebb 1972) regards an S→R

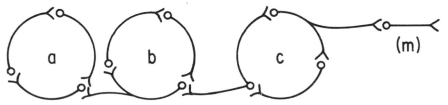

FIGURE 9.3: A phase sequence with a motor outlet. (After Hebb 1949.)

position as too simple to account for the complexity of behavior. Again, because of his neurological leanings, Hebb cannot be identified with those psychologists who are so obviously concerned with external world stimuli and responses. For Hebb, learning is not S⟶S or S⟶R but a matter of association of cell assemblies, an association that he attributes to simultaneous or immediately successive discharge, where the several assemblies keep reactivating each other until some kinds of changes occur in the tissues, which will facilitate mutual discharges in the future.

Summary of S⟶R Answers to the Question: What Is Learned?

We can summarize the positions thus far discussed in a formal display, as shown in Table 9.1.

✳ TABLE 9.1

The Components of Classically Conditioned Associations

Theorist	Associations Formed between:	Symbols
Ⓐ Pavlov	Waves of excitation in two sensory analyzer areas	CS and US
Ⓑ Watson	Stimulus and response	CS and UR
Ⓒ Guthrie	Stimulus complex and specific movement	$s\,{}^{s}_{s}S\,{}^{s}_{s}s \longrightarrow R$
Ⓓ Sheffield	Two sensory responses	$s \longrightarrow$ Image
Ⓔ Tolman	Sign and significate (via a behavior route)	Expectancy or S⟶S
Ⓕ Hebb	One cell assembly and another	A_1 and A_2

Source: Compiled by the author.

Instrumental Associations

We turn now to consider the associative components in so-called instrumental learning or instrumental conditioning. Here again, the basic orientation is based on the S⟶R formula, but two new developments must be examined. In the first place, a reward or reinforcement feature is included so that the formula is expanded to read S⟶R + R ± where the second R is the reinforcer. The reinforcer can be positive or negative, where, in the latter case, the *removal* of the reinforcer increases the probability of a preceding response. The second complication is the relative lack of concern about the stimulus feature, with a corresponding overemphasis on features of the reward or reinforcement, such as amount or intensity, its temporal proximity to the response, its quality or relation to drive or deprivation states, and so forth.

Role of the Stimulus

While Thorndike wrote specifically about S⟶R connections, he was rather general and vague in his treatment of the stimulus side of the bond. The Thorndike puzzle box *was* the stimulus, although whatever parts or aspects of it initiated responses could be designated as the proximal stimuli. Thorndike did not concern himself with *measurement* of stimuli, and the only response feature he recorded as the time it took for a cat to get out. In later word studies, a word would be the stimulus and words or numbers would be responses; here, the measurement would be one of success or failure or frequency of repetition. In such studies, as mentioned earlier, some awkward problems might arise, as the learner might learn or remember what he or she said on some prior trial but might not remember if his or her response was correct, or the subject might not remember his or her response, but remember that it was right or wrong. There would then be a question as to what was being reinforced.

Thorndike was rather unconcerned about the amount or quality of the reinforcer, considering food, for example, as a reward, even though he noted that his cats might not eat it; in the latter case, something that might be called escape or freedom would be the reinforcing state of affairs. In the case of rewarding or punishing students by saying "right" or "wrong" after they guessed responses, the amount or quality of reinforcement might be rather dubious.

Hull (1943) was much more definitive about all three features of the S⟶R ± R formula. The intensity, duration, and qualitative features of the stimulus would be specified where possible, as would response features, such as amount, latency, correctness, direction, and frequency. Rewards were also defined in terms of amount, relation to drive, frequency of occurrence, primary or secondary nature, and so forth. Hull strove for precision of measurement where possible, but in some situations, for example, the lever press box, there would be less specificity about just what the stimulus might be. Hull would also postulate unobserved (and perhaps even unobservable) stimuli, such as kinesthetic stimuli, stimuli from drives, and stimuli from hypothesized fractional goal responses. Such stimuli (while possibly potentially observable) could not be measured and were assumed where convenient.

For Skinner, the question of stimuli was of great theoretical moment. He took the position that in most instances of observable behavior, the actual stimuli are not observable. In the Skinner box, for example, it is unlikely that one can spell out or pinpoint the actual stimulus if there is only one. Rather than pretend to a knowledge of what the stimulus is, Skinner chose to emphasize the response. That could be seen and measured in some ways. In most human situations, attempting to describe the stimuli for all varieties of behavior would be a fruitless and/or impossible task. There are, of course, some kinds of events, for example, doorbells ringing, that can be identified as antedating some responses, but what is the stimulus for saying, "Good morning" to an acquaintanace when we meet someone? Sometimes, we do not say anything at all, we may not even nod; on other occasions we may say, "Hello" or, "How are you?" It would be an enormously complex task to discover the stimuli in such circumstances, and Skinner felt it was not essential, especially as he believed more could be learned by observing a response and its consequences. As we have seen, Skinner did make provision for discriminated stimuli, but he left the original inciters of activity out of his theoretical concerns. He agreed that something had to initiate a response, but he saw no way of discovering what this stimulus might be for an operant, emitted response.

All three of the theorists we are considering can be described as being concerned with *classes* of responses. While Hull was somewhat more specific in his interests, he did not actually concern himself with the details of a response in the manner of Guthrie. A bar press was a bar press, regardless of how the bar actually was moved. In this sense, Thorndike, Hull, and Skinner can be described as interested primarily in effects or outcomes of acts. This may prove to be an error in theoretical judgment.

WHAT IS LEARNED IN VERBAL LEARNING?

Another group of learning psychologists, whose laboratory interests were expressed in working with people, used words as their learning materials. We will deal with this kind of orientation later but note at the moment that their approach to what is learned reflects a belief on a practical level that associations are formed between verbal units or lexical units where both stimuli and responses may be some kinds of verbal formations, such as nonsense syllables, which could be pronounceable or not. Some verbal units, such as three consonants, would have to be spelled, as presumably something like *cxz* cannot be pronounced. Stimuli could be colors, forms, or pictures, but responses would be, normally, some verbal unit that was either spoken or written.

In paired-associate learning, pairs of words would be presented in various ways, with the learner required to provide the second word of a pair when the first was presented. In such a situation, the first word would be, somewhat arbitrarily, called the stimulus and the second, the response. Because the second word could be presented with a request for the first word, the S→R description becomes somewhat awkward. When the words are presented, both are stimuli. If both are called for, both are responses. In any event, the S—►R formula has been the basic orientation in such studies, and while the issue was never a serious problem, a reinforcement orientation also prevailed. It was commonly assumed that showing someone the correct "response" was a form of reward or reinforcement. Even if the learner was not shown the response or was reinforced directly by the experimenter, the learner could be considered to have been reinforced if he or she knew the response. Thus, knowledge of results (KR) came to be, perhaps unadvisably, accepted as a kind of reinforcement for those who believed reinforcement was necessary for learning.

If pressed, the verbal-learning psychologist would admit that words are not really associated with each other in the nervous system, that the words must, each in turn, arouse some neural activity, and it is such neural "representations" that become associated. But such neural surrogates were never of much interest to people working with words or nonsense syllables; they preferred to talk about the overt aspects of both stimuli and responses as the words the learner saw or heard and later spoke. Their interest in rewards can also be described as minimal; the appearance of the correct word in an exposure device was the only reward, if any, that the learner usually received beyond the "thank you" when the learning was completed. The verbal learning psychologists cannot be classifed as either Pavlovian or Thorndikian in any serious or meaningful way. Their answer to the question of what is learned is a rather empirical reference to words having become associated. A subject could be described as having learned to say one word when he or she saw another, or, as having learned a list of words.

We will delay consideration of the verbal-learning theorists until later and summarize the instrumental learning theorists' views on what is learned as shown in Table 9.2.

In Table 9.2, negative reinforcers and/or punishment effects are not included. In the case of Thorndike, his last views did not provide for effects of punishers. In the cases of Hull and Skinner, a negative reinforcer acted like a positive one, except that the necessary operation to make a negative reinforcer functional was to remove it, as in the case of stopping a shock after some desired response was emitted.

WHAT IS LEARNED? A PAUSE TO REFLECT ON THE ANSWERS

Despite the differences among the theorists on detail, there is general agreement that learning involves some association between contiguous events, presumably in the nervous system, whether or not reference is made to neural activity. Descriptions of stimuli and responses occupy different theorists to varying degrees, but they all agree or would admit that learning would occur without a precise knowledge of the stimuli and even though no responses were actually observed, as in the case of conditioning curarized

✳TABLE 9.2

The Components of Instrumentally Conditioned Associations

Theorist	Associations Formed between:	Symbols
Thorndike	Stimulus and response if followed by reinforcer	$S \longrightarrow R$ + Reinforcer
	Also possible:	
	stimulus and reinforcer	$S \longrightarrow$ Reinforcer
	response and reinforcer	$R \longrightarrow$ Reinforcer
	other stimuli and response (associative shifting)	$CS \longrightarrow R$
Hull	Stimulus and response if followed by reinforcer, but association is between neural surrogates ($s \longrightarrow r$) of observable stimulus and response	$S \longrightarrow (s \longrightarrow r) \longrightarrow R$ + reinforcer
	Other stimuli can be associated with response under some conditions	CS $S \longrightarrow (s \longrightarrow r) \longrightarrow R$ + reinforcer
Skinner	Responses increase in probability— no discussion of association	$\longrightarrow R$ + reinforcer
	Responses in discriminated stimulus situation	S^D $\longrightarrow R$ + reinforcer

Source: Compiled by the author.

animals. In such a situation an animal can be stimulated with a tone, CS, for example, and a shock US to the foot. It does not move during the stimulation. Later, after the drug effects are dissipated, the tone could lead to a leg flexion. Learning thus becomes a neural affair, even though no theorist deals directly with the brain in his or her experimental manipulations. The presumed neural activity must be regarded as some kind of change. One who has learned something, anything, is a changed person, and one's behavior will have changed, not necessarily immediately nor directly; the change may be recognized only in terms of how one behaves in later situations.

The learner may or may not be aware that he or she has learned anything. In the case of conditioning, the cessation of alpha waves, or the GSR, the learner does not even know that anything has happened except for recognizing that stimuli are being presented from time to time.

We have come some way from Aristotle and the association of ideas. We now recognize that many kinds of events (stimuli) may become associated in some way with many kinds of other events (responses) whether or not the learner knows what is happening or can talk about the associations involved. This last point brings us to another kind of association that has some aura of mystery because the only evidence for it is circumstantial or, perhaps, inferential; we refer here to mediated association.

MEDIATION AND MEDIATED ASSOCIATIONS

Suppose you arise with no special plans for the day, sit down to breakfast, and glance out your window. You see a dead tree. You have seen it many times before, but this time, the tree suggests a cutting-down operation, sawing up, stacking of logs, and so forth. The imagery of the stacked pile reminds you of the relatively small stack you have left over from last year, and you get up, go to the telephone, and order some fireplace logs. Whatever transpired between the original sight of the dead tree and the phone call, we have a chain of stimuli and responses, where one response generated the stimuli for the next. If we label the tree the first, most important, or obvious stimulus as S and the phone call the obvious, important response as R, then whatever went on in between could be described as of lesser magnitude, and we can label these s and r, so that we could represent the sequence as

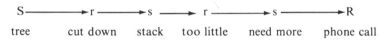

S————▸r————▸s————▸ r————▸s————▸R
tree   cut down   stack   too little   need more   phone call

There are many such occasions when a stimulus sets up a chain of events (either covert or overt) that terminates in some overt action. Any such events that are of no great significance of themselves but which are necessary links in a chain are called mediators. Guthrie, for example, in accounting for Pavlov's trace or delayed conditioning argued that the original stimulus, say, a bell, was not the true conditioning stimulus. It only looked that way. What really happened, said Guthrie, is that the bell initiated some response (unobserved), the response generated movement-produced (kinesthetic) stimuli, which led to some other response (also unobserved), which generated more movement-produced stimuli (m-p-s) which initiated another response, and so on, until at the appropriate time, some m-p-s was followed by salivation, the response that was important for Pavlov.

Shipley (1933), in a now classic experiment, conditioned human subjects to blink to a light when a tap on the cheek was the US. He then paired a shock to the finger with a tap on the cheek so that the former US was now a CS for finger withdrawal. Subsequently, he would ask his subjects to assume the position for the finger withdrawal arrangement, and he flashed the light stimulus. Several of his subjects now withdrew their fingers when the light came on, even though the light had never been paired with shock.

mediators — no great significance of themselves but which are necessary links in a chain

While we cannot be certain that anything of the kind occurred, we can suggest what might have happened. Thus, if the tap on the cheek was regularly followed by a blink, as it normally would, the blink would produce an m-p-s (regardless of how the blink was initiated). The finger withdrawal could then have been conditioned to the m-p-s and not to the tap per se. If this proved to be the case, the light, which was previously conditioned to produce a blink, would also generate the m-p-s. These, in turn, would initiate the finger withdrawal. Thus, for Shipley, the m-p-s following the blink would *mediate* the finger withdrawal to a light. This explanation could apply to many of the sensory preconditioning studies discussed earlier.

Verbal Mediation

In a different frame of reference, the writer (Bugelski and Sharlock 1952) asked college students to learn a list of 13 paired-associate nonsense syllables. The stimulus syllables can be called A and the response syllables B, and so the students learned a set of A-B associations. Two days later, they learned a new set of 13 pairs, where the B syllables of the first day were now the stimulus syllables for the new pairs. The response syllables of the new set can be called C, so that on the second learning, the students learned B-C associations. Two days after this second learning, the students returned to learn another set, made up of the first session's stimuli (A) and the second session's responses (C), so that they had to learn A-C associations. The learning proceeded apace, and the new list was learned relatively quickly. It was argued that what happened was that on the third occasion, the B syllables served as mediators. They had been learned as responses to A and stimuli for C. All that had to happen was for an A syllable to initiate a B response, which then, serving as a stimulus, could initiate C. One interesting sidelight of the study was the finding that the students did not seem to recognize the stimuli or responses as previously known and could be described as unaware of the mediation operation. They realized that the learning was much faster, easier, but did not know why.

Russell and Storms (1955), in a follow-up study, introduced a novel arrangement, which further points up the "unconscious" operation of mediation, as well as its effectiveness. They had previously ascertained the common verbal responses Minnesota students would give to 100 common words. Thus, *bread* would normally elicit *butter*, *grass* would normally elicit *green*, and so on. They now arranged for students to learn a set of paired associates, where the stimulus (A) was a nonsense syllable and the response (B) was one of the common words. They then *assumed* that the response word would arouse one of the common associates, for example, if the nonsense syllable was *rel* and the word was *grass*, they assumed that *grass* would arouse *green*. They further assumed that *green* as a stimulus would arouse some other common response, or at least would have an association with it, like *paint*. After the subjects had ~~larned~~ learned some pairs of nonsense syllables (A) with words (B), they were asked to learn a new set of words to the same syllables; now, they were learning A and D pairs, where the D word was an associate of an associate. To illustrate:

rel—grass—green—paint				*nis—army—navy—ship*			
A	B	C	D	A	B	C	D

or

The subjects learned the A-D associations much more effectively than unstructured pairs, that is, pairs where the D word was not a common associate of the C word. Observe that the subjects did not have any exposure to or trials with B-C· or C-D. Such associations were presumed to be part of the subjects' backgrounds. With such backgrounds, the learning proved to be simple. When pairs were arranged where the background could not operate positively, the learning proved difficult.

In the Russell and Storms study, the B-C and C-D associations were presumed to serve as mediators. The implication of the study is clear: any learner comes to a new learning situation with a background of associations. Some of these may be useful and others harmful. How quickly a new relationship or association will be mastered may depend on such backgrounds. Obviously, different individuals will bring different backgrounds and benefit or lose in any specific context.

Such verbal mediation was thoroughly explored in many experiments where the orders of A-B-C were altered in all possible ways (Horton and Kjeldergaard 1961) and where interference instead of facilitation could be demonstrated by introducing a competitive associations (Jenkins, Foss, and Odum 1965). Weaver and Schultz (1968) demonstrated that mediating words would tend to drop out after they had served their purpose.

The r_g as a Mediator

We can recall the Hullian construct of the r_g in this context of mediation. In any sequential chain, it is possible that r_gs and the stimuli generated by them can become conditioned to a variety of possible responses that we have previously performed in attaining goals. The stimuli from r_gs like any movement-produced stimuli, can help span the time between some original external stimulus (S) and some eventual or delayed response (R).

The old Watsonian S——►R formula has been found simply too simple to account for anything more than immediate reflex reactions. Critics of the S——►R view could point to the frequent instances where no response has occurred to a stimulus until some time has elapsed. They could then populate the organism with a variety of internal "cognitive" operations to account for the eventual R. The mediation concept is the behaviorist answer to such criticism. Behavior can be regarded as a chain of S⟶Rs, with some of the behavior involved going on implicitly, at some barely overt level, for example, the beginnings of a lip pucker, or even at some neural level, which cannot be observed at all with our present procedures for observing neural action. Hebb's cell assemblies are mediators and may well underlie Hull's r_gs or other imperceptible reactions and their m-p-s's. Whatever the actual form of mediating events, we can symbolize them as S⟶r⟶s⟶r⟶s⟶r⟶ s⟶R. We need not reject the S⟶R orientation, but we do need to expand it. We also recognize that the intervening (s⟶r)s are symbols for some kinds of neural activities with or without motor components.

With the addition of mediational activities to the S⟶R formula, we begin to see how some apparently rapid learning achievements might well be based on appropriate prior experiences. Such experiences need not be recalled by the learner as having occurred. The subject need not be aware of them, but he or she had to learn them in the first place. When we add the factor of generalization (which we will need to consider again), we can see how frequently we can respond appropriately to apparently novel stimulus situations.

In the above discussion, we have not emphasized emotions as possible mediators or sources of mediation. These will occupy us in the next section, and we mention them now only to fill out the picture of mediational activity, which has to be considered if we are to answer the question of what is learned.

WHAT IS LEARNED? THE NEED FOR INTEGRATION

Reflecting over the considerations of this chapter thus far, we find many nominees for an answer to the above question. In general, we find that there is no serious doubt that what we *do*, physically, whether it is to salivate or secrete from some gland or move a leg, an arm, a finger, or tongue, is not, in itself, learned. Such responses are made naturally, that is, we are capable of making them, and when the proper neural buttons are pushed, the appropriate glandular, muscular, or neural reactions occur. Such inborn or innate connections are not disputed. When learning is the issue, it is the occurrence of such responses to improper, unnatural, artificial, or substitute stimuli that is observed. Our capacity to observe responses may be somewhat limited if we classify Tolman's significates or Sheffield's imagery as responses. When r_gs are postulated, the capacity to observe is more restricted and largely inferential, as it is with most mediational reactions or operations. We may hesitate to assert that we ever learn or do anything if it is obvious that we are perfectly capable of the action without learning (any adult can lie down and roll over or say "ishkabibble"). Perhaps, it is a matter in such cases of learning to want to or want not to do things. Such was the view of O. Hobart Mowrer, to which we now turn.

10

Attempts at
Integrating
Learning Theories

The schism in the area of learning theory initiated by Pavlov and Thorndike and their followers was securely entrenched by the Hilgard and Marquis (1940) book. American psychologists had the options of following one principle (conditioning) or another (reinforcement). They could straddle the fence and accept the notion that there were two kinds of learning and go about their business, using whatever principle appeared to apply most readily to one kind of learning situation or another. The great majority took (reinforcement) the latter option. As a matter of convenience, they generally assigned acquired autonomic responses to conditioning and any learned striate muscle reactions to the workings of reinforcement.

We have seen that some psychologists (Kimble and Hilgard) despaired of any solution to the problem, because as they saw the matter, all learning situations involved both conditioning and reinforcement, and regardless of the arrangements, the same kinds of factual observations could be made. Other psychologists were not happy with the notion of two kinds of learning and hoped to reduce both to one kind of principle. It was mentioned earlier that Hull (1943) tried to account for Pavlovian conditioning as a "special case of learning by reinforcement." Hull noted that Pavlov generally used food as his US. The food would obviously also serve as a reinforcer or hunger drive reducer, and Pavlov always used hungry dogs, although he made no great point of it. Hull reasoned that any response that occurred in the presence of a drive reducer would enjoy an increment of habit strength, and therefore, even though the Pavlovian US occurred before the response, it would reinforce anything that the dog was doing or continued to do, notably, salivate. The fact that the US was also the instigator of the response only made it a special case. Many years later, Miller (1969), one of Hull's co-workers, would make another attempt to demonstrate what Kimble had believed to be unlikely, namely, to show that autonomic responses could be acquired by reinforcement procedures. We will look at Miller's efforts in connection with modern biofeedback studies later on (chapter 20), noting for the moment that they were not notably successful.

Hull's efforts to establish the priority or exclusiveness of reinforcement as the basic learning principle were not regarded as convincing, and the schism survived. No new efforts were made at deriving a one-principle learning theory until 1960, when O. Hobart Mowrer published two detail-packed volumes, in which he critically reviewed the then current views of learning and announced his own synthesis of the conflicting approaches.

THE MOWRER THEORY—AN INTEGRATION

The foundation for Mowrer's new interpretation of learning data that had been accumulated over the previous 60 years came, interestingly enough, from two standard and routine experimental paradigms, the Skinner lever press situation and the two-compartment avoidance situation. These two very familiar experimental setups provided Mowrer with all the ingredients for a new theory of learning.

As in Mowrer's exposition, we can begin with the avoidance problem. In the Mowrer-Miller box, a rat is placed on a grid floor that has been divided into two sections by some hurdle or a line painted on the back wall. Shock can be administered to the rat's feet in either or both sections. Lights or buzzers can be mounted appropriately above or below the grid bars and serve as conditioned stimuli. In the typical training situation, a buzzer is turned on, and after five seconds, the rat is shocked in whichever half of the box it happens to be. If·the rat gets into the other half, he *escapes* the shock. As trials continue, the rat becomes more and more successful, and by the tenth trial, it is likely to be in the "safe" section before the shock comes on. It has *avoided* the shock. Subsequently, with only occasional lapses, the rat continues to get into the safe area without experiencing shocks and may continue to do so for hundreds of trials.

The behavior just described presents a paradox. Why does the rat continue to avoid shocks it does not, in fact, get? Is conditioning with shock so powerful that it resists easy extinction? Is the rat being rewarded for crossing? If so, what is the reward—a feeling of safety, or of security, or of relief? These are internal states and not objective reinforcers.

Originally, the common explanation for such behavior included the construct of an acquired drive (of fear). When the animal is shocked, it was assumed that it was also frightened. The combined drives of fear and pain energized the animal into the only action available (get out of there). Arrival at the safe place would reduce such drives (primary reinforcement) and thereby reinforce the responses just made.

But this explanation has some problems left over. As long as there is a shock present, the account has plausibility. When the shock is no longer felt, however, why does the animal move when the buzzer sounds? An obvious answer might be: it is afraid. But why does it become fearful? It does not normally fear a buzzer. Pairing of shock and buzzer must be the responsible operation. If the buzzer accompanies both pain and fear, the fear (as a response) could be conditioned to the buzzer and account for the behavior if we make the additional assumption that fear leads to action. But this would be a straight Pavlovian account of the acquisition of fear. Such an account had already been proposed by Watson and Raynor (1920) in their famous study with Little Albert. In this study, an 11-month-old boy was conditioned to fear a rat through the procedure of pairing the presentation of the rat as a CS with a loud noise, created by striking a steel bar with a hammer. At first, the infant did not fear the rat but did shrink in fear to the loud noise. After two pairings, the infant began to shrink from the rat. He had acquired a fear. But this account would not satisfy anyone who insisted that reinforcement of a drive reduction variety was required for learning. We have seen that Hull (1943), in fact, suggested that fear or anxiety could be acquired in a drive reduction framework if the fear were suddenly initiated and suddenly reduced. Hull's explanation, however, was not widely accepted. Skinner and other sponsors of the two kinds of learning orientations were happy enough to assign autonomic, emotional responses to Pavlov. Fear could be learned by stimulus contiguity alone. This solution of the acquisition of fear was perfectly acceptable to Mowrer. It was the next step in the sequence that Mowrer challenged. Why does the rat jump over a barrier every time the buzzer sounds? Assuming that it has been made fearful by the buzzer, does the rat *learn* to jump over the barrier?

The Dual Theory of Learning

In 1947, Mowrer had proposed what he called a "dual theory of learning." In this theory, certain responses, primarily emotional, would be learned by Pavlovian principles, while any instrumental responses made in the context of such emotions would be learned, as Hull proposed, by reinforcement. Thus, the fear, regarded as a drive, would be reduced by the escape response; this response would then be acquired because a drive had been reduced.

By 1960, Mowrer no longer found this theory tenable. There had been too many demonstrations of weaknesses in the reinforcement view, notably, from the Tolman camp, and there was a growing recognition that instrumental responses were already well within the behavioral repertoire of the subjects who were called upon to "learn" them. Recognizing this point, Mowrer boldly asserted that no learning is involved in this operant or any other instrumental behavior. The rat already knows how to jump or run or whatever is required in the box (for example, to press a pedal or pull a chain). We might introduce a slight demurrer, here, in that the rat does get better at it, that is, faster, less erratic, more poised, but Mowrer argued the instrumental response is not learned in itself but, rather, is guided, controlled, directed, or motivated by the fear. In short, the animal, in fear, begins to engage in behavior that reduces the fear and continues doing what leads to fear reduction and stops doing what leads to more fear or fear induction. It is not learning to do anything. It is learning to want to do something it already knows how to do.

So far we have been describing what Mowrer calls "active avoidance learning." We may get a more convincing picture if we turn to passive avoidance learning. Passive avoidance amounts to refraining from doing something you are already quite capable of doing. If a rat is placed on a low box, about an inch from the floor, it can be relied on to step off; this, apparently, is a natural reaction in this situation. If the rat is shocked as soon as it touches the floor, it will get back on the box and refrain from stepping down again, at least for a time. This is passive avoidance. Experimental paradigms of passive avoidance learning are not so common, and we can illustrate more effectively by citing common human situations. Suppose a child blowing out birthday candles places his or her mouth too close to a lighted candle. The child may suffer some slight burn or pain. The child's approach to the next candle will be more tempered, more tentative. The child who gets spanked when reaching for a cookie in the cookie jar will withdraw his or her hand. The child may, on another occasion, start reaching for a cookie but withdraw even before contact is made. Why? Presumably, the jar is still attractive. Mowrer argues that at the moment of extending the arm (on the occasion of the spanking), stimuli in the situation have become conditioned to the pain-fear reaction created by spanking. Among these stimuli would be the spanker, his or her voice, but more importantly (because the spanker need not be there in the future), the movement-produced stimuli from the arm extension, as well as the sight of the cookie jar. Thus, stimuli from the reacher's body or the jar itself can now arouse fear. Fear will guide, control, and direct behavior that reduces the fear. In this instance, more extension will increase fear; less extension or withdrawal will reduce fear. Neither extension nor withdrawal are learned in themselves. Any child can do either.

To add an experimental example analogous to cookie-snatching, we can cite the numerous studies dealing with approach-avoidance behavior originally described by Bugelski and Miller (1938), Brown (1942), and Miller (1944), where rats are first fed at one end of an alley marked by a lighted lamp and then shocked in the same place upon arrival on some later occasion. As soon as they are shocked, they beat a hasty retreat. Now, the hungry rats are placed at the safe end of the alley and can be observed to start moving down toward the formerly feeding end. As they approach the now ambiguous or dubious goal, they slow down, stop, turn around, retreat, and, in general, vascillate at some relatively distant point. Miller has

meaning?

analyzed such behavior as showing conflict. Any approach begins to arouse fear, and retreat reduces the same fear. Assuming the animal does not reach the goal, the behavior can be described as passive avoidance. The term *passive* refers to restraint of action. Again, the animal does not learn to run. That it is perfectly able to do. It only learns *when* to or to *want* to run. Going back to the active avoidance situation, the rats do not learn how to do anything; they merely learn when to, or to want to, jump or run or whatever else they already know how to do.

passive - restraint of action

The Role of Positive Rewards

We turn now to the positive type of learning exemplified in the Skinner box. Calling it *positive* may be presumptuous, because only hungry rats will oblige us with a performance, and hunger is just as negative as the pain related to shocks or spankings. Such externally generated pains are perhaps sharper or more abrupt in onset, but hunger is clearly just as negative a state as fear (and, according to Mowrer, hunger is accompanied by a fear component—fear of getting no food, of never eating again, not getting enough, or not getting the right kind). Now, our rat's assignment is to press the pedal in the box if food is to appear. The rat already is fully qualified to press pedals or do anything else the experimenter may assign. Clearly, the rat does not learn how to press pedals. If it eventually does press the pedal at some above-operant rate, Mowrer argues that it has learned to *want* to press and nothing else. In this situation, an action produces a reinforcer (food). In the escape situation, a negative reinforcer (shock) produces the action. But this difference is only superficial. If we dissect the barpress operation, we discover that food not only reduces hunger, according to Mowrer, but also has a positive "value" or "valence" (in Tolman's language), which results in a positive emotional reaction. Every time a food pellet appears, the animal can *"Hope"* be presumed to feel better, that is, be in some positive emotional state. Mowrer chose to call such a state one of feeling better, or of "hope." The term need not be taken too seriously, but the suggestion that the animal feels better does not seem farfetched. It does not appear unreasonable to assume that the animal feels better in the presence of food than in its absence. But note that while the animal is pressing, it is also experiencing movement-produced stimuli. It also hears the clicking of the food dispenser. Such stimuli, coming as they do just before the arrival of food, can become conditioned stimuli for the positive emotional response that will be generated by the appearance of food. The animal feels better when it presses. It will also feel better as a result of any other stimuli that accompany the food.

What Mowrer has done is to reverse the role of so-called reinforcers. Reinforcers may, in some final analysis, reduce drives, but their appearance on the scene gives them the more immediate function of serving as unconditioned stimuli, stimuli for emotions. Thus, the appearance of food presumably makes the animal feel better at once. But the sound of the click in the Skinner box will also make the animal feel better. The click is not then a reinforcer, secondary or otherwise; it is a conditioned stimulus that evokes emotional reactions. It does not strengthen bonds or habits. Because it has been paired with food, the click becomes a CS for the same response that food, as a US, initiates. The click generates hope. It might be thought of as a secondary goal (Bugelski 1938). A buzzer prior to a shock generates fear. In the latter case, the buzzer is not a secondary negative reinforcer. It is a conditioned stimulus for a negative emotional response.

Learning of Skills

It is in the area of skills that Mowrer's theory is most easily appreciated. We can take as an example a basketball player in possession of the ball. He dribbles the ball down the court until he is in shooting range. The appearance of an opposing guard is a negative reinforcer, inciting fear, and he turns away. He maneuvers in various ways—approaching and avoiding, starting to shoot on numerous occasions and desisting as the hopes and fears within him rise and fall. Eventually, unless the situation is hopeless, he does shoot. But he does not always make an effort when the audience thinks he should. He maneuvers around until he is in a preferred spot, a spot from which he has been successful before, and when he is properly poised, he lets the ball go. Many players have their special kinds of "shots" and places from which they try to "make baskets." Unless they are in a certain place and in a particular body attitude, they will not shoot. The situation becomes even clearer with a foul shot. The player views the basket, bounces the ball, bends his knees, flexes his arms, tenses his lega, all in a rather individualistic style. When his body feels right, that is, when all the feedback stimuli are combining to make him feel just right, good, or "better," he releases the ball. He is not always successful, because feedback stimuli are not pronounced and are rather difficult to appraise. The beginner in foul shooting will experience many failures and slowly come to learn when not to shoot, when he is not set right, when the feedback stimuli that pour in are all conditioned to the negative (fear) response that seeing the ball go elsewhere than into the basket will generate. With an occasional success, certain patterns of stance and movement, including some (unnecessary?) preliminary bounces will begin to generate stimuli conditioned to hope, and the beginner will try his luck, getting closer and closer. With the professional player of 1,000 games, we have almost a machinelike precision. Each foul shot is a duplicate of the last, with a rare miss. In the basketball situation, seeing the ball going through the hoop makes the player feel better. Just as he makes the shot, all the movement-produced stimuli from the muscles involved in the shot are present. Such stimuli will be conditioned to the positive emotional reaction that will follow immediately upon a success. When the ball fails to drop into the basket, the kinesthetic stimuli that were present just before the shot will become conditioned to feeling worse. Learning to shoot baskets, then, becomes a matter of conditioning movement-produced stimuli to the consequences of the shot. On future occasions, the player reacts to such m-p-s signals and either tries to shoot or refrains.

Reinforcers as Unconditioned Stimuli for Emotions

In reviewing his proposals, Mowrer sides with Pavlov and Tolman in their stimulus-stimulus or sensory-sensory conditioning hypotheses. The second stimulus (the reinforcer, or unconditioned stimulus) is naturally associated with an emotional response, according to Mowrer, so that while the learning is a matter of stimulus association, the result or outcome of the learning is an emotional reaction. Here, Mowrer leaves Pavlov, accusing Pavlov of failing to recognize that it was not salivation that had been conditioned. It was hope. The dog, hearing the metronome tick, feels better if that tick has been associated with food. Feeling better is expressed or demonstrated by dogs by a secretion of saliva, among other responses. Pavlov mistook one indicant for the more complex reaction.

That salivation is an indicator of happiness or hope or feeling better may be difficult to accept for those unfamiliar with animals; cats and dogs when stroked or petted will slaver or salivate—in some instances, copiously. Again, the suggestion is by no means farfetched, though lacking experimental support from independent measures of happiness or hope. Probably no one will question the emotional glow humans enjoy when they are praised.

The One Kind of Learning Theory

With the above analysis, Mowrer was ready to assert that there is only one kind of learning, simple stimulus association along the Pavlov-Tolman model. Reinforcers are important, not for strengthening bonds but as generators of emotion. The emotion, in turn, guides, controls, and directs behavior, which ordinarily can only take the form of approach or avoidance.

We can illustrate the Mowrer theory with an example of everyday behavior. Anyone can write his or her name without looking at his or her pen or pencil. The signature will be reasonably close to the usual result. How do we come to have this skill? Originally, when we learned to write, someone had to present us with a model, and we laboriously constructed, first, block letters; then we progressed to cursive writing of individual letters; finally, we wrote words, including our names. As we write, we see the output. This output serves as feedback stimulation, and if it is adequate, we feel better and push on. If we are copying a sample, the circumstances are clearer. We see that our output corresponds more or less with the sample. If we move too far or not far enough in one direction, we feel worse; if we move just right, we feel better. Meanwhile, our fingers, hand, arm, shoulder are pouring in movement-produced stimuli. These become associated with hopes or fears as the visual product dictates. With sufficient practice, the movement-produced stimuli can guide the behavior to a conclusion. We write our names without looking. The same analyses could be applied to touch-typing or any kind of athletic, domestic, or, indeed, any of a broad variety of skills.

The example of writing our names was chosen deliberately to introduce the next stage or phase in Mowrer's theory. In many kinds of learning situations, movement-produced stimuli are not prominent. They need supplementation by other sources. Sometimes, in writing a word, we may misspell it—as we look at the word, it may look funny or wrong, and we may not know why. We write "seize" and pause; is it *ei* or *ie*—the rule says "i before e except after c," but *sieze* does not look right either. How do we ever decide on a correct spelling? Is it *immanent* or *imminent*, *stationary* or *stationery*? In such cases, no m-p-s will help us. Mowrer resorted to a then (1960) unpopular solution. He hypothesized that in much of what we learn, sensory impressions or reactions can also be conditioned. The result, a conditioned sensation, is an image. If a proper or correct image occurs, it can serve the feedback function and serve as a model to be copied, duplicated, assented to, or rejected. The image-model is not only a response, but it can also serve as a stimulus, and as a stimulus, it can be conditioned to feeling better or worse. Thus, we talk and hear ourselves talk; as long as our sounds are acceptable to ourselves, we can continue talking. The heard sounds are compared with imagery models of what we want to say. If our voice is heard through earphones with some short delay, we are unable to talk normally. The feedback and the model do not match, and we do not feel right. We begin to falter, hesitate, and otherwise break down. If we speak at some open-air meeting and the echo of our voices returns at a brief delay, we become confused, disoriented, and ineffective.

By introducing the image and other sensory feedbacks into learning theory, Mowrer was able to extend the emotional conditioning theory to encompass, presumably, the area of verbal learning, of symbolic, and/or cognitive learning and behavior. Where emotion was not prominent or important, perhaps even absent, images could carry the burden. It might be the case that the thousands of college students who have learned lists of nonsense syllables in laboratories did not experience much of an emotional excitement, but some research data might deny that the student "could not care less." In one study, for example, by Finesmith (1960), students were asked to learn nonsense syllables while their PGRs were being recorded. As the trials went by, Finesmith observed that on a trial just before a syllable would be reported correctly, there would be a significant rise in the PGR. The subject, on Trial 3 would report some syllable incorrectly or not at all, but the PGR would show an increase. On Trial 4, that syllable would be reported correctly. Something of an emotional nature was occurring that marked the acquisition. On the trial where there was a successful report the PGR would be normal with that syllable; it would remain so for the rest of the trials. While the learner may not care about nonsense syllables, he or she does care about getting out of the situation, making a good showing, not looking the fool, and so on. Such "fears," though of modest proportion, may underlie much of our intellectual learning efforts.

With the two tools of imagery and emotion, Mowrer proceeded to develop a theory of meaning and made some forays in the the area of psycholinguistics. These do not concern us now, and we can settle for Mowrer's answer to the question of what is learned. This answer is so simple that those who look for complicated answers to complex questions are loath to accept it. Yet, there appears to be no better answer: we learn to feel better or worse in relation to various stimuli. Some of these stimuli are within us—generated by our own activity or created as the consequence of the evoked imagery.

EVALUATION OF MOWRER'S THEORY

In the above presentation, we have not given a complete description of the Mowrer integration of the accumulated data from learning research. Suggesting that hope and fear are all that we learn does not do justice to Mowrer. We should mention that Mowrer considered that other emotions derived from hope and fear were also significant. He suggests that some stimuli can come to serve as warnings or indicators of future events, thus a cue can be provided that an ongoing shock will soon end. Such a cue should prompt the emotion of relief. The occurrence of a light might signal that a Skinner lever press will no longer be followed by food; this should generate the emotion of disappointment. We then have at least four emotional reactions as a basis for some kinds of responses.

Actually, relief is only a decrease in fear, and disappointment, a decrease in hope. The behavior in either case might not be seriously affected, and Mowrer does not spell out exactly what relief or disappointment might generate in behavior.

By way of summary, we see that although Mowrer came to view learning as unitary, a matter of conditioning along Pavlovian-Tolmanic lines, his theory involves multiple dualisms. He tends to think in pairs or dual combinations of factors. Thus, behavior is divided into escape/avoidance or approach; avoidance, itself, is active or passive; conditioning applies only to emotions or images; and drives can be incremental or decremental, that is, increasing or decreasing. Emotions are basically of two kinds—positive and negative (hope and fear). Stimuli are external or internal (m-p-s). Stimuli either occur or are removed. If they are removed, they result in either relief or disappointment, depending upon their nature (negative or positive). Out of these dual combinations, we might recognize a particularly significant one. Mowrer recognized the enormous influence and commonality of negative, noxious, unpleasant, punitive stimuli and their consequence of drive *increment* as of far greater impact on behavior then did earlier psychologists. Skinner and Thorndike were dedicated to a reward psychology of learning. Hull was preoccupied with drive *reduction* as a primary factor in learning. Mowrer showed that drive *induction* with its consequence of fear and the conditioning of fear to both external and proprioceptive stimuli was, perhaps, far more important in determining both learning and behavior.

CYBERNETICS AND FEEDBACK

In presenting the Mowrer view, we emphasized that feedback stimuli whether produced by muscle reactions or from external stimuli (the sounds of our own speech or the products of our activity, for example, a written word's appearance) are the cues or signals that become associated with our emotional reactions. In some (unspecified) way, these emotions now guide and control our behavior.

Mowrer likens our behavior to that of an airplane set on automatic pilot. As a wing dips, sensors in the wing react to this drop in terms of signals (movement-produced stimuli), which feed into a correcting mechanism, and the wing rises. Similarly, a thermostat in a house reacts to signals, indicating some change in status in a way to correct that change. So long as the temperature remains at a predetermined setting, nothing happens to change whatever is going on. Where there is a deviation, the "cybernetics" in the arrangement take over. It is this emphasis on feedback from one's behavior that distinguishes Mowrer's view from the many other theoretical approaches. In positive reinforcement situations, we keep on doing what we are doing because the feedback stimuli are conditioned to feeling better. In passive avoidance, we stop doing what we are doing because the feedback is conditioned to feeling worse. In active avoidance, we do what we must because it reduces the fear.

The Mowrer theory is a modified form of hedonism. It does not so much claim that we seek pleasure as it claims we avoid pain or fear. The neutral state of homeostasis is considered a working kind of objective in living, if not a goal. Thus, because of the nature of drives that are largely unpleasant, painful states, we are more often than not trying to restore a balance or status quo. But the cybernetic explanation is only an analogy to behavior, and it is not a really good one. The thermostat works by calling out a specific response, switch on or switch off, that is, there is a specific motor component involved. Mowrer's theory only allows him to say that an

Feedback on one's behavior

organism will approach or avoid in a general way. The specific responses and their relation to an emotional state are not accounted for. A rat can be made to stand on its hind legs when a light comes on and jump into the air when a buzzer sounds. In both cases, the emotion is fear. What determines the specific response to the different stimuli? The author has trained rats to press a lever when a buzzer sounds and pull a chain when a light comes on. Such a pair of avoidance responses is difficult for the rat to learn, but it can be done. Mowrer's theory does not provide an easy answer. It would have to call for a somewhat different fear of the light from that of the buzzer, and that may be the case, but it is in just this feature that the Mowrer theory falters. It does not explain why some specific response will occur when many are possible. Neither can it account for the initiation of action.

We can clarify this issue by looking at Mowrer's illustration of how a baby learns to talk. Mowrer derived his views on this subject from his efforts at trying to teach talking birds to talk (Mowrer 1950). People who buy myna birds or parrots might have difficulty following Skinner's procedures of waiting for a bird to say something and then rewarding it. Mowrer found he had to do something quite different to get his birds to speak. What Mowrer did was to talk to the birds while feeding them. Mowrer did all the talking. The birds ate and probably heard.

The food can be presumed to have made the birds feel better (hope), and this emotion would then become associated with human voice sounds. Now, and this is the awkward point, because certain birds, the talking ones, do vocalize, apparently spontaneously, they will emit sounds, some of which, by accident, resemble human speech. If the bird now hears its own sounds and these sound like human speech, it will feel better and tend to repeat these. Notice that we have to rely on spontaneity and accident, as well as on an assumption that the words that make the bird feel better will be repeated. The position is not too convincing.

Apply the same speculations to human infants, and we can make the case that babies hear human voices frequently and often when they are being fed or cuddled or otherwise made to feel good. Because babies do babble all sorts of sounds, again spontaneously, they will occasionally say something that sounds like the words used by the parents. These words have been conditioned as signals for feeling better, and now, the child, like the birds, comes to prefer such sounds and emits them more frequently than unfamiliar babbles, which are never heard in conjunction with stimuli for feeling good.

The limited vocabulary of a bird might be accounted for by the Mowrer view, but the vast human speech repertoire appears to present a problem in the selection of which words one comes to use in a variety of situations. Here, again, it is a matter of specific responses, as with the rats, and only a limited emotional repertoire to support the variety of responses.

Mowrer recognized these limitations and his difficulty in spelling out why some specific response would come to be the preferred mode of action.

In the case of a rat jumping a fence, we have no difficulty in accepting the rat's emotional state of fear and its need to get out of there in any way possible. Why does it come to favor jumping when that is the only response that will work? We can see with Mowrer that the rat will try a number of ways because it stays fearful until it does get out of danger, but why does it come to jump as the first response and in good style after a few trials? Mowrer can be credited with explaining why the rat tries one thing after another; it learns what it does *not* want to do. Must we accept that it finally learns to want to jump rather than anything else because nothing else works? This may have to be the answer.

There is another kind of limitation of Mowrer's theory, which he did not consider. As we will bring out later, we do learn a lot of things we do not care to know, do not want to know, or might even be displeased about learning. We learn television jingles and names of products we cannot even use. We learn bad news we did not want to hear and so on, but more importantly, we often learn in an atmosphere of anxiety, even fear, where no fear is reduced and where the things we learn about do not, in themselves, incite fear.

If we were to accept the Mowrer view that all learning is a matter of emotional conditioning, we would have to assume (or the emotion involved is not worth discussing) that a learner would feel better or worse after some learning experience and that in some way, subtle or otherwise, he or she would have felt some kind of emotional response that would mark the learning. That this is clearly not the case is readily demonstrable. Suppose that a student is asked to learn some assignment, for example, to memorize a short stanza of poetry read to him or her once or to give English equivalents in a vocabulary drill of ten items seen once. The student can be asked if he or she knows the material prior to a test. The student's answer will frequently be, or should be, "I don't know." In any number of situations, a learner does not know if he or she knows something prior to the test trial. There appears to be no way of appraising what one knows except on the basis of prior testing. Had there been any emotional impact of any proportion to mark the learning experience, one might be able to assert something about what one knew. The learning process itself is unconscious, as Mowrer himself points out, and emotional processes that occur at some kind of unconscious level are hardly worth the mention. What is an unconscious relief—or hope, for that matter? And how could they have been operating in the learning of the words? We can accept that the learner might have felt fear or uneasiness when trying to learn the words, but this should only make him or her fear the words. At the end of the trial, the learner does not know he or she has learned, and in subsequent recitation, the fear cannot be prompting correct responses unless these are now regarded as escape reactions.

We might end our review of Mowrer's challenging theory by citing experiments where the subjects do become conditioned but do not know that they have been changed in any way. It is possible, for example, to condition a cessation of the alpha rhythm by pairing a tone and a light. The light will normally block the alpha rhythm. After some pairings, the tone will come to block the alpha waves even though it did not do so at first. The subject in such experiments does not know when he or she has an alpha and when he or she has not. The subject's emotional state does not appear to matter in such studies. Similarly, a subject cannot tell when he or she is reacting with a galvanic skin reflex, yet such responses are readily conditioned, even though the subject is unaware of the fact that he or she is reacting. It may be, of course, that the PGR is only an index of some underlying emotion that was conditioned, which would be Mowrer's point, but the emotion in this case does not lead to any motor activity.

What Mowrer may have provided us with is a theory of motivation, really of acquired motivation, where the emotional status of an organism reflects the degree of motivational arousal. The fact that drives like hunger, thirst, sex, or pain lead us to some action should not lead us to overlook the fact that all such drives also have emotional components, and it may be the emotions and not the drives that are the prime movers.

We can view the Mowrer integration as a giant forward step if not a complete and detailed answer to the question of what is learned. We can now add emotional responses and imagery to the catalog of answers provided by previous theorists. The topic of imagery has kept coming up in our search. It has been mentioned by the early associationists, the mnemonists, by Leuba, Sheffield, and Ellson, and now by Mowrer. It may be time to look into the subject of imagery a bit more closely. It will be our next chapter's business.

mediation theory - the assumption that stimuli do not initiate behavior directly but that intervening processes are aroused by stimuli which in turn are responsible for the initiation of behavior

III

The Cognitive Approach

INTRODUCTION

During World War II, many psychologists served with the armed forces in the capacity of psychologists rather than as fighting men. They had come prepared to help solve the problems inherent in a military effort (selection of men for special duties, training, equipment design, treatment of mental casualties, postwar vocational counseling, and so forth). To some extent, some were successful, but the level of satisfaction with the results was not high. There was a general reaction that after all the promises of behaviorism and Neobehaviorism, we did not really know very much about human behavior.

By the 1950s, the dissatisfaction with the state of our knowledge in learning had become widespread. The old S⟶R formula did not appear to be adequate any more. Man appeared to be more complicated than rats and the methods of rat psychologists were not as attractive as they used to be. Human beings appeared to contribute something to a learning situation on their own. They were using "strategies" and following "plans," trying out different procedures or operations of their own; they were using their heads, or so it seemed. Some psychologists, for whom the "mind" had been a dirty word, now began to refer to mental activities, which had long been ruled out of psychology. The concept of meaning began to attract new interest, and words like *attention* began to drop from former behaviorist pens and lips. Some investigators began to look at man's capacities for selective attention—how people could ignore certain obvious stimuli and respond to a restricted field. The cocktail party phenomenon, that is, the ability to follow a conversation with a single person amidst the general uproar of a crowd of speakers, became a laboratory conversation piece, and experiments on human ability to "shadow" a message to one ear when both ears were receiving different messages became commonplace. Interest turned to what people did on their own with stimuli—how they manipulated them, categorized, stored, and retrieved them. A whole new emphasis arose. A person was no longer buffeted about by stimuli—he or she selected, organized, processed, and otherwise handled his or her world. By the early 1960s, the individual had become "cognitive" again, and cognitive psychology had been reborn, not in its old introspective form but in a form where *meaning* became the chief concern. No longer could there be any use for nonsense syllables; only real words were of interest, and because words were somehow the bearers of meaning, psychologists turned to words and verbal behavior. Learning psychologists now studied how lists of words were learned. The cognitive revolution somehow did not get rid of lists, despite the obvious fact that people in their right minds do not go around studying word lists.

In the chapters that follow, we will look into what has been learned by the psychologists who have been studying verbal learning and verbal behavior. Because old methods and tools are sometimes difficult to shed, we will occasionally find need to talk about nonsense materials and older findings with nonsense syllables, which have served to generate some more modern studies. Many principles about forgetting were first discovered with the use of nonsense material, and we will not ignore them, even though cognition might not have been of a high order in such earlier efforts.

11

The Role of Imagery in Learning

HISTORICAL BACKGROUND

No construct in psychology has had a more illustrious, yet checkered. history than that of the image. It has enjoyed the honored attention of philosophers from Aristotle on down to the earlier professional psychologists (Wundt, Stout, Bain, and James) and has always been the layman's reference for past experience or nonpresent objects, but from the time when Watson issued his challenge to introspective psychology in 1913, the image was exiled from psychology, not to return until the 1960s. In the intervening period, the "image builders" of Madison Avenue were the only prominent supporters of what may prove to be a primary principle for the psychology of learning.

The image had been a basic element of consciousness for Wundt (1897) and his student, Titchener (1909), along with sensations and feelings, but the structuralist approach to psychological investigation was never widely accepted by the more functional-minded American psychological world, which was more concerned with activity, behavior, and the control thereof.

Watson (1914) rejected this image on three grounds. First, the alleged demonstrations of the Wurzburg school that some kind of thinking could go on in the absence of images. This argument, of course, does not prove that images are not involved in other kinds of thinking. Second, the failure to demonstrate the existence of imagery types. Again, if there are no specific types of imagers (visualizers, for example), this is not evidence against the general operation of imagery; there is no reason why anyone has to be restricted to any one kind of imagery. Third, "the attempts of even the structuralists to reduce the so-called higher thought processes to groups of obscure organic processes." This is not an argument against imagery at all, merely a recognition that other psychologists had turned away from some kinds of subjective methods. Those weak arguments led Watson to reject "centrally initiated processes," which, for Watson, included imagery, as Watson had defined an image as a "centrally aroused sensation." For Watson, "central arousal" smacked of some "ghost in the machine." Behavior had to be aroused by stimuli in the external world. Watson later embraced the concept of conditioning because it appeared to represent external control over behavior, but had he stopped to think about it, he would have recognized that the unconditioned stimulus function must indeed be centrally aroused by the neural action initiated by the conditioned stimulus.

Watson's position on imagery can be summarized in two points: (1) the belief in imagery is a delusion, a superstition based on a wish for "this wonderful Aladdin's lamp, which, upon demand, illuminates the dark places of the human mind" (1914, p. 18); and (2) images, as described by the structuralists, were things, elements, static components of something called consciousness and not behavior, which was the only real concern of psychologists, whose aim was to predict and control behavior. Imagery became a seven-letter dirty word.

Washburn (1916), a firm believer in images as "centrally aroused sensations," addressed herself to the first point. If belief in imagery is a delusion, she said, it is so widespread a delusion that psychologists should really make a concerted effort to understand such a universal aberration. The second point had greater merit. It is improper to think of images as static elements. Had Watson chosen to consider the possibilities that images could be dynamic *activities*, he might have been more charitable and more correct.

Watson was reacting to the typical description of images that prevailed in his time. We illustrate with the definition from a popular textbook of the 1930s: in referring to the recall of some past experience, Boring, Langfeld, and Weld (1935, p. 344) say, "Conscious memories of this sort, which reproduce a previous perception, in whole or in part, in the absence of the original stimulus to the perception, are known as *images*." Not much progress had been made in the conception of an image by 1969, when Richardson defined imagery as consisting of "all those quasi-sensory or quasi-perceptual experiences of which we are self-consciously aware, and which exist for us in the absence of those stimulus conditions that are known to produce their genuine sensory or perceptual counterparts and which may be expected to have different consequences from their sensory or perceptual counterparts."

Such definitions could have been taken from James (1890), who referred to images as reproductions of earlier sensory experience: "Sensations, once experienced, modify the nervous organism, so that copies of them arise again in the mind after the original outward stimulus is gone." In fact, these definitions go back to Hume (1739), who defined images as "faint copies of sensory and emotional impressions."

Behaviorists who took a dim view of consciousness, the mind, and an even dimmer view of "the mind's eye" or the "inward eye" of Stout (1899) could not be blamed for shunning concepts so defined. They imply something like pictures in the mind that somebody can examine in a leisurely manner. Such implications can only be rejected out of hand by anyone with a minimal familiarity with the nervous system. But the definitions quoted above refer to something that could have been acceptable to Watson if we translate "experience" into a "reaction." Watson could have accepted the fact that some original stimulus is now missing but a reaction nevertheless occurs, and this reaction must then have some other origin, a different stimulus. Such a statement would amount to a description of conditioning.

We have already noted that the interpretation of imagery as a conditioned reaction was proposed by Leuba (1940), Sheffield (1961), and generally endorsed by Mowrer (1960b). There was a very good precedent for the reaction interpretation from results that had been reported from Titchener's own laboratory by Perky (1910) many years before. The Perky experiment is widely cited by supporters of imagery, but the important feature of her study is commonly overlooked. What Perky had done was to ask her subjects to look at a screen and try to project onto the screen their images of such objects as a banana or a tomato. Unknown to the subjects, an assistant began to project a slide of the to-be-imaged object onto the screen, slowly raising the illumination until the picture was above previously determined thresholds of illumination, that is, there *was* a picture on the screen, and the subjects could see it. The subjects did not detect the fact that there was an actual picture and reported that they had indeed "experienced" an image. Perky concluded that people could not tell the difference between an image and a perception, and therefore, images were somehow proven to exist. Wundt had made the same observation and arrived at the same conclusion years before. What Perky had really proved was that stimulation was required for a reaction. Nothing was proved about imagery. No one reported an image until the illumination had been high enough to see the picture.

Segal (1970) repeated the Perky experiment with a more sophisticated procedure. Unknown to Segal's subjects, a slide would be presented at a very low, nearly "subliminal" illumination on a screen built into a hood over the subject's head. The slide would be a colored shape of some sort, for example, a red square or green circle. The subject would then be asked to imagine a cup of tea or an elephant or some other object. In the cases where the subjects reported and described their imagery, Segal was able to demonstrate that the imagery had been basically affected by the colored shapes the subjects did not detect. Some of the features of the real visual stimulus were "assimilated" into the image. Segal accepted the reports of the imagery as representing that something was going on in the subjects when they were asked to image an object, but that something was not a veridical, or true, "copy" of the object—it was distorted by the real world stimuli, situation, and "sets," or attitudes, of the subjects.

IMAGERY AS A RESPONSE

What Segal was saying to us is that images are ongoing internal reactions to unknown stimuli but that they are not veridical, not copies, not templates of some previous unique perceptual experience, certainly not exact duplicates of anything, because they are affected by other stimulation also present. In short, images will be evanescent, unique, and never twice alike. Segal's view is not dissimilar to Neisser's (1967), who described images as "constructed originals."

The notion of imagery as a reaction, as a bit of behavior (unobservable to outsiders), had slowly become somewhat acceptable to some psychologists in the years since Watson's exile of the image. Even so ardent a behaviorist as Skinner (1953) felt obliged to recognize some kinds of "inner" behavior. The behaviorist position had always been a bit awkward about the stimulus consequences of sense organ activity. It was easy to describe a dog's reaction to a bell if the dog turned its head. That was a response. But if the dog's head does not turn, can we deny that it heard the bell? Skinner (1974) came to describe the results or consequences of some sensory stimulation that did not result in some immediate overt behavior in such terms as *seeing behavior.* Presumably, there could be hearing behavior, smelling behavior, and so forth. When faced with the question of imagery, Skinner could now fall back on "inner seeing" or "inner hearing." In short, Skinner could accept someone reporting an image of an apple as representing that the person was viewing an apple internally. Whatever else one may conclude, it is clear that an image had finally attained the status of behavior or a response.

Such a response as inner seeing is itself, at present, hypothetical, unidentifiable, and unmeasurable. We may feel privileged to describe it as an image, but we have not made much progress in understanding what we are talking about. Such images might have some motor components, as Jacobsen (1932) indicated long ago. If there are no motor components, the inner behavior would then, presumably, be largely of the nature of sensory activity and this, in turn, basically a matter of neural action in sensory centers. Data such as Penfield (1975) reported from the reactions of patients undergoing brain surgery to stimulation of sensory cortex would support the inner seeing and inner hearing hypotheses.

When Penfield's patients begin to describe a ball game or a neighbor hanging out clothes, they certainly give the impression that they are watching something happening, as if these earlier experienced events are being repeated before their eyes and ears. Because the patients are quietly lying on operating tables, if what they are describing bears any resemblance to a former experience, they must be "seeing" internally, without the use of their eyes. (See also Penfield and Rasmussen 1950.)

Other patients who have undergone amputations of legs or arms provide another kind of illustration, one that strongly impressed Hebb (1968). Such patients commonly report pains or itches in toes or fingers they no longer possess. Their complaints appear to be as genuine as those of people who have suffered no loss. Certainly, says Hebb, they are as genuine as a dog's yelp when its tail is trod on. They can be considered as sensory experiences that do not have the benefit of the specific stimulation usually associated with such reports.

IMAGERY RESEARCH

The validity of an imagery construct cannot be established by introspective reports, which vary from strong affirmations of detailed imagery to complete denial, as Galton (1883) had demonstrated with his famous breakfast table questionnaire. Galton (1879) had previously reported a great personal wealth of imagery in a word association test, wherein he tried to have two "thoughts" to each of 75 words he had prepared beforehand. He described his thoughts as largely consisting of various kinds of images.

From Galton's time on, that is, from the very beginning of the experimental science of psychology, imagery received sporadic attention, relying on subjective reports of its presence or absence as in the imageless thought controversy (see Boring 1950).

After Watson's polemical dismissal of images, which he called "the ghosts of sensation," discussion of imagery virtually ceased except in the dying Titchenerian camp. We have noted the famous but equivocal study of Perky. We have also seen Leuba's studies some 30 years later and the Ellson demonstration of hallucinatory hearing. The Brogden study (see chapter 9) could have been discussed in imagery terms but instead gave rise to the more respectable sensory-sensory conditioning investigations and the development of interest in mediating processes. A new hiatus followed until 1960, which saw the publication of Mowrer's work with his acceptance, indeed, need, for imagery to provide a base for denotative meaning as well as symbolic learning. In 1960, Miller, Galanter, and Pribram also published their very influential and cognitively oriented *Plans and the Structure of Behavior*. Miller and his colleagues did not hesitate to speak of images and showed how they could function as mnemonic aids. Before long, imagery became the subject to hundreds of experimental investigations, now with a new sophistication based on advances in the design of research that had taken place in the post–World War II period.

EXPERIMENTAL APPROACHES TO IMAGERY

Hull's advocacy of hypothetical constructs had prepared the way for the reacceptance of imagery. One could postulate any process that might be theoretically helpful, as long as it was operationally defined. Thus, images could be hypothetical constructs if a suitable operational definition could be developed. A number of working procedures were quickly invented.

Rating Method

Alan Paivio adopted the procedure of having college students rate words on a seven-point scale on the basis of how easily and quickly a word would arouse an image. Students apparently have no inhibitions about such a task, and Paivio, Yuille, and Madigan (1968) presented such ratings for 925 words. Lists of words with rated imagery values could then be learned by other subjects; there was a common, frequently replicated finding that high-imagery words were learned faster than low-imagery words. In such studies, nothing is said to the subjects about imagery. They are simply told to learn the words. Imagery here is operationally defined as the rating of a word.

Instruction Method

In some studies (see Bugelski 1974, Bugelski, Kidd, and Segmen 1968), subjects are asked to learn a list of words by trying to form images of the objects represented by the words, as in the "one-bun" procedure (see chapter 3, Appendix). Here again, imagery is not defined for the learners. They are merely told to employ it, whatever that may mean to them. Because differences in learning universally favor "imagers," as compared with matched groups of learners without the imagery instruction, the instructional procedure is presumed to support the operational definition of imagery. Admittedly, the procedure does not define an image, but whatever the subjects in such experiments do is supposed to represent something that makes the difference in learning. That something is the hypothetical construct of the image.

Test Method

Ever since Betts (1909) proposed a test for selection of high and low imagers, efforts have been made to screen subjects by some form of preliminary testing (Sheehan 1967). If two sets of subjects can be discovered to differ on some test that is intuitively presumed to indicate some imagery functions, for example, a spatial relations test, the subjects can now be put to some task presumably involving imagery, for example, judging which of a pictured pair of animals is larger or farther away, as Paivio (1975) has done.

In such studies, the high-scoring subjects on the original spatial relations test are presumed to be operating in terms of imagery. In such studies, the imagery test score is really an intervening variable in the Tolman sense and not necessarily a hypothetical construct.

In a variation of the test method, subjects can be shown visual stimuli that affect only the right cerebral hemisphere, which presumably does not normally have a language function. If the material can be responded to appropriately, imagery is alleged to be the functional agency.

Cross-Modal Method and Imagery Task Method

If you are asked to identify visual targets while listening to various sounds, there is no apparent difficulty. If you are asked to image some visual material in the same situation, again there is no problem, but if a visual stimulus is presented, the ability to image will suffer. Segal and Fusella (1970) were able to find such interference by and with imagery in both auditory and visual tasks. The implication of such studies is that when one images a visual or auditory event, the sensory areas of the brain are somehow involved and will not be available for appropriate processing of visual or auditory stimuli and vice versa. Other kinds of tasks, such as imaginal rotation of three dimensional objects (Shepherd and Meltzer 1971), have also been devised to demonstrate the presumed existence of imagery or icons.

While the various methods mentioned above have all produced data that demonstrate differences when something called imagery is presumed to be operating, they have not dealt with the nature of imagery itself; they have not addressed themselves to how the hypothetical construct is supposed to operate. Because of the potential value of the image in a number of learning contexts, it may pay to speculate as we do in the following section.

THE IMAGE AS A HYPOTHETICAL CONSTRUCT

For the present purpose, we can suggest that an image is an internal response which is largely if not primarily sensory in nature, that is, involving sensory cerebral areas or activities, as Segal and Fusella have suggested. The stimuli for such imagery activity cannot be the original, real, or external stimuli normally associated with such sensory functions. Thus, if we look at an apple, there is a good and sufficient basis for some kind of sensory neural activity. If we are asked to imagine an apple, or if something other than an apple reminds us of an apple, we are constrained to assume that some sensory neural activity similar to that following seeing an apple must occur. If we are looking at a real apple in good light we can report that we see an apple. This would be accepted by everyone as a proper remark, even though no one yet knows what *seeing* is. If we are told to imagine an apple, then the response, assuming there has to be some kind of response in the hearer of the instruction, would be an image, which we will label n, a neural activity, which would not be the same as the reaction in actually viewing an apple—it would be, as Segal (1971) has reminded us, a response modified by various possible sets, the verbal instruction, or other stimuli present (perceived or unperceived in the sense of one's being able or unable to report them).

THE IMAGE AS AN ASSOCIATED RESPONSE

The basic point, however, is that the image, n, is aroused not by an existent, present stimulus—that would arouise its own n. In short, an image is always aroused by some second or indirect stimulation. Seeing an apple is a direct external stimulus-related response; imaging an apple is a response to some other stimulus, perhaps the word *apple* or *tree* or *pie* or *sauce*, or it may be the product of some other n that was generated by any of an indefinite number of possible stimuli of internal or external origin.

For formal purposes, we can represent the definition of imagery, assuming the appropriate background in the imager, as

$$S_1 \longrightarrow n_1 \qquad \text{(real apple} \longrightarrow \text{seeing apple)}$$
$$S_2 \longrightarrow n_2 \qquad \text{(word "apple"} \longrightarrow \text{hearing "apple")}$$

With appropriate circumstances or conditions, S_2 can become associated with S_1, or more properly, n_2 can become associated with n_1, so that on a subsequent occasion, the arousal of n_2 might generate n_1 with some degree of efficiency. It might help to label the indirectly aroused form of n_1 as n_1'. The probability of n_1' occurring with anything like the clarity, efficiency, completeness, and so forth which follows an S_1 would be remote and certainly unlikely. We can represent the result of the pairing as

$$S_2 \longrightarrow n_2' \nearrow^{n_1'}$$

The above formal representation should be recognizable as the familiar conditioning paradigm. Thus far, the account is parallel to that of Leuba's (1940) description of images as conditioned sensations without the subjective reference that might have deterred some supporters. Note that the commonly reported fuzziness, vagueness, or lack of clarity of imagery is accounted for by this proposal. The n_1 is not generated in its usual manner; it does not have the benefit of the full input (S_1); it can only be partially generated by n_2. Note also that the frequent criticism of conditioning to the effect that the CR does not resemble the UR is also accounted for. It would be almost improper to respond with the full and complete UR given only the input from the CS→n_2.

But an even more serious implication must be considered. Pavlovian conditioning is itself a form of imagery association, where one is concerned over some externally observable response, for example, a dog's salivation. Thus, in Pavlov's situation we have

	After
Before Conditioning	*Conditioning*
The food US or S_1→n_1 tasting food→R_1 (salivation)	n_1'→R_1'
The bell or CS or S_2→n_2 (hearing bell)→ ?	S_2→n_2

What happens is that the conditioned stimulus (S_2) comes to arouse the response (n_1') indirectly; the dog still hears the bell (there has been no *replacement* of stimuli), but hearing the bell arouses imagery of the appearance, smell, and taste of food. The imagery will not be the precise equivalent of the original response (n_1) to food, but it may be sufficiently so to arouse the motor (glandular) response of salivation to some degree, again, not the precise equivalent of the response to n_1. Note that R_1' can only occur if there is some normal, natural, unconditioned response to n_1. Note also that it does not have to occur even though n_1' is activated. Whether or not the R_1' occurs might depend on other conditions, for example hunger, illness, and so forth. The imagery of food can very well occur without any salivation whatever. The household cat, hearing a can opener, usually, but not always, comes to the kitchen. Sometimes, it only opens one eye and goes back to sleep. Other conditions may be necesssary before overt action is released.

The R_1 deserves additional scrutiny. Pavlov's dog did not only salivate in response to food; at a minimum, it chewed and swallowed. It also, according to Mowrer, felt better; its emotional state would be more positive than before the food was presented. Pavlov chose to record only the salivary response, but subsequent researchers also looked for, measured, and recorded some observable consequence of stimulation. Suppose there is no immediate observable response when two stimuli are paired? Has there been no learning? Recall Brogden's study where tones and lights were paired. Brogden chose to call this "preconditioning" because there was no overt response. Actually, learning was taking place during these pairings, just as in the later pairings of light and shock. There was nothing *pre* about it except in a scheduling sense. Brogden had demonstrated simple sensory conditioning, or perhaps better, the association of neural consequences of sensory stimulations. To state the issue boldly, then, it can be said that Pavlovian conditioning, involving observable responses, is only a special case of the more primary law of association of sensory activity and imagery. Whether an overt response occurs or not is not necessarily important to a theory of learning.

To answer the question raised in the last chapter, then, we assert that what is learned is neither S-S, nor S-R, but n-n', where the n's amount to imagery, reportable or not. From the above account, any time associable components are activated in contiguity, images will be involved, and the consequence may be that n_2 will become capable of instigating n'_1 on a subsequent occasion. It is also possible, under appropriate procedures, that n'_2 can be instigated by n_1. The learner will have learned to the extent to which an image has been associated with some indirect stimulus agency.

VOLUNTARY BEHAVIOR—IDEOMOTOR ACTION

In previous chapters, we found occasion to suggest, along with Mowrer (1960b), that the concept of voluntary behavior, or its learning prototype, instrumental or operant behavior, was not a realistic construct. According to Mowrer, we do not learn how to do anything we cannot already do. There is no such thing as instrumental or operant learning. We only learn, perhaps, to want to do something or not want to do it. Put otherwise, perhaps we only learn *when* to do something. Mowrer could not explain, however, why wanting to do something would result in doing it. The initiation of behavior was left unaccounted for. At best, Mowrer could only account for not doing something in some situations.

With the tool of the image at our disposal, it might be possible to strengthen the Mowrer argument somewhat. Aristotle originally suggested that we do things when the idea of doing them occurs, that is, that the idea prompts or leads to the action. In our terms, we could translate this to read that actions follow images, images of the action. James (1890) stated this proposition in his description of ideomotor action.

James suggested that if you think of bending a finger, the finger will, in fact, begin to bend. You should, according to James, feel a tingle in your finger if you should think of bending it. If you do not feel the tingle, James could argue that you are not really thinking of bending it. If you do think of bending the finger and your finger does not bend, it is because you are also thinking of not bending it. That should result in a double tingle if you have two such thoughts at the same time or in rapid succession. The argument is not very persuasive to those who do not feel a tingle. James had to be satisfied with a simple statement of his conviction: "The bare idea of a movement's sensible effects produces sufficient impetus for a movement to follow."

That is about as far as James got and about as far as he could go in 1890. He had not yet heard of Pavlov. It will be recalled that Pavlov was the first to describe the antedating of conditioned responses. We have seen that Hull (1943) capitalized on the antedating feature in developing his construct of the r_g. In 1970, Greenwald considered the possibility that an r_g could be thought of in imagery terms as one feature of a more complex reaction pattern. Speculating along such lines, Greenwald then tried to integrate the thinking of James, Pavlov, and Hull by proposing that an account of voluntary behavior could be developed as follows.

When any stimulus is followed by a response, there will be some aftereffect, a response-produced stimulus (we can recall Guthrie's emphasis on movement-produced stimuli). We have, then, $S \rightarrow R \rightarrow s$ (the s represents a kinesthetic stimulus resulting from muscular contraction, such as bending the finger). Such an s can, Greenwald assumes, begin to antedate the responses that generate them upon frequent repetition. Something like this would have to happen if a response comes to antedate some stimulus; stimuli related to this response would also have to show this antedating feature. If the s is exercised sufficiently often, then, it will come to antedate the response itself, thus:

$$S \rightarrow R \rightarrow s$$

Time . . . . s . . . .

so that s will precede its own original generator. At this point, S and s are in a temporal relationship favorable to conditioning, and s can be thought of as a conditioned stimulus for the R that originally followed only when S was present. We now have the Jamesian situation. Hebb would have no difficulty here. He would consider the s as the anticipatory firing of a cell assembly related to the response, whether this be perceptual or motor. If we identify the s with an image (n'), we have the case where the thought (image) leads to an action related to the thought. To generalize beyond finger bending, s or really any n', can, with appropriate motor outlets, generate activity, or almost any thought can lead to a response, overt or otherwise. It could also lead to another thought.

To account for classical Pavlovian conditioning, we can review our earlier diagram. Thus:

Note that the conditioned response follows an indirectly generated neural activity (n'_1) and that this response will not be the full-fledged reaction that would occur to n'_1. Note also how this account would handle any, if only modest, personal control of some bodily function, for example, blood pressure. If some exciting event (S_1) results in a rise in blood pressure, then, if we can in any way make ourselves *think* of the event, that is, have an image of it (n'_1), we might increase our blood pressure. This would be an indirect way of controlling bodily functions. This procedure is one suggested by Miller (1972) as possibly effective for various kinds of organ control. It is, however, basically Pavlovian, because the thinking of the event (n') would be the result of some other form of stimulation. Something has to generate the image. Images are not voluntary, a conclusion noted long ago by Herbart in his textbook of psychology published in 1816 (see Herbart 1891).

IMAGERY AND INSTRUMENTAL BEHAVIOR

Coming now to any instance of instrumental learning, we can assume that any learning involved is strictly associational in nature and that only images (n'_1) are associated with certain stimuli (n_2) and that in the instrumental situation, the n'_1 has to be of the type that has a motor outlet.

To use the classical Skinner box situation as our example, a rat presses the bar because it has an image (probably numerous images are involved) of pressing (Greenwald's s), and this image is associated with the activity of pressing, and so, the animal presses quite automatically. Put loosely, we say the rat thought of pressing, and it pressed. It remains to show how the thought of pressing would occur to the rat in the presence of the bar. This should not prove difficult.

We begin by noting the fact that there is little to do in a Skinner box and that as the rat wanders about, it will in due course stumble onto the bar, and its weight will depress the bar. The immediate aftereffects of pressing will be of two sorts, one in the rat, the cutaneous stimulation from the bar and the kinesthetic stimulation from the movement, and the other in the box, the sound of the food release mechanism and, later, the food itself. A number of associations will now be capable of being formed.

The situation is not as simple as Skinner depicted in his (?)$\longrightarrow$R$\longrightarrow$ Reinforcement account, where some unknown stimulus results in the emission of the pressing response, which is immediately followed by a reward. The picture is actually much more complicated and calls for a depiction more like the following:

$$S_v \cdots\cdots\cdots\cdots\cdots\cdots\cdots\cdots\cdots\cdots\cdots\cdots\cdots$$

$$\longrightarrow S_f \longrightarrow R \text{ eating}$$
$$\longrightarrow S_a \cdots\cdots$$
$$S(?)\xrightarrow{\hspace{4cm}} R_{\overline{\text{press}}} \rightarrow S_k \cdots\cdots$$
$$S_c \cdots\cdots\cdots$$

where S_v is the visual stimulus, S_f is the food stimulus, S_a is the auditory stimulus, S_k is the kinesthetic stimulus, S_c is the cutaneous stimulus, and S(?) is the unknown stimulus in all cases.

Using this model, we can accept Skinner's view that the original stimulus is unknown. Whatever this stimulus may be, however, it occurs in the presence of the visual stimulus of the bar (S_v), which can persist for some time up to and beyond the time of pressing. Just before the bar is pressed sufficiently for it to activate the food release, cutaneous stimuli (S_c) must also be present. Such stimuli, the S_v and S_c, can qualify as meeting Skinner's definition of S^D or discriminated stimuli, as they will be present when the response is reinforced. As soon as the bar is pressed, the kinesthetic stimuli (s_k) will occur, followed almost immediately by the auditory stimulus of the food release mechanism, the sound of the dropping food (S_a), and the food stimulus itself (S_f), which should initiate the eating response.

With all the stimuli simultaneously present, the conditions for multiple associations of stimuli exist. All pre- and postpressing stimuli can be associated with each other, with each generating the image (n') of the others. Assuming with Greenwald (1970) that the s_k or n_k' will begin to antedate and that n_k' would initiate bar pressing, then if s_k is associated (conditioned to) S_v, S_f, S_a, or S_c and their corresponding ns, then any of these ns could arouse n_k', which would initiate the response. In the practical situation, the association of S_v with s_k would mean that seeing the bar would arouse s_k as an image (n_k'), and the rat would press. If the rat heard the click of the mechanism, this would also arouse n_k', but because the click is more likely to be more strongly associated with n_f' because forward conditioning is presumably stronger, the rat would be more likely to look into the food dish. In the author's (Bugelski 1938) study, rats were working in adjacent boxes, where the pressing of one rat would result in clicks being heard by other rats, which would promptly investigate their own food dishes. The clicks aroused images of food (n_f'), which would lead to behavior associated with food.

Presumably, any voluntary, operant, or instrumental response would be generated in the same way. The presence or absence of rewards would be irrelevant to the response itself; the food in the Skinner box instance would only serve as a stimulus for generating food imagery, which could be associated, in turn, with the box, the bar, the imagery of pressing, of hearing food drop, and so forth. The interpretation suggested here parallels that of Mowrer, who considered food not as a reinforcer for learning or strengthening bonds but as a stimulus for a hope response. In the present account, food is a stimulus that initiates eating in hungry organisms. This may well be accompanied by hope or positive emotion. It is the imagery of food, however, that is important in prompting the appropriate stimulation or imagery that leads to action.

In summary, it is claimed that what we learn is to respond in imagery (n') reactions to a variety of stimuli; some of this imagery can have motor outlets or can be associated, in turn, with images that are supplied with motor outlets. Given suitable associative conditions, we learn to do what we image. James was about 90 years ahead of his time; Aristotle, about 2,400.

IMAGERY AND MEANING

The account of the nature of imagery just presented differs radically from the philosopher's pictures before the mind's eye. It makes no reference to subjective experience, which, for the average person, is the heart and soul of imagery. It is time to consider this aspect of imagery, which we have left buried in the nervous system, with no way to get out unless there is some overt associated response. Fortunately, for imagery and for most people, there is a great range of such responses, namely, spoken or written words, which can describe some of the internal reactions we have conjured up to represent imagery. We use the word *describe* loosely, as there is no way to prove that what people are saying when they describe their imagery has any relevance to what is actually going on, however sincere they may be.

We must also hasten to note that the same kind of imagery reactions can go on in rats, cats, and dogs; in babies who have not learned to talk; and in mutes, aphasics, and people with split brains with activity in the right hemispheres, which they cannot talk about. When a cat comes to the kitchen when it hears the sounds of a can opener, does anyone doubt it has had some internal activity related to eating? Does anyone doubt that it had an image of food? When someone says, "What was that? Did you hear a noise?" and you did not hear one, do you doubt that he thought he or she heard a noise? You are more likely to say, "You must have thought you heard something" if investigation reveals no noise source. The individual did think he or she heard something. He or she had an auditory image. Something aroused the same (or similar) reaction that a real noise would. The present point is that the person need not have raised the question.

In our conversations, we use words, and if we are asked what we are doing, we may say that we are describing our thoughts. But if our thoughts are images, then we must be describing our imagery. We will not stop now to argue about Watson's notion that thoughts are words or that thinking is talking to yourself. That would make people who cannot talk for any reason unable to think. It took some heroic experiments with people paralyzed with curare and surviving with the help of iron lungs and unable to talk to convince some strong Watson supporters, but we can probably conclude now that there is merit to the notion that words describe thoughts or other internal reactions unless we use them deceitfully.

But how can you describe imagery? The answer is that you probably cannot do so very well and certainly not all of it, as new imagery is aroused with the words you pronounce. Words are probably the most frequent S_2s for imagery that we have. We have to accept the conclusion that most imagery is unconscious or at least indescribable. When we are able to say something, it will probably be no more effective than our efforts at describing a headache. We are never able to get the appropriate amount of sympathy for our toothaches or other (to us) excruciating pains because we cannot generate the corresponding imagery in our audiences very effectively. They tell us to take aspirin.

Skinner (1953) struggled with this problem of trying to describe internal reactions or conditions. He recognized the enormous difficulties and the limited success. Suppose you try to describe a toothache to someone who never had one. In such a case, where there is no suitable imagery in the listener, there is no communication. It is like describing a rainbow to a blind man. Skinner saw that language use depended upon social agreement and that objects outside of us could be described in mutually agreeable terms for speaker and listener. Internal reactions could not be socially observed, and suitable language could not develop. We can never tell anyone how much "it hurts."

Even when two people are asked to describe a present object, for example, a table, they will not use exactly the same words or the same sequence of words. In most cases, a description of something being looked at directly will not be complete; details will be missing, and personal values (emotions) will come into "the picture." When describing images, some people will claim, "I can see him clearly, just as if he were standing there." What this really means is hard to say, as the description would not be precise even if *he* were standing there.

Because of the widespread conviction that at least some people can describe their imagery to some degree, we can probably settle for the conclusion that they are describing something like what goes on when they are looking at, or listening to, some physically present stimulus in the absence of that stimulus. We do not deny the detailed reports of dreams, and we need not question the reality of the imagery that is described. The fact that the responses are not visible to other observers does not, per se, invalidate them. As Paivio (1971) pointed out, the evidence for any "implicit" verbal activity is just as tenuous; if we can accept a verbal report of some internal verbal activity, we need not shrink from accepting reports of imagery. We can question the completeness of the reports, references to vividness, and so forth without denying the probability of some partially describable internal reaction. To deny the reality of imagery is to deny the validity of anyone's report of what he or she saw when we were not present.

Mowrer (1960b) also worried over the problem of communication where the listener did not have appropriate prior experiences that could provide appropriate imagery. When we are trying to communicate, we cannot provide the meanings involved—we can only arouse them in people who are able to respond appropriately. A foreign language–speaking person cannot make himself or herself clear, no matter how slowly and loudly he or she speaks. In his discussion, Mowrer used a now famous sentence: "Tom is a thief." Suppose you hear this sentence and are expected to understand it, to "get" the meaning. According to Mowrer, the sentence is a meaningless collection of noises unless you react in certain specific ways. To the word *Tom* you must react with some image. If you know a Tom very well, it will help. If you do not, the imagery will be poor and inadequate; perhaps it will be some vague masculine figure or perhaps a young lad. Similarly, the word *thief* must arouse imagery of another kind, perhaps of some unsavory-looking character. But both Tom and thief must, for Mowrer, arouse some positive or negative emotion, perhaps both—positive for Tom and negative for thieves. The combination of reactions, that is, imagery and emotion, becomes the meaning of the sentence. The imagery provides the sensory-perceptual aspects, the denotative part of the meaning; the emotion provides the connotative part.

SEMANTIC DIFFERENTIAL

Mowrer thus made meaning dependent upon imagery aroused in a listener or reader. Without imagery, nothing would mean anything. Mowrer made his case by relying heavily on Osgood's (1957) work on the semantic differential, a word-rating technique wherein raters mark their reactions to names of objects, people, concepts, or any word, really, on a seven-point scale, where the ends of the scale are described by adjectives that are polar opposites, such as good-bad, hot-cold, pleasant-unpleasant, hard-soft, slow-fast, and so forth. Osgood used 50 pairs. A subject rating some object or person, say, would produce a profile of markings, which Osgood took to represent the meaning of the object or person to that subject. No two people would be likely to mark all 50 scales alike, suggesting that no two people ever have the same meaning for anything. By subjecting many ratings to factor analysis, Osgood concluded that three factors accounted for most of the meaning anyone had for anything. The factors were called evaluative, activity, and potency with the evaluative factor accounting for most of the meaning of anything. The evaluative factor derives from adjectives that relate to pleasant and unpleasant reactions and can be considered to reflect emotion. For Osgood and Mowrer, then, the bulk of meaning is carried by emotion—how you feel about something. But Mowrer did add the imagery factor to carry the descriptive, denotative aspects of the meaning of things— the features that distinguish apples from pears or this apple from that apple.

PAIVIO'S VIEW OF MEANING

In Paivio's (1971) approach, again considerable weight is given to imagery as the foundation of meaning. Words arouse meanings, whether in isolation or in sentences. One can describe a given event or scene in many words and in different languages and still refer to the same stimulus situation. The speaker describes his or her imagery, and the listener necessarily reacts with his or her own. The two may not correspond, and as with Mowrer, there need not be any exact communication.

What someone else thinks of when you say anything and how he or she will describe what you said to someone else may have little correspondence with each other. When the writer asked students to learn a list of words, which included *pen*, *baby*, *sofa*, and *river*, some students responded with *pencil, child, couch,* and *lake.* Such errors are common enough to suggest that the words were stimuli for reactions that differed from one student to another. In a variation of the Galton (1879) experiment, students were asked to describe their thoughts to 30 separate words (see Bugelski 1970). Of 75 students, no two had the same reported reactions to any of the words. It should be noted that Paivio prefers to think that words themselves can represent a separate set of reactions in a verbal system. They can, of course, be learned as such, and frequently long lists or long sentences can be reproduced on a strictly verbal level. When it comes to a meaningful reaction, however, imagery is required, and different words can be used in efforts to describe such imagery.

NOBLE AND MEANINGFULNESS

Noble (1952) proposed that an approach to meaning could be developed by noting the number and kinds of associations which occurred to people when they were asked to report any or all of the things they thought of when a given word or nonsense word was provided. Noble recorded all of the responses given to a word like *uncle* or *kitchen* in one minute. We will describe his procedure later (chapter 14) in another context. He considered the number of such associates to a word as representing its meaningfulness, signified by m. It turned out in numerous studies that words with high-m values were learned more easily than wrods with low-m values. The notion that m was in some way related to the meaning of words was at first quite well received. What it amounted to was that a word meant what it made you think of, that is, what associations it aroused, and one word might mean different things at different times. The little m construct did not flourish, however, and Paivio (1971) was able to show that when words were rated for imagery and meaningfulness, better predictions could be made about learning outcomes by relying on imagery instead of meaningfulness ratings. If words of equal m value but varying in imagery were used in a learning session, learning would fluctuate with imagery value, but if imagery were held constant and m varied, the learning would not fluctuate, all words being learned more or less equally. Such a demonstration does demonstrate that imagery ratings are superior to meaningfulness ratings in learning word lists but does not invalidate the significance of m, which still suggests that we think of many different things at different times, with each separate thought being, perhaps, another image.

PROPOSITIONAL MODELS

Some theorists, for example, Anderson and Bower (1973) and Pylyshyn (1973), while not denying the importance of imagery, preferred to work on the assumption that meanings are better considered as some kind of abstract

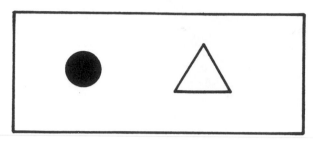

FIGURE 11.1: When you look at this display do you acquire information or are you undergoing a change which can serve to provide an image later?

representations of events or situations and that these can be described in the form of propositional statements. If we have someone look at Figure 11.1, even briefly, the subject is presumed to "store" a series of propositions about the stimulus in what we can loosely call his or her memory. Later, the person can answer a great many questions about this figure by "retrieving" the necessary information from the store. Such models are placed in opposition to image theory, which would simply imply that seeing the figure aroused some image (n'). When questions (S_2) are now asked about the figure, the image (n') would be activated and provide the basis for responses. Thus, using either theory, one could expect the subject to respond to the questions: What did you see? Which item was black? Which was on the left? Which was bigger? Presumably, a great many questions could be asked about the sizes, distances, shapes, colors, background size and features, and so forth. The propositional storage theory would require that an equivalent number of propositions was stored in a brief glance. The imagery theory requires only that something like the same reaction occur to the questions as occurred to the original stimulus.

The propositional model has been sharply criticized by Kosslyn and Pomerantz (1977). Anderson (1978) reacted to the criticism exhaustively and concluded that the image interpretation could not be ruled out on merely logical grounds. According to Anderson, "barring decisive physiological data, it will not be possible to establish whether an internal representation is pictorial or propositional." In the present treatment, images have not been described at any time as pictorial representations. There are no pictures in anyone's head. Images have been described as indirect activations of the neural operations, normally initiated by other stimuli. The fact that people commonly report their imagery in pictorial terms is beside the point. When people report hearing the voice of God or of various other gods or other nonpresent sources, we are inclined to regard them with pity, but we should appreciate that something is going on in their heads that is similar to ordinary auditory activity. This activity differs from normal behavior in that it was not initiated by external, audible sounds. We shall not pursue the issue here, as models are not really to be invalidated by criticism or disagreement.

They survive or die by their productivity and prediction value. We shall try to demonstrate the productivity of the imagery view in later chapters, where propositional explanations are not especially apropos.

IMAGERY AND CONCEPTS

Although the term *imagery* had been exiled from behavioristic psychology, the term *concept* retained respectability even though it possessed no greater objectivity. All through the behavioristic period, psychologists experimented with "concepts" with no eyebrows being raised. In an early experiment, Hull (1920) introduced such terms as *generalization* and *abstraction* to account for the learning of concepts. Hull used a paired-associate procedure, in which subjects learned to label or name Chinese ideographs. Each of a series of ideographs contained a common element or feature, and the subjects were required to somehow discover this common feature and ignore the obscuring aspects of the individual instances. When the subjects were successful, it was concluded that they had abstracted the unique element and were able to generalize to other instances. They now "had" the concepts.

In the same way, a label or name, such as *animal*, is alleged to be an abstraction from all possible instances of a variety of items, all of which possess some common feature or features; in this instance, the features might be life, motion, or reproduction (each of which is itself an abstraction). In the first chapter, we warned against reifying words. It is doubtful that anyone thinks of life, motility, or reproduction when he or she uses the term *animal* in ordinary discourse. In the study referred to earlier, when students were asked to report what they thought of when the word *animal* was mentioned, most of them replied that they thought of a dog, usually their own dog, that is, a specific, particular, animal. When they were asked to report what they thought of when words such as *justice*, *democracy*, or *communism* were presented, they again described highly specific, concrete imagery. Democracy was a polling booth or a particular president; communism was Red Square in Moscow, with troops parading before a line of commissars; justice was a courtroom, and so forth. Bishop Berkeley had stated the case long ago, namely, that we think in particular images related to our own histories.

ABSTRACT AND CONCRETE

In grammar school, we learned that there are abstract nouns and concrete nouns. The concrete ones are supposed to refer to ordinary observable objects or people; abstract nouns are supposed to refer to something else, perhaps not observable directly. Nothing is said about verbs or adjectives and adverbs, all of which are abstract in the sense of being unobservable. One cannot think of swimming, jumping, or walking without a swimmer, jumper, or walker. Nor can one think of beautiful, ugly, blue, fast, or slow without some concrete object present in imagery.

Verbs, adverbs, and adjectives are abstract in another sense. They can be applied to a great variety of objects; thus, fish swim, as do ducks, tigers, and people. And flowers, pictures, and roast turkeys all can be beautiful. Some parts of speech, then, are detachable from, or attachable to, objects, and in this sense, they are abstract. The same applies to nouns in that they can be attached to a variety of specific instances, which may not have much direct resemblance.

Most of Paivio's (1971) research suggests that abstract words are more difficult to learn or remember when used in lists—the implication being that they are less likely to spark imagery, which more concrete words are supposed to excite readily. Actually, Paivio (1971) himself found that abstract "peg words" (see chapter 3, Appendix), such as *fun* instead of *bun* or *true* instead of *shoe*, can be used very effectively as mnemonic devices, and the author has found that subjects can learn noun-adjective or noun-verb combinations just as easily, if not more so, than noun-noun associates. It is apparently easy for subjects to image "white-horse" or "strong table" or "boys shouting." It seems that any association of two nouns, for example, "cow-mountain," automatically invites a verb when subjects are asked to use imagery in learning the pair. They readily provide a verb to connect the two nouns in some meaningful way. There is no problem imaging verbs if nouns are provided, and if nouns are not provided, the subjects will supply them along with a host of adjectives. Every image will have some adjective and, possibly, verbal features. The noun refers to an object that has size, location, color, ownership, possible movement in a direction, and so forth.

The terms *abstract* and *concrete* are convenient for some purposes. If one does not wish to dwell on a specific instance but rather wants to talk about a number of cases, a collective or abstract term is useful. Thus, if a cat lover wants to collect money for an institution that will take care of stray cats, it is useful to appeal to dog lovers, too, and talk about "cruelty to animals." Nothing will be said about rats, of course. The term *animals* is supposed to be abstract, as compared to cats and dogs, but what is overlooked normally is that any word is abstract to begin with. Every word is, in Pavlov's language, a member of a "second signal system," a stimulus originally related to a direct, physical object, usually in some kind of motion and arousing direct sensory reactions. A ringing bell is a concrete stimulus. The word *bell* is abstract, a second-order stimulus that had to be learned in association with a real bell. Because there are all kinds of bells (temple bells, cow bells, sleigh bells, and so forth), the word can be used in a collective way to refer to any kind of bell. Such a grammatical usage or abstraction, however, does not change the word into a mentalistic "concept." Whenever the term is used, it can only arouse imagery of some specific bell or a succession of images of different bells.

Words such as *liberal, conservative,* or *democracy* all arouse their own acquired imagery in readers or listeners. They were all learned in concrete situations, and as the situations proliferated, so did the imagery. We should not ignore the attendant associated emotional responses Osgood emphasized. It is unlikely that any two people would have the same "meanings" for words like *peace, honor, justice,* or for that matter *cat.* Such words arouse complex imagery, some of which is quite beyond description because of commingled images, which Hebb (1949) described as some new totality of cell assemblies where no specific assembly was dominant and which could be made up of a number of different assemblies. We have chosen to describe such assemblies as images and suggest that "concepts" or "ideas," such as circle, triangle, or digestion, are or arouse imaginal responses. In a previous publication (Bugelski 1973a), I have described how such concepts, as internal responses, might be acquired. For our present purposes, we can note that concepts are intimately involved with imagery; they may very well include other behavioral features as Martin (1967) has suggested. Martin expanded upon Hull's construct of the r_g as a plausible vehicle for carrying the load of "meaning" that concepts are supposed to bear. Martin suggests that when various individual members of a class are observed, they may, when they share common features, arouse a common response. Fractional components of such a response, like r_gs, are likely to antedate any overt responses. As Hull had originally remarked, the r_g is the surrogate of ideas. What is being suggested here is that the common response that is aroused by any member of a class or category of stimuli is largely imaginal and, taking Osgood's emphasis into account, probably heavily weighted with emotional aspects. Words such as *dog* or *detente* will arouse imagery and emotional reactions, and these reactions are their meanings.

STATIC AND DYNAMIC IMAGERY

Earlier, we made the point that images, as responses, as "inner" behavior, need not and should not be considered as static "pictures" in the mind's eye. All of the early structural psychologists emphasized the fleetingness of imagery, the difficulty of "holding" the image "in place" for introspective observation. Paivio (1971) has proposed that images are somehow "parallel" reactions, as opposed to verbal responses, which are "sequential." It is not quite clear what *parallel* is supposed to convey, but the contrast with sequential suggests that images can be built up into complex organizations that, presumably, just stay there. Thus, Bower (1972) has suggested that one can image a whale, then add a top hat to the whale, then add a whale-size cigar for the whale to smoke, so that the resulting image is of a top-hatted whale smoking a cigar. Most people would agree that they could to this, but the fact that complex images can be formed does not deny their capacity for participating in sequential operations. Words, by their nature, must be used in sequence. Standing alone, they are of minor value for communication. We usually speak in something that passes for sentences, with one word leading to another. But images can function in the same sequential way, as one image can arouse another, in what has traditionally been called a train of thought. Earlier, I described an experiment wherein subjects learned under imagery instructions to sequentially report 20 words. Most subjects did relatively well when they followed the instructions. Subjects who tried to learn the same words as a verbal sequence did comparatively poorly. There appears to be no reason to maintain a distinction between verbal behavior and imagery based on a restriction that applies to language. Images can be dynamic and initiate action or other images.

LEARNING WITHOUT ACTION

In chapter 9, we described latent learning, which we noted occurred in the absence of any reinforcement operations. Over the years, some rather intriguing experiments have been reported (see Richardson 1969 for a summary) where subjects have been asked to learn some kind of skill without any physical practice. Instead of engaging in the task directly, the subjects are asked to sit and think about the skill for a number of imagery sessions, and it has been reported that such imaginal practice leads to improvement. Improvement has been reported for such tasks as dart throwing, free throws in basketball, high jumping, card sorting, mirror drawing, and playing new pieces on the piano, among others.

The usual procedure is to test the prospective learners first to get a base for measuring success. One group is then set aside without any further instruction or practice as a control group. A practice group is then allowed to practice for a number of sessions. A third group, the imagers, is given a number of sessions where they think about the skill, the movements, the situation, and so forth and imagine themselves performing competently. Then all three groups are tested, with the imagers usually outscoring the control group and sometimes showing up as well as the physical practice group. It is usually found that such imaging practice helps those subjects who are neither very good nor very bad at the original test.

Should such imagery practice prove effective in skills or operations that are costly to practice or involve expensive or dangerous equipment, it might prove of great value. At the present time, success in dart throwing does not appear to be a great social value, and we must await future studies should they be undertaken.

SUMMARY

We have tried to make a case for imagery as a prototype of learning as underlying both Pavlovian conditioning and instrumental behavior. There appears to be considerable heuristic value to the assumption that learning can be improved by instructing subjects to use imagery or by using materials that are rated as high in imagery value. We can talk about imagery objectively even if the history of the construct is fraught with subjectivity. We need not discuss pictures in the mind. Those who claim they have no imagery are referring to such subjective experiences, but even such people can give at least a rough count of the number of windows in their homes if asked for such information. They can also report the number of inside and outside turns in a block $\mathbb{F}$ (Brooks 1967, 1968), and they conduct their daily affairs without noticeable difficulties. Without imagery as described in this chapter, no one could survive a single day without constant supervision. The individual would not be able to recognize his or her own mother, a coffee cup, or the bathroom. All of our learned behavior involves recognition of stimuli and reacting appropriately. The only way we have to recognize anyone or anything is for the stimuli involved to arouse appropriate neural responses that they or their substitutes have aroused before. When the substitute stimuli arouse such reactions, we have imagery whether we know it or not.

12

Perceptual Learning

In the last chapter, we had considerable need to refer to visual processes. We talked of sensation and perception, of seeing and hearing, and of "inner seeing" and other "inner" perceptual responses in our effort to appreciate the nature of imagery. Learning psychologists have been used to ignoring the aftereffects of stimulation within the organism and have preferred to talk about the stimuli themselves. Other psychologists have been more than a little concerned about the problems of perception and its role in learned behavior, as well as the reverse problem—the role of learning in perception. Because of the many ramifications of these two questions, we must look into some of the issues that have emerged. We may well come up with more questions than answers.

THE NATIVIST ISSUE AGAIN

Many adjustment problems depend upon some appropriate reaction to a situation where the reaction must be more or less immediate and correct the first time, as in parachute jumping. A cat placed on a tabletop will not just walk off the edge. It will stop and "size up" the situation and jump down gracefully. A rat will not jump at all from such a height, even though it has never been there before. Psychologists usually mount their T-mazes on three-foot rods, so that the maze is up in space, and the rats do not jump off unless they are frightened. It is clear that they perceive depth. Do they do this naturally? Or was it learned? Animals can be reared in the dark and still be successful when tested on the Gibson and Walk (1960) artificial or "visual" cliff, which is a large box with a glass tabletop divided by a board, where the two sides are made to look (to humans) like two different heights above the floor. Some creatures, then, are judged to have an innate capacity for depth perception. Others may have to learn to perceive depth by using cues, such as interposition, clarity of distant objects, size factors, and so forth. Only the burnt child dreads the fire; a withdrawal reaction to fire seems not to be natural for human infants. They have to learn. What else do they have to learn? This is a question that has long preoccupied philosophers, who posed the question of what it would be like to be born blind and then have vision made possible by surgery or some other means at some later time. There have been two kinds of efforts to answer this question with somewhat inconclusive results.

The von Senden Study

In 1960, there appeared a translation of case studies collected by M. von Senden of people who had been born with cataracts and who grew up to various ages before the cataracts were surgically removed. At this point, fitted with suitable glasses, such people could be thought to have every physical capacity for seeing. Actually, there could be some failure of development of retinal structures or other physiological structures, because these might depend upon a history of light stimulation. In any case, such patients were commonly observed to see little, if anything, when the bandages were removed. They did report that something different was now occurring, but most were unable to identify by sight common objects they knew well by feel or sound. They could not identify figures such as squares or triangles or "see" any difference between them for months. Nor could they identify well-known people by sight, again for months. Some, slowly, over a period of months and even years, came to see perfectly well; others found it too much of a burden, put on their dark glasses and went about as before, blind, refusing the "precious gift" of sight because it was too much trouble to learn to use it.

Case studies are difficult to appraise, as the degree of blindness prior to the operation was not securely established. Most "blind" people are not blind from birth, and how much they were able to see in the early months or years is not known, but the dramatic results reported by von Senden suggested, if they did not prove, that we must learn to see objects as such. There appears to be some native capacity for responding to colors rather quickly and to detect lines and changes of direction of lines, so that the former cataract patient can say something like, "There seems to be something out there" without being able to identify the object.

The Riesen Experiments

In 1947, Austin Riesen began a series of studies in which chimpanzees were reared in the dark for periods of a year and more from birth, never seeing anything at all until some test day when they would be brought out into the light. Such chimpanzees, like the cataract patients, gave every appearance of being blind. They would not reach for milk bottles unless the nipples touched their lips. They could not avoid objects that would shock them strongly for many trials. They were functionally blind for periods of several months, but after daily experience in the lighted world, they became more or less normally seeing chimpanzees. There was some question about whether some illumination was required to foster development of visual mechanisms, and experiments with plastic helmets, preventing pattern vision, fitted on the heads of the animals indicated that they suffered less visual retardation. The results, again, were not conclusive, but suggestive of the importance of early learning that Hebb (1949) stressed and which we have mentioned earlier in connection with the Thompson and Heron (1954) studies of restricted dogs.

RESPONSES TO STIMULATION

The kinds of studies reported above led to a renewed interest in just what does happen when some environmental stimulus impinges on the organism. The earlier studies of Wundt and his structuralist followers had made this question the only question that psychology should consider, but the method of introspection had failed to gain acceptance from a broad spectrum of scientists, and the question itself was lost sight of until the "little German band" of Gestalt psychologists (Wertheimer, Koffka, and Köhler) revived it by a combination of experimental studies and phenomenological descriptions.

Gestalt Contributions

We shall not attempt to describe all the contributions and/or claims made by Gestaltist psychologists to the field of perception (see Gibson 1969 for a comprehensive review) but their nativist orientation frequently prompted incursions into the learning area, where behavioristically inclined psychologists felt their claims were unwarranted, unhelpful, and, indeed, wrong. The basic view of the Gestalt group was that one perceives one's world in terms of organization. We do not react to single, simple stimuli unless the environment is deliberately impoverished. We react to *patterns* of stimulation against backgrounds. If we hear someone whistling "Yankee Doodle," we hear this against a background of silence or some collection of noises. The melody stands out as a figure against the background. We do not hear a succession of single notes—we hear a melody, the same melody we would hear if "Yankee Doodle" is played on a piano or tuba; the melody is a pattern, comprising a whole. If the melody is transposed into another key, we would still hear it, but now there would have been a dynamic reorganization in our perception. We would hear the same thing in a different way. Such dynamic organizations and reorganizations of patterns of stimuli against grounds are the essence of Gestalt principles. We perceive the relationships of parts to each other and to the whole situation. When we are faced with a problem, we perceive a situation in some way; various stimulus components are reacted to in some patterned manner. As we continue to examine, inspect, or manipulate the stimuli or situation, the relationship of parts to each other changes; the organization of the pattern changes, and we see it in a new way. The new organization can represent a solution to a problem.

Insight

Suppose a caged chimpanzee sees a banana out of reach. A stick long enough to reach the banana may be placed in the cage. The chimpanzee sees the stick against the background of the cage and the rest of his world, which includes the banana. So long as stick and banana are viewed as separate stimuli with their own grounds, nothing much will happen. If the stick is at any time picked up and the "arm" is now perceived as *longer*, the chimpanzee may extend the stick toward the banana and rake it in. According to a Gestalt view, the stick was perceived in a new pattern, a new *relationship*, which happened to be useful. The chimpanzee *saw into* this relationship, that is, it had an "insight" and solved the problem.

The problem with this solution to a problem situation is that it says a lot but solves nothing. The Gestalt view, as stated by Köhler (1925) after his famous studies of *The Mentality of Apes*, is that learning is a sudden, all-or-none kind of operation wherein a relationship is perceived between or among the elements of a pattern, a relationship that was not originally perceived or there would have been no problem. Once this new relationship is perceived, it is retained more or less permanently. Learning is not a matter of practice; it is a one-trial affair. Köhler was reacting against the Thorndikian trial and error view and the notion that learning was a blind, mechanical result of accidental successful trials. For Köhler, learning was not an accident. It was an insight, accompanied, at least in humans, with an "aha" experience, which reflected a grasp of the situation—that is, "getting it" or "understanding."

The reaction of behaviorists to the Gestalt insight approach was to deny the "facts" by demonstrating the failure of other chimpanzees or other animals to show any sudden solutions to problems of the Köhler variety (Peckstein and Brown 1939) or to argue that in some situations, trial and error learning can occur with the trials and errors occurring implicitly, not overtly. Such an explanation would open the door somewhat to an imagery account. One could imagine what would happen if this or that were done without actually trying it. Eventually, something might occur in the nature of an image that might promise success, and an overt trial would ensue. If successful, one could claim insight. If unsuccessful, one could try again. Herein, we have the basic difficulty: any successful attempt can be interpreted as due to insight, although its mode of operation need not differ from unsuccessful attempts. Insight becomes the name for a successful trial, which might come first merely by chance.

Some American educators took kindly to the Gestalt view. One cannot learn if one does not attain insight. Insight happens or it does not. One cannot, therefore, teach anyone; one can only arrange a suitable setting and hope for the best. The Gestaltists took occasion to disparage all rote learning as dull, repetitive, and meaningless, and so teachers were discouraged from imposing drill and exercises on their pupils. The fact that much of our education really calls for drill and exercise was allowed to recede into the educational hinterland.

Response to Relationships

The emphasis placed on insight was illustrated easily by the Gestalt supporters through a variety of studies of choice situations where subjects appeared to be learning to respond not to the stimuli as such but to some obvious relationship between them. Thus, even chickens could learn to peck from painted dishes where food was available on the lighter (or darker) of two dishes. Corn would be glued fast to the "negative" dish and freely peckable on the positive dish. Children could be trained to choose the larger of two boxes to obtain rewards of candy or to choose the object on the right or the object in the middle of three or to choose the odd object in a group of three where two objects were alike. All of these situations can be described as calling for a response to some relationship. There appears to be little question that older children and adults can learn such appropriate behavior and do so very readily. The question may be raised, however, of just what has been learned and on what basis. Thus, if an older child is taught to pick the larger of two items, it can see the two objects and label them as *this* and *that* or *one* and *two* or *A* and *B*. He need not and may not label them *larger* and *smaller* or even *large* and *small.* If the child is now tested with two other objects of different sizes and picks the larger one, we are inclined to assume that it was the relationship between the two that was the basis for the selection. But what is a relationship? Here is the point of concern for the non-Gestaltist, or behavioristic, or physiological, psychologist. A relationship is something personal, that is, it is inside a perceiver and not inherent in the stimuli, or is it?

The Spence Answer to Realtionships

Spence (1937), a colleague and follower of Hull, chose to answer the problem of relationships by denial. When subjects chose the larger of two

FIGURE 12.1: Negative and positive stimulus objects differing in size. (After
        Spence 1936.)

stimuli it was not the relative largeness of the chosen stimulus but its specific
physical size and its actual physical impact on the perceiver in the context of
the smaller stimulus and its impact on the perceiver. Thus, if the original
training is between two objects like the squares shown in Figure 12.1, where
the selection of the large is followed by a reward, Spence assumes that this
object will be the base for similar positive responses to a range of objects on
the size continuum by virtue of generalization. Thus, if there are seven
objects and Number 3 is negative and Number 4 is positive we would have
positive generalization around Number 4, as shown in Figure 12.2. Any
object of any size would have some stimulus value for a positive choice. But
since the smaller object would not be followed by a reward, it would have
generalized negative values for any other stimulus, as shown in Figure 12.3.
Because the negative value begins on a lower position on the size continuum,

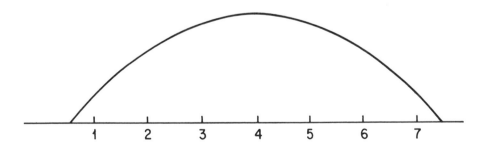

FIGURE 12.2: A positive generalization curve around stimulus item 4. (After
        Spence 1936.)

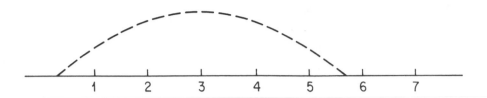

FIGURE 12.3: A negative generalization (extinction) curve around stimulus item 3. (After Spence 1936.)

it will not reach out as far on the larger size end of the generalization range. The negative strength cannot equal the positive strength to begin with because in that case there would be no choice. If we combine the two curves, with the negative generalization shown as a dotted line, we have Figure 12.4.

If we assume that the stimulus value of any object is the result of the algebraic summation of their positive and negative strengths, then Object 4 would be chosen over Object 3 and Object 5 would be chosen over Object 4 (the original positive stimulus). Note that Object 7 has very little positive value left from generalization, while Object 6 has a great deal more. Given a choice between Object 6 and Object 7, the subject should choose the smaller of the two stimuli. According to Spence, this is just what happened with

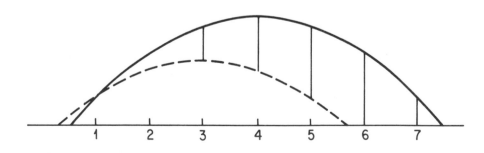

FIGURE 12.4: The algebraic summation of the positive and negative curves with stimulus item 6 more positive than 5 but also more positive than item 7. (After Spence 1936.)

chimpanzee subjects. The response to "relationships" disappeared because there was no relationship involved.*

The same results were obtained with young children by Alberts and Ehrenfreund (1951), who asked children to select one of two boxes, where the larger box contained candy. Young children (under age five) behaved like Spence's chimpanzees and chose the smaller box when the two boxes were at the large end of the scale, but older children kept on responding to the larger object. Were they responding to a relationship? Clearly, they saw that one object was larger than another. What these children did was to say to themselves, "The candy is in the larger box" (these were the stimuli in the study cited), and it could be said that they were responding to a mediational stimulus, the label of *larger*. But this only avoids the question, Why would they call the larger box larger?

Hebb and Relationships

Hebb (1949) proposed an answer that may have merit in this inquiry. As expected, the answer would be based on hypothetical processes in the nervous system. Suppose a chicken is looking at two dishes, one light and one dark, or one large and the other small, or one more circular than the other, or suppose *any* kind of relationship that can be expressed in visual terms. One object is made positive by the experimenter, the other negative. Now, as the chicken looks at one object, there will be a neural reaction of some sort. As it looks, then, at the other object, there *must* be a different neural reaction. If one dish is "brighter than" the other, the chicken must have two separate neural responses, one of which can be described as more than the other or different in some actual physical dimensions. Suppose we call the reaction to the dimmer stimulus a small or low reaction and that to the brighter stimulus a high reaction. Then, as the chicken looks from one dish to another, a high reaction will follow a low reaction and vice versa. At some point, the chicken will peck at the grain and be successful. The pecking will follow some change, either from high to low or low to high. It is this directional *change* of reaction, that is, increase or decrease, which becomes the physical cue that will be associated with a positive or negative reaction. The fact that the stimuli can be *described* in relational terms need have no connection with the behavior, which is still a matter of physical, not mentalistic, action. The true stimulus for the behavior is a specific neural reaction, or as Hebb suggested, a step up or step down of activity in the brain.

Such differences of neural discharges can underlie any kind of alleged relationships, for example, louder or softer, more or less pain, or of any

---

*The Spence explanation depends on the assumption that generalization curves follow the patterns shown. If this assumption is not valid, the explanation is debatable.

feature of any two stimuli that are simultaneously present. When stimuli are not physically present, the responses to "relationship" features begin to falter and break down. Which of two events happened *sooner* might be a question asked of some witness. Unless there are some kinds of additional markers, for example, calendar dates associated with the events, the answer may not be reliable. One might answer on the basis of "vividness" or some other extraneous factor and be quite incorrect. In such cases, one would be responding to changes of direction in neural patterns underlying images of the events, and such indirectly initiated patterns might be subject to many sources of variation in their characteristics.

The Contributing Organism

The general orientation of the Gestalt psychologists was to emphasize how much the learner contributes to any learning situation. How the learner will react depends on his nature, as much, if not more than on the situation.

The slogan of the Gestalt group was, "We see the world as we are, not as it is." Thus, how we react to any situation must depend on how we perceive it. A major principle determining how we perceive something is our tendency to make sense of any stimulation, to see a "figure" on a ground and to see as good a figure as possible even with fragmentary stimuli. A series of dashed marks like

is seen as a square even if the lines are not complete or filled in. Technically, there is no square, but we see one.

Such perception of "good" figures is assumed to be a reflection of basic, natural, organizing processes, where what is given by the world of stimuli is changed by the perceiving organism, which reacts to the various *relationships* among the elements and perceives organized wholes.

Retention

Many studies were reported by Gestalt supporters that suggested that we do not remember the actual appearance of some stimuli that were viewed earlier but that we remember instead how we perceived them. Even if we did note the physical features at the time and the features did not represent a good figure, with the passage of time, the figure would somehow become better, more organized, and more unified even though parts had to be omitted or supplied. Suppose we are told to look at something like

and we are told (or tell ourselves) that the first figure is a dumbbell or a pair of glasses and that the second is a broom or a shovel. Later on, we may not be able to pick out the precise figure from a set of alternate drawings similar to these because we will be looking for a pair of glasses and a broom. The behaviorist would say we remember a label response; the Gestalt psychologist would say we remember an organized good figure of our own construction. Experiments such as these are difficult to evaluate and remain controversial.

One of the early studies in learning that was commonly cited as supporting a Gestalt interpretation was that by Katona (1940), who tried to emphasize the principle of grasping relationships to show how it could result in very great differences in retention. Katona would ask people to learn a number like 14811151822252932363943. Some subjects would be told to study the number and think about it, and others would be told to memorize it. The thinkers would learn the numbers quite easily, while the memorizers would have an almost impossible time. If you look at the number, you will note that it is built on a principle of add three to the first number and four to the next and continue adding threes and fours. Katona held this out as a demonstration of the importance of organization and observation of relationships and, negatively, of the poverty of drill. What would Katona do with a number like 273548195751421391? It is obvious that his thinkers were not learning a 23-digit number. They were learning to add threes and fours, a simple assignment they were already experts at. Two different tasks were being compared, not two different methods of learning a 23-digit number.

Asch (1969), a contemporary follower of the Gestalt orientation, most directly represents the impact of the Gestalt position on learning and memory. Asch challenges the basic view that learning amounts to association of elements with each other by contiguity. He does not deny the importance of contiguity but claims it is not enough. What is important is the perception of relationships and the role such relationships play in learning. Thus, Asch illustrates with experimental data when he found that if subjects looked at a figure like A in Figure 12.5 and others looked at a pair of items like B as in Figure 12.5, and were later tested for recall of the item, A would be recalled more easily than B even though the parts of B would make an A figure. In another study Asch showed that two nonsense syllables, such as *hif* and *wug*, were harder to learn than a combination of the two into a single disyllable, such as *hifwug*. One does not question the data but the interpretation that the ease of learning reflects some

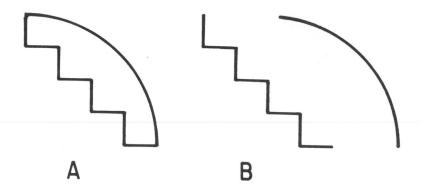

FIGURE 12.5: Organized and unorganized figures. (After Asch 1969).

powerful operation of a perceived relationship; this is not necessarily the only serious explanation available. After all, when the subject looks at figure A in Figure 12.5, he or she reacts in some way and quite possibly provides a label for the apparently single object. When the other subject looks at B in Figure 12.5, he or she finds two objects and can label each separately. In the recall task, the first subject has half as much to remember. Similarly, with the nonsense syllables, *hif* invites one reaction and *wug* another. The subject might well think of two separate items and attempt to find some suitable "association" via imagery or attempts to make some kind of words out of each that might take him or her far afield, as *shift* and *wugwam* (for wigwam), and hope to remember a sentence or phrase involving the moving of a tepee. The subject who has to learn *hifwug* might very well look for a single kind of representation or solution and settle for a "clang" reaction, wherein the mere sound of the syllables was being learned. The Asch experiments are really demonstrations of the fact that when people learn different kinds of things or different numbers of items, they are likely to differ. Asch (1969) complains that there was no place for relationships in the psychologies of Ebbinghaus, Thorndike, Guthrie, or Hull, but his strong conclusion that "the lingering belief that contiguity is the primary and sole condition of association deserves to be abandoned" is not justified by his demonstrations. The principle of contiguity does need some support, but it may not be from the perception of relationships. Relationships themselves may depend upon contiguity, as we have tried to demonstrate.

AN APPRAISAL OF THE GESTALT CONTRIBUTION

Except among some educators, the views of the Gestaltists on learning did not outlive their major proponents. Their specific principles were not incorporated into the broad body of American learning psychology, although their major thrust, that is, the emphasis on organization and the personal contribution of the learner to a learning task, was. In the late 1950s and subsequently, American psychologists began talking about subjective organization, a matter for our later attention (see chapter 14). The concept of insight was translated into one-trial learning, which became somewhat more respectable or acceptable when appropriate early learning or background could be taken into account. The phenomenological orientation of the Gestalt group was also effective in influencing various developments that came to be incorporated into what came to be known as cognitive psychology. The interest in imagery that Koffka (1935) favored may also have helped the growing respectability of that construct. The Gestalt views on retention played a role in some developments that stressed the retention of general plans, themes, or schema rather than the details of some experience of learning effort. We shall look into these later (see chapter 15).

TWO-STAGE LEARNING

The Gestalt influence was felt in another way, although indirectly and not necessarily with any specific recognition of Gestalt principles, in another development in learning theory. In some studies of rote learning, Hovland and Kurtz (1952) recognized that some subjects were having trouble pronouncing, and otherwise showing a lack of familiarity with, the nonsense syllables they were supposed to learn. The important operation in learning nonsense syllables in serial order is to recite them in order; some subjects might have a correct appreciation of the order but not have a correct control over the response or vice versa. Hovland and Kurtz decided to make sure that the serial task was not being affected by simple unfamiliarity with nonsense syllables, which had always been accepted as simple three-letter noises. Accordingly, they first showed each syllable to the subjects and then tested them repeatedly by making them supply the missing letter in a two-letter arrangement of the syllables; thus, a syllable like *zeg* would be shown as *z-g* or *ze-* or *-eg* with the subject required to fill in the blank. Such pretraining was regarded as providing assurance that the subjects knew the syllables. Now they had to learn only the order. It was found that such pretraining resulted in easier mastery of the list than that shown by control subjects without familiarization. We should mention that Underwood and Schultz (1960) did not find such facilitation with paired-associate learning.

The Hovland-Kurtz study demonstrated that subjects engaged in a learning task were really involved with two operations: one of getting acquainted with the materials and the other of learning the arrangement. We might suggest the analogy with a recipe. Ingredients must be known, but the order of their introduction might be important for the final product.

The recognition of the two-stage nature of learning had been anticipated by Hebb (1949) in his distinction between early and late learning and became of great theoretical importance to Saltz (1971). We will consider his views later. For the present, we will restrict the discussion to the first stage of learning and some subsequent developments.

THE OBSERVING RESPONSE

In our discussion of Pavlov (see chapter 6), we had occasion to mention the orienting reflex or orienting response. Pavlov had observed that the first presentation of a CS would normally arouse its own reaction. A Pavlov follower, Sokolov (1957), made a special study of these initial reactions, finding a rather complex pattern of activity when some stimulus, for example, flashing light would be presented to a dog. The pattern of responses would include some brain wave changes, movements of the head and eyes, changes in pupillary size, pricking up of the ears, heart and breathing changes, as well as postural adjustments. Such a pattern was dubbed the orienting response, and it was claimed that unless such a response was exhibited, there would be no conditioning. As trials continued, the orienting response would "habituate" to some degree, and the CR would come to replace it in part. The orienting response might be considered as an initial reaction in any learning situation, a kind of "let's see what we have here" adjustment. In a sense, it is a familiarization stage, a get-acquainted reaction.

Granting the immediacy and importance of the orienting response, we recognize that it refers to a single stimulus—a bell, a light, or a touch on the arm—and an immediate reaction. But many stimuli may impinge upon us at once. We recall Guthrie's stimulus complex and the fact that what we consider learning commonly occurs in a rather involved situation, as, for example, learning to drive an automobile or even a bicycle or swinging a baseball bat at a ball. Even a nonsense syllable contains three letters. We recall von Senden's patients, who had trouble learning to see objects. Much of our difficulty in learning may be a matter of responding only to certain stimuli out of a complex compound. We may not have to learn to see, but we do have to learn what to look for or at.

LEARNING HOW TO LEARN:
FORMATION OF LEARNING SETS

In this context of learning what to look for, we can reflect on some well-known experiments of Harlow (1949), who trained monkeys to select one of two presented stimuli, for example, a circle and a square or a long rectangle or a short one. When the monkey picked up the arbitrarily designated correct object, it would find a raisin. The problem is difficult for a beginner monkey. The beginner will take up to 16 trials before it makes the correct choice regularly. When one problem is solved, another is presented, that is, two new objects are presented. Again, a difficult learning period is gone through. After 300 problems of this nature, the monkey, no longer a beginner, solves the problem in one trial. The monkey is educated. It knows what to look for. What has happened? At first, the monkey chooses either stimulus for no known good reason. Perhaps, he prefers to choose the article on the right, but on the next trial, the correct object might be on the left. A monkey must get rid of, or extinguish, such a position habit. Once the position habit is eliminated, other irrelevant features must be eliminated by additional extinctions. A preference for big objects or small objects may be unsuitable. Color preferences must be eliminated if they are irrelevant. Easy-to-pick-up objects, light objects, preferred shapes, and so forth all must be eliminated through extinction. Eventually, there remains no difference except that of "this" or "that," however the monkey identifies "this" or "that." At such a stage, the monkey has solved that and all future problems. Harlow referred to the development of such appropriate reactions as the acquisition of learning sets. His more appealing description was phrased as "learning how to learn."

In the Harlow research, we have an example of learning what to look for or what to look at in a given setting. To the degree that such responses are important for us, we learn. More commonly, because there is so much that could be learned and because we have no need for universal knowledge, we do not learn what to look for and respond rather inefficiently in most areas of knowledge. Many people cannot tell one make of automobile from another. They may recognize some peculiar vehicle as different from others, but for the most part, they do not care and do not learn about different classes of objects, vegetation, or even groups of people.

GENERALIZATION AND DISCRIMINATION

We have returned to the problem of responding to stimuli as if they were all the same unless special extinction training has been undergone. Our concern now, however, is with discrimination in terms of classes of stimuli, with members of a class, and with preliminary first-phase learning, where we learn to react to specific features of some stimulus that will be paired later with some new stimulus or some different response.

We can illustrate the problem by citing a class of experiments where subjects first learn to make specific responses to specific stimuli where these stimuli will later be paired with new responses. Suppose you are called upon to identify ten fingerprints with the names of ten criminals. Would you do better by starting out trying to learn each name with each print, or would you be better off studying the prints first and classifying each in some fashion. If you look at a fingerprint, you can see some features that might not have occurred to you in the past. Each print will show a series of lines

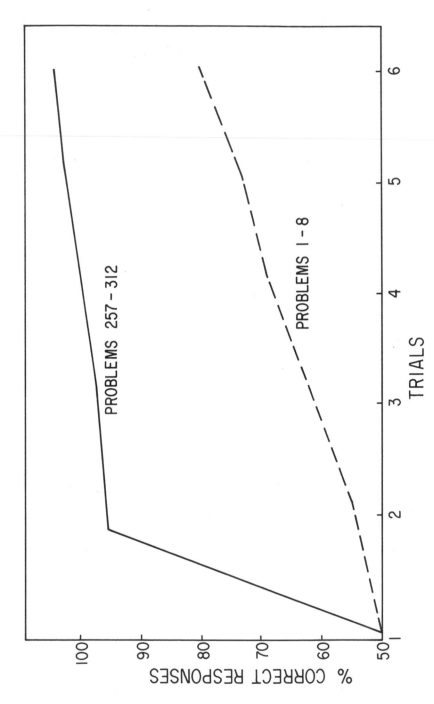

FIGURE 12.6: The formation of learning sets. The early problems are difficult. Later problems are easily solved. (After Harlow 1949).

PROBLEMS 257 – 312

PROBLEMS 1 – 8

TRIALS

% CORRECT RESPONSES

that are arched, looped, or whorled. The arrangements of the features differ, and you can count, locate, or otherwise classify a print as of a type and give it a name, a number, or a label of some kind. You will be doing what Hovland and Kurtz did with their nonsense syllables. When you, in effect, know the print, you can begin to associate it with the name of a criminal. The criminals' names should also be subjected to this process. What kinds of names are they? Are they one syllable or two? Are they foreign sounding? Are they common? Are any similar to each other? Wherein are the differences? With such a pretreatment, you are ready to learn the original assignment. Without the pretreatment, you will experience a lot of confusion and remember poorly.

In a study by Cantor (1955), children were shown pictures of girls' faces and asked to learn different names for the several faces. Later, the same faces were painted on different objects that had to be discriminated from each other. The children with the prelearning experience learned faster in the later learning session than did children faced with the final task to begin with. Similarly, Kurtz (1955) trained subjects to differentiate among pictures such as those shown in Figure 12.7. Note that the cartoons differ in two features: straight or wavy hair and straight or curved eyebrows. The subjects then had to learn specific names for some of these faces and other such prefamiliarized figures, as well as for unfamiliar pictures. There was a clear difference in the learning when the subjects knew what to look for. Saltz (1971) has reviewed a series of such studies and arrived at the strong conclusion that such predifferentiation of stimuli or items that are later to be associated is a primary operation for most kinds of verbal or symbolic learning. Association itself takes only a few trials or need take only one if the items to be associated are strongly differentiated. The association process, Saltz argues, can occur quickly if the ingredients or components of the association are really established firmly as distinct and are separated out from all possible confusing (generalizing) competitive stimuli. To learn something well, Saltz would recommend that the items to be associated be segregated, isolated, or differentiated as quite unique, almost one-of-a-kind. If this can be accomplished, we could have something like that shown in Figure 12.8; if we think of A and B as items to be paired or learned as "going together," then A and B must be walled off from the rest of the world of possible stimuli. The rings

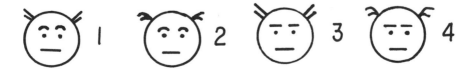

FIGURE 12.7: Faces differing in hair and eyebrow features. They all look alike but each is different. (After Kurtz 1955).

FIGURE 12.8: A and B are highly differentiated items walled off from sources of interference. (After Saltz 1971.)

around A and B represent barriers that would keep out any intruding, interfering, or otherwise disorganizing elements. The association between A and B could then be represented as shown in Figure 12.9. In this representation, another ring, which might be thought of as isolating the association, prevents any interference with its stability. The association, says Saltz, would occur quickly if the elements are appropriately differentiated. Our basic problem in learning, then, amounts to a failure to spell out exactly and precisely the features of the components that are to be associated. In short, we ordinarily do not make the necessary effort to observe how A differs from A', A", and so forth, and the same for B and its B', B", and so forth.

To learn the names of all the generals engaged in the Battle of Gettysburg on both sides is quite a little chore, because the names are not familiar at all or too familiar in connection with other battles. We have to segregate the battle itself, the two sides, and the separate generals. The fact that at least four Northern generals have names beginning with *S* is of no great help.

We are ready now to identify the observational responses we have been talking about as mediational habits acquired in specific situations where the interplay of generalization and extinction has resulted in a restricted or specific S⟶R pattern. Such mediational respones usually have no value in and of themselves and become important only in the second stage of a two-

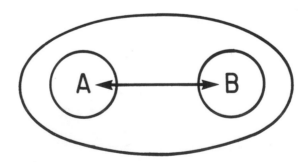

FIGURE 12.9: A and B are associated and the association is walled off from interference. (After Saltz 1971.)

stage learning or behavior sequence. When making a diagnosis, a physician looks for symptoms. The physician has long ago learned a general class of indicators of disease, and he or she knows what to look for as a final stage. The presence or absence of any one sign or symptom may or may not be crucial. As the symptoms are noted, they may mediate the important response, the diagnosis or naming of the disease.

UNDIRECTED FIRST-STAGE LEARNING

As we grow up or work in any specific environment, the features of that environment will come to impress themselves on us whether we take any special pains to observe or not. If changes in the environment are introduced, we may not notice them at once, but our behavior can be modified. If we are used to avoiding a piece of furniture by a characteristic turn we make frequently, we may still make the turn even though the piece of furniture is removed. We become familiar with our environment and its features.

As an instance of how such prior perceptual experience can affect learning, a study by Gibson and Walk (1956) might make the point most clearly. In their study, rats were reared in a cage outside of which metal cutouts of a circle and a triangle were hung. Later, the rats had to learn a discrimination involving cricles and triangles and did so more easily than did rats whose living quarters lacked such ornamentation. The implication, of course, is that even lowly rats notice their surroundings and learn something without any opportunity to manipulate or respond to those surroundings. It should be obvious that no reinforcements were related to the decorations in the preliminary phase.

The Gibson and Walk experiment raises many questions that we may not be able to answer for some time, if ever. We should note that the experiment did not work out in the same way when the circle and triangle were *painted* onto the surrounding wall (Gibson et al. 1958). Why should the rats be affected by metal cutouts and not similar painted decorations? This is one of the unanswered questions.

We need not quibble about the results of any one particular experiment. Many other studies have shown that prior experience with stimulus objects (nonsense syllables, words, light patterns, fingerprints, and pictures of faces) would result in more effective learning when these stimulus objects were now to be associated with some specific responses. Of course, the time devoted to such prior study must be taken into account when comparisons are made with other learners who are asked to learn to associate some new responses to unfamiliar stimuli. The point is, however, that *familiarization* might be a special kind of learning in itself.

Gibson (1940) argued for the need to recognize that before stimuli could enter into an S⟶R association, they had to be *differentiated*, one from another; otherwise, in learning a list of S⟶Rs, for example, paired-associate nonsense syllables, the stimuli would generalize among themselves and interfere with the associative process. The argument applies to the response items as well as in a paired-associate context; the responses are equally likely to generalize. We will look at the complications in such learning later when we consider Osgood's "transfer and retroaction surface" (see chapter 16). For the moment, we must take a closer look at what Gibson (1969) came to call "perceptual learning" as distinct from S⟶R or association learning. We can reduce the scope of the argument if we remind ourselves that we have already indicated in our discussions of Hebb's cell assembly formation, Tolman's latent learning, and imagery, that no overt response or reaction is required for an association to be formed, that associations are between neural activities and not necessarily between sensory inputs and motor responses.

In the context of learning nonsense syllables, whether in series or paired associates, it is clear that the final objective is to give an overt response (pronounce a syllable) when a prior syllable is exposed. If we recognize that the first syllable, a visual stimulus, evokes its own reaction, a visual inspection with some (possibly covert) verbal activity (pronouncing it, saying it to oneself), we can raise the question of whether some learning has been involved in this "recognition" reaction. The question answers itself. We have already learned to read before we can participate in such an experiment. The question then becomes one of how we learn to read. This question, even if it could be answered, is beyond the scope of this book. We can substitute a more basic question: What goes on when we look at anything?

The last question was the one addressed by Hebb (1949) when he considered the problem of how we come to know a triangle when we see one. In a broader context, the question becomes: How do we get to know or recognize anything as different from anything else? Verbal identification is not the issue, as animals and mutes clearly respond differentially to different objects. The differential response is the behaviorist or associationist answer to the general question. We learn to respond differently to different stimuli when the differences between the stimuli are important, that is, required by some circumstances. Reinforcement theorists emphasize or insist on some contingent reward. We have taken some pains to suggest that rewards are not the controlling factors in the formation of associations, and we need not repeat the argument. Hebb's answer to the basic question appears to be as good as any available. As we look at something, a particular neural circuit is activated. The more often we look at the same object, the more likely it is that certain specific neural components will discharge together (adding some, losing others), until a relatively stable neural circuit, identified by Hebb as a cell assembly, will be activated by any specific input energy. Any other stimulus will come to arouse its own specific assembly. Similar inputs may well activate assemblies with the same components and result in generalization, or lack of differentiation.

If we consider a child first learning to read and having difficulty responding correctly to *C* and *G*, we can assume that the little step on the *G* is not affecting the assemblies involved. We do whatever we can to force a change in the neural response. We are restricted to pointing, talking, moving fingers about, and so forth. We call it calling it to attention, but we are not manipulating attention—we are manipulating a stimulus input. In such a situation, we are, of course, interested in the additional association with a verbal response. But learning has been going on—new cell assemblies were being formed—while the child has been looking. According to Hebb, in such a situation, looking and learning are pretty much the same thing. Associations are being formed.

Gibson's contribution to our appreciation of learning is of major significance. We can recognize that learning is not restricted to associations between arbitrarily designated stimuli and responses. Both stimuli and responses may require development and discrimination through prior association and activity. The *discrimination*, however, is not necessarily a process in its own right. It is a term that describes the results of an associational history. Like *generalization*, it is only a name for the results of some neural processing and not a principle of learning.

ACQUIRED DISTINCTIVENESS AND ACQUIRED EQUIVALENCE OF CUES

Before we leave the topic of stimulus learning, we should note that in the post–World War II period, a variety of research procedures were introduced to evaluate the role of prior experience with stimuli, which were to be used in later learning situations. In some of the studies, for example, subjects might be shown a board with 16 light bulbs on it. Four lights in random locations would be turned on, and the subjects would simply be told to look at the pattern. Other patterns of lights would then be shown. The subjects could be told to do nothing except look at the patterns, which could be shown frequently or infrequently. Other subjects might be asked to learn to label each pattern by a number, letter, or in some other way, that is, a verbal response would be called for as part of this preliminary experience. Later on, the subjects would be asked to learn to press certain randomly arranged switches to turn off the patterns. The general findings in such studies (Gagne and Baker 1950) supported the expected conclusion that the pre-experience of naming patterns was helpful in learning the switch (motor) responses. Almost any kind of pre-experience was better than none. Such early experience was described as stimulus differentiation. The fact that subjects who merely looked but did nothing in the familiarization period did not benefit as much as those who learned labels for the patterns was explained by Goss (1955) on the assumption that any response would result in some feedback stimulation that would result from uttering a name. Such feedback stimulation would then add to the original sensory stimulation and increase the differences among the several visual stimuli. Not only would the original stimuli be different, but the different kinds of feedback would help increase the differences. Such improved differentiation would have been learned through the prior experience and could be called acquired distinctiveness.

On the other hand, the feedback stimuli might be somewhat similar to each other. If, for example, one stimulus is labeled *B* and another *V*, the feedback effects might be much more alike than vocal labels, such as *A* and *W*. If the feedback was similar, the original visual stimuli could become less distinctive because of this more similar feedback, and the subject might have trouble learning a new response to the visual stimuli. Such common feedbacks associated with different stimuli could be described as helping to develop an acquired equivalence of cues.

Many experiments involving such preliminary exposure or experience to different stimuli (and environments—enriched, deprived) were conducted in the 1950s and 1960s without fulfilling the (assumed) potential promise. It was shown that rats, dogs, and people can learn to attend to (or ignore) certain stimuli or stimulus features, to respond in the same way to different members of a stimulus class, or, as we already know, in different ways to separate members of a class. Lawrence (1949, 1950) demonstrated that rats would learn to respond to the white or black colors of a T-maze, to wide or narrow floors, to the presence or absence of chains dividing sections (and make use of these cues in other situations), or to *ignore* these cues when they were made irrelevant. Segal (1964) demonstrated that features of triangles (size, shape, or presence or absence of a cross in or outside of a triangle) could serve as cues that would later help in a recognition test. The theoretical framework guiding such researches usually was the general reinforcement and extinction view that Skinner followed in his analyses of discriminated stimuli. We know from Segal's work that some stimulus features are more noticeable or effective than others but cannot yet conclude why some stimuli or stimulus features originally have greater potency than others for different kinds of animals or different people. We still have much to learn about how experience (or lack of experience) with stimuli comes to affect our learning and behavior with respect to those stimuli in new contexts. We know that we can learn to ignore much of our world and be virtually unable to resist responding to other parts of it.

Because much of our civilized living depends on appropriate and specific responses to stimuli that might be quite alike, the importance of such discrimination learning or perceptual learning cannot be overemphasized. In the area of learning to read, the importance of such discrimination acquisition is of major significance. Gibson and Levin (1975), in their *The Psychology of Reading*, suggest that from infancy on we learn "the distinctive features of things and coded symbolic material, invariant relations in events, and structure, both superordinate and subordinate, which may also be thought of as higher-order relations and rules." There may be some process like reinforcement involved, but it is not through some external agent rewarding us; rather, it may consist in the discovery of structure and reduction of uncertainty. Such internal reinforcement may be part of the nature of organisms that must learn to adapt to their environments. It may well be that successive adaptations may even result in the acquisition of observational responses as a preliminary orientation to all novel situations.

THE OBSERVING RESPONSE AS A HABIT

The point has been made repeatedly that discriminatory reactions, that is, specific responses to specific stimuli, must be acquired for many kinds of effective adjustments. Much of our lives is spent in such preliminary activity that we must go through before we get to the "important" activity. Before you can study, you must get to your desk, get your materials, notes, and so forth. Before a pilot can take off, he must go through a "check-off" list. He learns to look at and adjust a whole series of instruments and switches in a patterned sequence, which helps assure efficiency and safety. Once he has the check-off list habit, he has made progress in learning to fly aircraft. The fact that a pilot has a list as a grocery shopper might have may mislead us about the importance of our own observational response patterns. We characteristically embark upon our own adventures, experiences, and operations with our own special package of learned mediational habits. We have our own way of doing things, and frequently, they are inefficient. We have learned to look at some things and not at others. In reading a newspaper, we may favor certain sections and ignore others. Some people may read a magazine backwards; others begin at the beginning. Some people study other people's apparel; others do not—and so on in all phases of living. "What you see is what you get" might well characterize much of our learned behavior. Many of us can walk down a street and see literally nothing. Others count the sidewalk divisions.

While much of our observational behavior is of no special importance, how we look at words or mathematical problems may be of some significance. If we have learned to look at words for spelling peculiarities, we can become good spellers. If we learn to make note of each item stated in a mathematical problem, we might also solve the problem. Information supplied in such problems is rarely irrelevant, as a student might wish. Only people who have learned to examine their dollar bills will detect counterfeits. It is obvious that where some learning requires reacting to specific stimulus features that we must observe those features. People who have learned to do so have an advantage over those of us who have not. When we see someone who seems to be smarter than we are about something, it is probable that he or she has learned some appropriate observing responses.

THE SECOND STAGE OF LEARNING

In this chapter, we have been concerned with stimuli and their function in first generating a perceptual response that could then lead to some innately prepared-for adjustive response. Learning psychologists, in general, have taken the stimulus for granted, that is, as not generating a response in its own right, and have been interested in how the original stimulus is connected with, or associated with, some subsequent response. Thus, in paired-associate learning, some nonsense syllable would be labeled *the* stimulus and another nonsense syllable *the* response. If the syllables are *ler* and *fim*, then *ler* is the stimulus and *fim* the response. We now know better, We know that *ler*, as a set of letters, invites its own response (seeing it, saying it, and perhaps distorting it into *lure, learn,* or *lair,* among many possibilities), and that *fim* is also a stimulus for its own response possibilities. We have also learned that the two syllables can arouse a mediational response, which might serve to bridge them, connect them, or otherwise play a role in the association between them. In future chapters, we will be more concerned with the second phase of learning, the new or artificial connection between the so-called stimulus and so-called response. We will try not to forget the immediate responses to the stimulus, nor should we ignore the observing responses that the learner has acquired, which control how his or her first responses to the stimulus will develop. We may find subjects who pay little or no attention to the stimulus. *Ler* may be reduced to *l* or *r* for all that the external observer or experimenter knows. That may be enough of an observing response to meet some learner's needs.

In the next chapter, we will examine more closely the kinds of behavior that are learned by observation alone—by being told or by seeing for ourselves—probably, the most common form of learning or education.

13

Learning by Show and Tell

Acquiring information and what we might call intellectual skills represents the bulk of what passes for academic learning. Thus, we expect students to learn some historical or geographical facts, biological facts, economic facts, and so forth. Facts might be distinguished from theories or principles or concepts in economics, philosophy, or science, but the ability to learn a theory, concept, or principle might not be essentially different from learning a collection of facts. We should be clear about what a fact is. According to Guthrie (1946), a fact is a statement on which those in a position to judge can agree. When people qualified to hold an opinion agree on a statement, we have a fact. In short, a fact is a statement. It is not necessarily a true statement. At one time, it was a fact that the earth was flat. The *American Heritage Dictionary* defines a fact as "something known with certainty," but then hedges with "something asserted as certain." Because we do not know what "known" is, the second version might be more useful for us.

Besides the facts students are expected to learn, they must also learn some skills of an academic or intellectual kind (as contrasted with some more physical skills, for example, dancing, pole vaulting, or gymnastics). These, too, presumably involve learning, and we will look into them later. An intellectual skill might be illustrated by use of a slide rule—here, the physical movements call for little more than some restraint and reasonable visual acuity. Long division or computation of a square root or a correlation coefficient might be suitable examples. Reading, writing, and grammatical speech might be included as academic skills.

How are academic facts and skills learned? Here, we find little help from learning theorists or researchers. Data on conditioning or instrumental learning are of little direct help. Facts about learning nonsense syllable lists do not help much either. Indirectly, however, data from traditional learning research provide some pointers, which we can explore.

As we have seen in the last chapter, we learn some things by simple observation, by just being around when things happen, or by simply living in specific environments. Babies learn a lot before they can respond to and with language effectively. They learn who feeds them and that some foods are good and others not so good. They learn, too, that certain people pick them up, dress them, play games with them, and sing to them, among thousands of other things.

As babies grow up and acquire language, they begin to ask questions about things they see and sense in other ways, and they are answered. A lifelong new procedure begins. We refer to it in the chapter title as show and tell. We constantly see and hear new things and acquire new associations that connect new stimuli to each other or to old or new responses. Such new associations are considered to be *knowledge* or *information*, but these terms are abstractions that are not necessarily helpful. You do not acquire knowledge; you learn to respond in a new way to some new or old stimulus or in some old way to a new stimulus. We have already reviewed what psychologists have had to say about how such associations are acquired in relatively simple situations. We can attempt now to look at the most common universal learning situation, which presumably has been implemented from the earliest humans on down, namely, that of someone telling or showing a learner something that will change the learner from someone who is ignorant or incapable into someone who is knowledgeable and/or skillful.

UNLEARNED KNOWLEDGE

Earlier in the text, we mentioned various nativist and rationalist proponents who argued that we are innately equipped to handle ourselves effectively in some situations. We left that subject with the conclusion that any such innate capacities were certainly welcome but that our interest lay in what we were not equppped for by birth, namely, such operations as answering questions abut the War of 1812 or any other subject where some prior experience had to be undergone before a suitable response was available.

There is an area of considerable interest for us that we must recognize before we move ahead. We are able to answer some questions that we were never asked before and never had any learning experience with in a direct and specific sense. We have already considered such factors as generalization to explain some responses to some stimulus situations. We have also taken fractional antedating goal responses and other mediators into account to explain some kinds of appropriate responses to novel situations. However, suppose someone asks us, Do canaries have skin? Or do whales give milk to their young? We may never have heard such questions before, and probably no reader of this book has probed under a canary's feathers or watched a mother whale nurse her calf. Is that what a whale baby is called? How do you know? Yet, you probably can answer the first question. Of course, canaries have skin. Did you know this? The fact that you answer "yes" to the original question does not prove you knew the answer before the question was asked. You had no prior knowledge of this fact. It had never been learned as such. But you did know something—canaries are birds; birds are animals; animals have skin; and you now "take a chance" and agree that canaries have skin. The process by which you come to answer the question is subjected to some kinds of analysis by logicians, who would argue that you reasoned your way to the answer by deduction from what they would describe as a syllogism or maybe, in this case, as two syllogisms:

Major premise:	All birds are animals.
Minor premise:	Canaries are birds.
Conclusion:	Therefore, canaries are animals.

Then, as a next step,

Major premise:	All animals have skin.
Minor premise:	Canaries are animals.
Conclusion:	Canaries have skin.

But logical reasoning is something that may or may not go on in some logic classes. The question is still, How did you get around to your answer? You could have imaged a plucked chicken or thought of fried chicken and in some way imaged a plucked canary showing its nudity. Whatever you did, it was unlikely that you went through the logical steps in a systematic order, but even if you did reason your way to the answer, you had to have a learning history relating to canaries and skin in your background. Similarly, to answer the question about whales, you must first know that a mother whale has mammary glands. You probably never saw a whale's mammary glands, and you may not have *known* they had such organs. But you may have known that a whale is a mammal and not a fish. The *only* way you could know that a whale is a mammal is if someone told you so by word or book. You also had to be told what a mammal is. With such knowledge, you could answer the original question event though you had never had any *direct* instruction or learning experience. This text will leave logic to the logicians and concern itself with how you learn the premises, the facts of life.

LEARNING BY SEEING—IMITATION

In the previous chapter, we considered the problem of perceptual learning in a somewhat passive sense. We are ready to talk about a different kind of learning, one that combines a relatively passive phase of observation—looking—with a subsequent active phase of performance.

Anyone who has seen children at play has observed what is called imitation. Children at age three or earlier turn steering wheels and turn on ovens, washing machines, and all manner of appliances; they cut cookies and apples with the sharpest knives—"Don't do as I do, do as I say" is standard parental language. Children imitate, adults imitate, and anyone in between imitates. They see what others do and repeat the action within the limits of motor development and sensory opportunities. They do not always see exactly what someone else did. But if the missing feature is pointed out, it may well be included in the next trial. Quite possibly, most of our behavior is based on observations of others. Even teachers imitate their former teachers, using the same stories, examples, mannerisms, and so forth.

In many phases of learning, perhaps especially in the acquisition of skills, the teacher demonstrates and the student tries to copy the master. Children continually ask, "Show me," "Let me try," or state assertively, "I'll do it" when they face new tasks or opportunities where they have observed adults operate. The demand for imitative opportunities almost bespeaks a natural need to copy, and such a native aspect of imitation is supported by the folklore, usually applied to humans, of "monkey see, monkey do."

Despite the pervasiveness and ubiquity of imitative behavior and its obvious role in learning (usually one trial, if conditions are right), learning psychologists have virtually ignored the topic if not taken a strong negative stance on the subject.

EARLY DENIALS OF IMITATION

Thorndike (1898) denounced the possibility of learning by imitation because of some superficial observations of failure to imitate on the part of some cats in his problem box situations. With even less reason, Watson (1924) joined forces and similarly denounced imitation as a possible form of learning. Imitation, like imagery, became a dirty word. Thorndike might have had some biases controlling his views, as he was committed to a law of effect principle, and rewards did not appear to play a major role in imitative behavior. Pavlov ignored imitation even though a conditioning explanation is most apt, and Guthrie, Hull, and Skinner similarly ignored the subject. Miller and Dollard (1941), associates of Hull, did make an attempt to examine imiation, but their studies with rats (perhaps not the species of choice) left them satisfied with a reinforcement of response-to-cues account.

Miller and Dollard would place two rats on a T-maze where the first rat would have previously been trained to make a left turn. If the second rat followed the first rat, it would be rewarded at a nearer food position. The rats would quickly learn to "follow the leader," but they could also learn not to follow and to make a right turn if that would lead to food. Miller and

Dollard concluded that the first rat was not being imitated, it was merely serving as a cue for an appropriate response. In the same way, they demonstrated that children would learn to do what others were doing because such behavior was then reinforced. The behavior only looked like copying behavior, but it was really individual behavior conditioned to specific cues.

Tolman, confined to rat subjects, perhaps had no occasion to look at imitation (whom will one rat imitate in a one-rat situation?), but his sign-significate theory lends itself obviously to the acceptance of imitative learning. After all, when you "show me," you demonstrate what leads to what, and that, says Tolman, is what we learn. Sensory-sensory conditioning espoused by Tolman is the basis for imitation, as will be proposed below.

Although the prestigious book of Miller and Dollard helped to discourage interest in imitation research, there were many studies (see the review by Flanders 1968) in which imitation was the central issue. We can look at a few. One might wonder why some psychologists were so concerned to demonstrate imitation in animals. Such determination might have been a hangover from the early Thorndike attack on Romanes. The later researchers seemed to believe that imitation was not admissible in people unless it could be first demonstrated in animals. They might have settled for monkeys with their notorious "aping" behavior, but some preferred cats and rats. Herbert and Harsch (1944) allowed "observer" cats to watch other cats (behind a glass partition) learn to solve problems involving a particular manipulation in a particular position in the problem box. When the observer cats "saw" all the trials of the learners, they too benefited from the observation, as opposed to seeing only the later trials. Whether such a demonstration deserves the label *imitation* can be questioned. The observer cats did work in the relevant areas and maybe responded more effectively to the relevant features of the situation.

Solomon and Coles (1954) trained rats to follow one another on a T-maze in the Miller-Dollard fashion. They then trained one group of these rats to avoid a shock preceded by a signal. The other rats were allowed to observe the first rats through a glass partition. The observer rats did not benefit in the new situation and had to learn on their own. Solomon and Coles concluded that the original training did not result in a general transfer of some imitation function (or learned habit of imitation).

Warden, Fjeld, and Koch (1940) had chosen monkeys as their research subjects and allowed observers (separated by a screen) to watch other pretrained monkeys solve four kinds of simple manipulatory problems on the other side. As soon as the accomplished monkey solved his problem, the observer was allowed to work out the solution on his own side. According to these investigators, there were 111 immediate solutions out of 144 tests, although the original learners took considerable time for their solutions. The conclusion drawn was that the monkeys displayed a high level of imitative capacity.

LATER STUDIES OF IMITATION

The subject of imitation, like that of imagery, languished until the 1960s, when Bandura and his co-workers began to study the imitation of aggressive behavior in children. Bandura, Ross, and Ross (1961) would arrange a variety of situations in which a child, serving as an imitator (I) could observe a model (M), another child or adult, of same or different sex, in real life or on film, and so on. After the observation period, the child would be allowed to enter the situation in which he or she had witnessed some interaction between the model and other children or a toy doll. If the model had kicked the doll, for example, the question of interest was, Will the child do the same? Commonly enough, he or she would. The facts of imitative behavior were convincingly demonstrated, but the explanation of imitation was left in rather abstract terms by Bandura and Walters (1963), who spoke of "activating properties" and information about probable contingencies of reinforcement.

Imitation is not an explanation; it is a term that itself needs explaining. When a child plays "patty cake" along with a parent, it is easy enough to call the behavior imitation and attribute some agency or process to the child that somehow activates the imitation. But we do not see imitation; we see only behavior on the part of two individuals where it can be said that one is copying or mimicking the other. Now, we must account for the copying itself.

IMITATION AS MODELING: THE MOWRER EXPLANATION

In 1950, Mowrer felt obliged to consider imitation. The need, Mowrer felt, was to explain imitation, not merely to accept it as a reality, and no previous learning theory could provide a satisfactory basic account of how or why imitation works.

Mowrer had already had the experience of teaching talking birds to talk (see chapter 10). He had experienced failure following the Thorndike-Skinner paradigm of waiting for speech, or some semblance of it, which could be rewarded. Skinner, like Thorndike, could find no place for imitation because a reward can only be applied after an action, and imitation is not a useful tool in the Skinner box for either rats or pigeons. When one works with one animal subject at a time, it is impossible to get the response by a show and tell method.

Mowrer attempted to extend his theory of how talking birds and babies learn to talk to account for the common Bandura imitation situation, which has the model performing some act while the imitator-to-be watches. Later, in a test situation, the child who has seen the model do something also proceeds to behave in a similar way even though it has never done so before.

The explanation of such behavior goes as follows: the model is someone the child has come to like, that is, the model is a CS for a positive emotional reaction. The model's actions, then, by generalization, also initiate good feelings in the observer. If the model, for example, kicks a doll, then observing the model results in a sensory-sensory association involving the model and his or her actions with the doll. Later, the sight of the doll arouses imagery of the model and his or her actions. The imagery then incites the kicking response. According to Mowrer, such imitative behavior would necessarily involve a prior emotional conditioning of the model as stimulus and some positive emotional reaction in the imitator. The imitator should like the model. Students should love their teachers. They do like their TV heroes and will copy their aggressive behavior in their play and real-life encounters. Congressional committees and broadcasters may "study" the problem, but their only problem is how to placate the objecting public. There appears to be no question of the fact that watching others aggress will be imitated under suitable conditions.

If the model is not liked, the opposite emotional conditioning would be present, and avoidance behavior would be generated by a later encounter with the doll. The child would not imitate. Such an interpretation would account for Bandura's findings about what kinds of models are, in fact, imitated.

IMITATION AND IMAGERY

As noted earlier, the Mowrer interpretation lacks a mechanism for initiating imitative (or any other) action. The Jamesian account of ideomotor action seems most appropos in this connection, and the interpretation by Greenwald (1970) (see chapter 11) is easily adapted to the issue.

Presumably, the same kind of ideomotor activity operates in all or most imitative behavior. The imitator is guided into action by his or her imagery of what he or she has heard or seen or done before. The explanation of imitation as a function of imagery may appear simplistic, but if we recognize that imagery functions as an antedating conditioned stimulus, we establish its kinship with Hull's r_g and the stimuli therefrom (recall Hull's proposal of the r_g as the surrogate of ideas, wishes, and so forth) and Hebb's antedating cell assemblies with their motor components. The explanation appears to be in good company. According to Aronfreed (1968), the Mowrer explanation is "the most sophisticated imitation viewpoint now available." Perhaps the ideo-motor account can add to that sophistication.

We can illustrate the explanation in a number of examples where imitative behavior is presumed. When one animal sees another animal respond in relation to some stimuli in a situation, sensory-sensory conditioning can result, and appropriate reactions can follow. Guthrie (1935) remarks upon the role of conditioned stimuli in his observation that when one horse in a barn began to urinate, many others would begin to do so, having been conditioned to the sound stimuli resulting from their own previous performances.

We can assume that a naive or untrained animal that watches another one eat in a given situation will later experience imagery of food, eating, or perhaps of the other animal eating and responding in some way to the situation. If the manipulation involved is not too complex, the imitator can begin to orient himself in the appropriate area, look for food, push things one way or another, and, perhaps, inadvertently solve the problem. The imagery would at least have the function of directing the activity to some restricted area where the solution could be affected. The imitator does not waste his time exploring other useless areas as the original learner probably did.

When a child says, "Show me" and a demonstration is provided, again, the child sees some manipulation and the solution. The imaged solution can be conditioned to the imagery of the manipulations, and if such manipulations are in the repertoire of the child, it, too, can now perform and will tend to do so if not otherwise distracted, or as James pointed out, if other imagery is not generating contradictory or conflicting activity.

The child doing "patty cake" must first develop the appropriate ideomotor patterns, and this is accomplished by the mother holding the arms of the child in a suitable manner and manipulating the hands to and fro. The movements, while relatively passive, generate the necessary kinesthetic feedback, which will become conditioned to the correlated sights and sounds and, as imagery, then initiate the clapping activity when the child now sees or hears someone else playing patty cake or even saying "patty-cake."

In the activity of copying, we have, perhaps, the clearest illustration. Suppose someone wishes to copy a drawing, a signature, or some other feature. We must assume a physical capacity for holding a pencil and moving it up and down, sideways, diagonally, in curves, and so forth. Now, in the original instance, the model lies before the copier. The copier begins a movement and compares the product to the model. If the movement is adequate, he or she moves on; if not he or she makes corrections—this is essentially an approach-avoidance situation. The movements are continued or inhibited as they generate pleasant versus unpleasant emotional after-effects. The first copy is likely to be erratic and ragged. With repeated efforts, the product will begin to resemble the model more and more. We say the copier is gaining confidence when what we mean is that the cues (kinesthetic and visual) are becoming more effectively discriminated and conditioned to fine changes in the emotional state—at first, a gross satisfaction at a reasonable facsimile; then, less satisfaction with even a fairly competent product; then, positive feelings only from a relatively perfect performance.

As the imitator continues his repetitions, he or she looks at the model less and less—the imitator's kinesthetic cues are becoming more refined, and the visual model is being replaced by an inner, imaginal model. If the latter becomes completely adequate, the copier can eventually produce the reasonably acceptable copy without any model at hand.

Consider the police artist who produces a sketch of a robber from a victim's description. We assume that the artist is highly skilled and capable of drawing reasonable portraits. In this situation, however, the only model he or she has is the victim's description. If the victim's imagery is inadequate, the sketch will be of little value. Both artist and victim are deeply involved with imagery: the victim with trying to match a developing sketch with his or her visual imagery of the robber; the artist, with his or her imaginal model generated by the victim's verbal stimuli.

The most common educational or instructional setting involves a teacher or coach who first shows the learner some step, posture, or position; the learner now tries to do the same. The voice coach, for instance, demonstrates a breathing technique, and the student attempts to duplicate the behavior observed. Or a note is sung or played, and again, the student makes an attempt to duplicate the tone. As the student hears the sounds he or she produces, he or she becomes conditioned to various cues in the setting and to the kinesthetic feedback generated by his or her activity. Later, the imagery of the tone can initiate the feedback imagery conditioned to the responses required for the production of the tone.

Professional voice mimics spend hours with recordings of voices of famous people, listening and trying to produce similar sounds. With some, they are successful, and a request for a copy of a specific person's voice can be met to a degree. The operation is the same, presumably, as in any other case of imitation—the conditioning of imagery to kinesthetic and other stimuli, which can release a response through ideomotor action.

We see then that imitation is not a special or novel type of learning. Imitation itself is not a learning process; it is a result of the kinds of operations that we have seen in all other forms of learning. This is not to say that "there is no such thing as imitation" in the sense of denying that people copy others; that is palpably untrue. It is, however, to say that imitation is a product of normal learning operations. These learning operations must be provided for. It will not do merely to say, "Go ahead, imitate me." The propsective imitator may not have the necessary preconditioning.

In the illustrations presented above, we have noted that copying behavior requires a model, but the model need not be alive or doing anything. We can copy pictures, recordings, or any other observable object. The principles are the same whether we are trying to paint a picture of a tree or trying to improve a golf stroke under some instructor's guidance.

The imitative process described above is perhaps the most pervasive activity in our daily lives. We are always matching things in our world with the imagery generated by verbal or other kinds of stimuli. The activity is so universal that it is perhaps not so strange that psychologists might not have noticed it, just as we do not pay much heed to the air around us. Even in our verbal behavior, we are always anticipating (imaging) what speakers are about to say, and as Skinner (1947) emphasized, we almost constantly echo the speech of others. Such imitative behavior obviously results in learning and probably accounts for most of it.

SUPERSTITION

In 1948, Skinner conducted a novel experiment. He arranged for a feeding tray to enter a pigeon's cage every 15 seconds regardless of what the pigeon might be doing. The pigeon was not required to do or learn anything. After a while, Skinner observed that six out of eight pigeons were behaving in a rather peculiar ritualistic fashion between feedings. One would raise one foot after the other in a marching-in-place pattern; another would swing its head in a pendulumlike fashion; the others engaged in their own unique activities. The pigeons behaved "as if" what they were doing was instrumental in bringing the food tray into the cage. Because the behavior was completely irrelevant to the feeding schedule, Skinner dubbed it "superstition." Such labeling might have been somewhat anthropomorphic, as the pigeons could have merely been marking time, that is, they could have been inhibiting eating behavior in the way that Wendt's (1936) monkeys actively filled in a delay period which was interposed between a stimulus and a response. The monkeys could not wait quietly and engaged in a variety of activities that, in a way, killed time.

Whatever Skinner's experiment proved, it illustrates the common human pattern of engaging in one form or another of unnecessary and pointless behavior, such as knocking on wood, avoiding paths crossed by black cats, spilling salt over one's shoulder, or expecting company if someone drops a fork. Refraining from walking under ladders might have some point, but stepping (or not stepping) on sidewalk divisions might be recognized as absurd. Breaking mirrors *is* bad luck; you have to pay for new ones, but the belief that one faces a seven-year stretch of misfortune is akin to a belief in the power of the stars to direct our lives. We dismiss such beliefs as those just mentioned as superstition and contrast such beliefs with those we feel have some more material or evidential base. A question we must explore is why we believe anything.

Skinner apparently believes that if a pigeon pecks at a disc mounted on the wall (where the pecking is followed by delivery of food) that such behavior is not superstitious. The general principle is that if reinforcement is contingent upon the action, then the behavior is not superstitious, while if it is not contingent, then *superstition* might be a reasonable label. But Skinner does not explain how nonsuperstitious behavior might be interpreted. It is not necessarily rational, intelligent, or even correct. The fact that reinforcement follows some response does not make that response qualitatively different from the superstitious responses; they, too, were followed by reinforcement. The pigeon is not an engineer and does not know that pecking the disc closes a switch that operates the food delivery mechanism. Some TV viewers believe that kicking their sets in a certain place improves or restores a picture. It might, at that, if the kick displaces some short-circuiting wire, but the kicker is responding at about the same intellectual level as the pigeon.

The implication of the above argument is that much, if not most, of what we believe does not necessarily have a solid foundation and is more casually then causally based. Skinner, along with many other psychologists, believes that one learns by emitting responses, which are subsequently reinforced.

During World War I, soldiers in trenches learned that it was not wise to try to light too many cigarettes with one match at night. The flare of a lighted match might invite a sniper's bullet, a rather serious negative reinforcer. A general rule or practice developed that discouraged "three on a match." Today, young people who know little about the origin of the practice might also follow the rule. It is a superstition that never enjoyed any contingent reinforcement for present-day followers. If we are to believe that all superstititions were originally based on some reinforcement, contingent or not, how do we account for the common superstitions of people who never had either? Skinner's answer would be to resort to "vicarious" reinforcement, but other people's historical experiences seem to be a rather shaky foundation for much of what we believe, superstitiously or not. Even our presumed scientifically based, experimentally supported beliefs may not differ in their acquisition history from superstition.

In previous chapters, we have suggested that reinforcement operations are really motivational and have nothing to do with the acquisition of associations. In the present context, where we are considering the acquisition of knowledge, information, or beliefs, it might help to mention the critical comments of Cook (1963), who pointed out that in learning paired associates, students learned faster when they were not required to pronounce the responses (this, of course, does not mean that they did not emit them in some covert way, but they were not reinforced for responding by the experimenters (Cook and Spitzer 1948)). If the appearance of the response syllable is interpreted as the reinforcement, then again, students learned better when they were shown these responses before saying them, that is, the reinforcement preceded the action. Cook concluded that Skinnerians are superstitious in their advocacy of an act-plus-reinforcement learning principle. Probably all scientists are superstitious; so many theories turn out to be wrong.

We may think that we believe what we believe because of some kind of evidence, but even the evidence of our own eyes is notoriously inadequate. It is much more likely that we accept most of our beliefs on the basis of being told that such and such is the case or that we have acquired the speech, manners, gestures, and other behavior patterns from our parents, teachers, and friends by observational learning, that is, by imitation.

SUPERSTITION AND IMITATION

It should be obvious that most of what we believe has been told to us by someone and that we adopted a given belief from a particular and specific source, a person, directly, in many instances, or indirectly from a book or other written source. But one hears or reads much and only believes some things while rejecting others. Why do we reject the spoken or written words of the people we do not believe?

When we endorse a supersitition or any other belief, we are, in effect, imitating. Just as we can imitate an action, we can imitate a belief or a statement. We say what certain others, our positive models, say, and when we do so, we are imitating. If our statement is accompanied by an emotional reaction—a positive or negative feeling—as is very likely in connection with religious, political, and moral issues, and the emotional reaction is similar to those expressed by our models, we are imitating a belief. Whether the belief is verifiable or supported by evidence is irrelevant for most of us in many spheres. There is no way to provide evidence to support or reject a position on capital punishment, abortion, contraception, women's liberation, or a host of issues we fondly support or strongly denounce. Such beliefs are basically emotional. Hunters can claim they are really conservationists because the animals they kill would otherwise starve. Those who consider hunting an atavistic and savage activity are not convinced. The same situation prevails about most beliefs. The emotional reaction is paramount, and facts do not apply, as they are used by both sides.

Recognizing superstition to be a matter of imitation allows us to fit it into the learning picture. Taking our earlier discussion of imitation into account, we see and hear a model expressing the belief. The expression is verbal behavior and, in principle, is like any other behavior. If the imitator likes the model, that is, has a positive emotional reaction to the model, the model's words will become conditioned stimuli for a postive emotional reaction. The imitator can now "feel good" when stating the same position. The model can even increase the imitator's positive feeling by expressing approval or otherwise reinforcing the imitator's statements. This has the effect of making the model even more powerful as a stimulus for initiating positive emotional responses in the imitator. Most religious groups have some kind of rituals for children at some age, where by behaving in certain ways, they are reinforced by gifts, recognition of adulthood, or in other ways. The reinforcement, however, has no direct role in the learning of the beliefs other than to generate the emotional reactions, which become conditioned to a whole variety of stimuli, for example, the models, candles, organ music, stained glass, vestments of religious leaders, and so forth.

Sometimes a belief is abandoned—the religious youth becomes an agnostic or atheist; the former Republican child is now a Democrat; a banker's son espouses communism. Such changes generally involve a conflict—some new source of stimulating positive feelings comes to serve as a more potent model. Earlier models may no longer be effective and as likable as formerly. Children find that their parents do not know everything while "teacher" does. A friend may be having a better time expressing contrary views. Tom Sawyer's admiration for Huck Finn was unbounded. Huck had freedom and knew so much more that was important, like how to get rid of warts.

We should not limit the imitation view to only matters of luck, faith, morals, or mores. Most of what we know we learn from statements made by people we trust (like, approve of). We believe that Columbus sailed across the Atlantic to San Salvador in 1492, although none of us accompanied him on the voyage. The veracity of the statement is not the issue. We believe it because we are told by a trusted source. In the same way, we come to believe in newspapers, texts, and radio and television news reporters because we would feel uncomfortable in a continuous state of disbelief. But many statements we hear or read are falsehoods. We can still believe them and repeat them because we feel better accepting and repeating them than we otherwise would. It is as easy to learn a lie as the truth; the same principles apply.

PROPAGANDA

A final word about negative beliefs is in order. When some statement is made that refers to some more general system of beliefs, for example, a statement by a statesman of some unpopular country, we sometimes dismiss it as propaganda. The term *propaganda* has acquired a negative value for American citizens, although in other countries, it is not a negative term and refers more to an activity in the sense of "propagating." Some churches, for example, actively strive for the "propagation of the faith." Their spokesmen obviously do not believe they are deluding or misleading anyone; quite the contrary. In some European countries, propaganda is only active education, namely, bringing the word to the unenlightened. In the United States, we try to make a distinction and consider education as dealing only with the truth. In education, we are supposed to look at all sides of issues and questions. The realities of time, skill, and knowledge rarely permit such luxuries, and there are only infrequent opportunities to consider more than one side. American schoolchildren might be a bit shocked to read about the American

Revolution of 1776 in a British history book. Children in Nazi Germany learned that they were the "Master Race," and Europeans generally regard Americans as uncultured, if not worse. Objective teachers are probably rather rare and not too popular. The teaching of Darwin's theory of evolution is not universally admired by school boards, and irate citizens frequently attempt to censor school libraries. We can conclude that *reason* is not significantly triumphant and that *emotion* rules the brain waves. The existence of multiple religions, political parties, social systems, and controversial issues should make the point. Some people will believe anything because they "trust," that is, like, or otherwise are positively affected by the models they follow. Superstition is not confined to beliefs about broken mirrors, spilled salt, or dreams; it pervades our lives.

SUMMARY

In this chapter, we have labored, or perhaps, belabored, over the obvious. People, if not animals, have always learned by show and tell, by demonstration, by example, and by illustration. To study such learning and discover the principles involved as not been easy. Animal research has not been productive precisely because we cannot show and tell animals very much. They have had to learn on their own. Animals do not have a culture or a history of successes and failures through which to teach their offspring. People obviously do, and it is that transmissible history which enables us to learn so much in one lifetime. Our verbal behavior allows us to teach. We do not yet know much about the teaching process. As a possibly necessary preliminary step, we may first hope to learn more about how verbal behavior itself is acquired. In the past two decades, learning psychologists have turned away from studies of animals and moved toward an examination of verbal learning and verbal behavior. In the next several chapters, we will attempt to see what they have learned.

14

Verbal Learning

In the last chapter, we began to talk about the learning of *facts*, *beliefs*, and *information*. These terms, of course, involve words, but we made no special point about the language factors themselves. It is time to look into what is referred to as verbal learning by contemporary learning psychologists.

NONSENSE SYLLABLES FROM THE TIME OF EBBINGHAUS

All through the years that conditioning and instrumental learning were being studied, primarily with animals, other learning psychologists were following the tradition started by Ebbinghaus and asking college students to learn lists of nonsense syllables. The variations on the theme were multiple and diverse. Lists were varied in length, difficulty, methods of presentation, presentation time of the units, and with or without rest periods between trials so that a list need not have a beginning or an end. Students learned one list or two or three in succession, seconds or months apart. Some might learn 36 lists over a semester. A great deal of information was accumulated about nonsense syllables in lists, although much of what was detailed had been anticipated by Ebbinghaus in his pioneer work. One innovation that Ebbinghaus did not introduce was that of paired-associate learning, where subjects had to learn a double list of pairs of syllables where the object was not to recite in serial order but to learn which (response) syllable went with which (stimulus) syllable. Becuase the number of researchers runs into the thousands, we cannot begin to consider all of the facets of nonsense syllable learning that were polished by aspiring graduate students. The interested student will find extensive reviews in Woodworth (1938), McGeoch (1942), Hovland (1951), Osgood (1953), and Hall (1971).

In the post-Ebbinghaus years, psychologists in the United States took the view that nonsense syllables would, indeed, allow them to study learning from "scratch." We now recognize this view as naive, that neither nonsense syllables nor their learners are evenly matched when a learning experiment begins. We also know that simple repetition, the basic principle of Ebbinghaus, is not the only one operating. But most of the work done with nonsense syllables prior to 1950 or so was done with repetition as the main learning activity. Subjects were instructed *not to think*, just look or listen, "and the learning will occur," slowly accruing, trial by trial. The kinds of problems that interested the early investigators were designed to reveal the broad general principles or laws governing verbal habit acquisition and the variables that might affect associations. The serial learning curve (see chapter 4), for example, became accepted as a genuine phenomenon, and enough experiments were conducted on this feature alone to provide material for a full-length book (Harcum 1975). The learning curve itself, that is, the course of acquisition, became a major issue as arguments came to be advanced favoring one-trial learning (Hayes 1953; Rock 1957), and much discussion was aired on whether or not there were plateaus in the "typical" learning curve (see Keller 1958).

By far the greatest amount of research was devoted to the problem of forgetting and the analysis of the nature of interference within and between learning lists because of the similarity of stimuli to each other. We shall look into these problems later (see chapter 17).

TIME AND LEARNING

The emphasis on repetition in rote learning was easily justified by countless observations that students could not learn a list of nonsense syllables in one trial. They always required numerous rotations of the memory drum to be able to recite eight or ten syllables in order. What seems to have been lost sight of is that exposing a syllable for two or three seconds did not leave the learner time to do much more than look at and pronounce a syllable (and not learn it). It was not until around 1960 that psychologists began to recognize that the presentation or viewing time might itself be important.

Because time of exposure or study time is so important in all verbal learning research, we must give it some detailed consideration. We should, at the same time, recognize that the time factor is a general one in all learning, verbal or not.

Anyone who wastes his youth in a pool hall may turn out to be a pretty good player and also do a creditable job in playing billiards. Any gaps or weaknesses in other skills or knowledge areas can be attributed to his failures to look into such matters because of his preoccupation with pool. He will know a lot about angles on a pool table and may not know much about triangles except for the one he uses to rack up the balls.

While some people complain that "there is so little time," everyone has the same amount, 24 hours per day, and it is not so much the time itself but how it is spent that matters in learning. The basic statement appears to be: it takes time to learn anything; when you spend the time at one task, you cannot be learning another. When some one appears to know more about something than we do, it is a safe guess that he or she has spent more time on the matter than we did. He or she is not necessarily more talented or intelligent.

Yet, given the same amount of time to learn something, different people will learn different amounts (or items) in the fixed learning period. We assume, in such cases, that the differences stem from different preparations (past experience), different techniques or procedures, or different interests. When we deal with groups of people, it appears that within some limits, the amount learned will vary with the time spent. A pair of experimental studies might illuminate the variables.

Murdock (1960) had subjects learn lists of words for one-minute totals of learning time. The lists differed in length, and so different presentation times were used. Thus, a 20-word list could be given at a three-second rate, a 30-word list at a two-second rate, and a 40-word list at a 1.5-second rate. Regardless of rate, the subjects were able to recall about nine words after the one-minute study time. There is a clear trade off—if you double the time per word, you work on a smaller number of words. You can only learn so much in a given time.

In a study by the writer (Bugelski 1962), students were asked to learn paired associates presented at different rates, ranging from six seconds to 19 seconds per pair. The longer the exposure (presentation rate), the fewer the trials to learn, as might be expected; but with longer exposures, a trial took longer. The students with shorter presentation rates needed more trials, to be sure, but if the presentation rate was multiplied by the number of trials, the total time taken to learn the list was not significantly different. In short, pt x t = k, where k is a constant, pt is presentation time, and t is the number of trials.

The same kinds of results have been found by Baumeister and Kistler (1974) and Zachs (1969). Cooper and Pantle (1967) reviewed a large number of experiements that gave general support to a "total time" law.

SPACED VERSUS MASSED LEARNING

Findings such as the above throw new light on what used to be a popular and controversial learning issue in the 1940s and 1950s, namely, the issue of spaced versus massed learning. It had long been claimed that spacing out or distributing a learning experience over a number of trials (days or weeks apart) was a better way to learn and retain some matter than putting in a heavy cram session and trying to learn something in one extended period.

Obviously, in such learning situations, one would be talking about something that could not be learned in one short trial. To memorize a long poem, for example, might take many readings. The question was, Should you try to cover the many necessary readings in one prolonged period or spread the task over a number of practice sessions? In many studies, it was quite clear that a series of review sessions proved more efficient (took fewer total trials) than the cram sessions procedure. What was not considered in such studies was the total time involved. In one case, a student learned a poem in one day, while in other cases, a week or more was required. In getting ready for the spaced sessions, a certain amount of time would inevitably be wasted—time to get the materials ready, getting set and warming up in the learning situation, not to mention all the intervening "rest" time. Still, the total number of trials could be fewer in number in the spaced situation. Such benefits might be due to something positive in spacing or something negative in massing. For example, in the spaced situation, the learner discovers from trial to trial that he or she actually knows some parts of the assignment quite well and need not go over them. He or she concentrates on the less well-learned material. In the massed situation, the learner cannot trust his or her retention of such recognized success and goes over the well-known material anyhow.

In the massed situation, the leanrer may become tired and inefficient, even developing conditioned inhibition, which in Hull's theoretical analysis would amount to a kind of negative learning. In Hull's view, the fatigue (see reactive inhibition, chapter 6) would serve as a drive, prompting rest efforts or responses, and the student would learn to avoid the work involved and become conditioned to rest when the learning stimuli were present.

In many studies where the learning task is short enough to permit a number of repetitions, the massed versus spaced issue becomes an empty matter. Here, the total time hypothesis appears to hold, and when the rest periods between trials of the spaced learners are taken into account, they need as much time to learn as do the massed learners (see Hovland 1938).

The total time hypothesis must be viewed with some care. It does not hold for very fast presentations (fractions of seconds) or for very slow presentations. In the latter case, students have difficulty maintaining attention on single nonsense syllables, for example, for 60 seconds per syllable, and part of that time is wasted.

TIME AS A "HIDDEN" VARIABLE

A study by Loftus (1972) might demonstrate how easily time can be ignored when it may be a determining variable. In the Loftus study, no great academic skill was being scrutinized. Learners were asked to look at pairs of pictures. The pictures would be shown in a larger collection to be looked at later. The test would include new pictures, which had not previously been seen. As the learners viewed the pictures (for three seconds per pair), they were informed that one picture, if recognized later, would pay nine points while the other would pay only three points. In the subsequent test, the learners remembered the higher-paying pictures significantly better. We should not jump to the conclusion that high pay has an effect on learning. While looking at the pictures, the viewers' eyes were photographed, and the numbers of fixations on each picture were counted. It turned out that the pictures with high fixation numbers were the ones remembered regardless of the pay off.

In a similar study, Atkinson and Wickens (1971) found that if a varying sum of money is promised for the recall of different pairs of paired associates, the learners will learn the higher-paying associates better than the lower-paying ones.

But what do the points or pennies really do? They clearly lead to more contact with, inspection of, or rehearsal of, specific items; this is obvious in the Loftus study but is also apparently equally true in the Atkinson-Wickens study. More rehearsal means more time spent interacting with the material. The importance of the time variable cannot be overlooked. From a variety of studies of both long- and short-term memory, it is abundantly clear that more is learned (remembered) if more time is spent in reacting to the stimulation (material).

A number of points, however, must be considered. Different kinds of stimulation or situations may require and, in all probability do require, different amounts of time for any individual (no one learns every kind of fact or operation in equal time). Further, no two people will learn all assignments in equal periods of time. We can accept individual differences here without worrying about why they exist. One extrapolation might be ventured, however; probably anyone with any pretensions to learn something can learn it if he or she takes enough time. Put another way, some people give up their study effort before they have given it the appropriate (for them) time. Remember Hull's continuity principle.

But in spite of its importance as a general factor, time, as such, does little or nothing for the learner. It is how the time is used that counts. In later sections of this chapter, the student will probably raise the time question for himself or herself in connection with a number of studies and theoretical forays.

ATTEMPTS TO INTEGRATE NONSENSE SYLLABLE LEARNING WITH CONDITIONING PRINCIPLES

From time to time, efforts were made to relate findings from nonsense syllable learning to conditioning or other principles. Gibson (1941), for example, found that Pavlovian generalization was a factor of determining the difficulty of learning paired associates. Similarity among stimuli could result in interference with learning appropriate responses. Hull and his associates (1940) tried to fit nonsense syllable findings into a general learning theory framework, where the same principles that governed animal learning might be found operating in rote learning. Some psychologists began to use nonsense syllables as a convenient material to test other kinds of variables in learning or performance. Spence and Spence (1953) and Farber and Spence (1953), for example, tried to demonstrate that anxiety as a drive would affect the learning of nonsense material, with the general finding that "high-anxious" subjects would learn easy lists better than "low-anxious" subjects, but with difficult lists, the high-anxious subjects would have greater relative difficulty. The anxiety concept in the work of these investigators derived from research on fear conditioning in animals.

The efforts of integrators to tie verbal (nonsense syllable) learning to animal-learning principles were not notably successful. Besides the principle of generalization, not much use was made of other conditioning principles. Mention should be made of attempts to apply the Pavlovian finding of spontaneous recovery to verbal learning. If a subject learned two lists of paired associates with the same stimulus items in succession, it would be reasoned that the first list would have to be extinguished for the second to be learned. If some time elapses, a test of the first list should reveal stronger retention than if the test is made immediately after second-list learning. Spontaneous recovery would be invoked to explain any improvement in first-list recall and, by implication, an extinction process, affecting the first list.

NONSENSE SYLLABLES AS USEFUL STIMULUS MATERIALS

Some researchers who were familiar with conditioning principles initiated some studies with human subjects where nonsense syllables would be used as stimuli but where the responses might be some physiological reaction to unconditioned stimuli, such as shock or hot or cold water. Thus, Roessler and Brogden (1943) asked subjects to say the syllable *wek* during a period when a 20-second buzzer was sounding. The buzzer was followed by an electric shock to the arm, which, in turn, would result in a vasoconstriction, a possible fear reaction. Four subjects showed conditioned vasoconstruction to the combined CSs (buzzer and *wek*), but two of them would respond to the pronouncing of the syllable itself. Later, the subvocal pronouncing of the syllable ("thinking" of it) brought on the vasoconstriction. Incidentally, one of the subjects would show vasoconstriction to *wek* but not to *zub*, which was never followed by shock.

Working along entirely different lines, Staats (1968) would have subjects learn paired associates where some nonsense syllable would be paired with pleasant words and some other syllable paired with unpleasant words. Later, the syllables would be rated by the semantic differential technique (see chapter 11), and it was found that the syllables had taken on the coloration or "meaning" of the words they were paired with. Staats attempted at least a preliminary approach to the entire problem of attitude, concept, and language acquisition along conditioning lines, but our present interest is directed toward nonsense syllables.

The samples and types of experiments described above illustrated the kinds of overtures or attempts at integration of two research fields made from one or another line of interest, but for the most part, the verbal-learning investigators stayed with their nonsense syllables and ignored the animal laboratory findings. The major interest throughout the period of 1880 to 1960 and beyond was the field of memory. The title of Ebbinghaus' book, *On Memory*, had set the pattern for almost 100 years. It was always appreciated by the nonsense syllable investigator that he or she was dealing with memory. Retention was an obvious test of learning, and whether one waited one second or 10 years, a learner had to remember to demonstrate his or her knowledge. Whereas Pavlov and his followers were interested in watching a conditioned response develop, most nonsense syllable experimenters were interested in what happened to the learned material with the passage of time. There was, to be sure, some interest in acquisition (in learning curves), but the basic concern was with variables or factors that influenced retention or "transfer" to other learnings. We will have occasion to look at those areas in later chapters. For the present, we will take note of a rather sudden change of interest on the part of learning psychologists from both the animal arena and the nonsense syllable researchers. In the 1950s, without any public resolutions or announcements, many learning psychologists appeared to have become fed up with both rats and nonsense syllables and turned to the study of "real" words.

THE NEW VERBAL LEARNING

In the post–World War II period, the psychologists concerned with learning saw the relatively rapid demise of the prominent leaders in learning theory and research. In the decade of the 1950s, one after another—Hull, Tolman, Guthrie, and Spence—died, and their systematic thinking died with them. Only Skinner (born in 1904) remained, carrying on without serious deviation from his 1938 views.

In 1954, in a book called *Modern Learning Theory* (Estes et al. 1954), younger supporters of the several schools subjected each other's views to a critical analysis, pointing up the flaws and weaknesses in the systematic thinking and leaving no theory unscathed, which led to a rather general disillusionment with the prospects for a "compleate theorie" of learning to which all would subscribe. Casting about for a safe haven, the learning psychologists turned to what must be called a new field or, at least, a new look. They discovered verbal learning. But along with the rejection of Hull, Tolman, Guthrie, and animal studies, they also rejected nonsense syllables. The new field of verbal learning was going to deal with meaningful materials, with real words. Psychology students would no longer be impressed into learning lists of nonsense syllables; they would now be impressed into learning lists of words.

The switch from nonsense syllables to words made some sense. Some psychologists had come to recognize that when the subjects were told to learn nonsense syllables, they commonly resorted to "strategies," which involved the translation of nonsense syllables into some meaningful substitutes, and it seemed sensible to let them learn meaningful words in the first place. Though sensible, it might not have been smart. Because nonsense syllables had proved to have some weaknesses might have suggested a search for materials that did not suffer from these weaknesses. The escape into words in lists could open a new area of research problems, but the research need not necessarily be productive.

The point made above about strategies was made the theme of a stimulating book, *Plans and the Structure of Behavior*, Miller, Galanter, and Pribram (1960), who suggested that when people are in a problem situation, they do not behave randomly but hypothesize solutions, trying something to see if it works and, if it does not, trying something else. Tolman (1948) and Krechevsky (1932) had endowed rats with the same operations, but their efforts did not have the same appeal. The 1960s became the decade for the study of learning strategies.

THE ANALYSIS OF LEARNABILITY

Before much could be done about strategy, the new learning material had to be evaluated, and a whole new line of research, which used verbal materials, was developed. The analysis of the learnability of different verbal structures, such as nonsense syllables, paralogs, words, phrases, and sentences, was initiated. We have already explored some of these (Osgood's semantic differential, Paivio's i).

An early exploration into learnability was the Glaze (1928) investigation of association value of nonsense syllables. Glaze would ask learners to report whether or not a given nonsense syllable appeared to be just that, nonsense, or did it make them think of something. For some syllables, for example, *zyw*, some, if not most, subjects would report no immediate reactions of an associative nature. If no one thought of anything, the syllable would be classified as of zero association value. With other syllables, different proportions of a subject population would report that some association had occurred, a syllable such as *jak* might have 100 percent association value; others would fall somewhere between 0 percent and 100 percent. Other investigators made additional studies (Hilgard 1951, for example), and lists of syllables of known association value became available to use in research. In an experiment, one could compare two methods of learning or other operations and know that the materials were equated for difficulty in at least some way—something that Ebbinghaus had ignored. Actually, association value of any individual syllable might not be the real problem. It might really be a question of how easily a given syllable might be associated with another given syllable (see Montague and Kiess 1968).

When Thorndike began his investigations involving words, he faced the same problem of equal word difficulty. He solved it by preparing the famous Thorndike-Lorge (1944) word list, which determined the frequency of usage of thousands of words by counting the number of times different words appeared in books, magazines, and newspapers. If a word appeared more often than 100 times in 1 million, it would be categorized as AA; if it appeared 50 to 100 times, it would be categorized as A; and below that, it would have a numerical value assigned, for example, 17 times per 1 million. Now, one could get comparable lists of words to use in research—words with the same frequency count. It was assumed, and supported by data, that more familiar words (greater frequency) were learned more easily than unfamiliar words.

It was becoming clear that nonsense syllables were not quite as nonsensical as they seemed. Some experimenters began to use three-consonant letter combinations, such as *xmv*, or digits and letter pairs, such as 26-E, but these did not become popular. Another attempt to find a substitute for nonsense syllables, at least as stimuli, was the use of nonsense forms or shapes, that is, line drawings that took various random turns. These random shapes introduce a problem of description, there being no common name for them, but even with such meaningless figures, subjects would try to label them and make them sensible. There was an underlying interest in the efforts of subjects to use the sense or meaning of the materials they were trying to learn. A more direct attack on this issue was launched by Noble (1952), who prepared a list of 100 verbal items consisting of common words, rarely used words, for example, tumbril, and paralogs (combinations of letters that looked like words but were not, for example *quipson* or *gojey*). Noble would present such "words" to his subjects and ask them to report everything that occurred to them as a response to the item in one minute. The number of responses made by the subjects to an item was considered to represent the meaningfulness (*not* meaning) of an item. Noble symbolized the meaningfulness score by *m*. Now, one could presumably use items of known meaningfulness vaue in verbal learning studies.

Along with imagery, Paivio, Yuille, and Madigan (1968) had secured ratings of concreteness-abstractness on some 925 words. Again, concrete words would be learned more easily than abstract words. Efforts were also made to evaluate pronounceability of words as a possible learning variable, but this did not prove of serious value (Lindley 1963). By the late 1960s, it would be possible to use words in experimental studies whose m, i, association value (AV), frequency (F), and semantic differential ratings were known. Various catalogs of common word associations to 100 common words were also available.

An additional contribution to word analysis was provided by Battig and Montague (1973), who classified words by categories (for example, furniture, food, animals, transportation, and so forth). The amount of information collected about words is rather staggering, considering how little is known about how they are learned.

THE INNOVATION OF FREE RECALL

The new emphasis on meaning and strategies led to a concern over what the subject was doing when he or she was learning (as compared with the old [Ebbinghaus] concerns over repetition), and some interesting discoveries were made with respect to what happened when a subject listened to a reading of a list of words or looked at a display and then was asked to recall the list. The established laboratory practice from the days of Ebbinghaus was to ask subjects to repeat the words in the order in which they had been presented. Bousfield (1953) introduced a revolution in this methodology by asking the subjects to report the words in any order.* This new procedure was labeled *free recall* (FR). Under such conditions, some subjects would deviate from the effort to respond in serial order, or "seriation" (Mandler and Dean 1969), and might report last words first or begin with any words at all and, with repeated trials, might come to report a completely new arrangement of the words. The subjects, in short, were doing something with the list, because it came out in a different order from the way it was presented. Because of the change in order, the subjects' activities (or contribution) was termed *subjective organization* (Tulving 1972). Such subjective organization was then analyzed to determine the strategies, plans, or manipulations of the learners. It should be noted that because the researchers were obtaining only recall data, they came to talk about the products reported by the subjects as functions of *retrieval* strategies. While the term may have some merit, it is possible that it was misapplied, as the subjects were probably exercising strategies only in the learning phases. We will look at retrieval strategies later.

---

*Actually, free recall had been practiced as early as 1916 (see Peterson 1916).

NEW METHODS IN VERBAL LEARNING

Along with the new information about words per se, new procedures were developed to study verbal learning, but again, psychologists were loath to break with the past. They still found it useful or practical to ask people to learn lists of words. Instead of presenting words by memory drum, words might be presented orally by tape recorder or be merely spoken; the subject might listen to a series of words or watch a series shown on a screen by a slide projector (the modern memory drum), sometimes, for only one trial. They might now be asked to recall all the words they could remember in a fixed or any random order. With the new freedom from the sequential restraints of a memory drum, subjects could be asked to look at or listen to different lists one after another, usually limited to two. The subject might then be asked to recall all the words from both lists or to recall from either list A or B or otherwise identify the words by list. If two lists of paired associates are learned in succession with the same words serving as stimuli, the learner later might be asked to recall *either* of the two responses to each stimulus word; such a procedure is called modified free recall (MFR). If the learner is asked to recall both responses in any order to the stimulus words, the procedure is called modified modified free recall (MMFR).

The Study-Test Method

Another innovation in procedure with some bearing on the reinforcement question was the study-test method (Izawa 1970). Here, a subject would be shown a list of paired associates with both items exposed for some interval. The subject would then be given a test trial in which only the stimulus items were shown; he or she would not be told, and therefore could not know, if he or she had given the right answers. The subject would then see the pairs together again, and so on. The study-test method differs from the anticipation method, where the stimulus item is shown first, then the response item appears whether the learner reported anything or not. Battig and Brackett (1961), using nonsense shapes as stimuli and two-digit numbers as responses, found the study test method superior to the anticipation method and questioned the propriety of using "knowledge of results" as some equivalent of reinforcement.

With the growing interest in linguistics, psychologists began some studies where syntax and grammar became the focus of interest. In the simplest form, subjects would be asked to learn adjective-noun or noun-adjective combinations—(the latter was better—Paivio 1967). Sentences consisting of grammatical sequences could be compared with a scrambled order of the same words—the former being found easier. This would be true even if the sentences were made up of nonsense syllables with suitable grammatical endings, for example "The lix goled umply over the ful"

(Epstein 1961). Some more innovative researchers tried out whole paragraphs containing some theme that, if recognized or provided, might result in more effective learning (Dooling and Lachman 1971).

In general, the new verbal learners were beginning to operate with the language as such, although the problems of working with this "new" medium are only now beginning to be revealed. Whether working with meaningful materials will prove to be meaningful cannot yet be assessed. We can begin, shortly, to look at a sample of the findings.

Concurrently with the new interest in verbal learning, psychologists had become acquainted with computers. Computers are obviously marvelous and (to most people) mysterious devices that solve problems. Because some people think they think when they solve problems, it was easy enough to think that computers also behave like people and also think like people. Such arrant nonsense hardly merits comment, but because computers are programmed to go through certain routines, a terminology had to be developed to describe these routines. Unfortunately, the terminology adopted made use of terms that appear to describe some human functions. Because computers could be supplied with circuits that could hold certain data (like a phonograph record holds a song, although so far no one has thought of saying the phonograph record remembers a tune), the computer was endowed with a *memory*. This would be no great fault if it had not been so easy to assume that if a computer had a memory, why should not a human? Completely circular reasoning overcame some researchers, and the computer came to serve as a model of a human learner. Other terms came into popular usage. A computer *stores* information (therefore, people *store* information); actually, it does no such thing—it has certain circuits activated. A computer *processes* information (therefore, people *process* information). A computer *searches* its memory (therefore, people *search* their memories). A computer *chooses*, *rejects*, *decides* (again, actually, the computer does no such things; certain switches are closed or opened, given certain other operations) and therefore, people *choose*, *reject*, and *decide*. A computer can process two or more kinds of trains of instructions at the same time, that is in *parallel* (therefore people can process in *parallel*), and so on. Perhaps the worst offender is the computer's *short-term storage*, that is, some circuits are set or programmed to hold certain information for a limited time, until something else happens, and the circuit is then *cleared*. The short-term storage concept led to an enormous amount of research energy on so-called short-term memory, a concept that even today is popularly discussed as if it represented some kind of reality. Actually, computers can hold any amount of data forever, but because some data are not needed after they are processed, they can be eliminated. The fact that humans cannot remember much for long if they hear it only once was taken as an analog of the temporary storage in a computer and human *short-term memory* was invented.

With meaningful materials (words), strategies and subjective organization, and "computerese," psychologists were able to spend the 1960s and the greater part of the 1970s busily at work building new roads to a hoped-for appreciation of learning.

Psycholinguistics

But there was a new development to quickly capture the attentive interest of the verbal-learning psychologists. Words were, after all, a part of language, and linguists had begun to develop their own field of linguistics beyond the old limits of cataloging languages, classifying phonemes and morphemes of different kinds of native speakers, and searching out the philological orgins of words. They had begun to discuss how language originates, how it is used (grammar, syntax, and semantics), and, in general, to make contact with psychology. Psychologists did not hesitate to join forces, and a new field of psycholinguistics began to emerge. The complexities of language and its use presented such formidable problems in relation to an understanding of verbal behavior that many students began to doubt the capacity of behavioristically inclined psychologists to cope with the issues. They, instead, sought refuge under the protective wings of nativists, who solved the problem by postulating innate capacities conferred on humans through genetics.

With the addition of psycholinguistics, it is clear that unless someone stumbles onto some serendipitous solution, there will be many busy travelers on all of the roads allegedly leading to a solution of the problems of learning. In the meantime, critics of the educational systems who point to deficiencies in teaching reading, writing, and arithmetic might well wonder if any progress is being made or if the new roads are only endless circles.

With the above introduction, we can examine the findings of the corps of verbal-leaning psychologists to determine if they have progressed beyond Ebbinghaus and/or if they have either invalidated or made use of the findings of the earlier learning theorists and their students who worked with animals. Because the range of topics to which the new roads lead is so vast, we can only look at a sample of the more provocative studies and lines of research. The extent of our review does not represent the relative importance or future potential worth. What looks like a tiny beginning today may turn out to be a giant step forward. We cannot proceed in a systematic way because there are no logical steps of development in the new approaches. We can only try to impose a sense of orderly progress and will start with animals and language learnings.

ANIMALS AND LANGUAGE

It is obvious that many domesticated animals can be trained to respond to language or verbal cues. Dogs are traditionally trained to sit, heel, and fetch. When dogs set up a search when someone shouts "Rats," one might begin to wonder how far their behavior represents some kind of meaning as divorced from some simple conditioning. But dogs do not use language on their own. To be sure, they can indicate some kinds of needs or "desires" by appropriate gestures and movements. Every dog owner can be trained by his or her dog to know when the dog would like to go out. While Clever Hans could "count" by tapping with his hoof and some dogs have been trained to bark out answers to arithmetical questions, the use of language by animals (perhaps excluding bird calls) is rather limited.

In recent years, two lines of research have developed to train chimpanzees in the use of expressive language. It appears from work by Gardner and Gardner (1969) that chimpanzees can be trained to use the American sign language of the deaf to a relatively considerable degree. Perhaps because of neural or other physiological (throat) differences from man, chimpanzees cannot pronounce words, but they can move their hands and fingers in appropriate ways to communicate with a relatively primitive grammar (largely in relation to personal needs). The chimpanzee, Washoe, for example, can tell someone in sign language that she wants a banana, a drink, to go for a ride, or to be played with or tickled. With a vocabulary of some 150 signs, Washoe and a number of other chimpanzees can function more effectively than some retarded humans.

Another technique has been used by Premack (1970) to teach chimpanzees grammatical expressions. In Premack's procedure, colored pieces of plastic, which can be placed on a magnetic board, can come to represent objects, actions, and people, so that a chimpanzee can, in effect, address a certain person and request a particular object or event. The order of placement is a syntax that is imposed by the trainer, and the success of such training again testifies to the fact that expressive grammatical communication is not restricted to humans. While the training is long and arduous and probably cannot approximate that of adult humans, the positive results suggest that the interpretation of language as learned behavior rather than as a native capacity is not completely out of order. The fact that a chimpanzee can communicate grammatically suggests that if grammars are innate, they are not restricted to humans. On the other hand, because the grammars have been taught to the chimpanzee, it might suggest that they are not innate in humans.

The suggestion that apes can learn some kinds of symbolic communication should be taken with caution. Limber (1977) has criticized the conclusion that the trained apes are actually using anything corresponding to genuine human language. Limber cites Descartes' conclusion that language is a uniquely human operation and believes that the best achievements of the apes amount to "naming" activities that do not surpass the earliest phases of human language functions, such as the two-year-old child might demonstrate.

The problems posed by the nature of language are indeed complex, and we must recognize that psychologists' efforts toward appreciating the nature of language are still only preliminary, if not primitive, approaches. We can excuse our present ignorance by pointing out that the subject of language has only recently become of serious concern and that learning psychologists in the past have either taken the subject too lightly or considered it too difficult to challenge.

THE BEHAVIORAL ORIENTATION

The behaviorist approach to language has never been seriously implemented. In this connection, it might be pertinent to note that Pavlov, basing his views on studies like those of Ivanov-Smolensky (1927), regarded language as a "second signal system," a different order of stimuli that could serve as conditioned or unconditioned stimuli beyond the lights, sounds, and pressures which could be imposed on a laboratory animal. What Ivanov-Smolensky did was to use a verbal command, such as "Press," for a child holding a rubber bulb. The child would respond by squeezing the bulb, the verbal command functioning, in this case, as an unconditioned stimulus. A tone or click could precede the command and serve as a conditioned stimulus. We can recall the Roessler and Brogden experiment (see chapter 9), where a nonsense syllable was used as a conditioned stimulus for a vasodilation response. The Pavlovian school did not develop the interest in language behavior as a conditioning operation and left it pretty much in the status of only a different variety of stimulation sources. Staats (1968) has offered a broad theoretical account of how conditioning principles operate in verbal behavior, and the interested reader can consult his work.

Watson (1924) treated the subject with some disdain and presumed that language behavior was subject to the same laws (conditioning) as any other responses. Skinner (1947) took what must be regarded as a preliminary look at language and also concluded that language is behavior that is "shaped up" and learned as a function of reinforcement by the community in which the learner grows up. Skinner did not launch an intensive programmatic research into language, and his possibly valuable contribution in the analysis of language behavior has been largely ignored. His invented terms to describe language features ("tacts," "mands," "autoclitics") are not commonly employed by modern psycholinguists, although they are rather careful descriptions of some language features. Much of the language as normally used by the average adult certainly demonstrates the importance of community reinforcement. When we look at various subgroups of our population, for example residents in various sections of the country, different age groups, and even different time periods within such subdivisions, we find evidence of changing practices not only in use of novel expressions but in having the same words mean different things to different people at different times. When a teen-ager says that something is "heavy," or "cool," he or she is not referring to its weight or temperature. Idioms change continually as do (un) grammatical forms. The innate grammar of Chomsky (1957) must be incredibly flexible to adjust to the changes imposed on linguistic components as new verbal fads come and go.

In spite of the changes introduced into a language community, the Skinner analysis does call attention to the common learning experiences that control verbal expression. Children do learn to "tact" things (that is, to identify). The Gardners' chimpanzees also learn to "tact," and they frequently make the sign for "What is that," although the sign may not represent precisely what the chimpanzee may be asking. The chimpanzee, like the child learning to talk, is expressing some ignorance, perhaps anxiety, when it makes the sign. The human child uses the words but may only be responding or behaving in a way he or she has learned to respond when meeting a novel object.

A great deal of children's speech and gestures amounts to obvious imitation of parental patterns. Children can run off long sentences that might even sound quite mature and intelligent to the auditor who has not heard the mother say the very same words, perhaps repeatedly. A three-year-old can say to someone (doll, pet, peer, or adult): "Now that's the last one you are going to get, believe me. That's final! I've had it with you." The child can say this with all the decorative inflections and gestures that make the sentence emphatic. The performance is impressive, but its history is quite clear. Such patterns of speech are called by Skinner "echoic," and such "echoic" speech makes up a large part of any speaker's repertoire. We are constantly mouthing what others say as we listen to them and repeating virtually the same words in response to their verbal behavior toward us. We fall into patterns of mimicking ourselves and frequently repeat the same sentences when reporting the same events or experiences to different people. Chomsky and his supporters continually express their surprise at the marvelous human capacity to formulate new sentences that have never been uttered before, but they keep saying this in the same old way. What should be described as surprising is the unusual commonality of speech patterns we encounter from the same person.

While it must be admitted that behaviorists have not made much of a contribution to the analyses of speech development and that they have not demonstrated any clear and consistent operation of learning principles operating in all aspects of the refined speech of highly articulate adults, it can be recognized that not much research has been devoted to this subject by learning psychologists, who have kept busy in other ways. Because of their penchant for working with animals, they have spent fruitless years trying to teach apes to talk (Cathy Hayes [1951] and Keith Hayes succeeded in teaching their home-reared chimpanzee, Vicki, to say "mama," "papa," "cup," and "up" after several years of patient toil—they might have made more progress watching a human child with the same care). We have seen how Mowrer (1950) approached the problem of training talking birds and emerged with some provocative insights that might apply to some aspects of human speech development. To denounce such preliminary efforts as representing the complete failure of a behaviorist approach and to take refuge in nativism might be regarded as at least premature. Not all problems are solved upon command; some problems can take centuries.

The modest efforts of Staats (1968) to find a stepping-stone to the central problem of how one learns to put words together into new patterns may eventually prove helpful. For the present, we must put the question aside and await the preparation of a reasonably large collection of children's biographies of language acquisition on a minute-by-minute (not three-month hourly samples) basis. When we have data about what words a child has heard and what the child says and the conditions under which the child says them, we will be in a more secure position to find out how the child learned them and how his or her grammatical transformations come into being.

We glanced briefly at the Mowrer theory of language acquisition (chapter 10) and at current attempts to teach language to the great apes. In this book, we will go no further with this complex subject and refer the reader to the work of Brown (1973) and Carrol (1953) as appropriate sources for an appreciation of the ramifications of the topic. We will assume with Carrol that language behavior represents an acquired skill without specific consideration of how that particular skill is acquired. Our own concern will be with the ways in which psychologists have studied the learning process using already qualified users of a language.

LEARNING AND READING

Just as we do not know much about how children learn to talk, we are not very sure about how people learn to respond to the written word. We do not know yet, despite the efforts of many educators and experimental psychologists, how people learn to read. Gibson and Levin (1975) have probed the problem intensively and have analyzed the perceptual learning factors along with the syntactic and semantic variables that are intimately involved. According to Gibson and Levin, reading involves a complex collection of skills and rules that govern our ability to process written information for a wide variety of purposes. Learning psychologists using college students learning lists of words have bypassed the problem of how the subjects learned the basic skill required for responding to the words as such. We will not attempt to go beyond them in this book and can recommend only that interested parties consult the Gibson and Levin authoritative work, with some additional inspection of Huey's (1908) classic on the subject, *Psychology and Pedagogy of Reading.*

STRATEGIES IN VERBAL LEARNING

The orientation of the new verbal learning investigators in post–World War II researches was to view the learner as someone who came into the learning laboratory with a background different from that of everyone else and who would not simply sit and absorb by repetition. Regardless of the nature or arrangement of the learning materials, the learner would approach the task in some personal, somewhat individual way. The learner would "do his or her own thing." What these "own things" were came to be known as learning strategies. To aid and abet such strategies, many investigators began to permit some freedoms. We have already mentioned free recall, and we can look at some samples of the new approach; starting with a free recall study by Glanzer and Cunitz (1966) may serve us well. In this study, subjects heard 20 words (at three-second intervals) and were asked to recall as much of the list as possible in any order by writing down the answers. Immediately, we encounter a question: Would the results be the same if the subjects were asked to report vocally? When subjects are given such freedom in writing their responses, how do they react? Frequently, they write down the last three words first (they might write them at the bottom of a list if they suspect that order will be looked at). The last three words are commonly remembered, compared with words in the middle of a list. If the results are plotted by original word order, there will be a sharp rise at the end of the list. Such a finding is very consistent and has received a label—the *recency effect.*

The first few words are also remembered better than the middle, and this consistent finding also acquired a label, the *primacy effect.* Both these effects or findings were well known to students of nonsense syllables, who described such findings as the serial-learning curve, which typically showed the progress of learning as one of working toward the middle from both ends. The analysis of such findings with words (or nonsense syllables) reveals apparently that subjects attempt to recite (repeat, rehearse) the first few words as frequently as they can, but as the list proceeds, the time becomes too short to go back to the beginning, and the middle items receive less rehearsal. At the end of the list, the last few items are still "reverberating as traces" and can be recalled pretty much on a "sound" basis, that is, the words need not even mean anything and still be repeated without having made any serious impact. If the recall is delayed for 30 seconds, the last three words will not be remembered any better than the middle items. If the primacy effect is really a rehearsal effect, it should be so labeled, and primacy can be dismissed as a principle (at least in such studies); because recency is so short-lived, it appears to be of little importance in accounting for learning (since, actually, no learning of significance occurs).

Active Rehearsal

Another form of repetition is that of active rehearsal as opposed to passive repetition. Active, in this instance, means trying to think of the materials instead of mouthing them or reading them. As far back as 1917, A. I. Gates had students read factual statements representing biographical facts about a person. Some subjects would read the statements over and over; others would read for a short time and then actively try to remember the statements. Gates found that recall improved more and more as the reading time was reduced and that the attempted recall or active rehearsal time increased up to a 90 percent to 10 percent ratio. Ebbinghaus had, of course, introduced the active rehearsal method with his nonsense syllables, but he did not study it as a strategy.

Intralist Associations

If rehearsal or repetition do not work too well, what else can the subject do? To some extent, what the learners can do depends on the nature of the items involved in the list perhaps more than on the learner, although some researchers do not draw such distinctions. For example, if the third word in a 20-word list is *bell*, the ninth, *book*, and the seventeenth, *candle*, a learner who is familiar with the phrase (also a book title, *Bell, Book, and Candle*) might, if he or she remembers any of these words, find himself or herself reporting the other two. What is happening is that any word has associated words in the learner's history and that if such associated words are included in a list, they can stimulate each other into existence, particularly since they have just been seen or heard, albeit not in a direct order. If a list contained the words *four*, *score*, and *seven*, it is likely that some subjects would report the three of these if they reported any one.

Clustering

The importance and extent of such intralist associations has been demonstrated repeatedly by Deese (1959). As mentioned earlier, Bousfield (1953) and Tulving (1972) reported that their subjects would tend (with repeated trials) to report words in a sequence (different for everyone) but becoming more and more systematic as trials went on. Bousfield found that words tended to provoke other words (as associates) and be reported together in clusters. Such clusters would be different for everyone because everyone's learning history is different. This observation of clustering has been found repeatedly and can be manipulated by constructing lists that consist of groups of related words (categories), with the words from any one category scattered throughout the list. Thus, if the words *north, east, south,* and *west* occur in the list among such words as *table*, *chair*, *bed*, and *lamp* and words such as *father*, *mother*, *sister*, and *brother*, almost anyone can recall all 12 words after one hearing. In effect, we have to remember only three words that are not even in the list (*direction*, *furniture*, and *family*). Any errors are likely to be inclusion errors—someone might mention *sofa* or *uncle*. Other kinds of clustering may occur, for example, all the words beginning with a certain letter or of a certain length may be reported more or less together.

Thus, clustering may be considered a strategy if the learner looks for such prospective associations within a list. Frequently, however, the learner may cluster without knowing that he or she is doing so. In the latter case, the word *strategy* would not be aptly used. In its place, the label *subjective organization* has been supplied to cover anything that happens to direct the course of recall. Because different subjects report different orders, it is subjective in the sense of being personal or individual, and because it becomes more and more systematized, it can be considered to be organization. What any given subject does may take a variety of forms, some of which are altered or abandoned in mid-course, and not much is gained by pursuing this kind of research.

Mnemonics

One form of strategy that has been pretty much ignored by psychologists is the effort by some learners to apply some deliberate (sometimes well-developed) scheme for recall of unrelated items. We have already reviewed a variety of mnemonic devices (see chapter 3, Appendix) and only mention them here to suggest that some learners will look for possible applications of previously prepared (or successful in the past) techniques. Thus, they might try to form a story from the unrelated items or at least run them into sentences. Even though a sentence contains more words, it is easier to remember than otherwise unstructured items. Thus, *man*, *sugar*, *box*, *car*, and *home*, can be formed into "The man bought some sugar, put it into a box, went to his car and drove home." Being sure to omit the verbs, the words can be remembered readily. Hebb (1949) pointed out that one can hardly remember "rec-com-del-lih-tob-bac-coh-har-til" after hearing these noises once, but "I can recommend the delights of tobacco heartily" is easily repeated. Forming sentences and stories can be effective with some word lists, but because the lists are randomly structured, some words cannot be fitted in easily and the strategy breaks down.

Imposed Strategies

When learners are asked to learn something and left to their own devices, they will usually approach the task with whatever old learning habits they happen to feel suitable. The typical laboratory task of learning a list of words does not appear to distress them too much, however silly they may regard it. They are generally acceptant of the assignment and proceed, within the strictures imposed by the experimenter. They exercise whatever freedom they can enjoy and usually embark on the effort as a chore that has to be completed in one way or another. But different people try different strategies or tactics, presumably on the basis of what has worked for them before. This is not the first time they have had to learn some collection of disparate items.

When the writer asked some 200 students to learn a list of 20 words, each word appearing at a three-second interval, the subjects reported at least 15 different approaches they employed, with some subjects trying different approaches on successive trials. The approaches or techniques included:

1. rapid repetition of as many previous words as possible (the most common report)
2. repeating groups of three or five words or repeating each word as often as possible in three seconds
3. repeating remembered words and ignoring the others
4. looking for words beginning with the same letter or similar characteristics, for example, length
5. looking for words that went together (belonged in the same categories)
6. making up sentences
7. making up stories
8. spelling the words, writing them out with a finger
9. imaging ("picturing" the words themselves)
10. imaging what the words meant

The fact that the subjects were certainly not all doing the same thing at the same time suggests that the usual statistical procedure of grouping the scores earned is at least dubious. We can also note that each procedure worked to some extent, although the scores, of course, differed. Some subjects remembered as few as ten words after five trials. Others remembered all 20 words after three trials. Did each subject use the best method or technique? Whatever the subject did, it might have been the best for him or her. We cannot judge from one effort.

THE ORIENTING TASK

What the subjects were doing in the effort to learn the 20 words can be described as an orientation in relation to some situation. What operations does one attempt or go through in any particular learning effort? Whatever it is that subjects do in such situations has been labeled *the orienting task*. In the experiment mentioned above, the subjects were told to learn something, and whatever they did as individuals amounted to a self-imposed orienting task.

Suppose the subjects had not been told to learn the 20-word list mentioned above but had been told to do something with the words as they appeared. Would they learn anything if they were not told to learn, had no desire to learn, no intent to learn, and did not try to learn? They could have been told to "check the following words for spelling." With such an instruction, we might be safe in assuming that most subjects would check the spelling and would not try to learn any of the words. If we now impose a test and ask for a recall of the list, any learning that occurred can be described as incidental to the spelling orientation. We would, of course, ask the subjects if any had tried to learn the words besides checking the spelling, and if any admitted such an effort, we could exclude their results. Such incidental or nonintentional learning holds great interest for us, because much of what we do learn was learned with no great desire or yearning for the knowledge.

INCIDENTAL LEARNING

The term *incidental* does not communicate much in itself. It has a nuance of unimportance, but this is most misleading. A great deal can be learned incidentally, as we shall see. The word refers to what happens when experimental subjects are asked to do something specific in relation to some material that other (control) subjects are asked to learn. Thus, in a simple case, some subjects (incidental) would be asked to count all the words in a list, while other subjects (intentional) would be asked to learn the list. Assuming equal time was given to both groups, we could expect that the counters would know how many words there were but not be able to name many, if any, while the learners might not know how many there were but would be sure to name some. If the counters remembered any words at all, such retention would be described as incidental learning because they had not been asked to learn anything. Any learning that took place would be incidental to the effort or assignment.

A great many studies of incidental learning have been reported, that is, studies where some subjects learned something when not asked to do so. This finding by itself is of no importance, but it is important to note that depending upon what the subjects do, they learn either nothing, a moderate amount, or as much as or more than the subjects who were instructed to learn. The point is that intention to learn, wanting to learn, motivation, interest, and so forth are quite irrelevant, as it is presumed that the experimental subject had no need, desires, or intention to learn. He or she was not supposed to learn or try to learn. We are not interested in whether people learn without intention; we are interested in what they do when they do learn.

We can get some leads as to how learning occurs if we look at the kinds of tasks experimental subjects have been assigned and how much they learned when they were not asked to do so. Because the studies done were executed by various researchers without any systematic grand plan, there is no organized set of tasks of a systematic nature that can be reported which would provide immediate analogs to classroom learning or individual study of various kinds of learning material; however, a review of such studies may be of service in theorizing.

KINDS OF ORIENTING TASKS IN INCIDENTAL LEARNING STUDIES

In general, there are two experimental designs in which incidental learning can be observed. In one approach or procedure, you can instruct someone to learn something and then test him or her on something else that he or she might have learned in addition. For example, if instructed to learn the content of several newspaper stories, you might recall that one story was in the lower left-hand corner of the right-hand page in the middle of the paper even though you did not try to learn this. If a story is read for general content, the reader might be quizzed on specific facts, spelling, or typographical errors.

In another paradigm or experimental design, some subjects (the intentional or standard control group) are asked to learn something, say, a list of words. The experimental subjects (incidental learners) are asked to do something with the material, but nothing is said about learning. The subjects might be asked to sort or classify the words; or they might be asked to alphabetize, count, or pronounce them; or they might be asked to judge or rate them on some kinds of scales. By forcing the incidental learners to do something, it is presumed that they have to look at, inspect, scrutinize material, or otherwise orient themselves with respect to the task. Whatever the incidental learners do is called the orienting task. After the learners have met some criterion, the incidental learners are tested; if they learn anything at all, it is assumed that the orienting task was responsible for the learning.

If the incidental learners learn more than the standard group, then it might be safe to assume that the standard group is operating under less efficient procedures, maybe even hurting its own progress.

The following illustration of an incidental learning experiment might demonstrate the issues.

INCIDENTAL LEARNING: AN EXAMPLE

In a study of how imagery might be used to remember a long chain of associations, the author (Bugelski 1974) asked his learners to try to remember 20 words in serial order. Some subjects (the control group) were told nothing else, and the 20 words were then pronounced in order at the rate of five seconds per word.

An imagery group was told to try to picture the second word in some interacting relationship with the first word; they were then told that they should picture the third word in relation to the second, the fourth in connection with the third, and so on.

An incidental learning group was approached with a request for assistance in evaluating some words to be used in an experiment that was being planned. The incidental group was asked to use a five-point rating scale and to judge the relative ease and richness of imagery that was aroused when the second word was imaged in connection with the first, the third with the second, and so on. These subjects completed the 19 ratings involved at a five-second rate and were then asked to write down as many words as they could remember and to try to write them in sequence. Nothing had been said about learning anything to this group, and not a single one suspected any kind of test. The results of the recall for the three groups are shown in Table 14.1.

Note that the incidental group learned more than the intentional group for the total recall (14.00 to 9.71) and for the sequence (9.52 to 5.46). In fact, the differences here are almost incredible. What these results show is that trying to learn this particular task by following some standard routine that had been acquired through grammar and secondary school results in a very poor showing. People who are not trying to learn anything but merely indulging in some imagery (which they do not take too seriously) learn almost twice as much. A glance at the imagery learning group reveals they were far superior to both other groups. Apparently, they were doing something more efficiently, or perhaps, the raters were hurting their recall by wasting time judging the imagery value. If one could get an imagery control

TABLE 14.1

Mean Recall Scores for 20 Words in or out of Sequence (Total) with or without Imagery Instructions

	Intentional Learning Group		Imagery Learning Group		Imagery Rating Group (incidental)	
	Total	Sequence	Total	Sequence	Total	Sequence
Mean	9.71	5.46	17.16	15.07	14.00	9.52
Number	39	—	43	—	18	—

Source: Compiled by the author.

group to engage only in the imagery operation, they would presumably learn as much as the group instructed to use imagery in learning.

In the illustration shown in Table 14.1, the incidental learners learned much better than the subjects who were trying to learn. Not all orienting tasks are equally successful for incidental learners. In Table 14.2, we shall list a number of orienting tasks with a variety of effects. In some of the studies, the subjects served in both roles, that is, as standard learners and incidental learners. In others, there were two or more groups of subjects. Our concern is with identifying the degree or amount of effect of the orienting task on the learning test. A review of incidental learning studies by McLaughlin (1965) provides many more illustrations for the interested student. McLaughlin stresses that incidental learning is not any special kind of learning in itself. The results obtained by incidental learners must be interpreted in terms of what they were trying to do.

It should be noted that all of the studies listed show some learning in the experimental (incidental) groups. The studies were selected because they do show these results. Some orienting tasks appear to have no value in producing learning. These include such activities as matching nonsense syllables with geometric forms, guessing a number to go with a nonsense syllable, rating voice qualities of speakers instead of listening to what they had to say, and writing out nonsense syllables as many as six times (this leads to worse results than writing them out twice [Saltz 1971, p. 358]). Presumably, many orienting tasks could be devised that produced no learning of the kind which the intentional group achieves. Such irrelevant activities have no interest for us unless someone practices them when he or she *intends* to learn. Recall the Gates (1917) demonstration that simply reading over and over some material is of little value, compared with attempting to recite it. This study seems to have had little impact on the average grammar, secondary, or college student, who still hopes to get by by reading over the material or, if misguided by some speed-reading salesman, into skimming the material. The only value of speed reading, if there is one, is to help you decide if you want to read what you are skimming.

ANTI-INTENTIONAL LEARNING

The notion that one must *want* to learn in order to do so is strongly embedded in our culture. Parents and teachers commonly complain about children who do not learn "because they do not want to." They may have a point, as just indicated; if the child does not get exposed to the material, no learning can take place. But the intent to learn may not go beyond that initial stage. Wanting to learn may have nothing to do with whether we learn or not. We must consider the fact that we learn a lot that we do not want to know. We do not want to hear bad news, but it takes only one telling to learn of a death in the family, that unwanted guests are arriving, that the Internal

TABLE 14.2

Some Samples of Incidental Learning Studies

Experimenter	Control Task	Incidental Learning Orienting Task	Outcome
Postman and Adams (1956)	Learn 20 nonsense syllables (Group 1)	Give meaningful associations to the syllables (Group 1)	Intentional best
	Learn same and give association values (Group 2)	Match list with geometric figures (Group 2)	Incidental with associations better than intentional with figure matching
	Learn same and match with geometric figures (Group 3)		
Postman, Adams, and Phillips (1955)	Free recall of nonsense syllables varying in association value (Group 1)	Rate syllables for association values	No difference on high association value syllables
			In recognition test, no difference on high or low.
	Learn and rate 30 adjectives	Rate for familiarity	Incidental learned 40 percent of intentional mean
Mechanic (1962)	Learn and rate adjectives for meaningfulness	Rate only	Incidental learning proportional to meaningfulness

Postman and Adams (1957)	Spell and learn 14 CVCs	Spell the CVCs	Incidental learned 62 percent of the mean of intentional group
Saltzman (1953)	Learn numbers associated with events—try to think of some connection	Think of connections between numbers and events	Both groups successful
Mechanic (1962)	Learn top syllable of a pair in a list of pairs	(1) Cancel certain letters in syllables (2) Guess which syllable experimental group selected—extrasensory perception (ESP) (3) Pronounce silently and judge similarity of meaning (syllable supposed to be foreign language)	Best incidental recall in task 3 Least in task 1
Silver (see Saltz 1971)	Put 20 noun-adjective pairs in sentence Learn in pairs	Same, no learning instruction	No difference between experimental and control groups
Postman and Adams (1960)	Fill 35 blanks in 214-word paragraph Learn the words	Same, no learning instruction	No difference Intentional 40 percent Incidental 40 percent

Source: As given by Silver in Saltz (1971). Compiled by the author.

Revenue Department wants to review our tax return, or that an aching tooth must come out. Most of us know about products that we never intend to use. We learn about them through obnoxious television jingles we find ourselves humming and hating.

In an experimental demonstration (Bugelski 1970), the writer asked college students to look at 32 words exposed on a screen for four seconds. When each word appeared, the students were told to recite it out loud four times. Half the words were marked with a plus sign, the others not. Some students were told that only the marked words were to be remembered and that they should ignore the unmarked words and try not to learn them, as they would interfere with the recall of the marked words. After all the words had been exposed, the students were asked to recall all of them, including the unmarked words. Despite remarks, such as, "You told us not to remember the unmarked words," all of the students remembered some of them, with an average recall of 4.2 of the unmarked words, compared with 8.9 of the marked words (total 13.1). A similar group of students with the same instructions were told to form an image of the object referred to by each word, marked or not. These students recalled 7.9 marked words and 7.4 unmarked words, despite their intent of not learning the unmarked words. It appears that if you perceive some stimulus and react to it in some way that you can learn something whether you want to or not. Simply seeing and saying a word will result in some learning. Adding some other operation, such as imaging, will increase the learning to the point where the intent to learn becomes irrelevant.

McDaniel and Masson (1977) take a more tempered view of intent. In an incidental learning study, they were able to show that intent to learn can be of some consequence when there is time for rehearsal in addition to processing operations. Thus, they found that exposing words at five-second intervals resulted in no difference between incidental and intentional learners in immediate recall. At a ten-second interval, again, there was no difference in immediate recall, but after a 24-hour delay, the intentional learners were significantly better. In a further control experiment, they discovered that such a difference would disappear if only one kind of processing (thinking of appropriate adjectives to go with the concrete noun stimulus words) was used. The original difference was found with a categorizing orienting task. McDaniel and Masson do not discuss the role of intent beyond suggesting extra rehearsal time. If intent means no more than that subjects will rehearse more, it becomes equivalent to rehearsal and loses any other intrinsic power. If incidental subjects do not process the material as long as intentional subjects, we should expect no more than McDaniel and Masson found. Obviously, a categorizing task can be completed within the five-second interval, and incidental subjects would turn to any other interest. The intentional subjects would spend the remaining five seconds with additional processing or repetition.

Our excursion into incidental learning supports the conclusion that intention to learn, desire to learn, or "motivation" for learning are all irrelevant to the learning operation. At best, such "states" might bring the learner to the learning situation. The learner might pick up a book; unless he or she does, he or she will not learn what is in it. From that point on, however, wanting to learn will be of no help. The learner might well give up wanting and start an orienting operation that will help the learning of that material.

15

Verbal Learning and Processing

In the last chapter, we noted that how much you learn or what you learn depends on how you reacted to the learning materials and the instructions or demands in the situation. In this chapter, we will look at the kinds of activities learners engage in and how the nature of the material or responses to be learned influence the course of learning.

WHAT IS ORIENTING?

In any orienting task, the learner responds to some kind of stimulation. Speaking loosely, we can say that the learner interacts with the material, or even more loosely, that the learner processes information. This latter phrase is a dangerous bit of psychological jargon, as no one knows what it means. It appears to be meaningful, but it raises embarrassing questions, such as: What is information? What is the nature of processing? If might be safer to stick to more operational language and look at the research findings.

We can illustrate an orienting task by reference to a standard psychology laboratory experiment, namely, the measurement of the span of perception (sometimes called the span of attention and, even, the span of apprehension). In such an experiment, a slide might be presented on a screen for a fraction of a second, perhaps 0.1 of a second. The observer, if looking at the screen and focusing on a fixation point will see some dots or other figures. The observer is asked to report the number of items and usually does fairly well up to about nine dots. Note that the observer is supposed to be looking at a specific point, usually designated by an X. If the observer is looking anywhere else, he or she may not be very successful.

If the task is one of looking at a brief exposure of 16 numbers in a four by four matrix, the observer can usually "catch" the top line of four and report that much. To report more numbers, more time is needed. With more time, different observers are able to report quite divergent results. Thus, at a five-second exposure, most observers will report only five (about one more than they could report after a 0.1-second exposure). With ten seconds, they might report six, indicating that they are able to add about one numeral in five seconds, whereas the first 0.1 of a second could provide about four numerals.

In such orienting tasks, the observer (learner) must do more than stare at the fixation point if he or she is to report something. What the observer does is difficult to discover, as his or her reports are not very helpful. Some information can be developed by noting failures—the observer can report "I wasn't ready," for example, suggesting that readiness is important. When 14 dots are flashed in a 0.1-second exposure, the observer reports, "There were too many to handle." This is of little help, but it suggests that only a limited amount of material can be reported correctly with brief exposures.

In a variation of such research, the observer can be shown three nonsense syllables or three sets of three numerals, as shown below:

H	ZAC			937	H
M	LOM	or		841	M
L	RIS			265	L

The slides are exposed for 0.2 of a second, and the observer is asked to report what he or she saw. Such experiments (Sperling 1963; Posner and Rossman 1965) indicate that for some brief moment, the observer enjoys some "iconic" memory and can report, when asked immediately, any of the syllables or any row of numbers, although he or she cannot report all three sets of letters or numerals. The letters H, M, and L, refer to high, medium, or low tones that can be sounded just as the visual exposure ends and indicate which of the three items the observer should report. If such exposures are repeated (more time), the observer can report more and more. Sometimes a "masking" slide is shown immediately after the stimulus slide has been exposed. The mask might consist of some cross-hatched lines. When masking material is used, the reports are less correct or extensive. Similarly, in so-called short-term memory experiments, (see chapter 16), subjects can recall over longer periods if they are shown material several times or provided longer exposures.

From such research, we can hypothesize that even when "ready," subjects can react effectively to only a limited amount of material per unit time. But the subject's ability to report correctly has not been explained except by postulating an icon, or afterimage, of brief duration. What is more important, perhaps, is to recognize that when there is a limited (feasible) amount of material exposed, the observer cannot be responding to other stimuli (distracters). The kinds of events that occur between exposure and test also have a marked bearing on the report. If the subject in a short-term memory experiment does some mathematical task (subtracting by threes from some given number), he or she will quickly forget what he or she saw; if the subject merely listens to a tone, he or she may not forget as much or so soon (Reitman 1971). In a later study, Reitman (1974) did find forgetting did occur during such intervals when rehearsal was more effectively prevented. She attributed it to "decay." In any case, effective learning requires that stimulation "impacts" on the organism without interference either from too much material in too little time or some other stimulation or activity following immediately. If learning is to occur, some limited stimulation must enjoy some freedom of entry and some after-period free from other stimulation.

Our review of incidental learning can now be looked at from the point of view of what the incidental learners were doing and what they learned. If the orienting task is to count the number of words in a column, the learner can report the number of words, but he or she cannot recite many of them. No one is especially surprised at such a finding. If the incidental learner is asked to think of the meaning of each word, he or she will be able to recite at least some but not be very accurate in telling us how many words there were. Again, this is not surprising. What accounts for the difference? An easy answer is to say that he or she paid attention to different things. The implication of such a statement is that attention has something to do with learning. It might be better simply to say he or she paid *for* something with his or her work. The trouble with *attention* is to identify attention.

ATTENTION AND LEARNING

We can begin as we did in the first chapter and question the existence of *attention*. Everyone knows that if you do not pay attention, you cannot learn. Teachers who see a student looking out the window or engaged in any activity other than looking at the teacher are inclined to suspect that the student is not paying attention. Incidentally, why must you "pay" attention? Is there a cost involved? To whom do you pay the price, and what is the price? If the teacher says, "Pay attention here," and the student looks in the teacher's direction, is the student now "paying attention"? At least, the student is not paying attention to what was outside the window—or could he or she still be thinking about what was outside (probably not as effectively as before)? But assume that the student is in no way any longer preoccupied with the outside and is doing his or her best to pay attention. What is the student doing? If anything, the student is responding in a rather general way, which Pavlov first labeled as "curiosity reflex" when he observed what his dogs would do at the first moments of the occurrence of a conditioning stimulus. We may benefit from a brief review of what we have already learned about the orienting reflex.

THE ORIENTING REFLEX

What Pavlov would see would amount to a general reaction that might be labeled *alertness*—the dog's ears would prick up, his body would tense, or his head would turn in the direction of the sound or light or whatever the stimulus source was. As we have seen (chapter 6), Sokolov (1963) later would attach recording devices to dogs and take motion pictures of dogs in this alert state. By analyzing the body data and the films, Sokolov was able to describe the rather complex reaction to, say, a bell. If the dog's brain had been generating alpha waves prior to the bell, such waves would stop; besides the ears rotating and pricking up, the dog's pupils would dilate. His heart might skip a beat or speed up, the breathing would become shallower, the limbs would tense, and digestive activity might decrease or cease. This package of reactions came to be called the orienting reflex or orienting response. The dog was *paying attention.* But note that this attention is a pattern of *responses:* it is not something that one pays or uses or refuses to give. It is also, in itself, a completely useless response if nothing else happens. At best, it could be classed as a preparatory response, a state of readiness for something else to happen. Thorndike once described the same situation in his law of readiness. In Thorndike's conception of readiness, the dog's nervous system would be in a state of readiness to receive certain stimuli (and not others). Thorndike's readiness was closer to a statement of motivation than to a law of learning, and its value for us is in the point that the dog is *not* ready for a lot of things that at that moment are irrelevant. A student paying attention to the teacher is not ready to hear a door opening at the rear of the room or to observe other students who may be engaged in trying to capture his or her attention. Sokolov found that the orienting response was crucial for conditioning, but in a paradoxical way—it had to be present originally, or no conditioning would take place. At the same time, it had to diminish (habituate) as training continued (or even before it started) if the animal was ever to emit the CR to the CS. If the dog continued to give the orienting response to the CS, conditioning would, of course, be delayed or never occur. The OR could be regarded as the original response to the CS and if the CS was rather strong, the US might never elicit its response. For this reason, CSs are normally of modest strength, that is, stimuli to which the subjects rather rapidly habituate or turn away from as of no direct importance.

What we are saying is that attention itself is not a thing that exists, and it is not a *cause* of anything like learning. It is, if anything, a result, a product, in a loose sense, of stimulation (conditions) that brought it about and, as such, a *condition* itself—a condition that has two aspects, positive and negative. Positively, the attentive learner is ready for stimuli of a certain class to occur, and presumably, he or she can react to such stimuli with greater than ordinary efficiency; negatively, he or she is not ready for other classes of stimuli to occur and will react to them with less than ordinary efficiency. Thus, if an observer is looking at a series of slides with numbers on them, he or she will be able to report them with some accuracy. If a slide with letters is shown instead, the observer will report fewer than if he or she had been looking at an equal number of slides with letters on them. The observer will say, "I did not expect letters." The word *expect* amounts to Thorndike's "readiness" or to attention, although, by itself, it does not contribute to our comprehension in any positive way. In earlier days in psychology, such a result would be attributed to set or preparatory set. Dashiell (1927) once spelled *attention* as *a tension* in describing the same kinds of operations.

We can accept a term such as *attention, set, orienting reflex, expectancy,* or *readiness* and recognize that such terms all refer to a condition that facilitates some kinds of consequent reactions and interferes with others. A pilot concentrating on his air speed meter may find he has run out of gas or landing strip. It is easy to be too careful. Carefulness, concentration, and attention are not agencies that operate on their own. They are, at best, conditions or states during which learning can take place. In summary and in short, attention is a response—one that can itself be learned (as when we develop an interest in something, for example, stamp collecting). We can become better at paying attention to some things and not to others. In much of our lives, we have to learn not to attend to stimuli that do not matter.

Granted all of the above argument, we now know that we can only handle a limited amount of material per unit time, and attention will help learning if it is properly directed, that is, if we are in readiness for certain consequences and are free of distractions, that is we are not attending (responding) to irrelevancies. All of the above statements merely set some ground rules for learning and say nothing about how the learning will now go on. What follows will attempt to approach this, the real, problem. A preliminary or tentative answer has already been implied earlier. We now have the orienting response in being or operation and are ready to look at the orienting task.

CONSEQUENCE OF THE ORIENTING TASK

What we learn is what we do, or, maybe better, what happens to us or in us. If our orienting task consists of estimating the number of letters in a list of words of varying length, we may not remember any of the words. We may remember some of our estimates. If our orienting task is that of judging a speaker's voice qualities, we may not remember what he or she said, but we may recall some of his or her vocal characteristics. The examples can be proliferated from our review of orienting tasks. In that review, we observed that people who were asked to fill in blanks in sentences or to make up sentences using certain words remembered better than people who merely tried to remember isolated words. Similarly, people who imaged words in connected pairs remembered more than people who tried to learn the pairs. As more and more of a creative effort or increase in working with the meaning of the material, as opposed to its form or structure, was involved, more and more learning took place.

PROCESSING

There is a strong temptation to follow the lead of Craik and Lockhart (1972) and to assert that the amount of learning depends on the amount of processing of the material. Craik describes what he calls "processing" as dealing with material at different levels. He considers looking at the material or even reciting it over and over as a simple, relatively unproductive or superficial processing which will not result in durable retention. Dealing with the meanings of things or words would be processing at a deeper level; thus, Craik suggests a hierarchy of levels. To do him justice, he is not committed to a hierarchical description and entertains the notion of "spread of encoding" operations, but the concept of encoding has its own problems. What seems more useful is to suppose that a variety of different kinds of operations can occur with different consequences. The concept of depth of processing is more mysterious than enlightening and might well be set aside. What we can say is that different operations will take place in different people, depending on their backgrounds, instructions, or the "demands" of the events (sometimes mysteriously attributed to self-instructions—but who instructs the self or whom does the self instruct?). Thus, we can demand that a learner recite each word of a 15-word list aloud three times in a three-second period, showing him or her a new word every three seconds. We know (we hear the recitation) that the learner does so, although he or she may claim to have done something else in addition. Whatever else the learner does in addition, it cannot be very much or systematic, as we move in with new stimuli every three seconds. We could shorten the period or require more repetitions to reduce any additional activity. When the subject is asked to recall the words, we can then evaluate the role of vocal recitation by comparing the performance with one when no such instruction was given. If the scores are identical, we can assume that the subject vocalized three times per word, but silently. The probability is that there will not be identity in the performance, and we can then explore other possibilities to discover what activity is engaged in and what leads to better or worse performances. Such variable activities are what we explored in reviewing the incidental learning research.

PROCESSING AS ACTIVITY

We have arrived at the conclusion that what you learn amounts to what goes on in the learner when he or she is affected by the stimulus components in a situation and how he or she reacts to them. It does not help much to say the learner learns as a function of what goes on in him or her. This may be true, but it is not informative and not subject to direct manipulation or verification. We have to work from the outside even though the work of the learner goes on inside the person, presumably in his or her head. We do not limit the learning activity to the brain—much of the rest of the body may be involved, depending on what is being learned—but we, of necessity, can note only the conditions under which learning does or does not occur and if it does, with what degree of effectiveness.

THE WORK OF LEARNING

By this time, the message of the first chapter that learning involved work should have become clear. The work involved, like more physical tasks, varies in the level of involvement, strain, or energy expenditure. Digging coal is work, but so is clipping bond coupons or rubbing on suntan lotion. The results vary in many ways. Pressing a button may not require much energy, but the results can be magnificent or disastrous, depending on what circuit the button is supposed to close.

Thus far, we have learned that what is learned depends on who the learner is, that is, what is his or her past experience, what state of preparation (attention) he or she is in, and what kinds of responses occur. The last item we have examined only superficially, listing such responses as looking, counting, listening, pronouncing, rating, or estimating in various ways—sorting and classifying, spelling, crossing out items, and so forth. These all help in varying degrees for some kinds of tests but not necessarily for all tests. Two activities or kinds of work we mentioned appeared to be as good as any compared with what people ordinarily do when asked to learn something. These were such activities as putting words into sentences and trying to form images of some interactive sort. In several experimental studies, image makers learned more than normally instructed learners, suggesting that normal operations (whatever they are), though strenuous and dedicated, are not necessarily the best ways of going about learning something.

Putting words into sentences or allowing images to occur appear to be related to something called meaning. In his discussion of processing, Craik places great emphasis on the importance of meaning as bearing on learning and retention. If a process involves meaning, Craik thinks of it as a deeper or more effective kind of process than, say, observing, spelling, or pronouncing. We can spell or pronounce to someone's instruction, but we may not learn much. Allowing or getting meaning into the picture, however, is the most effective processing operation. Craik and Tulving (1975) appreciate that a learner may react in many ways to any material, from simple sensory inspection to some semantic evaluation. When subjects are shown words with or without instructions to learn, they can look at them, try to find rhymes, consider their emotional impact, try to define them, make up sentences, react imaginally, and so forth. On later tests, it has been found that the different kinds of processing produce different results, with sensible, congruent, or semantic operations as the most effective for retention. Students will readily agree—they have always felt they learned something better if they understood it or got its meaning. The reverse of this proposition does not seem to occur to students: that they understand something only after they learn it. What Craik is talking about is that meaningful materials (that is, familiar, previously learned, already equipped with numerous association) can be put together in new combinations or settings more effectively than strange or novel items. This is not, by itself, very exciting. It amounts to the elimination of stage-1 learning when two stages are required (see chapter 12). But students will still protest. They know they learn better when they understand something. Their problem may be that they do not understand what understanding is.

UNDERSTANDING

The term *understanding* should probably be expunged from the dictionary, since it is a word that only creates confusion. It is often used in the context of instruction, where one person is trying to communicate an account of some nature to another who at the moment can be described as ignorant in the sense of not knowing. Thus, a mother may be telling a child why he or she should not say "Goddamn it." The child, having heard the phrase from his mother's mouth, asks, "Why not?" The mother proceeds to "explain" and continues her explanation until the child agrees not to say the words again. The session may terminate with, "Now do you understand?" with the child indicating his or her future compliance in some way. It should be evident that the child can only have learned that his or her mother is displeased and that the road to peaceful relationships with the mother calls for some restraint on language.

When the teacher explains the principle of gravity to a class, he or she makes one statement after another and watches the class for signs of concern or relaxation. The teacher winds up his or her explanation with, "Are there any questions? Does everyone understand?" If there are no questions, the explanation ceases. A later test will reveal that some students did not "understand." Clearly, *understanding* means that, assuming one is free to ask, one does not have any questions left. Not having any questions means that one is satisfied. Consequently, understanding equals satisfaction. But it is generally agreed by logicians that explanations are only descriptions, that fuller explanations are only fuller descriptions, and that ordinarily, one stops the line of description when no further inquiry is presented. Students sometimes argue that an explanation tells *why* something happens whereas a description only tells *what*. No one has yet told us why falling objects obey the law of gravity. Every *because* statement is only an additional description. The more complete a description is, the more one can do with an object or situation, the more one can predict about future consequences, and the happier one can feel. Understanding has nothing to do with the case. It always boils down to "that's how it is."

LEARNING AND MEANING

It is time to meet the issue of meaning and its relationship to learning. The meaning of meaning has always puzzled philosophers, who have not provided any solution that is not entangled with subjective mentalisms. Many psychologists blithely proceed to work with "meaningful" materials and have forsaken nonsense syllables as of little value for use in answering questions about man's learning and problem-solving adaptations. In general, there are two complaints against the use of nonsense materials that are commonly cited by verbal-learning psychologists. The first is a methodological or procedural complaint. Experimenters find that college student subjects refuse to treat nonsense syllables as nonsense material. They find meanings or associations to just about anything the earnest investigator tries to present as a meaningless stimulus. Given the nonsense syllable *mel*, the subject transforms it into *Melvin* or *melt*, and it is no longer nonsense. Only confusion can arise if the results of learning a list of such items are interpreted as reflecting basic learning principles. Perhaps, the answer is not to use the convenient college student as a subject and go back to the chimpanzee, who appears to be capable of learning some kinds of verbal or symbolic materials. The second complaint is that there is something in any message, spoken or written, that is learned or appreciated apart from lexical or phonological features of the words themselves. A message can be given in many forms. Thus, if we want someone to pass the salt, we can ask for it in any language the passer might know, or we can point to it with some other gesture if necessary. Some parental autocrats at the breakfast table merely have to look at the salt to have it passed, and others merely sit in stony silence until someone obliges. Usually, where words are employed, as in connected discourse, the words can say one thing and mean another. Puns and double entendres abound in our surroundings, and it is clear that meanings are communicated almost regardless of the words employed.

To make any real contribution to leaning or psychology, say these psychologists, one must deal with meanings, with semantic features, and stop the endless and pointless researching over the sensory level of word features. Even word features are better remembered if the words are meaningful, are in correct grammatical order, and are in relatively common usage (Marsten-Wilson and Tyler 1976).

The current total involvement of cognitive psychologists with semantics may hold some promise of bringing about some enlightenment, but the situation is not much improved over what the philosophers left us as far as any genuine forward steps are concerned. It is easy enough to demonstrate that more meaningful material is learned more readily than less meaningful or nonsense material or that correct syntax helps. Syntax and approximations to English can be manipulated, but when it comes to manipulating meaning, nothing is actually being done that does not simply assert the meaningfulness of some sentence, word, or message.

It might be better, instead, to approach the concept of meaning gingerly, step by step, objectively and operationally, and attempt to assess its role in learning along the lines introduced and developed by learning psychologists, who were also dissatisfied with nonsense materials and tried to work constructively but directly with the problem of meaning. We can grant, in advance, that the problem is not necessarily solved, but at the same time, it can be argued that the contributions that have been presented for consideration were not exploited. We have already described how learning psychologists have interpreted meaning. The reader will recall Mowrer (chapter 10) and his efforts to consider meaning as an emotional response with imagery as a denotative support. We have seen Hull place the burden of carrying meanings or r_g s, and we recall Osgood's (chapter 11) efforts to expand the r_g into ($r_m - s_m$) with his operational treatment of meanings through use of the semantic differential. We recall also Hebb's and Tolman's expectancies based on prior or early learning. We have also noted Noble's *m* measure of meaningfulness and Paivio's imagery interpretation of meaning. While no one of these accounts may be completely satisfying, collectively, they are impressive as reflecting an interpretation of meaning as an internal, mediational kind of response representing prior learnings. The apparently diverse set of mechanisms has a common base, including stimulating and/or motivational dimensions. Meaning is not necessarily a static reaction but a mediating one even though nothing serious develops in the way of action as a necessary consequence.

In a way, the old Wundtian description of perception as the addition of past experience to a sensation (where perception is regarded as somehow incorporating meaning into a stimulus) is borne out by the theorists listed above. It remains to show the relationship between meaning and learning and vice versa.

There appears to be no controversy among behaviorist or functionally minded psychologists that meanings are learned, not given. Starting with James (1890) who described the consciousness of an infant as a buzzing, booming confusion arising from environmental stimulation, American psychologists have consistently proposed that meaning can only be talked about when an organism has had a sequence of experiences such that some initial stimulation results in some preparatory response, set, r_g, cell assembly, expectancy, emotional reaction, or imagery that facilitates a subsequent response to some succeeding stimulus. When that happens, we speak of meaning even though the meaning, as such, is not a function in its own right and plays no role in any mentalistic sense. We could argue that meaning is irrelevant, although mediating responses are not. On the contrary, the mediating responses are necessary for some kinds of operations to occur. Meaning, then, becomes an immaterial term, in both common senses of the word (having no material body or form and of no importance or relevance, inconsequential).

Meaning and Learning

In relation to learning, we can appreciate the relevance of meaning in two ways: In the first place, we recognize that students commonly report that they do not learn something until they "grasp the meaning" of the material, assignment, problem or procedure; they argue that they cannot learn something until or unless they understand it. We have already dealt with understanding and can recognize now that it refers to some emotional reaction of a pleasant, relaxed, or satisfying nature—that no additional questions are occurring to the learner and that he or she feels ready to go on. We also recognize that the learner can be greatly deceived, that his or her readiness may be premature, that there are possibly many questions that could be asked but that he or she is not asking them, perhaps because he or she is too ignorant in the situation to have the questions arise, and that he or she has not noticed (been stimulated by) some features or aspects of a situation. The simple fact of the matter is that the feelings of understanding are exactly the same if one misunderstands, and they are irrelevant in either case, except that in the latter instance, the learner may stop learning (working at the task). If meaning has any role to play in this context, it is that of serving as a goal, but that goal should be carefully defined.

In the second place or role, meaning serves a descriptive function in relationship to the material. It has been demonstrated beyond question that so-called meaningful material is learned more easily than nonmeaningful material, at least when lists of words or syllables, forms, or other kinds of stimuli are concerned. Here, we have a different interpretation of meaning. We are saying learning proceeds efficiently when material is familiar; when it has been previously experienced, perhaps frequently; when a discrimination operation (extinction of generalized responses) has been effected; when there are suitable associations; when, in Hebb's terms, there has been considerable "early" learning; and where procedures have been perfected (as in the learning set studies) so that competing or conflicting responses are not generated. We are asserting that meaningful material is learned more efficiently when much of the learning has already been done before the present or immediate problem is approached. "Late learning," to return to Hebb's usage, can take place quickly—in one trial. When such learning does occur, we can assume it was accomplished by suitable prior experience. In discussing two-stage learning, we made the point that some time must be devoted to the first stage. If this stage is already accomplished, only one stage, the association, needs to be completed. If the second stage is also prepared for, the learning is complete as soon as the material is encountered. Thus, to learn to say "mother" to the stimulus "father" is no problem for anyone familiar with English. Even if the learner does not know Latin, he can learn to say "*mater*" to the stimulus "*pater*" almost as easily. To learn to say "*mere*" to the stimulus "*pere*" might give a slight pause, and to learn to say "*matka*" to the stimulus "*ojciec*" could create difficulties.

Emotions, Imagery, and Meaning

If we turn to the contributions of Mowrer and Paivio, we can recognize the virtues of additional aspects of meaning. To feel some emotional reaction at some level of intensity where it can become a conditioned response to some stimulation may be important in the learning process. To cite the earlier example of basketball free throws, it is probably the case that if one does not care whether or not the ball goes through the hoop, one will never learn to make foul shots. The reluctant participant in a bowling alley activity who could not care less about knocking down some silly-looking Indian clubs with a ball will never learn to roll strikes. The reinforcing stimuli of success and failure are fundamental to generate the emotions to which feedback stimuli can be conditioned.

Similarly, in terms of imagery, if one does not take time to allow imagery to occur, nothing much in the way of learning is going to happen. Here, we encounter a still unsolved problem. It is known that imagery takes some time to be generated. In securing his rating scores for imagery, Paivio defined high-imagery values in terms of whether an image was aroused quickly or only with difficulty. Bugelski, Kidd, and Segmen (1968) found that to associate images effectively, verbal stimuli should not be presented faster than about five seconds per pair. Some learners require more time. Sometimes, especially with children, a suitable pair of images is not aroused even after 30 seconds. The term *suitable* itself is a problem. Some imagery may occur quickly and not be recalled in a later test, because the imagery itself prompted new imagery immediately or because the imagery itself was capricious.

Numerous studies have pointed out that images, to be of any value, should represent an integration of stimulus events, an interaction such that both components of a pair have some functional relationship to each other. When imaging the pair "horse and man," it may not be fruitful to have an image of a man on a horse or a horse and a man standing apart (Bower 1970); a better working image might be one involving the horse trying to throw the man. In this latter case, each element is doing something to the other; such imagery is remembered.

The Operation of Meaning in Learning

How does meaning enter into a learning situation? A full account covering all possible situations is quite impossible, but some sample illustration might be of value. Suppose you are asked to remember a pair of words so that given one, you can remember the other. For an immediate short-term memory operation, all you need is one statement of the pair, but our demand is that you recall the other word tomorrow or next week. Now, you feel that learning is required. You will have to work at it. The pair of words, for example, is to be a password allowing you entry into some palace. The guard will say, "July" and you are to say, "fourteen." How will you remember that number of all the possible words you might use? Some readers will have no trouble—they already know that July 14 is a special day in France, Bastille Day, and that is all they may know or need to know to remember. They can even feel they *understand* the logic of such a password; in any event, they do feel good and are secure in their new learning. There is not much new (the association is already there), but there is some new learning in that they now know the phrase is a password. But suppose the second word is *banana*. Now what are you going to do? What has July to do with bananas? Now, you go to work. You can repeat July-banana, July-banana, and so on for some number of times, but your own experience will suggest this is not a surefire operation, although it might work. If you do not bother repeating the words but let yourself think about them, various thoughts will occur to you—July is warm and bananas are tropical fruits—aha! You might settle for that—just think of a tropical fruit—but can you be sure that will work? Maybe, next week, you will not think of July as warm (it is not always warm), or you might think of other tropical fruits, or the beach, or something entirely different. You can always stop thinking (by thinking of something else, that is, letting other thoughts occur), but you want to be more secure. Let's see. July—July is warm; that persists; accept it. Now, bananas—banana republic—that's it! Banana republics are warm, and they are always having revolutions (Bastille Day may come in here, too), and they do grow bananas. That should do it. Now you have worked, and you have learned something. You rejected an easy answer as insecure. You criticized and you evaluated.

The same kind of work can be allowed to occur for any learning, for example, when you learn a law in physics, say that of Archimedes on buoyancy. Archimedes' principle states that an object afloat or immersed in a body of water is buoyed up by a force equal to the weight of the water displaced. How do we teach and/or learn such a principle? Anyone who has held someone else up in the water already knows something useful to acquiring the principle (on past experience). People are lighter in the water than out of it. By generalization, so is anything else. Therefore, water helps. But why? Or how? We make more observations and accept or reject statements as they occur to us. Thus, we can see a ping-pong ball float, while a golf ball of the same size sinks. It cannot be a matter of size. Maybe, it is a matter of materials—some objects sink because they are made of heavy (sinking?) materials—but aircraft carriers are made of steel, and they float. Maybe, it is a matter of relative size and weight. Maybe, heavy things can float if they are big enough. We continue our observations until we notice that the water level rises to some degree when an object is dropped into (onto) the water. But we do not see the water rise in a swimming pool or lake. Archimedes could probably not have discovered his principle if he only had an ocean to serve as his body of water. He needed a tub, according to the story, but a laboratory beaker is better. We can measure the height of the water before and after introducing an object. We can see different objects displace (raise the level) different amounts (weights) of water. By weighing objects in and out of the water, we can relate their weights to the weight of the displaced water and find the relationship, which is Archimedes' principle. When we are all done, we do not understand any more than we did before, but we feel quite good about an ability to state facts describing floating and/or sinking bodies, and besides we know about specific gravity even if we do not know yet that we do.

What did we have to do to learn Archimedes' principle? We had to observe not one but a variety of things; we had to imagine (predict) the outcome of other events; we had to see that some predictions were correct and others wrong. We had to discuss the wrong statements (of which there could be quite a number). We experienced thoughts (imagery) of past experience and compared them with new observations. We continued working until we were satisfied (understanding). Did we at any time work with meaning? Or did not meaning result from the work?

It has been implied earlier that the same kinds of activities (work) go on whether we learn to strike a match without burning down the house or roast a pig without the same kind of sacrifice. What we learn depends on the kind of work that is done and how much work is performed. The results reflect the work. Our failure to recognize this stems from our misinterpretations of the successes of some and the failures of others to achieve equally. What that amounts to is our failure to take into account the past history (and present state) of the learners.

We can summarize the present issues by an educational proposal. Suppose we wish to "learn" a play by Shakespeare. We assign some students the task of reading the play. Other students are assigned to produce the play with any amount of money they need plus acceptances from any actors or personnel they choose to employ. We require from the latter group a report on the cast, stage business, props, music, sets, and characterizations they intend to have their actors develop. At the end of some study period (equal for both groups), we test them for knowledge of the play. Is there any question about which group will do better? At the same time, can we deny that the two groups went at the task differently? The readers could have read a lot and could even have worked harder, in some sense, but would they have learned as much or retained it as well?

Throughout the present chapter, we have been dealing with words— single words, words in pairs, and words in lists. We have not yet faced up to the kinds of learning that people undergo all through their lives, the learning that involves words in connected discourse. A little progress has been made in this area, and we can glance at it quickly.

RESEARCH PROBLEMS IN CONNECTED DISCOURSE

We recall that Ebbinghaus encountered the problem of equally difficult materials to use in his comparisons of learning procedures. In connected discourse, we meet the same problem. How do you find sentences or paragraphs of equal difficulty? We noted above that stories (narratives) are easier to learn than collections of facts in paragraph form. Children can learn a story in one hearing but would have great difficulty in listening to and learning an equally long collection of words describing the Panama Canal. In the latter instance, each sentence might describe a different fact about the canal—its location, length, cost, amount of traffic, history, builders, and so forth. One sentence would not necessarily arouse any anticipation of the content of the next. How can you construct equally difficult paragraphs or of known difficulty to use in research? Researchers have not yet examined this problem, although producers of reading tests have been measuring "comprehension" from sample paragraphs for a long time. Such tests do not inform us about *how* the content was learned.

How do we measure what someone learns or retains from a paragraph? Do we want a verbatim report? Will paraphrasing do? Do we want the main ideas only, or must secondary facts also be learned? There is some information from studies of reading that what is retained depends on the instructions or "sets" of the readers (Postman and Senders 1946; Rothkopf and Bisbicos 1967). When readers are asked questions as they read along, they will learn and remember the answers to the questions but tend to ignore other items. Such findings are relevant for instructional or educational purposes, but they do not reveal what went on in the learning activity, nor do they bear on the problem of relative difficulty of materials.

The problem of measurement of the learning of connected discourse has not resulted in the development of any standard procedures. Practices derived from learning lists have been adapted with subjects being asked for a free recall of the words in a paragraph or a recognition of the words from a mixed list.

STUDIES OF LEARNING OF CONNECTED DISCOURSE

As the revolution in verbal learning developed and as psychologists began to explore the problems of the learning of meaningful material, some researchers were audacious enough to try to deal with something more than a list of words. Most of the new efforts were modeled on the pioneer work of Bartlett (1932), a British psychologist, who wrote a most influential book, *Remembering*, on the basis of some rather unsystematic research. Bartlett explored a number of areas pertinent to recall, among them, the recall of pictures and ambiguous figure drawings, which subjects would view briefly and then try to recall at various intervals, some stretching into years after the original viewing. Bartlett is best remembered, however, for his study of the retention of stories. He would ask his friends, colleagues, and students to read a story (a folk tale) and to reread it a second time, then wait 15 minutes, following which they would write out as complete a recall as they could. Weeks, months, or years later (as they chanced to be available), Bartlett would ask these people for additional recalls. We might note his procedure as perhaps the earliest use of a free recall procedure, but we must also note his rather arbitrary use of two readings (why not one or five or ten?), his regular 15-minute delay, and his irregular later recalls.

One of Bartlett's stories has received more attention than some of the others, although this popularity might not be justified, as the findings with different stories were at some variance from each other. The frequently cited story was entitled *The War of the Ghosts*, a North American Indian folk tale. The story, as Bartlett's subjects read it, was rather confusing and incoherent. The reader cannot be sure of just who the ghosts were, for example. There is little logic to the tale, and it amounts to a succession of sentences that seem to make sense but not a great deal. Even a careful reader could not give a good account of the story immediately after studying it. Bartlett seems to have ignored this point and emphasized instead that in the recall protocols, the subjects attempted to *restructure* the story, to give it their own interpretations, omitting details and substituting some of their own invention, changing the language by fitting in English phrases and idioms. Considering the nature of the original story, this is very much what the subjects had to do if they wished to appear sensible themselves.

Bartlett introduced the notion that the readers of the story remembered something that he called a "schema" or "structure." We are all familiar with words like *theme*, *plot*, *gist*, and so forth and use these words as if they referred to something real. The words may have some literary value when they refer to some summary, précis, or major concern. We can reduce Shakespeare's *Othello* to one word, *jealousy*, if we wish to tell someone what the play is about, but no one unfamiliar with *Othello* would be much better off if he or she now tried to describe the play. There is no argument about the literary value of a word such as *structure*. The question of its psychological merit, however, is real. How does one learn a structure? How can a structure or theme be represented in the nervous system? A theme can only emerge after the fact as a response to some question, such as, "What was the story about?" The responder now knows he or she cannot reproduce the whole story, even if he or she wished to do so, and responds by describing the most potent imagery that the question provokes. If given time to reflect and organize his or her reactions, he or she, then, taking his questioner into consideration, can elaborate or reduce the report in many ways, depending upon his or her own history and experience. The reader or listener has to create or formulate the theme *after* the story has been heard or read. When children are asked the point of a story, they frequently appear to have missed it even if they enjoyed the story. A fable like the fox and the grapes can be reported as a failure on the part of a fox to jump high enough. On the other hand, adults can look for hidden meanings and find Hamlet to be struggling with an Oedipus complex. These are post facto interpretations and cast no light on the learning process.

Following Bartlett's suggestion that we remember structures, themes, or schemata, with "the central meaning stored in schematic form," some current research in verbal learning has again urged that psychologists look at the importance of "thema" in the learning of connected discourse passages. Dooling and Lachman (1971) for example, had college students read one of two paragraphs, one of which is reproduced below, and then asked them to recall it as fully as possible.

WITH HOCKED GEMS FINANCING HIM/ OUR HERO BRAVELY DEFIED ALL SCORNFUL LAUGHTER/ THAT TRIED TO PRE-VENT HIS SCHEME/ YOUR EYES DECEIVE/ HE HAD SAID/ AN EGG/ NOT A TABLE/ CORRECTLY TYPIFIES THIS UNEX-PLORED PLANET/ NOW THREE STURDY SISTERS SOUGHT PROOF/ FORGING ALONG SOMETIMES THROUGH CALM VASTNESS/ YET MORE OFTEN OVER TURBULENT PEAKS AND VALLEYS/ DAYS BECAME WEEKS/ AS MANY DOUBTERS SPREAD FEARFUL RUMORS ABOUT THE EDGE/ AT LAST/ FROM NOWHERE/ WELCOME WINGED CREATURES AP-PEARED/ SIGNIFYING MOMENTOUS SUCCESS

Some of the subjects were provided with a title for the paragraph, while the others were not. The title (*Christopher Columbus*) added an 18 percent improvement in the free recall of the 77 words of the paragraph over the recall of those subjects who were not given the title. The title presumably made the paragraph more meaningful or comprehensible, but we are unable to state how the title could do so. It does no good to assert that the title supplied a theme or structure. Such terms are literary abstractions. It might be that the title could provoke some imagery pertaining to prior experiences of the subjects with historical accounts of the discovery of America, with pictures of Columbus, portraits, movies, and so forth. If the readers had some image of Columbus at the court of Ferdinand and Isabella and then at the helm of the Santa Maria, the words of the paragraph might provoke other imagery, which could be associated with the more central or recurrent images of Columbus. A later recall could then benefit from such associated clues. The actual recall of the words was rather low (15.67), which might be a function of the abstract nature of many of the words.

Studies such as the one described above are a start in the right direction. A similar study by Bransford and Franks (1971) demonstrated that a paragraph of good English prose could be virtually incomprehensible if a title was not supplied for the reader. To say that the title furnished a context or a kernel around which the various sentences could coalesce does not offer much help. Again, an imagery interpretation might be more plausible.

At the present time, we can recognize that the efforts of psychologists in the arena of verbal learning have been prodigious and productive at the laboratory level in what might be described as the basics of the field. They are becoming familiar with the manifold syntactical and semantic features of language. They are beginning to cope with the problems of the nature of the units that comprise discourse, but many problems still remain to be probed before we can appreciate how a child learns a story or a college student masters the contents of a chapter of text.

All through this chapter, we have been skirting around the topic of how verbal learning is measured. We have made some tacit assumptions about memory and retention without stressing that from the time of Ebbinghaus to the present, all verbal learning has been measured by one kind of memory test or another. We now must look into how learning is evaluated and retained, how previous learning affects present learning, and how later learning influences the retention of earlier learning.

16

Transfer, Proaction,
and Retroaction—
or the Influence
of the Past

The fond hope of every parent sending his or her child off to school is that the child will learn something over the 16-year schooling period (of course, he or she will go to college) which will prepare him or her for what is left of his or her life. For at least half the population, "life" begins at 21, and for those who go to graduate schools, it may not begin till 25, 27, or with postdoctoral programs, until 30 or so. If present trends continue, college degrees will not be enough in the way of credentials for "life," and we may see "children" going to school until they are 40 or 50. Philosophers like John Dewey preferred to think of life as beginning at birth with education as a part of life—learning was living and vice versa and should be recognized as such.

TRANSFER OF TRAINING: FORMAL TRANSFER

How does one prepare for life? In the eighteenth and nineteenth centuries, one prepared by studying Latin and Greek, rhetoric, and mathematics, with added exposure to religion and some attention to the classics in literature. Such an education produced powerful and influential people, such as Alexander Hamilton, who were real-life testimonials to the efficacy of the program. Those who did not attain Hamilton's stature were conveniently forgotten. The argument that a classical education results in success is not very convincing when we recognize that Abraham Lincoln never attended more than 12 months of school in his life. Lincoln is a particularly irritating thorn in psychology's side, as his attainments and achievements cannot be traced to either heredity or environment with any great conviction.

Today's children shun the classics. Latin is a dead dead-language, and Greek attracts only a handful of scholars. Other courses, for example, modern dance, pottery, or poetry (modern) provide equal credit units toward a degree. And the schools continue to be regarded as preparations for life.

The concept of preparation for life rests on an assumption that some kinds of experience transfer, presumably positively, from one situation to another. "The tree will grow as the twig is bent" is the proverbial wisdom that covers the situation. Assuming that what the student learns in school will indeed prepare him or her for some nonacademic activities has been labeled as the *transfer of training*. We are ready to examine this parentally supported assumption.

PAST AND FUTURE EXPERIENCE

Up until now, we have been describing the learning operation as if someone came to it out of some kind of void, with no past and an uncertain future. The past, at least, is not uncertain, if largely unknown. Every learner has a past, however, and it may affect his or her present learning operation and his or her future in at least two ways. It may make the present task easy or difficult to learn and easy or difficult to remember in a more distant future.

If we symbolize a present learning task as A and future learnings (experiences) as B, then we have the situation as shown below:

Entire previous history	Present learning task	T I M E	Future learning or experience
X	A		B

We face the following considerations:

1. Because X is largely unknown, we find that different prople learn A at different rates of efficiency. Because it is too difficult to trace the influence of the past, even with a two-year-old, to say nothing about college students, we put this down to individual differences and move blithely on. It is obviously inappropriate to assume that X is the same for people who learn with the same degree of efficiency, although in such cases, X might be ignored. It might not be so safe with respect to the next question.

2. The learning of A is of no importance unless we have some interest in the learner's future. Sometime in the future, maybe only seconds after learning A, we may test the learner for the retention of A. Here, we will find more individual differences, and X may be an important variable, one, however, which we cannot or do not manipulate regularly or easily.

If any meaningful period of time passes after the learning of A, the learner may have new experiences or acquire new learnings, B. Again, we face two major questions. First, will the learning of A have an effect on the efficacy of the learning of B? (Note that it is really the effect of X + A.) If it does, and the effect is positive, we can label it *proactive facilitation*, or positive transfer. If the effect is negative, we can use the label, *proactive interference*, or negative transfer. Of course, there may be no effect, in which case we do not need a label.

Second, will the learning of B have an effect on the retention of A and on the retention of X? If the effect is negative, it will be labeled *retroactive inhibition* (RI). A positive effect would be difficult to demonstrate, as it could only amount to a perfect retention, and any hypothetical gain would be obscured. A schoolteacher learns the names of his or her students in 1976. A year later, the teacher learns the names of the 1977 class. The following year, he or she learns the 1978 roster. What happens to the schoolteacher's retention of the 1976 names (X) and the 1977 names (A), and how easily did he or she learn the 1978 list (B)? (Note that the X should really apply to all the names ever learned before 1977.) A third question should be included here. How well will B be retained? If the effect is negative, we would label that *proactive inhibition* (PI).

RETROACTIVE AND PROACTIVE INHIBITION

Literally thousands of experiments have been done in which subjects would learn something, for example, a poem or a list of nonsense syllables. Such learning would be called original learning, frequently symbolized by O or referred to as Task A. The subjects would then learn another poem or another list of syllables. Because such learning would be followed by a test of recall of the first, or original, learning, such a second learning task would be called interpolated learning, symbolized by I or referred to as Task B.

With such an arrangement, it is possible to see if any particular kind of interpolated learning has an effect on the recall of the original. It is also possible to discover if any particular original learning has an effect on the ease of learning or retaining Task B.

We can illustrate the typical experimental approaches to studies of such positive and/or negative effects of past or future learnings by diagramming the following paradigms.

Retroactive Inhibition

Experimental group	Learn A	T I M E	Learn B	T I M E	Test retention of A
Control group	Learn A	T I M E	Rest	T I M E	Test retention of A

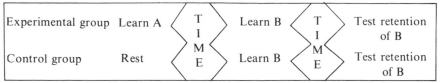

Proactive Inhibition

Experimental group	Learn A	T I M E	Learn B	T I M E	Test retention of B
Control group	Rest		Learn B		Test retention of B

Note that in the typical studies, there are two groups—an experimental group that learns two sets of materials (A and B) and a control group that learns only one. Normally, the period marked *Rest* in the retroactive inhibition design lasts as long as it takes the experimental group to learn B. In the proactive inhibition design, the rest period amounts to the entire prior history of the learners.

We should also note that the time at which B is learned in the retroactive inhibition design can vary from seconds after learning A to years. Similarly, the retention tests in both designs can vary from short to long periods of time. You never know when something you have learned before might help or hurt.

During the rest period, the control group can, of course, engage in many activities, and such activities can be "controlled" only within the retroactive inhibition design, and there only to some modest degree. It would be ideal to quick-freeze or immobilize the control groups (this was actually done with cockroach subjects by Minami and Dallenbach 1946) or put them to sleep (Jenkins and Dallenbach 1924), but usually the only concern is to keep the control group from rehearsing. Sometimes, humor magazines are provided, with the subjects instructed to pick out the best cartoons or best jokes. The basic intent is to prevent any new learning in the control subjects.

The outcomes of such experiments are numerous and varied and will engage us shortly. For the present, we can recognize that any difference in the retention of A in the retroactive inhibition design can be referred to the learning of B. If there is no difference, then B is not a variable of importance. Should there be an improvement in the experimental subjects, again the learning of B could be considered the responsible variable. There need not be any difference in retention, of course. Not everything we learn is forgotten just because we learn something else. It is, among other factors, the nature of what we learn in B that matters, but this matter will be discussed later.

In the proactive inhibition design, the same considerations apply with respect to retention of B. There may be no, little, or a great deal of loss of B, depending upon the time of the test after B is learned (which opens the door to additional kinds of learning experiences and, consequently, some retroactive inhibition possibilities). The X factor discussed earlier may be of greater prominence here because any laboratory learning of A can only represent a trivial addition to X, and although in the laboratory, such learning can be demonstrated as highly important in creating proactive inhibition, much ordinary forgetting can be blamed on extralaboratory experiences of a cumulative nature. In a sense, the more you already know, the more you will forget of newly learned material. At the same time that you may be learning easily, because of experience, you are also doomed to rapid forgetting.

Caught between the effects of retroactive and proactive inhibition, the student might wonder about the virtue of learning anything new. The concern may not be justified. Not all learning is forgotten, or we could not survive for a day without help. Retroactive and proactive inhibition effects are to be considered only as factors responsible for what we do forget. As we grow older and learn more and more, X becomes larger and larger, and we could expect that sooner or later we might reach the stage of being unable to remember anything because of proactive and retroactive inhibition. While some old people might suggest just such a state, there are probably many other variables of a physiological nature operating that might account for old people's memory troubles.

INTERFERENCE HYPOTHESIS

What we have been discussing above in terms of retroactive and proactive inhibition is commonly referred to as the interference hypothesis commonly assumed as a basis for explaining forgetting. For the moment, we will ignore the forgetting issue and return to the question of transfer (of which forgetting is only one negative aspect if we take the interference hypothesis for granted).

The general statement of negative transfer was proposed in interference terms by McGeoch (1942). It can be symbolized as

$$\text{Learn } S_1 \longrightarrow R_1 \qquad \text{(early learning)}$$
$$\text{Then learn } S_2 \longrightarrow R_2 \qquad \text{(later learning)}$$

If S_1 and S_2 are the same or close on some generalization dimension, S_1 may begin to arouse R_2 instead of R_1, and interference is the result. According to McGeoch, the $S_1 \longrightarrow R_1$ association could remain intact, but if $S_1 \longrightarrow R_2$ should become a stronger association, R_1 would not emerge. We all have had the experience of interference when we try to recall something we are supposed to know. Our problem is not a blank mind. We usually think of something—the wrong answer. If we try to remember which president followed Grant, we might think of Garfield or Arthur instead of Hayes. Garfield might have some higher strength—we are reminded of him occasionally when newspapers review presidential assassinations. We rarely if ever hear of Hayes and might even reject the name as not in the presidential list.

THE OSGOOD ANALYSIS

Osgood (1949) expanded upon the McGeoch suggestion by recognizing that not only might the stimuli be identical or similar but so could the responses. In such a case, we could have a whole catalog of conditions, some of which might favor retention, while others would lower it or increase forgetting. Osgood's basic concern was with the problem of similarity.

Many studies of retroactive inhibition had demonstrated a very firm finding that it increased when the second material (B) to be learned was similar to the original learning (A). Thus, if A is a list of adjectives, there will be more loss in retention if (B) is another list of adjectives rather than a list of nouns. If (A) is a list of words and (B) a list of nonsense syllables, there will be less loss of A. The problem of measuring *similarity* has never been solved by psychologists despite numerous attempts (for example, Gibson 1942). Once one leaves *identity* and introduces some change, the question of how similar are the two items arises. Thus, if we change a nonsense syllable from *zel* to *zil*, we can probably agree that they are similar, but we cannot say to what degree. Because one letter is altered, we might propose that there is a 66.66 percent similarity. Such a procedure will not carry us far, however, in discussing the similarity of meaning of words, for example. If we take words like *joy*, *elation*, and *happiness* or *hate*, *loathe*, *detest*, and *abominate*, we recognize the similarity, but we can give no numerical scale points. There are no yardsticks by which to measure similarity.

Osgood chose to approach the problem rather broadly. Considering words as possible stimuli and responses in paired-associate learning, Osgood suggested that one could consider some five degrees of similarity. He could have chosen ten or 20. Thus, Osgood proposed that in original learning some pair could be considered as the base, where $S_1 \longrightarrow R_1$, and in subsequent learning, another pair would represent a new association, where $S_2 \longrightarrow R_2$. The Ss and Rs could be classified for degrees of similarity, as follows: S_2 and R_2 could be identical to S_1 and R_1 or S_2 could be very similar, similar, or neutral, and R_2 could be very similar, similar, neutral, opposite, or antagonistic to R_1. If we take all the possible combinations that Osgood proposed, we would have at least 24 different kinds of interpolated learning, using only the crude distinctions of similarity Osgood proposed. There is probably no real limit to the steps in a similarity scale. Even with Osgood's program, he omits an opposite step on the stimulus side, and one could wonder why it should not be included. For example, the word *adore* might be the original stimulus word, *love* could be a very similar item, *like* might pass for similar, *swim* might be neutral, but *hate* could be an opposite, along with degrees of opposites, like *abhor*, *detest*, *dislike*, *disapprove*, and so forth. Roget's *Thesaurus* illustrates the problem of dealing with word similarities.

Osgood never explained what an antagonistic response might be, as compared with opposite, nor did he stipulate how close on a scale similar might be to very similar or to neutral, but even with such restrictions or limitations, the suggestions of Osgood indicate the intricacies of the situations that govern either facility or difficulty in learning and forgetting.

We can now state the problem of this chapter in a more formal manner. Given the situation as above, where $S_1 \longrightarrow R_1$ is some current or "original" learning (A) and we now learn something else (B) before we test ourselves on the retention of (A), we can examine the following questions. With respect to transfer, what is the effect of A on the learning of B?

1. If positive, we can talk about the transfer of training, that is, the possible benefits of practice or prior experience.
2. If negative, we can talk about proactive interference; something is difficult to learn because we have learned something else that keeps us from learning the new material. Old habits are operating.
3. If the concern is with the retention of B, we have proactive inhibition to consider.

With respect to retroaction, what is the effect of learning B on the retention of the original learning (A)?

1. If positive, that is, if the original material is remembered better because of (B), we can look for facilitative features in B (perhaps some kind of practice effect or learning how-to-learn has occurred; this would only be evident in a relearning type of test).
2. If negative, we blame the loss in retention on the intervening or interpolated learning (B). We look for competing elements or consider possibilities of fatigue, changes in motivation, failure of discrimination, and so forth.

EFFECTS OF PAST EXPERIENCE ON NEW AND OLD LEARNING

With the formal considerations out of the way, we can now look at the facts. How does past experience affect us in our current learning, and how will it affect us in our future learning experiences? We can see from the formal presentation above that the consequences can be good, bad, or indifferent. Taking the last possibility first, it appears that we can learn some kinds of skills or materials as if the past has never existed. This is probably not strictly true, as there may be some general effects that are common for most people which result in some average level of operation. But if a new situation involves neutral stimuli and neutral responses relative to anything else we have learned before, then we are, in effect, (though not in reality) starting from scratch. In the laboratory, if we learn a set of paired associates where the stimuli are various shapes and the responses are colors (names), it is probable that except for some warm-up effects, there will be no impact of such learning on the subsequent learning of a set of paired associates where both stimuli and responses are words. The later learning should also not affect the retention of the earlier learning.

OSGOOD'S TRANSFER AND RETROACTION HYPOTHESIS

Osgood reviewed a great many studies wherein subjects had learned two sets of materials that could roughly be rated for degrees of similarity of the stimuli and responses involved. From his review, he arrived at a general proposition that there was a strong relationship between the ease of learning B and the recall of A. We can readily see that if $S_2 \longrightarrow R_2$ is exactly the same as $S_1 \longrightarrow R_1$, that is, if both stimuli and responses are identical in A and B, then the learner is merely *repeating* the original learning or practicing it some more in the B stage. The learner can only get better at B and will, of course, remember A better. If the stimuli in B begin to differ in similarity from those in A while the responses remain identical, the ease of learning the B task will begin to decrease as the stimuli approach neutrality. If both stimuli and responses begin to deviate from identity, there will be a gradual decrease in ease of learning B and efficiency in recall of A until the responses approach some "similar" level, when B learning will become more and more difficult when the B stimuli are identical or very similar. Recall of A will become correspondingly more difficult.

Osgood described the changing effects on both learning of B and recall of A in what he called the "transfer and retroaction surface" (see Figure 16.1). A number of attempts to verify this surface (Bugelski and Cadwallader 1956; Kanungo 1967; Martin 1965) resulted in mixed findings. None of the efforts has been entirely in correspondence with Osgood's hypothesis, and no real proof could be expected without precise measures of similarity. The surface, however, is a convenient device to remind us of the need to consider possible facilitative and interference effects as we move from one learning task to another. Some things we will learn easily and some with difficulty. Learning some things will hurt the recall of some other things. Much of our learning, however, will not suffer in either regard because the stimuli and responses will be sufficiently different to qualify as neutral.

As soon as we leave a contrived laboratory situation, however, we can say little with confidence about situations we might judge to be neutral. Actually, we are defining neutrality in a circular way—by pointing to no effect on or of the interpolated learning. Does a prior course in history affect our learning of physics? Would a prior course in chemistry have a more positive effect? Here, the problem of similarity arises in numerous, sometimes subtle, forms. In their early studies, Thorndike and Woodworth (1901) claimed that there could be a positive transfer if, and only if, there were

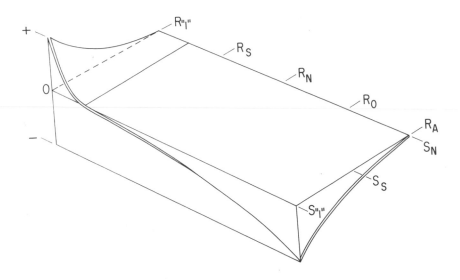

FIGURE 16.1: The Osgood transfer and retroaction surface. Stimulus similarity is shown to the right and response similarity to the rear of a flat surface. Effects of various combinations on recall of original learning or interference with new learning are shown as deviations above or below the flat (after Osgood 1953).

identical elements in the two situations. But Thorndike and Woodworth did not spell out what an identical element might be and even suggested that such factors as motivation, study habits, and attitudes might be identical and carry some positive transfer weighting. Consider how this might apply to studying Latin and its effects on future courses. The student who has some moderate success in Latin must acquire a number of attitudes, orientations, and work habits. He or she learns that a translation cannot be dashed off, that one must plan on a suitable time of work, that some words will have to be looked up, and where such looking up can be done. He or she picks up much grammatical lore about cases, voices, and moods; he or she learns to make words agree in number and gender. The student learns some history, geography, and cultural facts along with a lot of words that have cognates in English and other languages. He or she may learn, even without realizing it, something about style. In short, the student of Latin learns a great deal more than Latin, and some of what he or she learns may transfer in some future situations, even if he or she never has any use for the language itself. These remarks are not an argument for studying Latin. Had the student spent the same amount of time in other pursuits, he or she might be better prepared for a different set of future activities.

Athletics provides many illustrations of transfer. While there is much specialization in professional sports, it is still the case that if one can ride a bicycle, he or she can "transfer" to motor scooters and motorcycles, even airplanes, with some finesse. Roller skating and ice skating share some features, as do most activities involving balls. Tennis, squash, badminton, and volleyball have common elements. The all-around athlete is not just a figure of speech.

Positive transfer is readily observable in such matters as driving different cars or trucks after a bit of preliminary fumbling, moving from one accounting system to another, from one computer language to another, and so on. In short, we observe positive transfer wherever useful preliminary training has been experienced. The current trends of specialization, however, prepare people for rather restricted kinds of activities, which leave them unprepared for even simple jobs in other fields. When apartment dwellers buy a home of their own, they often do not know how to light a furnace or even what to do with the garbage.

Because the future is unplanned and likely to be capricious, it is difficult to train or educate young people for an unpredictable occupation or mode of life, and curriculum planning in schools is likely to remain a sea of controversy.

We turn, then, to negative transfer in its two forms, first in the difficulties encountered by learners in new situations because of what they have learned in the past and, later, to the problem of forgetting.

NEGATIVE TRANSFER IN PROACTIVE INTERFERENCE

When we encounter a new learning task, we face it with all our past experience. Sometimes, the past counts against us. If we are accustomed to loosening nuts by turning to the left, we are in trouble with nuts that call for right turns to achieve the removal. Old habits interfere with necessary new adjustments.

It has been suggested that the standard typewriter keyboard is not the most efficient arrangement possible in terms of which fingers do the most work. Any new keyboard arrangement that was designed for efficient learning and operation would not get to the market because current typists would have to relearn to type. Powerful old habits would interfere. Similar problems arise when a nation like England changes its currency to a decimal system. Two years of public preparation were required before the public was considered ready. The United States in planning to introduce a centigrade system of measurement faces the united wrath of the citizens. In Canada, a change from Fahrenheit to centigrade temperature measurement called for considerable preparation and, when introduced, confused the citizens, who required both readings for some time.

When a student is having trouble with his or her academic work, it can be presumed that something is interfering with the student's learning. The something may not be prior academic achievements but feelings of despair, even learned helplessness, faulty study habits, competing interests, various kinds and degrees of resentment, expected failure, fear of competition, or a kind of childish "machismo" in resisting discipline—all can be considered competitive operations. No teacher can succeed in an academic assignment if the learner is more interested in attracting attention than in being attentive. We have already considered the role of attention and mention it here only as something that may be being misapplied, providing a source of proactive interference in terms of habits that are not conducive to learning.

When we address ourselves to more specific kinds of interference in new learning, we find the similarity factor the most important variable. In earlier days of aviation training, for example, in one aircraft, the pilot had to reach down with his left hand to pull up a lever that raised his wing flaps. This is a task the pilot does after landing while taxiing on the runway. Adjacent to this lever was another identical lever. A slight difference in hand location and the wrong lever would be pulled, which resulted in the wheels coming up, something not desired on a runway. In the air, the same levers would create new problems. The pilot might want full flaps when climbing, but pulling on the wheel lever when the wheels are already up is not helpful, or lowering the wheels when one wants to lower flaps might lead to disaster. Numerous other sources of confusion were built into airplanes, so that pilots transferring from one plane to another had additional learning to do because levers, buttons, switches, indicators, and so forth were not placed in the same positions in different planes. In academic matters, one can experience proactive interference when learning new foreign languages after having learned others. Appropriate words might occur when needed but from the wrong language. Mathematics text writers sometimes are idiosyncratic in their choice of symbols and may use symbols that represented something else in an earlier course. Such difficulties may be only trivial and temporary but they illustrate the sometimes insidious nature of past experience.

In a simple experimental demonstration, the writer (Bugelski 1948) had some students learn in immediate succession ten lists of ten paired associates where the stimulus terms were the same nonsense syllables in all ten lists. By the time the students reached the tenth list, they were confused and exhausted, declaring the task the most impossible ever attempted. The results are shown in Figure 16.2.

A glance at Figure 16.2 shows the more or less steady decline as new responses were learned (or not learned) to old stimuli. All through the effort, mistakes kept occurring from previous lists. Even on the tenth list, the students were giving responses from the first list. Two points of interest might be mentioned. The tenth list shows an end spurt, which commonly appears when we know we are approaching some goal. More interesting perhaps is

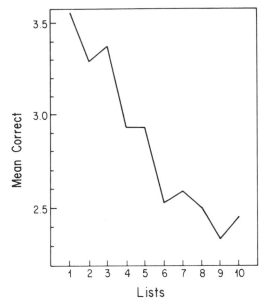

FIGURE 16.2: The effect of identical stimuli in learning successive lists of paired-associates.

the zigzag nature of the course of learning. Ebbinghaus (1885) had reported something of the same nature. It might be accounted for by assuming that if on some trial only a little is learned (see trials 2, 4, 6, 8), there cannot be as much interference as from the more successful trials (1, 3, 5, and 7). It should be noted that the stimuli were identical and that the responses were somewhat similar in that they were all nonsense syllables. The responses were different enough, however, to show a powerful interference effect.

The central point of the above example is that we can expect to have more or less difficulty in learning B, C, D, and so forth, depending upon the nature of A, B, C, and so on, in terms of their relative similarities. In our day-to-day lives, we are constantly exposed to a succession of stimulations requiring responses (same, neutral, or different), and we should not find it strange that some learnings give us more trouble than others.

The picture is not totally negative. As Osgood pointed out in his review of the effects of similarity, if the stimuli are identical or very similar and the called-for responses are also similar, the new learning can proceed at a faster pace than could occur without the background. Thus, some authorities suggest that one might learn Spanish, French, Italian, and Portuguese languages as a group without much difficulty and with a savings in time because of the great similarity of the languages. A few rules about spelling and pronunciation would handle a great many apparent differences. The student of French who learns that *school* is *école* should be told that many

French words beginning with *ec* can be transformed into English by trying out an *s* as a replacement for the *e*. In a sense, many rules in language and science are reflections of the positive transfer when stimuli and responses are very similar. The rule of *i* before *e* is based on the similarity of sounds (neighbor, weigh, freight), or in the case of *c* words, (receive, conceive) and opposed to non*c* words (believe, relief, siege, sieve).

In Osgood's judgment, if new responses were opposite to those originally learned and the stimuli identical or very similar, there should be great difficulty in the new learning and considerable RI for the old. This may be the case in some S$\longrightarrow$R situations, but for learning words of opposite meanings, again, the rule principle might apply. The learner can, perhaps, recognize that opposites are called for and can proceed to engage in appropriate opposite types of behavior. One need not learn anything more than the rule: do the opposite. If a prior response was "up" the learner can say "down" without much if any thinking in between.

NONSPECIFIC TRANSFER

Up to now, we have been concerned with the effects of experience with specific stimuli and specific responses on future learning efficiency or on the recall of past learnings. Two additional kinds of transfer operations must now be considered to complete the picture. These are of a more general nature, dealing more with procedures and approaches to learning or problem-solving situations. We have already considered one of these operations, learning how to learn (see chapter 12), and we will touch only briefly on it. The second general transfer factor is that of warm-up. We will start with that.

Warm-up

Anyone familiar with sports activities has discovered for himself or herself that athletes typically engage in some activities related to what they will shortly be doing in some more serious or competitive way. The relief pitcher warms up in the bullpen. The prospective batter swings his or her bat(s) in the air. Athletes usually refer to this as loosening up, although this is probably incorrect usage of the language. They may, in fact, be tightening up in the sense that they are getting ready for certain specific actions. Whatever the terminology, the facts seem to indicate that some preliminary activity similar to that to be employed shortly is beneficial to the later performance. Such benefits can be seen in the laboratory when subjects perform some simple task, such as following a moving target on a pursuit meter (Ammons 1948). The performance improves more or less steadily until the performer reaches some reasonable level of efficiency. If the subject stops now and rests a while, he or she cannot start at the level at which he or she stopped. The performer may have improved greatly over his or her initial efforts, but in the second or later trials, he or she always shows less efficiency at the start of a trial than at the end. The difference can be attributed to both practice and warm-up. The practice effect can be observed by comparing the final moments from trial to trial, while the warm-up effects can be observed from the difference between the final moments of one trial and the early moments of the next. The loss, if there is one, indicates what can be made up by warm-up.

Warm-up is not confined to the athletic arena. In the laboratory, a subject can learn nonsense syllables better if he or she first looks at a rotating memory drum that presents different samples of common colors. The subject names the colors as they appear. The subject is not learning anything about colors, but as he or she sits there and names them, he or she is getting set for the session, for a looking and naming operation. Even guessing colors helps (Thune 1950).

The student facing an examination does well to use "scratch" paper to doodle, write, draw, compute, or engage in whatever kind of activity is to be performed in the immediate future. Various expressions are employed to describe the virtues of such activity—"getting into the right frame of mind," "getting organized," and "getting into the act." Musicians demonstrate the operation in a most obvious manner just before the arrival of the conductor, who has been preparing for his or her effort in the dressing room. Even some instruments must be warmed up to play properly.

What warm-up does, presumably, is to prepare the operator to respond to certain signals and not others; it amounts to what we described earlier as the response or state of attention in a preliminary form. The performer is opening certain gates and closing others.

Learning How To Learn—Learning Sets

We are indebted to Harry Harlow (chapter 12) for his original demonstrations in which monkeys were given the same problem over and over again in different forms. Slowly, over a period of a year or so, the monkeys solved one problem after another and got better and better at it. Slowly, the monkeys eliminated all tendencies to react to features that were irrelevant to success. What these were cannot be stated but the generalization is warranted that the monkeys learned what *not* to do. Such learning can come, presumably, only from experience, at least in such a situation (no monkey ever solved the early problems by intuitive analysis or by the operation of categorical imperatives).

In many academic and professional situations, a great part of the learning consists of learning what not to do. Firemen learn where you do not pour water or lean ladders. Painters learn not to paint themselves into corners. Doctors learn what medicine not to prescribed, and so on. The average parent uses the word *don't* far more often than *do*. The student in algebra learns what not to use x for, and after he or she has solved the "John and Joe take two hours to dig a 12-foot trench" problem with Henry and Frank and Jack and Jill, he or she can solve it again, even if the new diggers are Sylvester and Otto and the ditch is 16 feet long.

Both positive and negative learning goes on all our lives, and our reaction to a new situation depends on what we have learned to do and not to do in our past experience with similar situations even if the similarity is not evident to some observer or sometimes even to the learner. If he or she does the correct thing quickly, we call him or her bright. If he or she stumbles along, we have our doubts about his or her genetic background. It might be more appropriate to think of the stumbler as a monkey who did not go to college.

The landmark studies of Harlow have been replicated with children with essentially similar results. On the adult level, Keppel, Postman, and Zavortink (1968) have shown that even such tasks as learning lists of paired associates (words) benefit from successive learnings of one list after another, with steady, though decreasing, benefits as learners master one list after another. Learners kept improving up to about 35 lists. With all their practice at learning, the subjects did not improve their ability to remember from one day to the next. Should such an experienced learner show up in a new laboratory, he or she would confound the experimenters until his or her experience was revealed. Many learners we observe do not or cannot describe all their relevant experiences, and we proceed to classify them as bright or dull when it might be better to think of them as better or worse prepared by their backgrounds.

We have now considered both negative and positive transfer with respect to new learning. We are ready to consider what happens to that learning in terms of retention of both the new and the old learning—in short, the problem of retention.

17

Retention and Forgetting

At the present time, despite the warnings of the functional psychologists, we still speak of memory—good memories and bad memories (sometimes good for faces but not for names)—and a lot of folklore surrounds the subject: "He only remembers what he wants to remember," a remark that Sigmund Freud built into a system of therapy. The general notion prevails, aided and abetted by computer-sophisticated psychologists, that there is such a thing or entity as a memory with its own features, mechanisms, and structures. We might, instead, recognize that the evidence we have allows us to say only that some people, some of the time, remember some things (immediately or with some aids) and not other things we have some reason to believe they should remember. Remembering is an activity. What underlying structures are involved or how they work is completely unknown, and any resemblance to a computer is simply a forced analogy of little merit for an account of how we do remember what we do.

The problem of retention is as old as psychology. We met it first with the ancient mnemonists with their efforts at improving memory. For them, memory was an agency or faculty with some internal locus, and it could be described as good or bad, the way many of us still do when we say, "I don't have a good memory for names," or, "I can't memorize very well." When you see advertisements that offer to "improve your memory," again some faculty is implied with some properties, such as muscles, which can be improved with exercise or certain practices.

MEMORY VERSUS RETENTION

Nowadays, psychologists do not use the term *memory* except in casual conversation, where it should also be banned, as it perpetuates a myth. It is much more appropriate to talk about retention, which covers the same behavioral phenomena without assumptions about faculties. Either we retain something or we do not. If we do, we do not raise any questions about memory, although someone who does not retain some shared experience might ask, "How did you remember that?"

The statement made above about either retaining or not may be somewhat misleading or confusing. In any event, it needs considerable evaluation, and that will be the business of this chapter. There are many caveats to consider before we can reach a satisfactory position.

AVAILABILITY AND ACCESSIBILITY

When Ebbinghaus (1885) began his studies of memory, he already had surmised, in agreement with many predecessors, that the problem was complex—some things were quickly forgotten, while other things were remembered by some people for long periods; this almost, if not quite, justified an assumption that perhaps nothing learned is really forgotten even though it is not immediately available for report. The concept of accessibility as different from availability (made prominent in modern times by Tulving 1972) is at least as old as Ebbinghaus. His findings with relearning and the usual savings score (see chapter 4) testified to the fact that *something* of what was once learned had been retained. It needs only getting at. Ebbinghaus was inclined to believe that once something was learned, it would remain in "memory" but might be difficult to bring out, if possible at all. This is the kind of proposal that generates theories, as we shall discover.

In the current state of the science of retention, psychologists have recognized the need not to talk of retention as some yes or no or single on-off operation, and their explorations have enlarged the range and scope of the problem beyond the relatively narrow restrictions followed by the early successors of Ebbinghaus. Out of a voluminous mass of research, there arose the concept of various kinds of retention or kinds of memory. Perhaps they could be more correctly described as different kinds of tests with different kinds of results, arising from different kinds of procedures.

KINDS OF MEMORY

If we are to talk about kinds of memory at all, the labels employed should be carefully noted as referring to either different kinds of content or different testing conditions. A clear distinction is offered by Bahrick, Bahrick, and Wittlinger (1975) in their findings that even old people can recognize, that is, identify, photographs (pick out the correct name out of five) of high school classmates very effectively (71 percent scores at age 65), whereas they can *recall* only about 6 percent of the names of these classmates. Such tests, by the way, are conducted with adequate time to reflect, inspect, and otherwise "jog the memory." Unless we routinely consider the content and test procedure, we are likely to reify some types of memories into substantive agencies.

We can begin a classification of memory types by recognizing two general distinctions, one based on time factors and the other on content.

Time-Related Memories

Iconic Memory

Memory or retention can be talked about in terms of the duration of stimuli or the time since something has been learned. In the case of the former, we have so-called iconic memory. If a stimulus is flashed before us for about a tenth of a second, we will be able to report its existence and some of its features if we are tested immediately. You can test yourself easily. Walk into a dark room at night, flick on the light and flick it off as fast as you can. For a few moments, you can still see the room illuminated even though the lights are out. Now, describe what you just saw. You will be able to say something about the icon you just retained while the room was, in fact, dark. Such positive afterimages are of extremely low duration but, in one sense, can serve as the basis for a description of a previous experience and, thus, qualify as a kind of memory. Classifying the operation as a memory test is not especially fruitful. Any learning involved has to be of a one-trial variety with an extremely short trial duration. At best, the measure involved is one of some kind of perceptual or sensory capacity following an extremely brief exposure, too short to allow even an eye movement. People do not ordinarily go about learning anything by arranging for extremely short exposures of the stimuli. We should note, however, that even with such short exposures, more and more can be learned if the stimuli are repeated.

During World War II, servicemen were trained to recognize aircraft, tanks, warships, and so forth by looking at flashed pictures and/or silhouettes of such items, and after a suitable number of training sessions, they could identify pictures of various airplanes, for example, even if granted only a momentary glimpse of a picture never seen before. Whether such speed of recognition had any value is not the question. The point is that such exposures do show a cumulative effect. Even icons can add up. There even appears to be something one might call visual rehearsal that improves recall if some delay is introduced before a test (Weaver 1974; Twersky and Sherman 1975).

Short-Term Memory

Suppose the duration of exposure is extended to a second or a few seconds. Now, more can be remembered if the stimuli are limited and if the retention period can be extended for a short time. In a provocative experiment, Peterson and Peterson (1959) presented their subjects three consonants, for example, *xkl*, at the rate of one per second. They then asked the subjects to start counting backwards by threes from some number like 347. After a few seconds of such subtraction, the subjects would be asked to recall the consonants. At the first trial, most subjects would remember the letters (or unrelated words, Murdock 1960), but after a few such tests with different letters, most subjects would forget within about 18 seconds. Such a finding was described as an instance of short-term memory. After a number of researchers had verified the short life of retention under such conditions, it became common practice to use the label *short-term memory* or STM, as referring to some kind of processing or processing agency that was somehow different from what went on when we remember something for a longer interval—that, by the way, became distinguished as *long-term memory*, or LTM, something that was presumed to operate on some other basis.

The fact that we do not retain indefinitely some things that are briefly experienced was built into a problem area of great proportions in the 1960s and early 1970s. Everyone writing on the subject seemed bound to mention that we forget telephone numbers after we dial them (if we looked them up just before dialing), and this common experience was built into a separate kind of memory with its own features instead of being treated for what it was, namely, the effect of a short exposure of unfamiliar combinations of material, immediately followed by some other activity. Extensive debates developed between researchers who felt that short-term memory was a meaningful concept and those who saw it only as inefficient one-trial learning of meaningless material, presented for a short time with an immediate distraction task. It was pointed out, for example, that even with distracters, people would remember three letters or nonsense syllables on the first test. Failure to recall after several tests on different letters or syllables would be ascribed to proactive inhibition (Keppel and Underwood 1962). The interference task could be considered as interpolated activity leading to retroactive inhibition (Posner and Rossman 1965). Smaller amounts of material, for example, one letter or familiar combination, for example, IBM, would not be forgotten (Meton 1963), and repetition of the material would lead to improvement (Hebb 1961), suggesting more and more strongly that STM was not a viable concept and that the effect was only what one would expect from a one-trial situation involving rapid exposure and immediate distracters.

The STM concept was strongly fostered by psychologists with a fondness for models. Flow charts of memory would be drawn with STM in one box, LTM in another, with various arrows showing the course of transfer, effects of rehearsal, storage capacity, and so forth. As the research findings began to accumulate, the acceptance of a separate "storage" bin for short-term memory began to wane. Critics such as Postman (Keppel, Postman, and Zavortink 1975) and Wickelgren (1973) found the same processes operating on both alleged kinds of memories, with the general conclusion that the postulation of short-term memory as a special kind of operation had little or no justification and that, if anything, the postulation was premature. At present, there appears to be no reason to consider short-term memory as anything but a label for what happens when one has a brief exposure to some unfamiliar sequence of materials that one cannot rehearse because some other activity follows immediately. We might summarize by suggesting that there was not enough time for the learning to occur or that for whatever reason (possibly interference), the exposure had not made sufficient impact on the learner.

Long-Term Memory

The label long-term memory (LTM) has no special merit except as a contrast to STM. If STM seems to range only over an 18- to 30-second period, LTM would describe any retention of anything beyond 30 seconds. Because we do not ordinarily talk about retention for such limited times, the label LTM might also be abandoned. We should then look for the factors and variables that effect any retention of any kind of material for any length of time, including the retention of childhood experience by centenarians.

Content-Related Memory: Episodic and Semantic

In recent years, another distinction or classification of memories has been proposed (Tulving 1972), namely, that between episodic and semantic memory. The former refers to any kind of relatively isolated events (including words or nonsense syllables that are shown to a learner) that have no organized relationship to one another. Any sensory event occuring in one's history could be considered episodic in contrast to organized information about events, words and language, rules, principles, and other meaningful relationships, for example, causes and results, logical steps, and so forth. On a simple level, a spoken word in an experimental setting, for example, *bird*, would be episodic. On the other hand, one could be asked, "What do you know about birds?"—the information volunteered in an answer would represent semantic memory, as all that one knows about birds could be brought out in some kind of sequence. How such semantic memories are acquired is the research question that is posed. As of now, some answers are available for episodic types of learnings, as those are the kinds that have been studied in the laboratory since Ebbinghaus. Semantic memories are just now being investigated in exploratory studies of how people remember information provided in a paragraph of connected discourse, that is, how a story is remembered and how themes might guide our organization of information.

It goes without saying that semantic memory is at present just a label for the kinds of learning experience that count in everyday life and about which we know the least. The difficulties in the way of getting useful data are enormous, and it will be some time before sound principles are discovered that will allow us to write practical prescriptions for teaching the kinds of things people learn. At present, model makers appear to be caught up in problems of reasoning, the nature of concepts, and unsupported assumptions about how bits and pieces of information are acquired and organized. The critical assumption is commonly made that there *is* organization in our knowledge—that, for example, all we know about birds is integrated somehow, someplace. That this is actually the case should be demonstrated and not assumed. It may turn out that anyone's knowledge about birds (barring some ornithologists) is a messy collection of unrelated episodic facts mixed in with considerable episodic memory of an autobiographical nature.

THE NATURE OF LONG-TERM RETENTION

Retention is the only test of learning that we have. Whenever we attempt to measure or observe learning, we depend on retention, whether the time interval is short or long. Thus, if someone says something and asks, "What did I say?" immediately, he or she is measuring learning or determining something about learning while, at the same time, he or she is measuring or determining retention. Earlier, (see chapter 6), we made the point that *antedating* is the criterion by which we judge whether learning has taken place. But antedating can only occur in a retention test situation. Retention becomes virtually all-important in considering learning because there can be no learning, that is, we cannot talk about learning, if there is no retention, and of course, there can be no retention without learning.

Retention involves consideration of many variables beyond those involved in the immediate learning situation and is, if anything, a more complex problem area. Thus, two people may learn the same thing, at the same rate, to the same criterion, and the retention can vary, depending upon such factors as age and sex of the learner, the time(s) of testing, and the different experiences of the learners before and after the learning. Beyond such interperson variables and the time factor, we run into such problems as the kinds of material involved (nonsense, meaningful, or familiar), and the similarities involved. Learning procedures, for example, massed versus spaced and whole versus part, and learning strategies, for example, the use of imagery, form another set of variables.

THE COURSE OF FORGETTING: FORGETTING CURVES

In 1885, Ebbinghaus published his famous curve of forgetting. This curve has been frequently reproduced in other texts but will not be shown here because it is misleading. In view of the points made above, it should be recognized that whatever Ebbinghaus found, it was not *the* curve of forgetting. It was, instead, a graphical representation of what happens with regard to retention of a particular serial list of nonsense syllables of a particular length, learned by a mature male, with considerable experience at that kind of learning (Ebbinghaus used a complete exposure procedure, that is, he would have a list of syllables before him all at the same time, and he would go over the list for a fixed time before testing himself). Ebbinghaus learned his lists to a criterion of one perfect repetition. His shortest test was 20 minutes, his longest, 30 days. We cannot accept his curve as the correct depiction for different kinds of materials, age and sex of learners, different criteria, different experiences of learners, different kinds of learning operations, different periods of testing, and different kinds of test (Ebbinghaus used *relearning*).

The variables become quite striking if we investigate as a sample problem the retention of grammar school teachers' names. The writer asked suitable samples of people averaging 12, 22, 45, and 68 years of age to try to recall all the names of their teachers in grades kindergarten to six, with the following results.

The first and most obvious finding was that not all people attended kindergarten. This is of no special importance, as such, but it is mentioned to point out that we cannot remember something that we did not learn or could not learn. Many of those who did attend kindergarten did not recall the teacher's name. This does not mean it was forgotten—it might not have been learned by four-year-old to five-year-old children, who might have called the ever-present adult "Teacher." In parochial schools, such a practice might continue on into the higher grades, where a nun (teacher) might have been addressed as "Sister." All the seventh graders recalled the names of their sixth-grade teacher. Here, we have a base—100 percent recall—from which to appraise the retention of older groups. As the groups change in age, more and more people forget the names of the teachers at each grade. We can be reasonably certain that at one time they all knew the name of the sixth-grade teacher, and we do find the steady decline (in virtually a straight line— Ebbinghaus' curve dropped sharply at first, then very slowly). What does such a drop mean? Are we measuring forgetting or retention? Actually, it is the latter that is graphed in Figure 17.1, as the points represent percentages of a group's members who did recall. While it would be possible to plot the curve in reverse, the point should be made that some people remembered *all* of their teachers at any test age. Consequently, in this situation or test, they had perfect recall at age 68, say, even though others had zero scores. The best that can be said here is that some people forget more rapidly than others. Instead of wondering about why so many forgot, we might do better trying to find out why some remembered. We note from Figure 17.1 that more women remembered the names than did men. Why? Do they have better memories? Did they learn better? Teachers were predominantly women (virtually 100 percent). Did the girls identify with the teachers more?

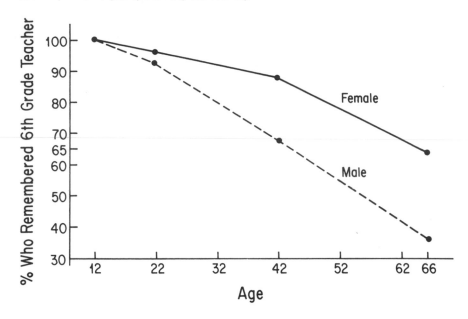

FIGURE 17.1: The retention of the name of the sixth-grade teacher by people of different ages.

Or did the boys go out into the world and learn more names, which could act as interpolated learning in retroactive inhibition? With the older groups, more males went to high school and college than did females. The data show no special effects of such additional schooling, but schools are not the only places to learn new names.

Is the forgetting that is represented a function of time because the abscissa is time? According to the curve, there will be fewer and fewer people remembering the sixth-grade teacher's name and hardly anyone by age 94. Is this because of deterioration or disuse or, as suggested above, from added competition or interference from further learning of new names?

If something so overlearned and well known as the name of a sixth-grade teacher is forgotten over the years by most people, what questions can be raised about other names? What if the names of high school or college teachers are the subject matter? Here, the learners are older, and that might make a difference. But, in high school, there are more teachers, possibly as many as 32 (four or five subjects per semester, eight semesters) or as few as 16, but even 16 is a large number. In college, the number of teachers could easily be 32 or 40. Comparisons become difficult to assess.

What of the method of testing? In the Bahrick study (Bahrick, Bahrick, and Wittlinger 1975) mentioned earlier, a distinction was drawn between recognition and recall with rather dramatic findings. We will look at testing methods shortly. It should be noted that Bahrick and his colleagues also found strong sex differences. Males recalled more male names than female names. Females recalled both sex names about equally and, in general, remembered more. More than the method of testing is involved.

METHODS OF MEASURING RETENTION

The ordinary situation involving retention is one where a question is asked and someone is expected to volunteer an answer. Such volunteered answers are usually described as recall, and the answers may come quickly, slowly, or not at all. But recall is just one measure of retention that we shall examine. There are others that are possibly of greater practical and theoretical value, for example, recognition and relearning, and we might look at recognition as a primary concern.

Recognition

If we consider this method informally first, we should recognize it as the almost constant and daily operation in virtually all aspects of our lives. From the moment of awakening when we recognize an alarm clock throughout our daily routines, we operate on recognition. Only encountering a novel object or person may give us some hesitation. If we did not recognize our coffee cups or breakfast tables, we would be off to a bad start. Our lives depend on recognition so obviously that we need not labor the point.

Formally, a test of recognition is applied by presenting a learner with a choice between previously experienced events and new ones. Students are familiar with multiple choice and true-false tests. These are tests of recognition. If a student picks the one he or she experienced before, we credit the student with retention. In experimental situations, such a test is not customary with one out of two items—the chance element is too potent. In experimental practice, if a person has seen or been asked to learn 20 items, he or she might now be shown 40 items, 20 of which are new. If the person merely guesses, he or she will pick right items about as often as wrong ones. Scores above chance will reflect his or her learning. A good test of the recognition type is not easy to arrange. It can be made so easy that 100 percent scores can be attained. For example, a person could be shown the names of 20 flowers and then tested with 20 Chinese ideographs added to the list. The person's choice of the 20 flower names would prove only that he or she knew or remembered that he or she had not seen any Chinese writing before. It is also possible to make the test so difficult as to make it virtually impossible. Thus, if the original learning is of common names of girls and the new "distracter" items are more common names of girls, the test would be far more difficult than if the distracter items were of rare names of girls or names of boys. A list of synonyms might be a more difficult set of distracters than some unrelated words in a test of retention of common words. A proper test would require some kind of confusability index for the distracter items. So far, we have none.

It is commonly assumed that a recognition test is the easiest test of retention, but as just noted, this is not necessarily the case, and it can even be more difficult than other forms of retention tests, depending upon how the others are arranged (Tulving 1974). Students who prefer "objective" tests on the grounds that they might recognize a correct answer can be very disappointed if the test maker produces items where the choices are different in only subtle ways.

Recall

In a test of recall, the learner is expected to volunteer the material, for example, recite the Gettysburg Address, as a total effort, or he or she can be quizzed or cued with various stimuli. The usual serial list or paired-associate learning paradigms can illustrate typical laboratory studies using recall. In paired-associate learning, a syllable is presented, and the learner is required to pronounce its partner in the list before it appears in a memory drum, that is, announce the associated syllable before it is shown. This is a form of cued recall, because a stimulus is provided. In serial learning, the subject must cue himself. Each syllable the learner reports becomes the stimulus for the next. If the learner cannot recall by himself or herself, the next syllable will appear and be a cue for its follower. In trying to recall names, we sometimes "sound" the letters of the alphabet to ourselves, thus providing cues that might spark a recall. In some experiments, the experimenter supplies various cues, or probes, to determine whether some response has been learned. The probe might be a picture, a synonym, or any other kind of hint. Usually, the recall method has been employed when the order of events or items is of interest.

Free Recall

In some studies, an entire list of words is presented in some sequence. After the list has been shown or read, the learner is asked to recite the list in any order. As seen earlier, this procedure is known as free recall. The list may be repeated in some new, random order and another free recall required. The emphasis here is not on the sequence, but the way in which the learner responds is observed. We have already learned (see chapter 14) how subjects engage in various organizational operations.

Sometimes, a learner listens to two lists of words, one after another. The learner is then requested to respond with words from one list or the other. This is called modified free recall. If asked to respond with words from both lists, modified-modified free recall has been used. The learner may be asked to identify the lists in which the words appeared in a variation of the same procedure.

Relearning

The favored method of Ebbinghaus was designed to study forgetting and not learning. Before you can relearn something, it must be forgotten first, at least in part. The general procedure for using the relearning method is to count the trials it takes to learn something the first time; then, a time period to permit forgetting follows. A second learning, the relearning, then is undergone, and the trials are counted again. The results can be treated in various ways, but if the second learning takes fewer trials, the difference in trials is known as a savings score. You have seen the formula for a savings score in chapter 4. With the formula, one obtains the percentage of savings. The percentage of savings may vary from small to large and be surprisingly great for material long since forgotten. The college student may not remember much high school French on which he or she originally spent two school years. Should the student begin to restudy the subject, he or she might get back to his original level of competence in just a few review sessions. Burt (1932) reported a curious case of savings when he demonstrated that his eight-year old son learned passages from Greek poetry that had merely been read to him at the age of 15 months more easily than he could learn control passages. Here was a savings without prior learning in the usual sense. When college students master any material, they should not despair at its apparent disappearance with the passing semesters. They might be able to relearn in little additional time. Studying is like putting money into a bank, which keeps it where you cannot get at it without a little trouble. The memory bank will not pay interest, but it keeps your investment for you at a slight charge.

VARIABLES IN FORGETTING

The several measures of learning described above are used as the occasion requires. If one cannot recall directly, one can be cued, or probed, with various stimuli that are presumed to be related to the response. If cueing is of no effect, a recognition test might be in order. Failure with recognition might call for a relearning session. Whatever success is revealed, especially with relearning, supports the general notion that you never really forget everything. If you did learn something at some earlier time to some degree, there may be some residual effect upon which you can relearn, with, sometimes, considerable advantage. Such a hypothetical proposition, however, is of little comfort to a person who is unable to remember something of consequence. In the following sections, we will consider some of the variables that underlie the forgetting that does occur. Controlling such variables should help to prevent the forgetting in the first place.

Degree of Original Learning

How well must you learn something before you can be sure of knowing or remembering it? No one knows the answer to this question. It has been reported that some people forget their own names under conditions of stress. In genuine cases of amnesia, a person may forget his or her entire prior history—curiously enough, the person usually remembers his or her language skills and can tell us that he or she cannot remember. Professional singers who are called on to sing the "Star Spangled Banner" cannot be trusted to come through the assignment every time and would be well advised to have a copy of the words at hand. Well-practiced multiplication tables can be forgotten in part and nine times eight or seven times eight might not come out quite right despite thousands of repetitions.

When we ask how well something should be learned, we are raising the question of criterion. If we learn anything to one perfect recitation, we have learned it to one perfect recitation, and that is all we can say. Another test immediately after the perfect recitation might show some loss. In nonsense syllable list learning, one can learn a particular syllable on one trial, forget it on the next, regain it, relose it, and so on. In the laboratory, it can be demonstrated that over relatively short retention periods, one does not gain much by raising the criterion to two perfect recitations, but if one continues to extend the criterion in terms of test trials, there will come a point of diminishing returns. Thus, if it take ten trials to learn a list to one perfect recitation, doubling the number of trials to 20 will not improve the retention appreciably over adding five more trials. When we learn to some criterion beyond one perfect trial, the operation is called *overlearning*, although there probably is no such thing. Overlearning to 150 percent is about as good as overlearning to 200 percent. Such results come from short retention period tests, such as are used in retroactive interference studies.

The point just made is that you suffer less retroactive interference the better you learn the original material. It is also correct to say that you suffer less retroactive interference if the interpolated material is well learned. What this amounts to is to say that poorly learned material will be interfered with, while strongly differentiated material will not interfere or intrude because it is recognized as improper. No one is likely to say that Lincoln was the first president of the United States. Both Washington and Lincoln are too well differentiated. However, it is possible for the average college student to say almost anything about the presidents who are in between because the succession of presidents is not likely to have been learned in any serious way.

Nature of the Interpolated Material

We have already considered the significance of similarity of stimuli and responses in relation to transfer. In connection with retention, we have the same factors at work. If early learning is similar to the present learning assignment, there will be difficulty in learning and retaining the present learning if the stimuli and responses involved are similar but not identical to those in the early learning. Not only will there be trouble in learning the new task but the early learning will not be remembered as well. We recall Spinoza's (chapter 3) warning about seeing or reading too many plays by the same author and finding that we cannot remember any one as well as if we see or read only one.

The college professor may assign some readings to his or her students and find that the students may remember the material better than he or she does and this material could be in his or her own specialty. While a little knowledge may be a dangerous thing, it will be remembered.

Again, we come up with the same point discussed above under overlearning. The overlearning may itself be an indirect way of producing some necessary discrimination or differentiation of materials. The singer who forgets the "Star Spangled Banner" never forgets the "Oh, say, can you see." The difficulty comes in with "the rockets and their red glare"—did they give proof through the night or through the fight? Do the broad stripes come before or after the bright stars? To learn such a song effectively, one could well afford to spend some time thinking about (imaging) the successive features, noting that rockets illuminate the sky, and so forth, instead of doing what most people do, that is "memorizing" the words without reacting to the meanings. Children who sing the song may not know what ramparts are, and some have been known to sing "ram parts." Any imagery involved could only be confusing.

We have considered the need for differentiation of stimuli and responses in earlier chapters and need say no more at this time. Perhaps, only one more variable needs to be considered in connection with our present concern, the prevention of forgetting, and that is the role of intent to remember.

Intent

McGeoch (1942), as already mentioned, emphasized the need for proper stimulation and the appropriate settings as potent variables in remembering. When he explored the powerful effects of retroactive inhibition, he was puzzled about what could be done to prevent forgetting. The study of Lester (1932) on the influence of instructions on retroactive inhibition led him to propose that the intent to remember might be of some value. What Lester had shown was that people who knew about retroactive inhibition and its possible effects suffered less from subsequent learning than people who did not. The more they knew and the more they tried to overcome possible interference, the better they remembered. The worst retention was demonstrated by students who did not know they were going to learn anything else before a subsequent test.

What the Lester study appears to show is that most of us go about our learning in terms of today—we may have no great expectations about remembering, but we fail to take into consideration the prospect of forgetting, the almost inevitable probability of forgetting because of something else learned earlier or later interfering with retention. Simply recognizing and taking account of the fact that we will forget at the time of learning seems to help retention. When we meet a new person and learn his or her name, we should recognize at that moment that the name will probably disappear fairly quickly; this might prompt some additional effort, for example, rehearsal. If we know why we will forget (interference), we might extend the learning effort to include some mnemonic device, for example, examining the name and face and looking for some connection. Popular entertainers (Lorayne and Lucas 1974) indicate that they use imagery to connect the name with faces—they allow themselves to react to facial features, for example, a shaggy beard, and then look for something in the name that could be set off by viewing the beard again. Suppose the name is Feldman. Feld is "field," and fields have sheep, and sheep are shaggy, and the name is remembered. The system may not work with all names—or easily; the point, however, is that something is done to differentiate Mr. Feldman from all other men, bearded or beardless, because of the probable forgetting unless something is done. What the notion of intent implies is that steps must be taken to prevent forgetting. Obviously, this is not always possible, but it appears that any steps are better than none.

After mentioning the factors or variables of the degree of initial learning, the nature of the stimulus as a suitable access agent, the interference from prior or later learning (proactive and retroactive inhibition), and the operations present at the time of learning that might be described as guided by intent, we can say little more to help the student remember the contents of this chapter.

THEORIES OF FORGETTING

With the appreciation of the variables determining learning and retention behind us, we can turn to some theoretical explanations of why or how we forget. We can start with some popular generalizations, none of which should be unfamiliar.

There are at least three broad views of how we happen to forget something we at one time might claim to have known.

Disuse

Assuming that some reasonable criterion of learning has been met, one theory of forgetting, known as the disuse or decay theory, holds that if the material is not practiced, it will somehow fade away due to some presumed deterioration of the brain or other kinds of neural changes. This would be a direct decay theory. If some neural cells that are involved are taken over by new experiences and are no longer available for the old material or experience, the theory would be closer to a disuse view. The learning would no longer be there. With a disuse or decay theory, we could expect that as we grow older, more and more fading away will occur, and we will no longer remember much because it was so long ago. If no other theory had support, the disuse theory might be acceptable, as much is forgotten with the passage of time, and just as our senses and muscles deteriorate with age, there could be justification for assuming that the neural foundations of memory also suffer.

Our immediate problem with the disuse theory is that as people grow older, they sometimes appear to remember events from childhood better than more recent happenings. Such paradoxical recall may be misleading in that we may not be sure that there is as much being remembered as being fantasized. It may be that old people have rehearsed these items many times and remember the rehearsals rather than the original events. There may also be a difference in the amount of learning and attention old people devote to recent events. A war in some far-off area may not interest a senior citizen, who is not going to be drafted to fight in it. He or she may not bother learning anything about such a war, and even though he or she can be observed to be looking at a television screen showing a news story about the war, he or she may not even see or hear it, much less remember it.

When events or items can be authenticated, there will still be some recall after many years by some people. We cannot, however, pick and choose the evidence to support a disuse theory. If some very old people do remember some items from a distant past, we cannot postulate a general deteriorating function without taking some indefensible stand, such as: all people deteriorate as they grow older, and if we live long enough, we will forget everything. We have to account for differential forgetting or retention.

The Sherlock Holmes or Displacement Theory

A variation of the disuse theory is the common folk view that the "head can only hold so much." Sir Arthur Conan Doyle expressed this through his renowned detective, who explained to Dr. Watson that the brain is like an attic, which can only hold so much material. As it gets fuller and fuller, something has to be removed to make room for more valued items. We forget, therefore, because something had to give in order for new learning to have a chance of survival. This theory may have some appeal for reluctant students, but it has no apparent biological base. There do not appear to be any limits on what one can learn, at least not in terms of brain tissue. One may not have the time to learn all that could be known, but one presumably has more than enough room to accommodate any learning that does occur.

Interference Theory

The most widely endorsed view of forgetting is the one we have already described in the formal discussion of negative transfer. According to this view, time has nothing to do with forgetting (McGeoch 1942). It is what happens in time that counts. If we forget, it is because the stimulus for some response is now actively inciting a competing response, which can even be one of "I don't remember," if that is how we have learned to respond when a question is asked and the correct answer does not occur at once. In recent years, this interference view of retention has generated a new concern—that of the significance of retrieval. It is argued that whatever we learn is not lost for all time just because we cannot respond immediately with a correct answer. Our problem may be one of retrieving the answer from a large repository of many possible answers.

The view that we never really forget anything was given a strong boost by the reports of Penfield (1975) on the observations he made while operating on the temporal lobes of epileptic patients. He found that if he stimulated some point on the cortex with a small electrical charge, the conscious patient might report experiencing a rather involved and detailed "replay" from his or her past. The patient might recount a conversation, some vacation trip, a visit to a ball game or concert, and so on, presumably in faithful correspondence with his or her actual history. Penfield suggested that perhaps all our experiences are stored, as if on a tape recorder, and it is only a matter of proper stimulation that is needed to tap any memory.

The same suggestion was made by McGeoch (1942) when he argued that often we cannot provide a suitable response in a memory situation because the proper question was not asked. Given the precise stimulus to which a response was associated, we might respond appropriately unless that stimulus had, in the meantime, been associated with some other, new response. McGeoch made much of the necessity for suitable cues (as Guthrie would have) if we are to get the appropriate response to run off. Suitable cues might involve generating appropriate imagery or an actual return to the original scene of some learning. To remember a name, we might have to see the live person, or perhaps a picture might do. Playing a piano concerto in a concert hall might not be as fine a performance as one might give in one's own living room with one's own piano. Amateurs rehearsing theatrical lines at home might suffer memory lapses on a stage even though they were "word perfect" in their lines at home. Bilodeau and Schlosberg (1952) provided an experimental demonstration when they found that whereas people learned nonsense syllables in one room when standing up and reading cards, they did poorly when tested in another room when sitting down, with a memory drum providing the cues.

Tulving (Tulving and Pearlstone 1966) has made a strong case for the proposition that our prior learning may be available but not accessible without the right stimulation. Tulving makes much of the proposal that if we are to remember something, it is not only necessary to learn the material but, also, to associate some kind of retrieval tag with it. This suggestion amounts to recognizing the inherent danger of forgetting anything unless we make provision for getting to the correct responses by selecting and associating appropriate cues. Our big problem is that when we do learn something, there is usually no developed system operating to make sure of retrieval. When a library book is shelved by a librarian, it is placed in a specific place keyed to the card catalog by certain letters and numbers. If the book is properly shelved, anyone who knows the catalog number can find it. If the catalog is vandalized, the whole library will be out of order and useless until the catalog is restored.

The basic problem in retention is that our experiences are not always, or even commonly, formal, regular, or systematic. According to Landauer (1975), our memories are rather random in that we learn one thing after another with no necessary connection between sequences. Landauer describes a model of a memory space where our experiences are randomly stored. If something is repeated, it is likely to be stored in some "place" that may be quite remote from the locus of the first experience. With many repetitions and many storage places, we are more likely to "tap" a memory than with few such repetitions. Because of the multiple, unorganized experiences we all have, our "memories" become somewhat cluttered, uncataloged libraries, where novels are side by side with textbooks or films, television shows, and baseball games. To get at or to some particular memory may be easy or difficult, but it is largely a chance matter unless some very handy cue is provided. We may be lost in some memory search forever even though the sought after memory is there, available but inaccessible.

The view that nothing is really (or completely) forgotten is basic for the interference theory. The situation reduces itself to the statement: you did not forget—you just do not remember. While the statement may sound paradoxical, it should not be for the reader who has followed the arguments of the interference theorists. Their basic position is that when the question involving retention is posed, that is, when a stimulus occurs, it will generate a response. If the response is wrong or useless (for example, "I don't know"), it is because the stimulus is not prompting the correct response. The "forgetter" is suffering the effects of either proactive or retroactive inhibition or both.

If it is granted that the original learning was adequate, then the interference theory has wide appeal and considerable endorsement from learning psychologists. At almost any age, a learner has acquired some background or learning experience to a wide range of stimuli, which will serve to generate proactive inhibition, and the older the person, the more likely he or she is to have had potentially interfering experiences. As time passes, we all add to our learning experiences, thereby assuring some potential retroactive inhibition for earlier learning.

FORGETTING AND EXTINCTION

The interference theory has some close affinities to the observations made on deliberate extinction of conditioned responses. We already noted (see chapter 6) how conditioned responses *replace* other responses in the original conditioning procedure and how these original responses return during extinction trials. Extinction and forgetting may be two sides of the same coin. It should be remembered that extinction does not refer to some decay or permanent inability to make the response in question. We have seen that extinctions are marked by spontaneous recovery and that conditioning can be rapidly re-established (relearning on the basis of savings).

The fact that extinction will be followed by spontaneous recovery has been proposed as an explanation of the forgetting of verbal material in terms of extinction. Suppose that someone learns two lists of paired associates in succession where the stimuli (A) are the same but the responses in the first list (B) differ from those in the second (C). We then have someone learning A-B and later A-C. To learn to say C to A, the subject must somehow inhibit or prevent himself or herself from saying B to A. Because B is now the wrong response, it will not be followed by the US (or, if one pleases, it will not be reinforced). Not being followed by the US should lead to extinction. The new response C to A is reinforced and, therefore, learned. If we wait a while, the extinguished responses (B) will begin to recover spontaneously, and a test some time after the A-C learning should show many B responses occurring. Just such an account has been proposed by Barnes and Underwood (1959).

If we view interference as a matter of having learned some new response to some "old" stimulus, the parallel between extinction and forgetting is striking. Such parallels between verbal learning and conditioning have not been prominent in learning research, but this may be due, in part, to the kinds of operations and opportunities to observe. The verbal learning studies have used lists of words; the conditioners have favored single stimuli. When college students are asked to recite a list of words or nonsense syllables, they frequently sit silently before the memory drum instead of reporting the items that they think of. Such omissions were at one time (Melton and Irwin 1940) taken to represent an "unlearning" operation. When students are encouraged to produce "wrong" answers, they can respond to every stimulus, usually with an "error" indicating that extensive interference is occurring. Failure to note such unemitted responses can lead to speculations that are opposed to interference or extinction theories.

It would be remiss to fail to remind the student of Gibson's (1942) (see chapter 12) study of generalization effects in paired-associate learning. Here, we have another instance of conditioning principles being applied to human learning. We might also recall the concept of the stimulus trace, which had its origin in the philosopher's speculations about association but attained its fullest developments with Pavlov and other physiologically minded investigators. The stimulus trace was a major working assumption of Hull and his associates (1940) in relating human verbal learning to conditioning principles.

We can conclude this section by recognizing that we have dealt with only the simplest kind of verbal learning, namely, that of single words or lists. Multiple lists do not add much to our appreciation of how human beings learn the kinds of things people learn in everyday environments.

RETRIEVAL

It is argued by Tulving and Pearlstone (1966) that failures of memory are primarily failures of retrieval. Something forgotten only appears to be forgotten because we are not going about the business of reinstating the original experience correctly. It is not gone permanently, although we may die before we can re-establish the desired response. The basic assumption made is like that of Penfield (1975), namely, that every experience is recorded some place in the brain and that suitable probing will revive it.

McGeoch's Proposal

The general proposal was made by McGeoch (1942) that if we do learn something (to whatever degree), it can be thought of as some response having been made to a stimulus. If that same (or suitable) stimulus recurs, we should make the same response. It has been mentioned in an earlier section (see discussion of Rock's 1957 experiment) that the writer's subjects in a replication of Rock's study were able to *recognize* the nonsense syllables that had been shown once and discarded because they were not recalled in the next test trial. In this case, McGeoch would feel justified in saying that learning had occurred to a *recognition* level and not to a *recall* level and that his principle still ruled. In the case of a recall of some syllable to a stimulus, the argument would be that the stimulus was indeed appropriate enough. A later test, in which the subjects could be presumed to have forgotten the earlier learning, would call for a more appropriate test.

In support of McGeoch's position, the writer once had subjects learn 20 nonsense syllables in a serial list—a really taxing job—in September. In May of the following year, the subjects were asked to recall the syllables. The first reaction was to label the request as ridiculous. No one seemed to remember any of the syllables. The writer then urged and encouraged that each subject try. After a few minutes, some syllables were produced, but the remainder seemed long and far gone. The writer then asked the subjects to recall the day in September, the laboratory cubicle where the learning took place, the memory drum used, the experimenter involved, and so forth. More syllables were recalled. A final measure was then introduced: each subject went back to the room involved with an unloaded memory drum; the subject was seated where he or she thought he or she had been before; the drum was started and made its characteristic clicks; and more syllables were recalled. One subject, the best, recalled 18 syllables in one-half hour. McGeoch would have argued that it was not September, but May, that other variations in the stimulus situation had been introduced, and, in general, like Guthrie, McGeoch would want the exact stimulus complex repeated.

The Probe Technique

Tulving (1972) and Murdock (1968), among others, have employed another method to facilitate retrieval. While the technique has many other uses, in the present context, it amounts to providing additional cues to elicit formerly learned responses. If the task is a list of words, for example, and the subject cannot recall the word *apple*, which had been in the list, one could ask: Was there a fruit in the list? Such a question includes the probe *fruit*, which might arouse the correct response. If the list contains words such as *child*, *chicken*, and *river*, the subject could be helped by probes such as *baby*, *bird*, *water*, and so forth.

The probe technique is commonly used when we search for a familiar but presently unavailable name. We run through the alphabet and hope the sounding of the letters will initiate the name, and it frequently does. As we run through the alphabet, we easily dismiss many letters as unlikely. The name is on the "tip of the tongue" and we need only a slight jar (probe) to have it emerge.

When no amount of probing results in a success, we still do not need to abandon the hypothesis that the response is available; it may need more direct or fuller probing. We can provide the material in the original form, for example, some forgotten name. If the forgetter accepts the name as correct, that is, recognizes it, there had to be something there to be recognized. If a single presentation fails to arouse the recognition, the forgetter can always *relearn*, and the forgetter's savings score will again testify to some degree of retention.

If the savings score is low, one can legitimately ask, Was there then not some forgetting, elimination, or disappearance of the S⟶R association. McGeoch and his loyal followers could still argue that the presumed neural traces involved could have been shunted into new associations, which kept up a strong interference. The argument is foolproof and untestable at the same time. Whatever the realities, it is reasonably safe to conclude that much that is learned becomes unavailable even with heroic efforts at improving the accessibility.

IV

Applications

INTRODUCTION

In the early 1970s, students were preoccupied with relevance—they wanted their education to be meaningful, but teachers, in most cases, did not know what the students wanted. For teachers, their work was, and always had been, meaningful and relevant. Was not biology meaningful, or mathematics, or philosophy? Was it not meaningful to ponder the origin and nature of the earth, of the cosmos, of the mind? Were these areas irrelevant?

The students were reflecting an ancient conflict between "pure" and "applied" knowledge, a conflict of long standing between physiologists and physicians, between physicists and engineers, and between academic psychologists and clinical practitioners. The academic psychologists had not discovered enough useful truths to please clinicians, educators, penologists, reformers, social workers, or mothers trying to bring up their children. How true such an assessment may be is difficult to resolve. People are never satisfied with answers to questions because new questions keep developing as old ones are answered, and we can always declare ourselves to be ignorant. It is common enough for senior students to feel they know less than they did as freshmen, and education is frequently described as the process of discovering how little we know "when you get right down to it." As Conant (1953) put it, the answer to any question merely opens up new questions, and science escalates our ignorance. Landing on the moon, a technological triumph, only stirred our curiosity about Mars. The moon is no longer exciting to many men, although the landings and soil samples raised thousands of questions we never knew enough to ask before.

In the psychology of learning, we have learned a lot. Whether it is considered useful or not has not always concerned investigators, although everyone would like to believe that his or her research might some day find some valuable application.

On a pure-to-applied scale, many psychologists fancy themselves closer to the pure end and tend to ignore practical problems; they believe that basic research is the foundation for any application, and they concentrate their efforts on what they perceive as basic questions. They like to describe psychology as an infant science that may require centuries (Spence 1951) to mature. Some, like Pratt (1937), feel that psychology belongs in the library and in the laboratory "for a long time to come." When will the baby grow up? Maybe, it has grown more than its parents think. Parents are always protective of their children even long after the children have children of their own. Perhaps, psychology has already accomplished someting of value. We can take a look at what we have learned and then see what some psychologists have suggested as solutions to some practical problems in certain areas of education and behavior problems. In the next chapters, we will look at education, delinquency, and psychotherapy.

18

A Theoretical Recapitulation

In the chapters remaining, we shall look at some practical applications that have arisen from the mountain of theoretical labors of learning psychologists. A student of learning might feel some responsibility for advising interested parties about real-life problems where learning seems to be involved. In some such problems, there may well be situations where learning is only apparently involved, and misguided efforts at training or teaching could do more harm than good. Before we turn to the real world, however, it might serve our interests to review the theoretical developments our examination of learning research and thinking has produced.

A THEORY OF LEARNING

The nature of a theory is a topic of considerable debate among philosophers of science. Some think of a theory as a formal collection of postulates from which deductions about new discoveries are drawn; others, like Russell (1927), think that theories contain no more than is put into them and that they serve only as summary statements, purporting to account for some restricted area of empirical findings. A theory need not predict; it might only explain or order some sets of observations in a systematic way. Others think of a theory as a pedagogical tool that serves to organize some accepted statements concerning observations in a given field.

The theory to be described here partakes of all of these suggested reasons for the existence of theories, with the inclusion of the general warning that all theories are temporary and are subject to change, as observations warrant. We will be considering a tentative explanatory account of the common observations garnered by learning psychologists over the past century. We should take note that philosophers of science prefer theories that are as simple as necessary and as simple as possible with the fewest possible postulates (assumptions) from which the greatest number of observations can be accounted for or explained.

BASIC POSTULATES

In our examination of the speculations of earlier workers, we have recognized that whatever else they found of interest, their basic concern was the problem of association. When learning occurs, it is because something is associated within (not by) the learner with something else. In every theoretical account that we have examined, there was agreement that something that could be described or referred to as association did, in fact, occur. Disagreements arose as to why some things might be associated and others not and as to what was associated with what (stimuli with stimuli, stimuli with responses, responses with rewards, and so forth), but the basic agreement on association is common to all.

Principle of Contiguity

In an early chapter (see chapter 3), we noted that Aristotle had proposed a universal and necessary condition (principle, postulate, law) for association, namely, contiguity in space or time. There appears to have been no disagreement with the philosopher on this point. The only issue was whether it was a *sufficient* condition. Aristotle, himself, felt that it was not, because he added another law, that of similarity and contrast. Skipping over a couple of millenia, we find E. R. Guthrie, himself a philosopher, agreeing with Aristotle on contiguity as necessary but disagreeing with him on insufficiency. For Guthrie, contiguity was all that was required for learning to occur. It, of course, behooved Guthrie to reject similarity-contrast and all other proposed principles, and he did so in the case of similarity by pointing out that the real, the genuine, components in the association were actually the same, even though they were not recognized as such by the experimental observer. In the instance of Pavlovian conditioning, for example, the issue that tests the principle is that of generalization. If a dog salivates to a tone similar to, but not identical with, the original conditioned stimulus, then not only is similarity apparently operating but contiguity itself is questioned, because the "generalized" tone had never been presented in contiguity with the unconditioned stimulus. Guthrie points out, however, that the actual conditioned stimulus may not be the tone at all—it could be, for example, a movement-produced stimulus initiated by some response to any tone. If the movement-produced stimulus should be identical, in such instances, there would be no case for *similarity* whatsoever—the notion of generalization would be not only unnecessary but erroneous, and contiguity would reign as the sole and sovereign principle.

So Guthrie dealt with all other alleged and proposed secondary principles, for example, frequency, which as we have seen, gives way to a one-trial learning interpretation. More trials merely mean that more conditioned stimuli are becoming involved or "getting into the act," an expression that might give Guthrie a momentary pause, but only that. Any other suggestions Guthrie would greet with denial and rejection. His strongest denials would concern the role of reward, but that is not the present issue. Guthrie's endorsement of recency or postremity was not meant to suggest another law of learning. Postremity was meant to be a factual statement that was relevant to prediction of future behavior but irrelevant to learning. It is a behavioral postulate, not a learning principle.

Guthrie was not alone in his endorsement of contiguity; on the contrary, as indicated above, he was a member of a universal society—his differences with fellow theorists were on subprinciples—almost everyone else had some use for frequency as a principle (Thorndike, Hull, Spence, Skinner, Watson, Pavlov, and Tolman). Among more recent theorists, I. Rock and E. Saltz, as well as the Gestalt school in general, might be included as supporting one-trial learning.

In the present theory, then, we can see no evil and only good in accepting the principle of contiguity as a basic law of learning. No one can be found who now or ever before disagreed with it. Do we need any other basic principle?

Factor of Time

The problem of frequency we have already disposed of (see the discussion of time in chapter 4) by arguing that the contiguity must exist for some minimal amount of time, during which the association components must coexist within the learner (presumably as activated neural traces). In short, instead of making frequency either a first- or second-rank principle, we reduce it to a corollary of contiguity in the dimension of time. We state, then, a general law of learning: components in an association will enter into an association if the components are in contiguity over a sufficient period of time.

This principle is stated in such a fashion to account for the fact that many possible associations fail to survive primarily because the components do not coexist for an adequate period of time. No one remembers (learns) everything he or she conceivably might have learned. Not all contiguous experiences are associated.

Isolation

We can now suggest a second corollary or modification, derived from Spinoza and elaborated by Guthrie's supporter, Virginia Voeks. Spinoza had proposed a principle of association that we labeled *isolation* (see chapter 3). Voeks (1954) experimentally demonstrated one-trial conditioning of the human eyelid blink when the circumstances were so designed as to virtually restrict the potential components of the prospective association to two stimuli and the reactions thereto. In short, when only two potential components are active within a learner, the association occurs. By inference, any failure of an association suggests that the learner is being subjected to other, undesirable inputs that interfere with the formation of the association. We can now rephrase the basic principle as: components in an association will enter into an association if the components are relatively isolated and in contiguity over a sufficient period of time.

What is meant by *relatively isolated* should not prove to be difficult to appreciate by readers of this text. Relative isolation is what Saltz (1971) described as discrimination, differentiation, or segregation. The components cannot be multiple, complex events if any precision of learning is to occur. One cannot be expected to give correct answers in a paired-associate experiment using nonsense syllables if one is preoccupied with the apparatus, the purpose of the experiment, or the impression one is making and merely reacts to one syllable after another as, "Oh, I saw a mess of nonsense syllables; they were in pairs, I think." It should be noted, of course, that this unworthy subject did learn something—that he or she had seen a mess of nonsense syllables—but the point that Saltz would emphasize is that each nonsense syllable or component of an association must be responded to specifically as different in some way from every other possible nonsense syllable if any specific learning is to occur. We have already dealt at length with the problem of discrimination, discriminated stimuli, differentiation, familiarization, and so forth and need not belabor the issue.

We come instead to the question of why should two isolated components coexisting for a suitable period of time enter into an association? For this question, there are a variety of answers that bear comment.

THE QUESTION OF WHY ASSOCIATIONS OCCUR

Some investigators, for example, Watson, Guthrie, and Tolman, chose to ignore this question as a serious issue. Associations occurred because they occurred. It is the nature of the beast, or man, to have associations form when components are simultaneously present in isolation for a sufficient period of time. This may still be the best answer. After all, the behaviorist's preoccupation was with the *conditions* under which learning would occur, and they described those conditions to their own satisfaction. Pavlov's (1927) inadequate physiological accounts were ignored.

Some investigators—Thorndike, Hull, and Skinner—chose to argue that association formation depended additionally upon the presentation and/or consumption of a satisfier, drive reducer, or reinforcer *after* a response had been made in some stimulus situation. We noted earlier that Guthrie had the good sense to ask how anything that came after something could affect what went on before. He was never answered. His question was ignored or misanswered by pointing to the empirical facts that future responses would be of greater probability if prior responses were reinforced. Such an answer (Hilgard and Bower 1975) is on another level of discourse and bears no direct relation to the question. Both Thorndike and Hull indulged in speculation that the satisfactory state of affairs might, indeed, in some way strengthen a neural "bond," but they never could spell out the operation. Skinner (1938) left the question and answer to the physiologists.

Hebb (1949) chose to ignore the issue of reinforcement and went back to the simple Pavlovian setup to propose a possible reason for the formation of associations. His suggestion amounts to the postulation that when adjacent neural fibers are in some state of activity, growth processes occur, for example, enlargement of end buds or terminal boutons on neural fibers can increase in size and make closer contact (reduce synaptic distances) or otherwise facilitate transmission of neural energy from one (or set of) neurons to another. While Hebb's account is plausible, it lacks hard evidence and leaves us no better off than recognizing that something must go on in the nervous system when we learn. Fortunately for psychologists, it is not necessary to provide a neural account of learning. We can be content with an account on a behavioral level. We are obliged only to demonstrate that under certain conditions, learning will occur and that without such conditions, it will not. Thus far, we have identified three conditions that are necessary (contiguity, isolation, and time). Those may be all that are required. Other questions may then represent technological issues in how best to set up the necessary conditions. Consider the original Skinner teaching machine. This consisted of a device that, in effect, at any one time, presented a single question which was normally answerable by a suitable learner. The question and/or the answer contained the two components that had to be associated if the next question(s) were to be answered correctly. Here, we had contiguity and isolation, and because the arrangement allowed for it, all the time in the world. People using such a device with a suitable set of questions (called the program) could and did learn. The program was difficult to construct because it had to have the associable components appropriately discriminated (isolated), and program constructors could not devise suitable items without a great deal of labor and testing.

It must be concluded that other features of the device or program, particularly its built-in reward or reinforcement features, were irrelevant and extraneous to the learning process even if they had other uses, primarily those of keeping the learner at the task. It is argued here that such reinforcers as lights, buzzers, candy, or knowledge of being correct are all irrelevant to learning, if highly relevant to motivation. But motivation's function is only that of bringing the learner to the learning situation. No one can learn the contents of a book unless one opens the book. We can concede that motivation leads to opening books and looking at their contents. From that point on, motivation is of no further interest as far as learning is concerned, and contiguity, isolation, and time take over. Any rewards involved come after the learning takes place.

The theory or principle sketched thus far may be satisfactory up to a point or as far as it goes. It may not appear to go very far, although it might account for simple Pavlovian conditioning, without too much spelling out of what is implied by the broader interpretation of contiguity. Thus far, we have indicated that two component events must coexist for a period of time in relative isolation. If we go no further, we can account only for very simple learning, probably of a rather primitive nature—the learning of infants, perhaps, where they learn some associations like that of the general appearance and sound (vocalizations) of the mother. For any more involved learning, we must consider the nature of the coexistence of components more seriously.

PROCESSING

In an earlier chapter, the concept of processing was introduced. In the present theory, *processing* refers to anything that is going on inside the learner, including any emotional or other kinds of physiological reactions, for example, brain wave changes, electrochemical activities, feedback stimulation from muscular or glandular activity, and so on. The learner may not and need not be aware of any such activity in the sense of being able to describe it. Learning, itself, is an unconscious process—we do not feel ourselves learning.

In the area of perceptual or verbal learning, we can extend the processing operation, as Craik and Lockhart (1972) have done to the kinds of activity that a learner might describe in a learning situation if asked, "What are you doing?" The learner might answer something like this (assume that the task is that of learning to recite 20 words in any order):* "I say the words over to myself as rapidly as possible." "I look for words beginning with the same letter." "I look for words that fit into certain groups, like animals, vegetables, and minerals." "I try to group words in fours or fives." "I try to make up a story from the words."

Such reports sound realistic enough. We all know what the subject is talking about—that is, all of us but the subject. What the subject is actually doing is talking about what he or she thinks is occurring inside himself or herself with his or her lips or eyes, yet, clearly, he or she is not inside himself or herself and there is *no one* directing his or her lips or eyes. These are responses the subject has learned to make somewhere along in his or her

---

*The reader is reminded that these are actual questions from subjects in such a study (see chapter 15).

learning history in such situations. Any one subject could engage in any of these activities if instructed to do so, but in the absence of specific directions from outside, certain activities will occur (it does no good to say the subject instructs himself or herself—this just gets us into an identity inquiry, namely, Who is instructing whom and how?). Perhaps at present, we can go no further than to say that when someone is learning something (trying to or not), certain kinds of "operations" (processing) are going on whether the subject is aware of them or not. Thus, it is perfectly possible for a subject to be repeating words, silently or aloud, in serial order or by groups of two or three, that is, reciting the first, second, and third words and coming back to the first, and so forth. An experimenter might call this a strategy. The subject would, more likely, describe it as "That's how I always try to learn such an assignment."

Regardless of how the subject reacts to the components that are to be associated, the efficiency of the learning (how quickly he or she learns or how well he or she retains) will depend on what, in fact, is occurring in him or her. What this amounts to is to recognize that the time factor in our learning principle is of interest only insofar as we take account of what is going on in that time. The mere passage of time is presumably irrelevant. It is unlikely that any two events can coexist in time in some passive, noninteractive way, and whatever does occur by way of interaction will determine the efficiency of the learning.

Suppose, for example, that the learner responds by allowing images of what each word represents to occur. It will then be the case that he or she will remember more words than if he or she simply mutters each word to himself or herself. Allowing images to occur, however, is a relatively mature reaction, a reaction to instructions from the experimenter or from cues related to prior experiences of such learning efforts. Inexperienced learners do not usually think of working with images.

What we are talking about now is that our principle of learning will operate more *or* less efficiently depending upon the reactions occurring within the learner and that these reactions themselves are dependent upon prior learning. Such reactions would also include what is commonly called attention. We have already treated the concept of attention in some depth and need not review it. At this point, we are merely stating that the efficiency of learning depends upon how the time (of association) is being spent, and this now can be described as reflecting the nature of the attention "being paid." From an earlier chapter, we recall that learning *costs* something besides tuition fees.

THE WHAT OF ASSOCIATION

Here, we face the question of what is associated with what? We have already examined this question in terms of what different theorists favored in the past (the S $\longrightarrow$ S, S $\longrightarrow$ R, S $\longrightarrow$ R plus reinforcement views, the cell assembly approach of Hebb, and the earliest of all, the association of ideas, Aristotle's original proposal).

Hebb's translation of ideas into cell assemblies appears to be the most attractive view. It explicitly recognizes that learning takes place within a person and not in some external world of observed stimuli and observed responses. Hull had approached this conclusion in his emphasis on the notion that an external world stimulus, S, necessarily generated some sensory neural process, s, which presumably led to some neural activity, r that could initiate the observable response, R. Because s and r are very likely to be of the same qualitative nature, although varying perhaps in location, complexity, or other quantitative ways, it will facilitate discussion if we refer to either s or r as n, a neural reaction or activity, and consider the possibility that learning amounts to associations between ns. Such a position absolves us from concern over over Rs, which need not occur in learning, as when responses are blocked by suppressive drugs (Pavlov 1927; Black 1965) or when they are not *performed* for appropriate reasons as in latent learning studies.

The recourse to ns as the units of association allows us a further luxury. We can identify certain ns with images. In the chapter on imagery, we suggested that when a neural reaction was initiated indirectly, that is, not by its normal stimulus, such an n' would be an image whether or not the subject involved could describe his or her internal reaction with any adequacy. The subject could not, of course, describe the actual neural activity; he or she could only refer to the original stimuli that would normally elicit such a reaction and which are now absent. In discussing such imagery reactions, we mentioned the split-brain patients who can respond appropriately (but not verbally) to stimuli that are processed by the right hemisphere. When such patients can recognize by feeling with their left hands some object that was "seen" by the right hemisphere, we can assume that the felt object is initiating some reasonable facsimile of the object as seen, original stimulation, in short, as imagery.

We made the point that Pavlovian conditioning was a special case or subclass of the general principle of the association of images where investigators were concerned about overt behavior. We can now recognize that while learning may involve overt behavior, as in the acquisition of skilled motor performances, where feedback stimuli are generated, it is these stimuli that, in turn, generate the ns and n's that are the critical activities in learning.

LEARNING AND PERFORMANCE

In the first half of this century, the expression "predict and control" was commonly cited by textbook writers as the aim of psychology. It was the aim of the behaviorist movement, as expressed first by Watson (1924) and more recently by Skinner (1971). There was a sense of the expression that could be generally accepted, that is, a science must operate in terms of *experimental* predictions and must be able to *replicate* its observations under *controlled* conditions. But Watson and Skinner were interested in a more direct interpretation of the prediction and control statement. They were interested in social progress and improvement—in making the lot of mankind more suitable than they perceived it. In Skinner's famous debate with Rogers (1956), Skinner stated that he wanted people to be more adjusted, more creative, healthier, happier, and more productive. We can sympathize with these goals, although Rogers indicated some reluctance to see Skinner become happier, presumably because of some assumption that only unhappy people are creative and productive. But the only apparent way to behaviorists to bring about suitable changes in society is to change *behavior*.

The concern with prediction and control led to the concern with the observations of overt behavior and performance rather than learning. It was obvious that rewards (and punishments) could change behavior, and the all-consuming interest in behavior change led to an overpreoccupation with the function of rewards and punishments (aversive stimuli) on the part of hundreds of psychologists, who described their efforts as a concern with learning. Because rewards and punishments can be employed only as consequential events, following some behavior or performance, performance became the equivalent of learning, whereas it can only serve as an inferential base.

We have seen how Tolman (chapter 9) strove to distinguish learning from performance and how Hull came to agree with him. Guthrie and Skinner never did. They stayed with behavior, as was true of all the followers of Pavlov. By continuing to use rewards and/or aversive stimuli and regarding the preceding behavior as *the* learned response, they failed to recognize the real role of rewards and punishments as stimuli for emotional reactions, an interpretation that we owe to Mowrer. We can see now that Skinner, Hull, and Thorndike were operating primarily with *motivational* situations and with behavioral control, and whatever real learning was going on was obscured or misinterpreted.

If emotional responses are reactions to rewards and punishments, we must examine the implied questions of whether emotional responses are themselves learned. We have seen how Mowrer argued that the emotions of hope and fear were conditioned to external and feedback stimuli, but we also pointed out that Mowrer had adopted the Pavlovian-Tolman view that conditioning was a stimulus substitution operation. Emotions as responses are not then learned; they are the consequences of unconditioned stimuli. When such unconditioned stimuli are associated with conditioning stimuli, the latter will come to arouse, indirectly, the emotional responses that are directly related to the unconditioned stimuli. In short, we do not learn *to respond* emotionally or in any other way. The responses are already available. What is learned is an indirect arrangement for activating the response. For practical purposes, of course, we can ignore the theoretical operations and proceed to condition emotions or instrumental acts through the presentation of "reinforcements." Theoretically, we are forced to recognize that reinforcements are only unconditioned stimuli, as Pavlov recognized in his original use of the term *reinforcement* (with a small *r*). For Pavlov, a reinforcer was something that strengthened an association and the withholding of which (extinction) would weaken the association. In both cases, he was referring to an unconditioned stimulus.

MEDIATIONAL RESPONSES

We started our inquiry into learning by accepting a broad or general S $\longrightarrow$ R position. That position, however, was shortly amended by introducing the concept of mediation, of m-p-s's, or r_g's and of imagery. While we spent much time in dealing with observable stimuli and observable responses, we recognized that a great deal of learning and of behavior occurs between the initiating stimulus (S) and the concluding response, (R) of some S $\longrightarrow$ R sequence. Much of our behavior consists of unobservable reactions, in fact, chains of such reactions, where attention to only the external components leaves us ignorant of what went on. If our only concern was how paired associates, such as "grass" and "green," came into being, we would have an impoverished science. It is to Skinner's credit that he spent so much time on the concept of chaining and on how one step in behavior leads to another, as he demonstrated in his programmed learning efforts. Skinner was reluctant to indulge in some of the speculative operations that broaden the notion of chaining into the more encompassing concept of mediation. We remind the student that the principle of learning involved in chaining is the same as that in simple paired associates but that the operation of chaining cannot be ignored.

Besides carrying the burden of linkage between steps that bridge the gap between S and R, mediational responses, such as the r_g, for example, have the feature of producing stimuli that not only lead to the next step but also add to the energizing of the ongoing activity. Like emotions, r_gs can be motivators and play the role of incentives. With associated imagery, r_g's and their stimuli can serve to initiate behavior (including emotional responses). We saw how the concept of ideomotor action could be exploited (chapter 11) to account for the acquisition of instrumental responses. While the research support for mediational operations, such as imagery and r_gs is not as robust as might be wished, we cannot get along with only a bare S $\longrightarrow$ R interpretation. Too much of our learning is done while we merely sit and "think."

SUMMARY STATEMENT

The theory spelled out above has been reduced to one basic postulate—that of contiguity of the neural consequences of stimulus events. In an earlier proposal (Bugelski 1973b), the theory was embellished with some formal statements about the factors of time, isolation, and processing. These have now been incorporated into the expanded statement of the continuity principle. The construct of imagery has played an important role in the discussions of various learning arrangements in earlier parts of this book. Imagery is to be recognized as a major factor in the processing operation that *is* learning.

In discussing processing, we recognized that attention was basically a negative or subtractive matter. We are attentive when a minimum number of events is being processed or when we are responding to a minimum number of stimulus consequences. When our attention is wandering, we are responding to other stimuli than those someone else might wish us to process.

We recognized that time, per se, is irrelevant, but unless sufficient processing occurs during a learning period, there will be little learning. We can state that *time* and *attention* are basic requirements for learning if we carefully note that neither term should be taken as referring to anything in itself.

We have found that the contiguity postulate as presented above has been sufficient, and presumably necessary, to account for learning in various situations that called for motoric responses and verbal activities. We have been able to account for learning by show and tell and to interpret so-called imitation, mnemonics, and one-trial learning.

What we have tried to emphasize throughout the book is that we need not try to explain all behavior through learning. Many kinds of activities or behaviors are not learned, although they may make use of prior learning or are modified by learning. Man does other things besides learn, and his behavior may change for other than learning reasons all through his lifetime. We leave the discussion of other processes, agencies, or influences to others to explain.

19

The Nature and Function of Punishment

When we discussed Thorndike's law of effect (chapter 7), we noted that he originally included a negative counterpart to the positive impact of rewards. Punishment was supposed to weaken bonds, break habits, and otherwise play a role that was equal but opposite to that of rewards. Thorndike did not support this view with any evidence, and we did not pay serious attention to it at that time. Because punishment (or negative consequences) is such a universal practice and because we all encounter negative consequences, it is incumbent upon us to see what relation there is, if any, between punishment and learning.

SOME PHILOSOPHICAL VIEWS

Throughout history, some people who have been in a position to do so have punished some others. Throughout that same history, philosophers have pondered the meaning, purpose, and effectiveness of punishment. For some people, punishment is the proper operation when someone sins, commits a crime, or otherwise offends. For those who follow the Bible in guiding their conduct, sin is natural enough; it started with Adam and Eve, who were punished for the first sin. In Biblical times, the eye-for-an-eye formula was adopted as a reasonable guide for regulating human affairs. The motivations of the sinner and the punisher might not be too seriously examined. Divine example was a sufficient guide.

For some philosophers the notion that sin was natural did not appear obvious—in fact, for Jean Jacques Rousseau (1712–78), it appeared contrary to nature. For Rousseau (1762), man was born good, but an ill-regulated society corrupts some men. Society should be adjusted so that the individual would not be inclined to crime, because his or her will would be part of the total social will. The individual would have accepted the general rules of conduct.

The Social Contract of Rousseau is an echo of Hobbes's *The Leviathan* (1651), which also described a proper society as one where individuals exchanged some of their personal rights for the protection offered by a state or sovereign. Such an exchange was presumably based on mutual agreement by rational men. Hobbes chose to ignore the fact that no such contract had ever been agreed upon.

LAW AND THE RATIONAL MAN

In modern societies, legislators or lawmakers define crimes or other levels of offenses and sometimes prescribe penalties for infractions of what are considered appropriate standards. The approval of all the citizens is not assumed. The basic foundation of the law is the *rational man*, who is considered personally responsible for his behavior. The rational man is assumed to be able to choose to obey or disobey laws (whether or not he knows of their existence—"ignorance of the law is no excuse"). Such a position suggests that certain modes of conduct should be naturally perceived as good or bad by a rational man. When a defense lawyer can find no other alternative for freeing a client, he or she may challenge the law by arguing that his or her client was not "responsible" in the sense that he or she could not choose. Inability to choose can be supported by arguing that the client is or was insane or otherwise incompetent because of mental deficiency or defect, because he or she was drunk, senile, too young, sick, tired, drugged, emotionally upset, threatened with death or injury, or whatever else can be proposed to explain the behavior as irrational, that is, irresponsible or excusable.

To appreciate the solemnity and potency of this legal base of rational choice, we need only to recall the trials of war criminals who were judged guilty after entering the defense of following military orders. It is not easy to be a soldier when one is commanded to kill. Even in such a situation, one is expected to be able to make the right choice. Failure to follow orders is, of course, another (military) crime.

THE DETERMINIST VIEW

In contrast to the rational man theory, most modern psychologists follow a determinist position, which holds that everyone behaves as he or she must or as he or she has to because of his or her nature, taking into account heredity, history, and environment. The position has been strongly presented by Skinner (1971) in his *Beyond Freedom and Dignity*, where the crucial social implications are spelled out. No man deserves credit or praise for his good deeds, and no one deserves blame or condemnation for his or her misdeeds. In neither case could the individuals involved have acted otherwise.

From a determinist, view all behavior is caused by factors beyond any individual's control. All of one's choices and decisions are forced upon one. One can no more help being "good" than being "evil." The lawmakers cannot help making the laws they enact anymore than they can stop thinking that their laws are proper conclusions of rational men applied to the behavior of rational men. The fact that laws are enacted that commonly serve the interests of some other citizens is either overlooked or excused as representing the will of the majority. Those who will be most likely to violate the laws will also be most likely to be in the minority—those who might have little use or respect for the law.

From the determinist position, law-abiding people are those who are reinforced for behaving in ways that conform to the legal structure. Those who are not reinforced for conforming will be inclined to violations of some laws. If the violation results in reinforcement, such criminal behavior will become more probable.

REASONS FOR PUNISHMENT

The usual catalog of reasons for punishment includes the following reasons.

Revenge, Retribution, and Retaliation

Nowadays, the term *revenge* has acquired negative connotations for many people, especially public officials. For the famous Hatfield and McCoy feuding families, it was, of course, natural to retaliate (*lex talionis*—the law of retaliation). Some modern judges accept the retaliation principle without any grave concern on the general ground that one must pay for one's crimes when one breaks the law. Some philosophers, such as Kant and Hegel, assumed a need for retribution because it represented a natural balance, a quid pro quo. Criminals who serve their time come out saying they have paid their "debt to society" (although not to the person(s) they might have offended). The driver who speeds pays his or her fine when caught as a kind of debt settlement if he or she knowingly "took a chance" when he or she raced along. The philosophical basis for revenge or retaliation is some notion that citizens have entered upon some social contract with the society and that a violation of a contract calls for penalties. Because no citizen ever made such a contract, the basis for retaliative punishment is hardly rational. When individuals attack those who have injured them in some way, we describe the behavior as aggression, not punishment. Such retaliative aggression might be natural enough, but it is not our present concern. An angry mother beating up a child is aggressing, not punishing. To qualify as a punisher, the mother would have to be quite calm and rational.

Deterrence

The administration of punishment is often excused as a preventative operation. The punishment is intended to introduce restraint should the occasion to commit the crime recur. Sometimes, the punishment of an apprehended culprit is supposed to deter others, who might otherwise engage in the illicit behavior. The deterrence notion is frequently derided by psychologists, criminologists, and other citizens, who point to the high rate of recidivism as proof of its failure. How many others are deterred is, of course, unknown, but in all probability, many people are deterred. It is the rare motorist who does not reduce his speed when he or she notices a police car on the highway. Deterrence deserves another look and will receive it shortly when we discuss passive avoidance.

Rehabilitation and Reform

The underlying view here is that the criminal simply has not learned to cooperate with the appropriate authorities and that some kinds of treatment (penance, solitude, beatings, training, and/or separation from his current environment) will either "teach him or her a lesson," "make a new man or woman out of him or her," or otherwise refit the criminal for society. There is an inherent inconsistency with this view, as the criminal or miscreant may never have been "habilitated" to the society in the first place. The concept of *re*training suggests that original training has failed "to take." Actually, the original training may never have occurred. Retraining in this situation refers to some new or different training program calculated to make someone respect rules or laws he or she previously had no respect for. Unless the reasons for the former lack of respect are eliminated, so-called reformation in terms of new skills may be meaningless.

Current appraisals do not support the reform concept seriously; in fact, prisons commonly are considered training schools for more successful criminal behavior. Some reformers, however, keep the faith.

DEFINITIONS OF PUNISHMENT

When the original penitentiaries (later, prisons, now "custodial facilities") were established, the religious orientations of officialdom led to the view that the criminal needed time to reflect over his or her crime(s) and would become penitent after "seeing the light." How long that would take was never rationally established. When it became customary to sentence criminals to prison terms, very little was determined or stated officially about how prisoners should be treated. In the case of capital punishment, the judge might describe the method of disposal ("hanged by the neck until you are dead"), but in lesser sentences, except for the occasional hard labor, nothing was specified about what might be done to a prisoner beyond locking him or her up. Treatment was left to wardens or other officials, who made their own rules. Such rules could vary from having conjugal visits to solitary confinement with anything in between (work, sports, schools, libraries, entertainment, or idleness).

In noncriminal situations, where parents or other authorities (for example, teachers) administer punishment, again, there is no specific treatment that the term defines or defines the term. A parent may slap, belt, bruise, or abuse a child with varying degrees of force or violence, or he or she may simply frown (which might devastate some children) or withdraw love, deny privileges, or send the children to their rooms. We have to ask, What is punishment?

AVERSIVE STIMULATION

It should be clear that inflicting pain or otherwise putting stress on another does not always qualify as punishment. Punishment is presumed to be an after-the-fact affair; thus, a threat of punishment is not, in itself, a punishment, although it arouses some stress or disturbance. Usually, we say we punish someone for, or after, he or she has done something not desired by us.

If we hurt someone before he or she does something and he or she now does what we want him or her to, the appropriate term is not punishment—it might more properly be *torture, coercion,* or more politely, *aversive* or *noxious stimulation*. If a rat is minding its own business on one side of a box divided by a fence and we wish it to jump over the fence, all we need to do is shock it where it is. There is no point to saying the rat was doing anything that was wrong by minding its own business, as we can now decide to drive it back to where it was by shocking him again on the side it just jumped to.

In Nazi or other concentration camps, the prisoners could be made to do just about anything the captors wanted by the imposition of any of a variety of measures, for example, hunger, pain, humiliation, threats, and so forth. Pain is obviously a powerful persuader, and as Hollywood would have it, every person has his or her breaking point. There are famous exceptions, of course—various religious or other martyrs who met death with smiles or prayers and would not submit. We can accept them as exceptions without trying to explain their behavior. The far more usual case is to comply.

We have already learned that the normal reaction to noxious stimulation is that of escape or avoidance (see chapter 10) when some signal precedes the pain. We have also distinguished between active and passive avoidance on the grounds that in the former case, the pain precedes an action, while in the latter case, the pain follows the action in the early stages of training.

The only real laboratory paradigm for punishment is the passive avoidance situation. It will be recalled that in such a setup, a laboratory animal first does something, for example, steps off a box onto an electrified grid floor and quickly returns to the box. In a lever press situation, a rat is first trained to press the lever, and when it is doing so at a suitable rate, the experimenter can shock the rat when it does press. In such experimental situations, we can speak of punishment. If, on the other hand, we shock the rat until it presses a bar, we are not punishing it, we are inflicting pain.

A DEFINITION OF PUNISHMENT

As in the case of reward or reinforcement, what is a punishment for one person may not be for another. Some children are alleged to "ask for it" as a form of attention getting. Some can absorb or accept more drastic treatment than others. Even extreme maltreatment may not discourage some people from "misbehavior." Appreciation of such observations led Skinner (1953) to define punishment in terms of its consequences. Only such treatment that is followed by a reduction in some response qualifies as punishment. In short, unless a response drops in frequency, whatever abuse or aversive treatment is administered is not punishment.

The definition of punishment in terms of its consequences is dictated by experimental, operational requirements. It includes a measurement feature—in Skinner's situation, a change to a lower rate of response. The definition may appear paradoxical, as one might choose to reinforce some competing response at some more effective level and bring about a reduction or cessation in the original response. Such a procedure would amount to calling the rewarding of a new response a punishment of the original.

Skinner's definition appears to be suitable, however, as he restricts it to situations where the original response is occurring at some rate and is being reinforced, at least periodically. When, in such a situation, some new factor is introduced that lowers the response rate, it can be considered a punishment. In practical situations such new factors will normally be some kind of aversive stimulation, for example, electric shock, a slap, and so forth.

The practical value of Skinner's definition is to force us to look for a behavioral change before we decide that something we do to someone else is punishment. If the behavior does not change, our behavior has been fruitless. We have accomplished nothing, and perhaps, we have not punished. Or the punishment may not have "fit the crime" in the sense of being inappropriate in some ways or inadequate in others.

THE ROLE OR FUNCTION OF PUNISHMENT

In his original statement of the law of effect, Thorndike (1898) assigned an equal (though negative) role to punishment as a weakener of connections along with the positive or strengthening effect of rewards or satisfiers. Thorndike did not like the term *punishment* and changed it to "annoyer," defining it as something an organism did nothing to attain and frequently sought to avoid. At first, Thorndike did not have any observations of actual weakening effects of annoyers and merely asserted the negative function of punishment. Later criticism by Tolman (Tolman, Hall, and Bretnall 1932) led him to make his own observations where he found that punishment apparently did not, in fact, weaken any bonds or tendencies to repeat incorrect responses. In a typical Thorndike experiment, Thorndike (1932) would have college students guess numbers as responses for words or have them select foreign words from a set of five, one of which would be the translation of an English word. When the subject chose a number or word that was not correct, Thorndike would say, "Wrong." It was assumed that "wrong" was an annoyer for college students. Repetition of the exercise revealed that the same wrong choices would be made, more often than chance, and Thorndike concluded that punishment simply did not work, that is, it did not weaken bonds. From such studies, the relatively strong conclusion was accepted by many psychologists that punishment (in other forms and in other situations) also was useless, fruitless, and, therefore, unwise. Skinner might have pointed out that saying "wrong" was not a punishment, as it obviously did not lower the response rate.

Skinner (1938) approached the problem of punishment by using rats in the lever press box. After training some rats to press a lever for food, Skinner started an extinction procedure, but if the rats pressed the lever at all, they would be slapped sharply by the bar. The result of such slapping was an immediate suppression of pressing. After a while, however, the rats would return to the bar and proceed to press as if nothing had happened. They would produce normal extinction curves. Later, Skinner's student, Estes (1944), would use electric shock on the paws of his rats for any presses in the first ten minutes of extinction.

Shocks could be varied in frequency, among, and duration. Normally, the rat would withdraw and cease pressing the bar after a shock. In a subsequent extinction period, it was observed that the number of bar presses emitted by shocked rats did not differ appreciably from the number emitted by unshocked rats. Estes and Skinner then concluded that shocking rats in this situation had no enduring effect, and the strong conclusion was then widely accepted that punishment was, in effect, a waste of time and energy. Punishment would temporarily inhibit responding, but in time, its effects would dissipate, and the animal would act as if it had never been shocked or even more effectively emit its quota of extinction responses.

Following these observations, Skinner adopted an antipunishment, antiaversive treatment view. In human situations, the punisher could readily be identified and would acquire a bad ordor as an unpleasant, cruel, tyrannical person, and this might as well be avoided, as the punitive treatment did not work anyhow.

For a time, the Skinner-Estes view seemed to receive general acceptance, and interest in punishment waned.The Mowrer theory in 1960, heavily based on the laboratory findings in aversive situations, revived interest in punishment to some extent. Reviews of the literature by Church (1963) and Solomon (1965) called for more research. Punishment was so much a factor in daily life that its detailed effects should be known. Solomon reported on his attempts to instill guilt and temptation in dogs by punishing them when they chose desirable food over less desirable dishes. He would then leave the room and observe the dogs to determine if they would avoid the punishable food. In most instances, the dogs approached the previously punishable food dishes. Solomon emphasized the scarcity of evidence on the effects of punishment on people in the face of its ubiquity. Following these reviews, new studies were undertaken, largely with rats, as these were the only creatures that could be treated harshly without public resentment. Boe and Church (1967) were able to cast some doubt on the Skinner-Estes position. They found that the effect of electric shock on bar pressing, for example, depended on the amount of punishment. If the shocks were severe and/or long in duration, the suppression of bar pressing could be relatively prolonged. Behavior therapists, for example, Azrin (1960), began to experiment with intermittent (periodic) punishment and found that continuous punishment was more effective than periodic punishment, in contrast to positive reinforcement effects. Increasingly, the view developed that punishment could be used to suppress behavior, at least for some time, during which some other action could be taken along more positive lines while the side-effects of punishment, for example, fear of the punisher should be avoided.

If the object of punishment is to change behavior, Skinner argues that more effective, stronger, longer-lasting changes can be achieved by positively reinforcing desired behavior than by punishing undesired behavior. This was also the view adopted by Thorndike, who felt that punishment might temporarily inhibit undesired behavior, during which period positive effects could be introduced for correct or desired behavior. Note that the purpose of punishment for Skinner is to reform, not to exact retribution. Deterrence would be automatic, of course, if new behavior replaced the old behavior.

Earlier, it was suggested that the deterrent notion might have some merit. There might be cases where we might not be interested in developing counterbehavior of a more desirable sort or where we might be unable to do so, and all we might hope to accomplish would be to prevent some undesirable behavior. Here, we come back to the Mowrer view about passive avoidance learning. According to Mowrer, if a person is punished *in the act* of misbehaving, of whatever nature, the kinesthetic stimuli from the activity, along with all other environmental stimuli, can be conditioned to the ensuing fear response. On future occasions, any attempt or effort to perform the behavior, that is, any activity that could initiate the appropriate stimuli, could arouse the conditioned fear, and the response should then not occur. Such conditioning, of course, depends on the actual arousal of fear, and thus, the punishment must be of sufficient quality, quantity, and duration to generate fear. If the fear does not develop, the punishment is either unworthy of the name or useless. The argument between the Skinner and Mowrer views boils down to the strength of the CER. If it is strong enough, it might suppress the behavior forever or at least for a long time. It cannot be said that punishment does not work. It may be that we did not work hard enough at the punishment.

In general, psychologists concerned with behavior problems tend to avoid aversive control operations for various humanistic reasons. In very difficult cases, where some urgency (or necessity) requires it, aversive treatment has been used to control undesirable behavior. Autistic children who may bang their heads against the wall to the point of serious damage may be given strong, brief, localized shocks that momentarily hurt more than the head banging; they can be made to stop the undesirable behavior, at least for a while. Alocholics can be made sick enough in some situations to stop drinking in such situations, but the successes are by no means assured, especially in other situations.

Because the effective use of punishment calls for cathing the culprit in the act and for creating a strong conditioned emotional response (fear), the limitations of punishment are fairly clear. Frequently, the behavior is over and done with before the punishment can be administered. The behavior could be reinstated, but that might be more troublesome than desired. The frequency, intensity, and duration may be too high a price in the light of other considerations.

While laboratory psychologists were working with rats and electric shocks, many developmental psychologists were observing the effects of relatively mild punishment (reproof, removal of toys, and so forth) on the behavior of children. The observations of these researchers have been summarized in a unique way by Walters and Grusec (1977), who tried to compare the various laboratory studies on rats with those on children. In general, the findings tend to parallel each other. Such variables as timing, duration, and consistency are important with children, as they are with rats. Again, the interest seems to be on *suppressive* effects and their duration. Punishment does not appear to be a learning variable so much as a mode of temporary behavior control.

The conclusion that might be drawn is that punishment can work under some circumstances if you wish to pay the price. The Thorndike-Skinner view that it does not work is not completely acceptable. Their remedies of instituting rewards for desirable behavior while either temporarily suppressing undesirable behavior or letting the latter extinguish are not very practical. Such remedies may be available with laboratory animals where their food can be removed by the experimenter with no great concern over the creatures' comfort. On the human level of misbehavior, we have other factors to consider. It is illegal to abuse people and extinction, with people, calls for some kinds of abuse. Besides, some criminals of whatever age or character are remarkably resistant to extinction, and some behavior is too dangerous to be ignored. We cannot arrange for a bully to extinguish by letting him beat up a population without reinforcement. We do not even know how he is being reinforced. In such cases, the psychologist has little or nothing to advise beyond what anyone else can say.

The suggestion or conclusion that punishment does not work in the sense of some kind of negative learning or weakening bonds should not have come as a surprise to anyone unless he or she at the same time accepted the conclusion that rewards affect learning. Throughout the text, we have been concerned to point out that positive reinforcement (rewards) has nothing to do with learning. The role of rewards is to serve as stimuli for positive emotional reactions. When such reactions do occur, we can expect some energizing of ongoing behavior and some positive ideomotor action. When aversive stimuli are present, we can expect negative emotional responses and negative ideomotor activity (withdrawal, escape, or avoidance).

If we recognize rewards and punishments as motivational stimuli, we can appreciate Thorndike's definition of such stimuli as satisfiers and annoyers and, using his descriptions, allocate suitable functions to them without any specific relationship to learning itself. What someone who is rewarded or punished learns is what kinds of behavior may lead to reward or punishment. Whether that someone now behaves in a particular way will depend on the ideomotor stimulation that is generated in the situation.

We can expect that someone who has been reinforced for some behavior and also punished for the same behavior will be in some state of conflict when some stimuli related to the behavior are present. The relative strengths of the reward and punishment components of the associations involved will presumably resolve the conflict. A youthful burglar who has successfully burgled 30 homes without being caught will be tempted by a new target. If he is now apprehended and treated lightly by the law as a first offender, he may well return to his felonious behavior. Someone caught at his first attempt may think twice, as James (1890) might have it, and not give in to the temptation (an ideomotor "tingle"). Certainly, the history of reinforcement is important for learning, but it is a question of what is learned.

TEMPTATION

The term *temptation* is usually employed when someone is allegedly contemplating some activity that he or she knows is supposed to be "bad," "evil," or illegal. The restriction to illicit behavior does not appear to be warranted. We do not talk about temptation when a professional car thief is planning a particular coup. The professional is merely doing his or her job. We all learn to call certain behaviors good or bad depending upon our reinforcement histories. For the car thief to fail to drive off with his or her selection would be bad. Temptation does, however, refer to prospective behavior. Such prospective behavior involves hesitation or conflict between ideomotor stimulations. The "temptee" images some action and begins to initiate it when other imagery prompts some inhibition or counteraction. If the positive ideomotor activity is stronger, the temptation is implemented, and the forbidden act is performed. Commonly enough, the performance of the activity is not fully satisfying and may even be regretted. We will see shortly how the conflict features of behaving in ways we have come to label *bad* might have serious consequences. For the moment, we can recognize that social training is obviously the foundation for our views of what is right and wrong.

MISBEHAVIOR AND MORALITY

For the learning psychologist to admit that he or she can offer no sound suggestions with regard to such universal behavior as crime is to admit that perhaps criminal or delinquent behavior is innate, natural, or, at least, inevitable. Crime, aggressive or antisocial behavior occurs in all societies. excluding, perhaps, some select ones, where like-minded people might choose to live together, as in a monastery or some commune or where a vast army enforces a dictator's views with regard to suitable behavior. Some organized groups of adults who create a relatively small social group on the basis of some contractual principles might survive for some time by selecting new recruits who "fit in" and expelling misfits, but most such newly created societies have foundered. Utopias have had a rather depressing history of failures. Even groups founded on Skinner's (1948a) views, as described in *Walden Two*, have not been without their problems (see Kinkade 1974).

Children, even in affluent families, have trouble in learning the difference between "mine" and "thine," and "right" and "wrong," and have to be trained to keep such distinctions meaningful as they grow up. With less affluent children, the problem is apparently more difficult. Crime appears to be more prevalent among the poor, who rob and assault each other more frequently than do residents in more prosperous groups.

Over the centuries, various devices have been invented to control antisocial behavior; chief of these has been the development of moral codes, sometimes under dictatorial edicts and frequently with the introduction of appeals to supernatural forces, as in religious orientations. Religious institutions commonly are based on beliefs in some kinds of rewards or punishments after death, if not before, and they normally provide a moral code for earthly behavior. To a considerable degree, they have been successful and have been a stabilizing influence for centuries (see *The Story of Civilization* by Will and Ariel Durant). When adherence to some religion and its moral code weakens, antisocial behavior increases.

THE MOWRER THEORY OF NEUROTIC CONFLICT

Among his other contributions, Mowrer (1967) has written extensively on the significance of a moral code as a factor in maintaining personal integrity and the prevention of neuroses. His views are diametrically opposed to those of Freud. According to Freud, neurotics have become so because they have repressed their id impulses too severely or rigidly because of a strong, censorious superego (conscience, moral principles). The continuing battle between the id and superego expresses itself in neurotic symptoms, inefficiency, and unhappiness. Freud's advice, according to Mowrer, appears to be to unleash the id and grant it some occasional relief or satisfaction by not taking the superego too seriously—"after all, we're only human" appears to be the appropriate Freudian slogan. Freud's views on religion as based on illusion fostered by a repressive culture suggest that he thought of the overdeveloped superego as the chief problem with neurotics.

In contrast to Freud, Mowrer argues that it is essentially the weakness of the superego that allows some people to indulge themselves in ways the well-developed superego would not countenance. When an individual with some moral (religious) training misbehaves, sins, or commits a crime, he or she knows he or she has done wrong but had been unable to resist the desire, impulse, or "need." The individual's moral training has been insufficient or inadequate. Because the individual has violated the moral code that he or she believes he or she was *supposed* to endorse or comply with, the individual now feels guilt, remorse, and misery, and these emotional reactions lead to the neurotic symptoms, inefficiency and unhappiness. The "sinner" becomes a neurotic if he or she feels guilt.

To restore the neurotic to some semblance of personal integrity, Mowrer advocates punishment of the neurotic—the neurotic has sinned, and he or she must atone for the crime. As part of the treatment, Mowrer advocates confession of the crime to the injured parties, not to a privileged priest or therapist. The notion that neurotics do not know what they have done or what their problem is (that is, unconscious conflict) is dismissed by Mowrer as Freudian fantasy.

To prevent delinquency, crime, or other antisocial behavior, Mowrer advocates strengthening the superego, that is, moral, ethical standards. Such strengthening is normally left to religious institutions, but as is apparent in rising crime rates, religion is apparently not as effective as it used to be. We note that "normal" people do not commit crimes; they may be tempted, but their moral training restrains them. Psychopaths or "sociopaths" do not subscribe to moral training, and punishment will be ineffective. Only neurotics should be punished, and that is for their own good, as they cannot be cured otherwise.

To develop strong moral codes in children without the aid of appeals to supernatural agencies is not an easy task. For parents to tell children that something is bad for them or wrong, especially when the parents behave in the ways the children would like to follow, is to appeal to reason, when frequently, there is no reason that is meaningful to the child. Parents resort to lies or bribes, but the bribes offered usually promise some future reinforcement of a vague greater good in the face of present sacrifice or dissatisfaction. One of the most difficult responses to learn is to turn the other cheek. To teach children not to cheat when they see cheaters get high marks introduces them to mockery. Such misbehavior could be eliminated by changing testing procedures, but to generate the proper conditions could be expensive.

NONNEUROTIC CRIME

The fact that a large proportion of delinquent or criminal behavior is found among the poor, the unemployed, and the uneducated (in general, among those of lower economic status) makes the problem more than difficult.

How can one expect a "have not" to subscribe to the morality of the "haves"? A poverty-striken subculture in a slum develops its own rules, morality, and laws. Such laws may bear little resemblance to those of the majority culture and may, in fact, amount to a systematic negation of the majority "establishment." The realities of the situation have been slowly impressing the courts, which now not only take into account but also recognize lack of education, broken homes, and poverty as prime factors in crime. The doctrine of personal responsibility is slowly surrendering to the recognition that people behave the way they do because of conditions outside themselves.

There may be solutions to the problem, but they cannot come exclusively from learning theory. Those who have not must be able to get more; those who have may have to want less. But we are getting somewhat beyond our field. Learning theory can only suggest that a moral code must have a foundation of reality, that people cannot be tricked into moral behavior that works to their disadvantage, at least not for long. Those who are concerned about the morals of someone else must recognize that but for the grace of the environment, they would be the objects of someone else's concern. What we must appreciate is that human nature is neither good nor bad by nature—it is human nature, and *goodness* or *badness* are labels we apply to the behavior of those who please or displease us, while they label our behavior in like manner. The labels we learn are products of our histories and circumstances. To label someone who rapes, robs, and kills his victim and then burns down the building to hide the crime as *evil* may be satisfying, but it will do no good. Such criminals must be taught not to need to rape, rob, kill, and burn. Such teaching, however, calls for a different set of experiences than the malefactor had in his or her background, and time cannot be rolled back. The necessary training will have to be done in the early years with some kind of realistic attention to reinforcement opportunities.

20

A Learning Approach
to Behavior Disorders

When someone behaves in a manner that displeases us, we are inclined to assume that there is something wrong with him or her. If he or she displeases enough people or people powerful enough to take some action, he or she may be put away, sometimes in a jail or sometimes in a hospital, where if there does not appear to be anything wrong with his or her body, he or she might be classified as having a mental illness. The psychiatrist Thomas Szasz considers such a term a misnomer, a label for some mythical thinking. Szasz (1961) prefers to say simply that someone's behavior is regarded as unsuitable or undesirable to those he or she lives with or with whom he or she has contact.

Since this book has had no use for such concepts as the mind or mental activity, the notion of mental illness is also of no particular value, and we can look at people classified by others as neurotic, psychotic, or mentally ill from the point of view of behavior.

STRUCTURAL AND FUNCTIONAL DISORDERS

For a long time, psychiatrists have distinguished between structural (organic) and functional disorders. The structural disturbances are explained away or accepted as related to some kind of brain damage due to physical trauma, disease, growths, or chemical disturbance. Some assume that heredity plays some role in faulty development of neural structures. Efforts toward therapy in such cases involve physical means (surgery, drugs, convulsive shocks, or other physical treatments, for example, freezing or generating fevers) that might eliminate or destroy possible viral or other agencies. When no organic base can be found or assumed, a person manifesting undesirable behavior is considered to be a functional case.

Functional has come to mean that the personal history of the individual has been such that he or she has been exposed to various kinds of environmental stress and has developed reaction patterns as defenses or adaptations to such stresses. Sometimes, as in the Freudian interpretation, the stresses are assumed to have occurred in childhood and are forgotten (repressed) but continue to work unconsciously in determining symptoms. In the Freudian view, the symptoms are not the disease or the trouble—they merely indicate a deeper set of forces at work, and removal of symptoms is considered ineffective, as they will merely be replaced by other symptoms unless the basic cause is rooted out through a process of making the unconscious forces conscious with a new adaptation to the factors generating the original stress.

TREATMENT OF SYMPTOMS

The notion that treating symptoms themselves is useless has a long history and a wide acceptance. A kind of rationale can be presented by using the analogy of taking aspirin for a headache. The headache might be relieved, but the aspirin presumably has had no basic therapeutic value. It merely suppressed the pain. The original cause of the headache has not been attacked, and the person who took the aspirin instead of finding out why he or she had the headache might do himself more harm than good by "masking" the headache. Still, millions of people take aspirin for headaches; the headaches go away, and the people go about their business. Only when headaches fail to go away does it occur to most people to look more closely into their problems.

The analogy described above, however, is no proof of the generally accepted belief among psychiatrists, especially those of a Freudian or functional persuasion, that treating symptoms is foolish or useless. As a matter of fact, there is no proof or evidence that relieving symptoms is unwise or useless. The standard argument is that if one does have a symptom relieved or eliminated, another symptom will take its place. This is evidently a persuasive argument for some people, but it has no support in fact. There simply are no data on this issue, and until some evidence is obtained, it must be regarded as an old wives' tale.

LEARNING AND MISBEHAVIOR

The general Freudian functional position has been accepted by some psychologists as translatable into the notion that undesirable behavior is learned. Symptoms are viewed in the same way as habits, and it is commonly accepted that bad habits are learned in the same way as good habits. If they are learned, they can be unlearned or replaced by desirable behavior or habits. Note that it is rather generally accepted that if a particular habit, say, a conditioned response, is extinguished, it will probably be replaced, usually by whatever was the previous action to the CS (see chapter 6), usually, again, a response of no importance. Sometimes, however, as in the case of habits that have some physiological features (smoking or taking drugs, including drinking coffee or other addictive refreshment), eliminating the behavior may leave the person with a kind of vacuum, uneasiness, or "withdrawal" symptoms, and a specific effort should be made to fill the newly created gap with some more desirable or acceptable reaction or habit. The methadone treatment for heroin addicts is based on such a principle. People who gave up smoking after long addiction sometimes find themselves eating a great deal more, chewing gum, or behaving in other less than attractive ways. Guthrie (1935) tried to give up smoking by eating apples every time he felt like smoking. He found himself doing both.

We find then that symptom treatment is not considered an undesirable operation, and behavioral psychologists are rather commonly committed to the notion that bad habits or undesirable behavior can be *replaced* by good behavior or good habits. This amounts to symptom substitution as a basic operating procedure.

How the replacement of one set of behavior patterns by another will be carried out becomes the business of psychotherapy. In the following sections, we will describe psychotherapeutic practices of those psychologists who take the behavior as the problem and not the reflection of something else (for example, an inadequate personality or the manifestation of unconscious conflicts). Some psychologists of the client-centered school (see Rogers 1951) operate on the basis of beliefs about personality or human nature that assume some kinds of inner sources or resources that a person can bring to bear on a situation—that he or she can be helped to develop a different view of himself or herself and of his or her role in the world. We will not consider such views, as our own interest is in a pure learning theory approach where some behavior, now considered to be undesirable and believed to have been learned, can be eliminated and/or replaced by more desirable or acceptable behavior.

LEARNING AND PSYCHOTHERAPY

There are two basic approaches to psychotherapy from a learning perspective. Interestingly enough, the two methods go back to the old distinction between Pavlovian and Thorndikian learning orientations. In one method, the approach is strictly Pavlovian, using principles of conditioning. This method is now generally called behavior therapy. The other method, practiced by followers of Skinner, relies on reinforcement as the basic tool. It is generally called behavior modification or behavior mod, for short. Both terms are really specific to the practices mentioned, namely, conditioning *or* reinforcement, but many critics have carelessly described all kinds of practices, including brain surgery and drug administration, by either or both of these terms—the terms themselves are probably too general and might better be changed to specify just what is being done in order to avoid improper criticism by lumping them with unrelated practices.

We shall start with the historically earlier approach, behavior therapy, which was first publicized as a new treatment by Wolpe (1958), who was a psychiatrist and not a psychologist. As with almost anything else, there is a history of prior developments. Pavlov (1927) himself did not use a behavioral approach in his psychotherapeutic ventures; he preferred to use drugs. Pavlov did demonstrate to his own satisfaction how neurotic behavior could be acquired, namely, by forcing his dogs to make extremely fine discriminations, a procedure that sometimes, with some breeds of dogs, would result in what Pavlov called "experimental neuroses" (see chapter 6); but, it was in the United States that the first therapeutic applications of conditioning were attempted.

Counterconditioning

In 1924, Mary Cover Jones succeeded in treating a young boy (Peter) for his fear of rabbits. Her procedure was described as counterconditioning. It amounted to presenting Peter with candy when a rabbit was brought into a room (at a considerable distance from Peter). Slowly, day by day, the rabbit was brought closer and closer to Peter, who was always distracted from reacting negatively to the rabbit because of the positive reaction to the candy. Eventually, Peter was able to sit comfortably in the presence of the rabbit and was pronounced "cured." The Jones's treatment was introduced to support the claims of Watson and Raynor (1920) that their study of Little Albert which demonstrated that fears could be acquired could be expanded into a program for elimination of fears.

Behavior Therapy

Wolpe adopted the formula presented by Jones, namely, that of introducing a negative stimulus in a situation where a positive reaction could be initiated, and developed it into a general therapeutic practice which, presumably, could be used to relieve any kind of fear or anxiety that might trouble anyone. In the early practice of his procedures, Wolpe and his followers concentrated on rather specific fears that are common in our society. Two popular fears, those of snakes and spiders, have been widely studied. What the treatment requires is some way of presenting a fear stimulus (the CS) gradually or, at least, without exciting a strong reaction and generating a positive reaction (UR) to serve as a substitute response. For the latter, Wolpe chose another old technique, namely, that of relaxation. Subjects were first taught to relax, following methods previously developed by Jacobsen (1938), who had found that people could learn to relax by going through a set of exercises in which they would systematically tense various muscles, from toe to head, and then relax them. Following instructions, people could come to relax rather generally to the simple command, "Relax." Once a client or patient had learned to relax, Wolpe would then bring up the subject of the person's fear in some fashion (this now serving as a CS) and instruct the subject to relax while the subject of the fear was introduced. Because some fear situations could not be brought physically into a therapist's office, for example, a fear of crowds or heights or death, the CS had to be presented in some substitute form. Wolpe hit upon the procedure of asking his clients to imagine, or image, the fearful situations or objects. To forestall any panic or uncontrollable fear, Wolpe decided to arrange the images of the fearful stimuli in a hierarchy, ranging from tolerable to threatening. Thus, if a client was afraid of heights, he or she might be asked to imagine standing on a footstool as a first step. If even this initiated a mild fear, the subject would be told to relax. The pairing of the image of the footstool situation and the relaxation instruction would continue until the subject was comfortable when imagining himself or herself on a footstool. A second stage would then be introduced, for example, standing on a low ladder, and again, the subject would be instructed to relax while thinking of standing on a ladder. If this proved unsuccessful, retreat to the footstool would follow; if successful, a higher step on the ladder could be suggested. Slowly, the therapist would introduce imagery of escalators, elevators, roof tops, high buildings, airplanes, or even rockets to the moon while the patient was conditioned to relax while imaging these formerly threatening situations.

With more specific or concrete feared stimuli, such as snakes, spiders, or rats, the stimuli themselves could be introduced at a distance (as in the case of little Peter) or in image form—first, perhaps, as a cartoon, than as a picture, then as a plaster or other kind of model, then in some real form at a safe distance or in a cage. Wolpe claimed some 90 percent therapeutic success with such treatments for fearful subjects. We can accept the general success of such efforts and procedures, although many critics are not convinced that the method is general enough to handle the wide variety of behavioral problems that arise among people. Some critics claim that a subtle kind of personal psychotherapy is also operating when a therapist sees a client frequently (perhaps nine or ten sessions for a snake phobia) and that the therapist's example of courage plus his attention and the information that might be generated are also effective. Some find that the therapy is rather specific to specific situations. Lick and Unger (1975), for example, found some of their clients could be relaxed in the presence of a snake in a box, and could even touch it there, but if the snake was placed on the floor, the client might panic. Obviously, the real test of a cure is in a real-life situation, and therapists do not accompany their clients into jungles or airplanes with any frequency. One might also argue that only some of the overt behavior has changed but that some anxiety or fear might still be experienced by the apparently cured person.

Behavior Modification

The Skinnerian approach to undesirable behavior, as might be expected by now, is to observe the behavior, wait for signs of desirable behavior, and reinforce the emission of the desired behavior in a systematic way. We can take the case of some grade school boy who is misbehaving as an example that might illustrate all aspects of the behavior modifier's approach.

In the first place, we find an unhappy teacher who complains of misbehavior. The therapist is not satisfied with such a general description. He asks the teacher, What is there about this boy's behavior that you do not like or want to continue? Any remarks about how bad the boy is—how disruptive, ill-natured, troublesome, irritating, no good, and so forth—are unacceptable. Only specific references to specific behavior are acceptable. It is not enough for the teacher to say, "I don't like his attitude." The teacher must come up with something specific. Suppose that the boy is described as getting out of his seat without permission. Here is a concrete example of the kind of complaint the therapist wants to hear. He next inquires into what the teacher does about this. If the answer is that the boy is spoken to, yelled at, asked to behave, kept after school, or forced to present reports, and so forth, the therapist suggests that such approaches obviously have not worked and should be stopped. If the teacher asks, Should I ignore it? the answer is a firm "Yes, but." The *but* refers to the alternate approach to be proposed. The objective is to keep the boy in his seat. The method of choice for accomplishing this is to reward the boy for seat-keeping behavior.

The method just mentioned involves a number of questions, as well as a number of procedural steps. Suppose the behavior is seriously disruptive to the class and is really intolerable? In such a case, the therapy cannot be conducted in the classroom. How shall the boy be rewarded? This is a serious question, as the reward must be more reinforcing than the reinforcement the lad gets from leaving his seat. It obviously cannot be more expensive than the teacher can afford or arrange. It cannot be chocolate or chewing gum, or the rest of the class will get into the act. How long must the new reinforcement be continued? Can it be dropped without a return to misbehavior? Will the boy become "good" only for this teacher and only if the rewards continue?

The behavior modifier is a little weak on answers to all of these questions, but he has a procedure to follow, and he follows it. The procedure amounts to several steps. The first step concerns the operant rate. A count is kept of every instance of seat leaving over what is called the base period. This might last for several weeks in some problem situations if the behavior is not frequent. When a count is established, the second step comes into operation. The modifier introduces reinforcement for defined amounts or degrees of desirable behavior. Here, the question of what reinforcement is to be used becomes crucial. (In some situations, prisons, for example, inmates can be given cigarettes, TV time, or other "privileges.") Because it might be awkward for the teacher to go to the student to proffer a reward or even more awkward for the boy to leave his seat to get it, the therapist might recommend a "token" reinforcement. In such cases, the former misbehaver is given "credit" or "points" or actual tokens of some kind for x minutes of seat keeping. The tokens can then be exchanged for some concrete and desirable object, for example, a baseball or hockey puck, or for gym time or free time, or anything else that is desirable to the boy and suitable for the teacher. The behavior modifier continues to count the instances of the behavior. Under the reinforcement conditions, the good behavior should rise to some peak and level off at a desirable level. Now, because the behavior could have changed for any of a number of other and unknown reasons, it behooves the modifier to test his or her program by withdrawing reinforcement. (This is the third step.) As the modifier withdraws reinforcement, the prior misbehavior should re-emerge, thus demonstrating that it was the reinforcement program and nothing else. When the desired behavior declines sufficiently to prove the point, the reinforcement is reintroduced to build up the desired behavior again. Finally, as the desired behavior becomes more and more firmly established, a program of partial or periodic reinforcement is introduced to save the time of the teacher and, presumably, to establish the behavior on the basis of some more intrinsic reinforcers, which are thought to be almost inherent in most situations where the modification might work in the first place.

Although the example involved only one boy and one kind of behavior, the principles and procedures are supposed to work for any number of people—certainly, a whole classroom, a hospital ward, a prison community, a commune, or society in general. The behavior can be of any sort desired from toilet training to politeness toward prison guards. Psychotics have been modified to keep their rooms neat and tidy, appear at the dining room on time, and to participate in other varieties of therapy. Behavior modifiers have attempted to change almost every kind of behavior describable, from fasting to losing weight to altering sexual inclinations. Willis and Giles (1976) have compiled a catalog (in abstract form) of the many varieties of behavior change that have been reported.

Critics of behavior modification approaches have found the procedures to be superficial and not as powerful as sometimes claimed. The method works best in situations where the subjects are confined under some authority (schools, orphanages, prisons, and hospitals) and where there are obvious alternatives of a negative sort (deprivation, isolation, and physical abuse). Prisoners who are paroled because of good behavior often return to crime almost as soon as they "hit the street." Schoolchildren, too, may behave in one classroom but not in another. The reinforced behavior is said not to transfer to other places or times. In one instance, a behavior modification program using a token economy worked in the afternoon when the program was in effect but not in the morning when it was not (Krasner and Krasner 1973).

The modification involved in this approach appears to be a matter of behavior control rather than one of learning. We can accept the general notion that some kinds of reinforcement can get people to do some kinds of things they are not now doing, but we should not be beguiled into thinking they could not do them if they wanted to in the first place. They know how to do what the modifier wants (to go back to our example, our boy knows how to sit in his seat); they are reinforced more for doing something else. What behavior modification appears to amount to is a matter of changing motivation for different responses.

The significance of the behavior modification movement is in its insistence on specifying what is meant when some behavior is called good, bad, or undesirable. Such a requirement forces the complainer to deal with realities rather than with fictions. It is reminiscent of Guthrie's insistence upon spelling out just what is involved in such alleged behavioral attributes as kindness, forcefulness, politeness, generosity, and so forth.

The importance on establishing the frequency count of behaviors is also noteworthy. We are too prone to use expressions such as "always" or "never" instead of getting specific about the number of occasions something happens. Finding out when something happens is also helpful in possibly suggesting the controlling stimuli for some behaviors.

The lack of generality to behavior modification suggests that generalization be taken into account as part of the program if it becomes desirable. The sailor who keeps his locker shipshape may be a slob at home. It may not matter at home; it does matter on a ship. Some behaviors might be undesirable in some circumstances and less so in others. The lesson of behavior modification is that you get what you pay for and not much more.

The behavior modifier calls attention to an important feature of most of our efforts to control others: we are unsystematic. While periodic reinforcement will prolong behavior, the periodicity itself must be carefully and systematically controlled. The random reinforcement parents give to their children or husbands and wives to each other cannot be relied on to prolong desirable behavior. Reinforcement, like punishment, must be administered at appropriate times and not when we think of it.

Extinction Therapy

In presenting our case of the lad who left his seat, we expected the teacher to ignore the behavior when it did occur. A stronger point is involved, of course. The lad presumably left his seat because such behavior was being reinforced. If we want him to stop leaving his seat, we might be just as successful if we could eliminate the reinforcement that came with leaving. Our earlier interest in extinction (see chapter 8) led to the conclusion that organisms stop behaving in certain ways if no reinforcement follows. To stop any habit, then, the trick would be to find out what the reinforcer is and eliminate it. If the reinforcement for smoking is nicotine (Schacter 1977), then smoking could be stopped by producing nicotineless cigarettes. Because the manufacturers are not interested in stopping sales, they obviously will not produce such items.

To eliminate the reinforcement is not always easy or wise. Suppose a baby cries when being put to sleep and stops crying when picked up. The solution is easy: stop picking up the baby. Such a procedure works, and in a few days. What the consequences are one will never know; there is no way to control the situation with that baby.

Negative Practice: The Beta Method

Guthrie (1935) concerned himself with the problem, following upon some procedures described by Dunlap (1930). Dunlap knew that the control over reinforcers was not easy, but he also knew that too much of a good thing is also not rewarding. He accordingly suggested that the way to get rid of an undesirable habit was to practice it, but to practice it in such a way that it became troublesome, tiring, boring, or negative. He referred to this negative practice as the beta method. It amounted to simply forcing yourself to do something that you did or liked to do on occasion but not repeatedly. Thus, to use his example, if you happen to type *the* as *hte* on the typewriter, you should deliberately type *hte* over and over until you get tired of it. You say with each occasion, "This is not how you type *the*." This should work for a while. You can permanently eliminate the habit by putting a fresh piece of paper into your machine and typing *hte* often enough to cover the sheet—about 600 times. To stop smoking, smoke an entire pack of cigarettes by lighting each cigarette from the stub of the previous one. After 20 cigarettes, you should not care to smoke for several days (if you live), and another pack then should finish you or the habit.

Guthrie applied this reasoning to his own learning views. To get someone to break a habit, he suggested tiring him or her out by forcing him to repeat the response until it could no longer be performed. The competitive response of wanting to rest or escape from the stimuli involved would thus be learned. The essence of the Guthrie procedure was to prevent the desired response from occurring. The procedure is sometimes applied to children whose eyes do not work in synchrony by placing a patch over one eye, forcing the other eye, the "lazy one," to do its share of the work. Tying the right hand behind the back will force people to use their left hands for responses they might need to do with the left hand. A military anecdote describes how ignorant and illiterate soldiers were taught to salute with the right hand by forcing them to hold bricks in their left. Such suggestions, of course, are not following the Pavlovian extinction procedure directly, but it is sometimes difficult to control reinforcers, and prevention of the response seems to work equally well.

Summary

We have seen that the attempts of some psychologists to apply learning theory principles to problems of psychopathology are not marked by great successes but that they do have some modest place in handling some problems of adjustment. Basically, they amount to eliminating (extinguishing?) one set of responses and substituting more desirable responses for them either through the use of straight conditioning procedures or by reinforcement of the new behavior. Such practices might might have their proper role, and where they work, they might very well serve as substitutes for more involved kinds of therapies, whose histories of successes are not especially noteworthy (Gross 1978).

BIOFEEDBACK

In recent years, we have seen the development of interest in another form of therapy less directly related to psychotherapeutic problems but with some connections to areas of personal awareness or different levels of consciousness. Where interest in consciousness-expanding drugs waned, a concomitant interest in meditation, transcendental or other, quickly took over. Some people became enthused over various Eastern philosophies based on some techniques for "clearing the mind" by suppressing bodily activities. Whatever the goals of practitioners of Zen Buddhism or other meditators, the Western interest in the techniques had its origin in learning principles.

The controversy that developed from the clash of Pavolvian and Thorndikian principles had settled down in the 1950s to a general acceptance of both views as dealing with separate spheres of influence. Thus, Pavlovian learning was generally accepted as (or relegated to) dealing with functions of the autonomic nervous system, bodily secretions, and visceral activities. Thorndikian learning was supposed to deal with the more voluntary (instrumental or operant) type of behavior, implemented through striate muscles under the direct control of the central nervous system.

Learning psychologists more or less specialized in one kind of research or another, rarely combining the two deliberately. Pavlov, following the work of Konorski and Miller (1937), indicated that he had long recognized instrumental learning. He referred to it as covering conditioned reflexes of "the second type," that is, reflexes initiated by the experimental animal to previously conditioned stimuli related to food, but Pavlov paid little attention to instrumental learning. Researchers like Mowrer (1947) at first classified avoidance behavior as instances of dual mechanisms or types of learning where fear is conditioned (according to Pavlovian principles) and then serves as a drive for instrumental responses that reduce it. Later, as we have seen, Mowrer (1960a) came to believe that there is only one kind of learning, namely, Pavlovian conditioning.

In the late 1960s, Neal Miller, at Rockefeller University, reopened the question. He took the working position that there is indeed only one kind of learning but that contrary to the Mowrer view, it is the Thorndikian principles that really govern all learning. The principles in question are basically those of drive and its reduction through some behavior that directly or indirectly reduces the drive, that is, where reinforcement *follows* the behavior. In short, according to Miller, all learning is based on reinforcement for some emitted response. To demonstrate the truth of such a view, Miller believed it necessary to demonstrate that visceral activity, that is, functions under automatic nervous control, could be modified, altered, and controlled through reinforcement operations. We noted earlier (see chapter 10) how this problem troubled Kimble.

It had long been known that some people could effect changes in some of their autonomic functions—some could control their heart rates, for example; others could reduce their intake of oxygen and their respiration rates to such low levels as to be barely observed. Indian yoga practitioners had always been a puzzle to academic psychologists. Miller observed, however, that nearly everyone does control the vital functions of urination and excretion to a relatively high degree and that such control appears to be acquired by very young children. Why should one not be able to learn to control any of the vital visceral functions? One problem remained, for Miller. It is possible that any control demonstrated by anyone was indirect, that is, via some voluntary muscular activity, which would have the effect of increasing or decreasing some autonomic function. In the simplest instance, for example, anyone can raise his or her blood pressure by running up stairs. Relaxing muscles can be learned, and such an operation might lower blood pressure to some measurable degree. To eliminate this possibility, Miller decided to use a paralyzing drug, curare, on his subjects. The drug affects the central nervous system and prevents any voluntary muscular activity. For subjects, Miller chose rats, which could be surgically prepared for careful recording of a variety of autonomic functions, such as heart beat, blood pressure, blood volume, and peristalsis. With the voluntary musculature controlled (and artificial control over breathing arranged for), only one other problem remained, namely, that of reinforcement. Miller had to demonstrate that by presenting a reinforcer whenever blood pressure, for example, declined (or increased), the change could be brought about when a S^D such as a light or tone, was presented. Because the paralyzed animal was incapable of an instrumental response that could be rewarded, Miller chose to reinforce his subjects by using a special procedure involving stimulation of special areas of the brain with small electrical charges. It has been reasonably securely established (Olds and Milner 1954) that such electrical shocks appear to serve as rewards or reinforcers for rats in that rats will manipulate levers which will result in such shocks to the brain apparently for long periods of time. Olds (1956) referred to areas in the brain where such stimulation seems reinforcing as "pleasure centers of the brain." Assuming that such shocks are reinforcers, Miller could now sound a tone and wait for an increase in blood pressure, which would normally occur from time to time, and then provide the shock. If over a series of trials, the rat would show a relatively rapid increase of blood pressure to the tone, the point would be made.

For some ten years, Miller and his associates reported one successful demonstration after another in such "instrumental" learning of various visceral responses. In one dramatic report, a rat was described as learning to flush one ear and blanch the other to an appropriate discriminated stimulus. Numerous other researchers began similar studies, ignoring Miller's careful controls and jumping directly to human subjects, whom they reported to be able to control heart beat, blood pressure, galvanic responses, and brain wave activity. In the human cases, the subjects would be connected with various kinds of monitoring devices (biofeedback machines) so that a lack of alpha waves, for example, would result in the occurrence of a tone. Reappearance of alpha would stop the tone. Subjects would be instructed to keep the tone on or off and apparently were able to do so with some success.

Great expectations were fostered by such research, with the prospect of people curing themselves of hypertension and other conditions by controlling their internal functions. In 1972, however, Miller began to have difficulties in replicating his studies and found fewer and fewer successes. After making all the changes he thought likely, he reported that he was no longer convinced that his prior successes could be reproduced. Interestingly enough, Miller concluded that it might be possible for some people to voluntarily control some of their autonomic activity through the use of imagery. By imaging situations where some increase or decrease in some function would be a normal consequence, some people could bring about the increase or decrease. Such an explanation of successes in bodily control, however, can not be attributed to instrumental learning, except by some stretch of the imagination. There are no reinforcements operating either, and the conclusion which must be accepted for the present is that there has been no successful serious demonstration of the learning of autonomic responses by a reinforcement procedure.

The many other investigations in this area have not demonstrated the virtues of a Thorndikian approach to autonomic control. The research is difficult to control, and Katkin and Murray (1968) have criticized the experimental procedures of many reports of alleged successes as lacking in one or another kind of control.

Meanwhile, various entrepreneurs have advertised and sold to a more or less innocent public a variety of kinds of devices that are supposed to provide monitoring signals from various bodily organs to represent their state of activity. Thus, one can monitor his or her brain waves and attempt to achieve a state of continuous alpha, which more or less represents a blank mind. The same state can probably be achieved by reciting a mantra, and those people who aspire to the attainment of blank minds are welcome to follow the promotions of dispensers of biofeedback monitor salesmen.

As a form of therapy, there appears to be no great promise from biofeedback research. As an attempt to demonstrate instrumental learning of autonomic responses, we must regard the research as unpromising if not a failure. This is not to denigrate the importance of feedback stimulation from either autonomic or striate muscles. Such feedback has been central for the Mowrer theory of learning and, presumably, plays a considerable role in all of our learning, as well as our normal functioning, particularly in such matters as walking or talking and hearing ourselves talk. Without our normal feedback from the muscles and structures involved in walking and talking, we would become jibbering idiots and basket cases.

21

Education and
How to Study

The effective and efficient student will have investigated this chapter first. Note that we did not use the word *read*. He or she will have looked over the table of contents, found this heading, and will have taken advantage of whatever might be useful for himself or herself before bothering with the rest. If this chapter proves somewhat trite and useless, he or she can make some judgments about the rest of the book. Of course, if the student already knows how to study, he or she can skip this chapter, although he or she cannot be too sure—maybe there are some tricks he or she has not learned the hard way.

The first thing to recognize is that different people study or go about their learning in different ways. Earlier in the book, an investigation was described in which the author asked some 200 freshmen students to learn a list of 20 words. They were given five one-minute trials to look over the list. By the end of the five trials, some students had learned the list perfectly; others came through with as few as seven words. All of the students were asked to describe how they went about the task, and the answers that were intelligible could be classified into about 15 different approaches. Obviously, some of these "methods" were followed by good learners and some by poor learners. At the moment, all we are interested in pointing out is that some 15 different methods had been picked up by these people by their average age of 18. Perhaps, each followed the method best for himself or herself. The suggestion, however, remains that some methods might be better than others. Efficiency experts are fond of saying that there is always a better way to do something, and they may be right. In this chapter, we will look at some of the principles covered earlier in the text that might suggest the "better way."

LEARNING AND BEING TAUGHT

From our review of various procedures and data gathered by learning psychologists, we saw little if any evidence of any teaching. No psychologist ever taught a rat to get through a maze or a sophomore to get through a list of nonsense syllables. Yet, both rats and sophomores learned. In no learning experiment does a psychologist ever teach anyone anything. At best, he tells human subjects what to do and expects them to do it. The psychologist might ask you to learn something. If he does, you might proceed; it is unlikely that you will ask him how to go about the learning or that he or she will tell you how to learn. It is presumed that you know how to learn. Usually, if not always, the subject acts as if he or she knows what to do and does what he or she is told as opposed to doing something else—the latter does happen; sometimes, subjects in experiments are somewhat perverse— they suspect things and try to outsmart the experimenter. Sometimes, they try to help him or her. This is called subject bias when it is noted.

Perhaps, psychologists do not teach subjects in learning experiments because they do not know how to. Perhaps, no one knows how to teach, and, again, perhaps that is because there is no such operation as teaching. But there are teachers in various kinds of schools getting paid for something, and they are doing something to earn their salaries. Perhaps, what they are doing might better be called educating. The word *education* has a Latin root, *educare*, which means to rear or bring up; it comes originally from *ducere*, which translates into *lead*, and *e* meaning *out*, and education, therefore, means to lead out or draw out. Perhaps, that is what teachers do. It is what psychologists do when they put a rat into a maze. They draw out of the rat a series of responses that the rat is perfectly capable of making. Actually, of course, they cannot draw out anything. They merely arrange circumstances or conditions where the behavior has a chance or likelihood of emerging. But even to do this much calls for some suitable background and experience. Not everyone knows how to handle rats properly. Nor do all teachers know how to arrange conditions of learning for all kinds of students.

So, the first thing a student might learn is that no one is going to teach him or her. The student must do the learning; the teacher can only arrange conditions so that the learning can occur. What are these conditions and arrangements? We can offer some negative answers at once. They are not those found in schools with classrooms where one teacher tries to teach the usual allotment of 30 or more students. McKeachie (1976), the president of the American Psychological Association, suggested that what we need most in our educational effort are more teachers and smaller schools. He was limiting himself by realistic considerations, because he really meant one teacher per student, a condition once described as ideal by a supporter of Mark Hopkins, the famous nineteenth century U.S. educator, when he remarked that the ideal teaching situation was one where Mark Hopkins sat at one end of a log and a student on the other. The ideal should be adjusted to the subject matter, however, and if the subject is piano playing, the teacher should be close at hand while the student plays, and the student should not practice without the teacher being there. If the subject is horsemanship, the teachers should ride alongside. Such conditions were met in the education of Queen Elizabeth II of England with notably successful results. Because we cannot all be royalty, which would make the status useless, we might like to settle for McKeachie's more teachers and smaller schools. Because we have little choice in the matter, we might recognize that we must do what we can with what we have. Most of our learning will not go on in the classroom anyhow.

THE FUNCTION OF TEACHERS

Anyone who is to teach must either be able to do what is to be learned or know how it must be done, how it should not be done, and how it cannot be done. Many opera stars of great accomplishment continue to take singing lessons, sometimes from former stars who cannot now match their pupils; they do know, however, how something can be done and how it should not be done and can be very helpful. Swimming teachers do not commonly enter the water, and parachute jump instructors do not accompany their students. What do these teachers do? They save time by pointing out errors, thus preventing errors, that is, they criticize the performance by providing, in one way or another, a model of the correct performance, or of a good approach, or a correct answer.

The Criterion Problem

What the effective teacher does is to arrange for a model of an acceptable performance, product, or answer. The student cannot normally be trusted with his or her accomplishment—he or she may produce just enough "to get by," and getting by might, for the student, be a shabby performance. The teacher establishes an acceptable model of achievement and a "passing" standard. Obviously, many factors can enter here to prevent a match between performance and model (social expectancies, time, values to the learner, and so forth), but unless there is a model, there will be no learning. A proper teacher provides specific indications of what students are supposed to learn.

The issue described above is better put, perhaps, in this way: the student must know what is expected of him or her (and in modern educational operations, the student rarely does). If we were to put it in terms of rights, the student has a right to know what the right answers are and, in a related way, what the questions are. Some teachers approach this basic need by providing a list of questions (and answers or sources for answers) from which a sample is chosen for a test. Auto operator license bureaus do the job properly. They provide prospective license earners with a booklet containing a number of questions, some of which will be used in a test. The answers are in the booklet, and the examinee knows that there will be no surprises. There is no place for surprises in proper education. Teachers who "spring" tests are engaging in disciplinary operations that pervert the proper function of tests. No one should take a test for which he or she is not prepared, and no disgrace should be associated with failure. There should be no failing grades. The student should be regarded as not yet ready; the student merely took the test before he or she was properly prepared. The student is simply not licensed, certified, or recognized as a passer. He should be allowed to try a test as often as he or she needs. In England, one candidate for an auto operator's license took the driving test 123 times before she passed. Boy Scouts earn their class and merit badges when they pass tests that they schedule for themselves when they are ready. They also know what they are supposed to know. The requirements are spelled out with some precision. Our educational system frequently works in exactly the opposite way—it follows the policy: here comes the test, ready or not.

On this same point, we might notice that in the situations described above, the examiners were not the teachers. Teachers should neither test their own students nor make up the tests. Incidentally, homemade, that is teacher-made, tests are rarely pretested for reliability and validity and may bear little relationship to what is taught or should have been taught. Students should be supplied with detailed syllabi, which inform the student of just what he or she is supposed to learn. The tests should be prepared by outside experts. The teaching program contains many occasions for informal testing, and the teacher might be able to advise a student about when he or she is ready for a test. The old artisan guilds worked on this principle. An apprentice was judged by the guild, not by his teacher. If a candidate failed, the teacher was responsible. The candidate was not presented until the teacher felt he was ready. Skinner (1968) endorses this general view by his remark that all students should get As. If they do not, the teacher has failed. Before we go failing all of our teachers, however, let us make sure they are working with legitimate students, who are properly prepared for the teacher's efforts and who are diligent and that the teacher decides when they are ready to take the test. Most students are not ready for an A grade in a one-semester period in any course. It must be recognized that teachers work within a system governed by boards, parents, and governmental bureaucracies.

Teacher as Model

In the Mowrer (1950) theory, learning becomes a matter of emotional conditioning. The learner, in effect, models himself on, or imitates, the teacher. We have seen (chapter 10) how Mowrer illustrated this in his effort at teaching talking birds how to talk. The procedure amounted to the teacher talking to the bird when the bird was hungry and being fed. Presumably, the bird felt "better" or "good" when it ate. It was feeling better, however, in the surrounding context of the teacher's body and voice, and according to Mowrer, the human voice became a conditioned stimulus for the "feeling better" response. Now, because talking birds do spontaneously emit vocal sounds for whatever unknown reasons, they would occasionally vocalize some sound that would correspond to a human voice, a sound like the teacher had made. Should this be the case, that sound, which would be similar to the teacher's vocalization, would make the bird feel better by initiating the same emotional reaction. Because the bird felt better when it heard the sound it made, it might continue to repeat it. That sound, at least, would have more value than any others in its repertoire.

Mowrer described this situation loosely as one wherein the teacher "made love" to the student. More strictly speaking, the teacher was establishing himself as a "good" stimulus, a desirable object to have around, a source of feeling better. Many teachers do try to get their students to like them or, at least, not to dislike them. Regardless of what the teacher is like or does, some students do get to like some teachers and even get "crushes" on some teachers. When there is a positive feeling, there may be signs of imitative behavior as well. If the student does imitate the teacher well, he or she will also be showing signs of learning.

It is not necessary, however, that teachers be liked. However, there is no point in their being threatening, abusive, or primitive—this will only result in a reluctance to imitate, as the results of the imitation will only make the student "feel worse," and this may generalize to other aspects of an educational program. Some stern and hard-nosed teachers are successful without being popular, and some popular teachers do not produce students of quality. The personalities of the teachers are probably not significant variables, as they have undergone a great deal of prescreening before ever becoming teachers. What matters more is whether the teacher provides the necessary conditions of learning, to which we can now turn.

CONDITIONS FOR LEARNING

Time Factor

It takes time to learn. This simple fact seems to have escaped the attention it merits. Earlier in the book, we considered this problem and recognized, of course, that time, per se, is not the issue, but, rather, what is done *during* the time. Still, in broad general considerations, we must note that we become better and better at something if we spend enough time at it (under good instructional conditions). Olympic champions are made in childhood. Tennis champions might start at age four. A concert violinist might start at two, and in general, as Norman (1977) suggested at a seminar at the State University of New York at Buffalo, it takes 5,000 hours to learn something well. At ten hours a week, we can get good at something in about ten years. It probably is not worthwhile to go to a concert where the performers have not put in at least 5,000 hours of practice, and to appreciate the performance probably takes the same amount of practice in appreciation. The average class and study time for a semester course might approach 135 hours or so, and no student should feel he or she has learned a lot in that time in just about any course.

The point under stress is that learning does not happen instantly nor does it attain permanency from brief, casual contacts with the material. True, some people learn faster than others, but the presumption of the learning psychologist is that the faster learner has put in the necessary time prior to the present challenge. It should not surprise the beginning piano student if his or her teacher plays a new composition faster or more effectively after merely looking it over than the student will be able to do in a year or so. The "bright" students in the class have spent the necessary time somewhere in the past.

Intent to Learn

Earlier in the book (chapter 15), we concluded that intent to learn is of no special importance. We will not waste time here on this topic and simply remind the student that the desire to know can only bring him or her to the learning situation. If you want to learn how to play tennis, you must get to a tennis court (and put in ten hours per week for ten years). To learn what is in a book, you must open the book and expend an appropriate amount of effort. That is about as far as intent to learn will get you. What matters now is what you do.

LEARNING STRATEGIES

The typical college assignment of "read the next chapter for next time" should get the student off to a bad start. Some students have picked up the notion that reading is equivalent to studying. The instructor should have said, "Study the next chapter." It is by no means rare that students will come to an instructor following a failure on a quiz and report, "But I read the chapter three times." Some instructors rejoin with, "You should have read it four times," an obviously inadequate bit of advice. Something can be learned by reading, to be sure, but it has long been known (Gates 1917) that reciting is far more rewarding than reading. Reciting amounts to trying to recall. The procedure is simple: you look over the material for some time and then try to remember it. The more time spent (up to 90 percent) on trying to remember or reciting, the better the learning. Ebbinghaus (1885) followed this procedure with nonsense syllable lists. He would read over each syllable and put the list aside while he tried to recall the items. In more recent times, this has been called the study-test method (Izawa 1971), and it is generally found to be more effective than other procedures. In modern laboratory studies, however, the learners are not given the freedom to try to recall for as much time as they would like. For experimental purposes, the study and recall times are strictly controlled, and the benefits of the method are obscured.

The recitation strategy is definitely a good one—better than merely reading—but it is not the only procedure of merit. From many studies of incidental learning, we know that what matters is what the learner does. Craik and Lockhart (1972) called this "processing" (see chapter 15), and the term covers any operation the learner applies to some study material. In the past, processing was called the orienting task. The best processing operation appears to be one where the material becomes meaningful to the learner, that is, where the learner imposes some meaning on the units involved.

When we considered meaning (chapter 15), we remarked on the importance of imagery and its role in both learning and retention. We noted that a whole paragraph of otherwise apparently meaningless verbiage could become meaningful by having someone provide a suitable image. With the appropriate image available, all of the statements in a paragraph suddenly make sense. If the author of the material to be studied does not provide the appropriate stimuli for adequate imagery in his or her readers, the material can be difficult; the learner must provide his or her own imagery. Writers frequently are enamored of their own literary skills and use abstract words to excess. They may not take the reader into account and seem to fear simple, concrete words that would result in communication. If the material is unfamiliar or too abstract, the appropriate imagery cannot be sparked, and the learner is helpless. A paragraph in a foreign language that is unfamiliar to the reader is an extreme example. It means nothing. Unfamiliar terms in England present the same problem; they cannot generate appropriate imagery and must be looked up. We are back to Thorndike's equation of vocabulary and intelligence. The reader of a paragraph must have the necessary vocabulary in a working sense—it must generate useful imagery.

What is being suggested here is that the student attempt to "picture" everything he or she reads—people, events, or materials, in the interactions that are usually described in texts. If the student can schematize, draw, or create a physical model, so much the better. All this takes more time than reading, of course, but that is the point, namely, reading is not studying. It is obvious that all unfamiliar words should be looked up and not only looked up but made effective and useful by the student finding his or her own examples. All this takes time, as was just stated. There are no short cuts. Study is work. The 35-hour work week is for the factory employee. Students should expect a 45-hour work week with a 15-hour course load. That might be a minimum for passing grades.

LEARNING THROUGH READING

We mentioned earlier (chapter 12) that reading is a complex skill serving many purposes and calling for different activities, depending on the purposes. Reading a newspaper may amount to glancing at headlines, ignoring whole pages or sections, selecting some articles or features for more detailed inspection, skimming here, concentrating there—it is a completely personal matter. Unless we note something we wish to tell someone else about, we usually spend only a little time with most of the paper.

Reading aloud to someone is another kind of operation and varies with the content. Reading poetry is a special art, as is reading a radio script or a part in a play. Reading a technical chapter in a textbook has its own special problems. A textbook or technical article is not meant to be read so much as studied. Study in this case is to be interpreted as analogous to what a watchmaker might do when he opens a watch that will not run or what a wine taster does with a glass of wine. Such experts examine the objects under study. Textbook chapters are to be examined, not read like novels.

The student with text in hand cannot know what he or she is supposed to know or retain from the content. The student knows, of course, that he or she is not expected to memorize the text, but beyond that, there is no basis for deciding what is to be retained and what can safely be ignored. If a workbook accompanies a text, the student has an immediate ally. Workbooks commonly include a kind of summary of a chapter consisting of sentences with blanks to be filled in. It can be assumed that the author believes that the blanks represent the key contents of the chapter and that filling in the blanks represents a mastery of the content. If the student can fill in the blanks without reading the chapter, he or she probably can afford to ignore the text. If the student cannot answer the questions, he or she should appreciate that his or her responsibility is to find the answers.

Reading a text, then, should be a matter of finding answers to questions. If the questions are not supplied by the author, the student must raise them for himself or herself. As the student reads, he or she must constantly be asking himself or herself, What question is being answered by this sentence, paragraph, or section? Starting with the title chapter, the question might be phrased, What is that chapter about? The answer, that is, the title, might not be too satisfying, but the student can ask himself or herself: What do I know about _____? What would I want to know about _____? What am I expected to know about _____?

The same process can be repeated as the student glances at or skims over the pages and notes topic sentences in paragraphs, section headings, illustrations, and so forth. The last paragraph of a chapter frequently includes some summary statement or conclusion. Questions can be raised at how one might reach such conclusions. With such a preliminary scouting expedition completed, the student is ready to return to the first page and start the questioning process all over again—this time in detail. The point, of course, is that the text reader is looking for answers; the reading itself is a skill used to find the answers. What the student should be busy with in reading is best exemplified by what it would take to satisfy him or her that someone else had learned the content of a paragraph or section. How would you decide that some friend had "read" the material? You would quiz him or her to the degree to which you held the material to be important. If he or she cannot answer your questions, you can charge him or her with negligence. If you cannot answer the same questions, charge yourself. The concept of programmed learning introduced by Skinner is at base a question-and-answer operation. In programmed learning, someone else asks the questions in a systematic way. In reading a text, you do your best to ask and answer the proper questions.

The practice of underlining with colored pens sells a lot of colored pens, but that is about the only value. What might be tried, instead, is to prepare an abstract—a shorter version—or a detailed outline of a chapter. This is essentially a question-and-answer operation, too, even though it may not have the appearance. Unfortunately, the detection or recognition of the important items cannot be pinpointed beyond what the author indicates by relative space, repetition, italics, or other clues.

When the student is finished with a chapter, he or she should be ready to give a lecture on the subject to anyone prepared to listen.

LEARNING FROM LECTURES

Much of our education occurs in classrooms where a teacher fills 50 minutes, frequently with talk, some diagrams on a chalkboard, exercises, demonstrations, or other activities. The fact that lectures have been given in universities for something like 600 years suggests that they may have some survival value and even educational virtue. We could raise some critical questions about lectures, but most of the criticisms would relate to bureaucratic institutional and scheduling arrangements. It is unlikely that 50 minutes represents anything like an ideal time for someone to talk or someone else to listen, but that is not the lecturer's doing. Someone has scheduled the lecturer.

One obvious difficulty with lecturers, as compared with reading, is that the lecturer moves along at some pace and the pace may not match everyone in the class. The reader can go back to pick up something missed or move ahead if the writer is dawdling. Lecturers serve a number of purposes, as do books, but usually, the reader cannot tell what is coming or what points are to be made. Considerate lecturers might provide outlines of their talks and save students the trouble of taking notes. With an outline in hand, the student could expect to follow a lecture, making additional notes where the outline is not completely satisfactory.

The value of a lecture is frequently a function of the preparedness of the listeners. If the audience is ready to receive the message, a lecture is a convenient way to give the message to many people at a time. A television lecture can reach millions and be excellent if the audience is in a position to appreciate the points being made.

The probability that anyone will retain much from a lecture consisting of many new facts is rather low. Studies with short (paragraph) lectures of two minutes that include 30 facts suggest that the average college student will remember about seven facts from a single hearing. Obviously, the lecturer should not provide many facts in verbal form. His or her purpose might be one of bringing some cohesion to a number of previously learned facts, to point out the significance of some facts over others, or to provide a frame of reference for facts to be learned outside the lecture hall.

The basic function of the lecture is to provide a rehearsal for the student of what the student might wish to instruct others about. In short, the prepared student (who has studied the preassigned material) should antic-ipate every word of the lecture (excepting attempts at humor). The student should know what is to be said and should find himself saying it along with the lecturer as a test of his or her own mastery of the subject. Some new twist or novel interpretation can then be appreciated for its value.

Some lecturers, because of style, manner, appearance, or other personal features, can serve a motivational function that encourages students to study more on their own; this is obviously a value when it works. A lecturer might as well be liked, although this should be a minor consideration. It will not help the student who is not prepared to listen.

DISCRIMINATION

In chapter 12, we considered the problem of discrimination or differen-tiation, namely, the need to ensure that materials we are learning are free from interference from other learnings. Many facts, personalities, principles, theories, and so forth are similar in some respect, and such similarities may lead to difficulties both in original learning and in later recall. When stimuli and/or responses are similar from one situation to another, there is likely to be interference among the components entering into association. The student should take account of this and ask such questions as, How will I remember that it is Henry II and not Henry III, or General Johnson and not General Jackson, or the second Battle of Bull Run and not the first? There is no easy answer to such problems, and where it matters, the distinctions must be established by looking for the differences. To the casual stroller in the park, all squirrels look alike, and it does not matter. Yet, every squirrel is different from other squirrels, and the differentiating features need to be considered should the individual identity of squirrels become an issue. At this stage, we can only warn the student that if something matters, he or she should make certain what that something is and how it is different from anything else that might resemble it. Again, this takes time and effort. You cannot learn while you are sleeping even if you are in class (see Simon and Emmons 1956).

EXAMPLES AND TEACHING

We can extend the studying operation somewhat more "creatively" by noticing that textbook writers usually offer examples. The student should never settle for the writer's examples unless what is being described is unique. Every effort should be made to develop at least another example—several examples would be better. When the student has his or her own illustrations, he or she is in command of the material and is equipped to teach. If you can only parrot the text, you have not learned much.

STUDENT AS TEACHER

Teaching others is often suggested as a fruitful and effective way of learning. Beginning teachers often report that they had never really learned the material before they began to teach. While this is an exaggeration, probably, it merely refers to the fact that the responsibility of teaching forced the teacher to now learn the material better than he or she knew it before. The teacher puts in a great deal more time on the subject than does the student. Yet, the suggestion has merit in a possible extension. Students should discuss material and raise questions with other students. Such discussions and questions can clarify points or inspire new approaches. Every student should be a teacher. He or she will soon find out how little he or she knows.

LEARNING AS INVENTION

What the above suggestions imply is that learning is an activity that involves consideration (attention, processing) of previously unfamiliar relationships. It is a creative process in that it results in knowledge. It is like a process of invention, where old items are put together in a new way. We can pay some respect to the old saw that there is nothing new under the sun, but for individuals, the result of a creative learning experience can be an invention. It is new to them even if it was invented millions of times over by previous students. We can consider the educational process as one wherein each learner invents everything he or she comes to know even if someone does help the learner or show the learner some positive or negative features of a problem or process. In the history of mathematics, it took some 1,200 years to invent the zero. You do not have 1,200 years, and so someone has to tell you about it. Thus, most students coming to algebra for the first time find it new or novel to hear the teacher say, "Let x be the unknown." But someone had to invent even this phrase, and given enough time and need, a student might invent it for himself or herself. Teachers merely hasten the process of invention. Once the appropriate expression is processed (comes to "mean" something), the student can start solving some problems he or she could not previously solve. Leibnitz and Newton invented the calculus (at about the same time) because each needed it to solve other problems. By doing so, they saved succeeding generations of students enormous amounts of time they would have had to invest if they had invented it for themselves. But in studying calculus, the modern student must, in effect, duplicate their efforts. A textbook or teacher merely restricts the field of processing, keeping the student from wasting time on fruitless approaches.

It should be obvious by now that no one has time to study everything that history has developed as a field of learning. The student is forced to specialize and be content with knowing rather a small part of the world's knowledge. There are no more Renaissance men. The modern student will be, inevitably, grossly ignorant about many things some other people will know extremely well. One settles for what one has time for.

In the discussion above, we have not treated all the strategies that are useful for learning. What works for one may not work for all, and each student develops his or her own stock of procedures with his or her own history of successes and failures. What might be of value is to consider the retention of the material learned because, sooner or later, the student will be tested.

LEARNING AND FORGETTING: THE NEED FOR TAGS

Have you ever forgotten where you left something or where you parked your car? Did it happen more than once? The first thing to know about learning is that you are liable to forget and that the more you learn the more you will forget. We have mentioned earlier in the book (chapter 17) that you can always relearn anything you ever knew with a probable great savings score, so do not despair. One of the reasons for learning is so that you will have something to relearn when necessary. But to avoid the necessity for extensive and expensive (in time) relearning, one can help himself or herself in two ways. First, if the matter is minor in quantity, such as where did you park your car, you can help by realizing that anything, including your name, can be forgotten. If it can be forgotten, then steps can be taken at the time of learning to assist in a later recall. When you park your car, look around for landmarks. A big lot will have sections and/or rows lettered or numbered. The easiest thing to do is write down the location, but sometimes you forget to carry a pencil; in that case, you might notice how you leave your car, whether you turn left or right, or how far you walk (you can even count your paces if you have nothing better to do). By such an effort of tagging, you provide a retrieval cue, which may pay off. Remembering to mail a letter that you have in your pocket may be more difficult, but again, you can image the mailbox you expect to use, arrange to pass it but do not pass it, and mail your letter. It does not always work to image such a prospective event, but sometimes it does. If you are going to the store to buy something and are asked to bring something else, the two items can easily be imaged together, and arrival at the store and reaching for the original item may prompt the appropriate imagery of the other. Tagging amounts to using mnemonic devices (see chapter 3, Appendix), and such devices can be very potent.

When it comes to textual material, it may be more difficult to develop suitable tags, but it will help to realize that anything can be forgotten and probably will be and that it pays to ask the question, How will I remember that? about almost any statement of fact or theory. Asking the question may prompt a suitable mnemonic device. If you do not ask the question, the whole operation may be lost.

When material is extended and relatively complex, it is important to recognize that the passage of time will introduce retroactive interference (see chapter 17). If there is time, it becomes important to review and to relearn. Learning of this kind is considered to be spaced as contrasted with massed. When you cram for a test, having never studied the material before, you are massing. If you have learned it before, you are taking advantage of the benefits of spaced learning. Reviewing at frequent intervals is more like the spaced learning of the laboratory. You find that each review takes less time; you discover what you know well and need not work on; you do not get so tired, which might lead to some extinction through conditioned inhibition (see chapter 6). The good student reviews; the poorer student waits until all the material is in at the end of a course.

THE PROCRASTINATION PROBLEM

One additional point might be made. In an affluent society, students own textbooks; they are always there and available for study. If the student could see a text only once for a limited time, he or she would take every possible measure to learn the material before the book was taken away. The shrewd operator in today's society would Xerox it, to be sure, but then the Xerox copy would lie around waiting to be consulted.

If you can imagine a situation where you had only the one limited chance to study something, what would you do? You would get rid of all distracters first. You would then go to work, asking yourself questions and looking for their answers. You would, in fact, do everything suggested here earlier except for the speedup in your activity. The best thing for any student would be to be placed under a constant and real threat that his or her text would be taken away from him or her. While this is a bit difficult to arrange, he might follow the practice of Joseph Conrad, who spoke no English before the age of 21 but who learned to write beautiful English by reading two pages (one sheet) of a small print, fine paper Bible every day. He would do his reading while off duty on a sea voyage to the Far East. When he had read his daily stint, he tore out the sheet and rolled a cigarette with it and let it go up in smoke while he reflected over the passages he had read, rolling the smoke and the words over his tongue. (This is probably an apocryphal tale.)

WARM-UP

The practice of athletes who spend some time and energy in warming-up was described earlier (chapter 16) as a nonspecific form of transfer. The student will find that it pays (in study and in examinations) to spend some time in more or less idle, that is, nonserious, activity related to the learning or test material. Flipping the pages of a book, reading random passages, and checking the index for related material all help set the stage or create the mood for a more serious effort. Even sharpening pencils will help if it does not become the chief preoccupation. If writing is involved, a few minutes of penmanship flourishes will also help.

Some writers save on warm-up time by following a bit of advice offered by George Bernard Shaw, who suggested that when the writing is somewhat extensive, say, beyond the level of a single work session, the writer should never stop with a completed paragraph or even a complete sentence. Always stop with a partially developed sentence, which you can be sure to be able to complete when you return to the task. Rereading the last paragraph should reset you for the sentence you failed to complete and restore the appropriate stimuli for continuing. The advice is sound enough if you can stop at just the right point and not find yourself wondering what you meant to say in the uncompleted sentence. It is a short form of warm-up.

THE TIRED STUDENT

Last, we come to the most acceptable advice, which should not be taken too eagerly. Never study when you are tired; certainly, do not study in bed.

You will either learn to sleep in the presence of books or find it difficult to sleep in beds. Because the average student might identify a state of fatigue long before it is really operating, the advice here is difficult to specify. A regular schedule of switching activities as they begin to pall might be considered. You might benefit by quitting when the subject begins to get interesting and turn to another subject. Sometimes, a change of activity is as good as a rest. But as every student knows, a little rest and relaxation never hurt anyone.

Bibliography

Alberts, E., and Ehrenfreund, D. 1951. "Transposition in Children as a Function of Age." *Journal Experimental Psychology* 41: 30–38.

Ammons, R. B. 1948. "Acquisition of Motor Skill: Quantitative Analysis and Theoretical Formulation." *Psychological Review* 54: 263–81.

Amsel, A., and Roussel, J. 1952. Motivational Properties of Frustration: I, Effect on a Running Response of the Addition of Frustration to the Motivational Complex." *Journal Experimental Psychology* 43: 363–68.

Anderson, J. R. 1978. "Arguments concerning Representations for Mental Imagery." *Psychological Review* 85: 249–77.

Anderson, J. R., and Bower, G. H. 1973. *Human Associative Memory*. New York: Wiley.

Aristotle. 1931. *De Memoria et Reminiscentia*, translated by J. I. Beare. In *The Works of Aristotle*, edited by W. D. Ross. Vol. 3. Oxford: Clarendon Press.

———. 1964. *On the Soul* (De Anima), *Parva naturalia*, and *On Breath*. Translated by W. S. Hett. Loeb Classical Library. Cambridge, Mass.: Harvard University Press.

Aronfreed, J. 1968. *Conscience and Conduct*. New York: Academic Press.

Asch, S. 1969. "A Reformulation of the Problem of Associations." *American Psychologist* 24: 92–102.

Atkinson, R. 1975. "Mnemotechnics in Second Language Learning." *American Psychologist* 30: 821–28.

Atkinson, R. C., and Wickens, T. D. 1971. "Human Memory and the Concept of Reinforcement." In *The Nature of Reinforcement*, edited by R. Glazer. New York: Academic Press.

Azrin, N. H. 1960: "Effects of Punishment during Variable-Interval Reinforcement." *Journal of the Experimental Analysis of Behavior* 3: 123–42.

Bahrick, H. P.; Bahrick, P. O.; and Wittlinger, R. P. 1975. "Fifty Years of Memory for Names and Faces." *Journal Experimental Psychology: General* 104: 54–55.

Bandura, A., and Walters, R. H. 1963. *Social Learning and Personality Development*. New York: Holt, Rinehart and Winston.

Bandura, A.; Ross, D.; and Ross, S. A. 1961. "Transmission of Aggression through Imitation of Aggressive Models. *Journal Abnormal and Social Psychology* 63: 572–82.

Barnes, J. M., and Underwood, B. J. 1959. "'Fate' of First-List Associations in Transfer Theory." *Journal Experimental Psychology* 58: 97–105.

Bartlett, F. C. 1932. *Remembering*. Cambridge, The University Press.

Bass, M. J., and Hull, C. L. 1934. "The Irradiation of a Tactile Conditioned Reflex in Man. *Journal of Comparative Psychology* 17: 47–65.

Battig, W. F., and Brackett, H. R. 1961. "Comparison of Anticipation and Recall Methods in Paired-Associate Learning." *Psychological Reports* 9: 59–65.

Battig, W. F., and Montague, W. E. 1969. "Category Norms for Verbal Items in 56 Categories: A Replication and Extension of the Connecticut Norms." *Journal Experimental Psychology* 80: 1–46.

Baumeister, A. A., and Kistler, D. 1974. "Study and Retrieval Interval Effects in Paired Associate Learning." *Journal Experimental Psychology* 102: 439–42.

Beach, F. 1951. "Instinctive Behavior." In *Handbook of Experimental Psychology*, edited by S. S. Stevens. New York: Wiley.

Bekhterev, V. 1933. *General Principles of Human Reflexology*. London: Jarrolds.

Berkeley, G. 1709. *An Essay Towards a New Theory of Vision*. (See any modern edition.)

Betts, G. H. 1909. *The Distribution and Function of Mental Imagery*. New York: Teachers College, Columbia University.

Bilodeau, I. M., and Schlosberg, H. 1952. "Similarity in Stimulus Conditions as a Variable in Retroactive Inhibition." *Journal Experimental Psychology* 42: 199–204.

Black, A. H. 1965. "Cardiac Conditioning in Curarized Dogs: The Relationship between Heart Rate and Skeletal Behavior. *Classical Conditioning: A Symposium*, edited by W. F. Prokasy. New York: Appleton-Century-Crofts.

Blodgett, H. C. 1929. "The Effect of the Introduction of Reward upon the Maze Performance of Rats." *University of California Publications in Psychology* 5: 113–34.

Boe, E. E., and Church, R. M. 1967. "Permanent Effects of Punishment during Extinction." *Journal of Comparative and Physiological Psychology* 63: 486–92.

Boring, E. G. 1950. *History of Experimental Psychology.* New York: Appleton-Century-Crofts.

Boring, E. G.; Langfeld, H. S.; and Weld, H. P. 1935. *Psychology.* New York: Wiley.

Bousfield, W. A. 1953. "The Occurrence of Clustering in the Recall of Randomly Arranged Associates." *Journal of General Psychology* 49: 229–40.

Bower, G. 1970. "Imagery as a Relational Organizer in Associative Learning." *Journal of Verbal Learning and Verbal Behavior* 9: 529–33.

———. 1972. "Mental Imagery and Associative Learning." In *Cognition in Learning and Memory*, edited by L. Gregg. New York: Wiley.

Bransford, J. D., and Franks, J. J. 1971. "The Abstraction of Linguistic Ideas." *Cognitive Psychology* 2: 331–50.

Breland, K., and Breland, M. 1961. "The Misbehavior of Organisms." *American Psychologist* 76: 681–84.

Bridges, K. M. B. 1932. "Emotional Development in Early Infancy." *Child Development* 3: 324–54.

Brogden, W. J. 1939. "Sensory Pre-conditioning." *Journal Experimental Psychology* 25: 323–32.

Brooks, L. R. 1967. "The Suppression of Visualization by Reading." *Quarterly Journal of Experimental Psychology* 19: 289–99.

———. 1968. "Spatial and Verbal Components of the Act of Recall." *Canadian Journal of Psychology* 22: 349–68.

Brown, J. S. 1942. "Factors Determining Conflict Reactions in Difficult Discrimination." *Journal Experimental Psychology* 31: 272–92.

Brown, P. L., and Jenkins, H. M. 1968 "Auto-shaping of the Pigeon's Keypeck." *Journal of the Experimental Analysis of Behavior* 11: 1–8.

Brown, R. 1973. "Development of the First Language in the Human Species." *American Psychologist* 28: 97–106.

Brown, T. 1820. *Lectures on the Philosophy of the Human Mind.* Edinburgh: Tail, Longman.

Bugelski, B. R. 1938. "Extinction with and without Sub-goal Reinforcement." *Journal of Comparative Psychology* 26: 121–33.

———. 1948. "An Attempt to Reconcile Unlearning and Reproductive Inhibition

Explanation of Proactive Inhibition." *Journal Experimental Psychology* 38: 670–82.

————. 1950. "A Remote Association Explanation of the Relative Difficulty of Learning Nonsense Syllables in a Serial List." *Journal Experimental Psychology* 40: 336–48.

————. 1962. "Presentation Time, Total Time, and Mediation in Paired-Associate Learning." *Journal Experimental Psychology* 63: 409–12.

————. 1970. "Words and Things and Images." *American Psychologist* 25: 1002–12.

————. 1973a. *An Introduction to the Principles of Psychology.* Indianapolis, Ind.: Bobbs-Merrill.

————. 1973b. "Human Learning." In *Handbook of General Psychology*, edited by B. B. Wolman. Englewood Cliffs, N.J.: Prentice-Hall.

————. 1974. "Images as Mediators in One-Trial Paired-Associate Learning: III, "Sequential Functions in Serial Lists." *Journal Experimental Psychology* 103: 298–303.

————. 1975. *Empirical Studies in the Psychology of Learning.* Indianapolis, Ind.: Hackett.

Bugelski, B. R., and Cadwallader, T. C. 1956. "A Reappraisal of the Transfer and Retroaction Surface. *Journal Experimental Psychology* 50: 360–66.

Bugelski, B. R., and Miller, N. E. 1938. "A Spatial Gradient in the Strength of Avoidance Responses." *Journal Experimental Psychology* 23: 494–505.

Bugelski, B. R., and Sharlock, D. 1952. "An Experimental Demonstration of Unconscious Mediated Association." *Journal Experimental Psychology* 44: 334–38.

Bugelski, B. R.; Kidd, E.; and Segmen, J. 1968. "Images as Mediators in One-Trial Paired-Associate Learning." *Journal Experimental Psychology* 76: 69–77.

Burt, H. E. 1932. "An Experimental Study of Early Childhood Memory." *Journal of Genetic Psychology* 40: 287–94.

Bykov, K. M. 1957. *The Cerebral Cortex and the Internal Organs*, translated by W. H. Gantt. New York: Chemical.

Cantor, G. N. 1955. "Amount of Pretraining as a Factor in Stimulus Predifferentiation and Performance Set." *Journal Experimental Psychology* 50: 180–84.

Capaldi, E. J. 1958. "The Effect of Different Amounts of Training on the Resistance to Extinction of Different Patterns of Partially Reinforced Responses." *Journal Comparative and Physiological Psychology* 51: 367–71.

———. 1966. "Partial Reinforcement: A Hypothesis of Sequential Effects." *Psychological Review* 73: 459–77.

Capaldi, E. J., and Capaldi, E. D. 1970. "Magnitude of Partial Reward, Irregular Reward Schedules, and a 24-Hour ITI: A Test of Several Hypotheses." *Journal Comparative and Physiological Psychology* 72: 203–9.

Carmichael, L. 1926. "The Development of Behavior in Vertebrates Experimentally Removed from the Influences of Stimulation." *Psychological Review* 33: 51–58.

Carrol, J. B. 1953. *The Study of Language.* Cambridge, Mass.: Harvard University Press.

Chomsky, N. 1957. *Syntactic Structures.* The Hague: Mouton.

Church, R. M. 1963. "The Varied Effects of Punishment on Behavior. *Psychological Review* 70: 369–402.

Cohen, I. 1962. "Programmed Learning and the Socratic Dialogue." *American Psychologist* 72: 772–75.

Conant, J. B. 1953. *Modern Science and Modern Man.* New York: Anchor Books.

Cook, J. O. 1963. "Superstition in the Skinnerian." *American Psychologist* 18: 516–18.

Cook, J. O., and Spitzer, M. E. 1948. "Supplementary Report: Prompting versus Confirmation in Paired-Associate Learning." *Journal Experimental Psychology* 38: 168–72.

Cooper, E. H., and Pantle, A. J. 1967. The Total-Time Hypothesis in Verbal Learning." *Psychological Bulletin* 68: 221–34.

Craik, F. I. M., and Lockhart, R. S. 1972. "Levels of Processing." *Journal of Verbal Learning and Verbal Behavior* 11: 671–84.

Craik, F. I. M., and Tulving, E. 1975. "Depth of Processing and Retention of Words in Episodic Memory." *Journal of Experimental Psychology: General* 104: 268–94.

Darwin, C. 1859. *On the Origin of Species by Means of Natural Selection.* See any modern edition.

Dashiell, J. F. 1927. *Fundamentals of General Psychology.* Boston: Houghton Mifflin.

Deese, J. 1959. "Influence of Inter-item Associative Strength upon Immediate Free Recall." *Psychological Reports* 5: 305–12.

Descartes, R. *L'Homme.* See any modern edition.

Dewey, J. 1910. *How We Think.* Boston: Heath.

Dooling, J. L., and Lachman, R. 1971. "Effects of Comprehension on Retention of Prose." *Journal Experimental Psychology* 88: 216–22.

Dunlap, K. 1928. *Repetition in the Breaking of Habits.* Science Monographs Series, no. 30: 66–70.

Durant, W. and Durant, A. *The Story of Civilization.* New York: Simon and Schuster, 1935–1975.

Ebbinghaus, H. von. 1885. *On Memory.* New York: Teachers College, Columbia University.

Ehrenfreund, D. 1948. "An Experimental Test of the Continuity Theory of Discrimination Learning with Pattern Vision." *Journal of Comparative and Physiological Psychology* 41: 408–22.

Ellson, D. 1941. "Hallucinations Produced by Sensory Conditioning." *Journal Experimental Psychology* 28: 1–20.

Epstein, W. 1961. "The Influence of Syntactical Structure on Learning." *The American Journal of Psychology* 74: 80–85.

Estes, W. K. 1944. *An Experimental Study of Punishment.* Psychological Monographs Series, no. 57, whole no. 263.

———. 1975. *Handbook of Learning and Cognitive Processes.* Vol. 2. New York: Halsted Press.

Estes, W. K.; Koch, S.; MacCorquodale, K.; Meehl, P. E.; Mueller, C. G.; Schoenfeld, W. N.; and Verplanck, W. S. 1954. *Modern Learning Theory.* New York: Appleton-Century-Crofts.

Farber, J. E., and Spence, K. W. 1953. "Complex Learning and Conditioning as a Function of Anxiety." *Journal Experimental Psychology* 45: 120–25.

Finesmith, S. 1960. "Systematic Changes in the Galvanic Skin Response during Paired-Associate Learning." Unpublished manuscript. University of Buffalo.

Fitzgerald, R. 1963. "Effect of Partial Reinforcement with Acid on the Classically Conditioned Salivary Response in Dogs." *Journal of Comparative and Physiological Psychology* 56: 1056–60.

Flanders, J. P. 1968. "A Review of Research on Imitative Behavior." *Psychological Bulletin* 69: 316–37.

Gagne, R. M., and Baker, K. E. 1950. "Stimulus Predifferentiation as a Factor in Transfer of Training." *Journal Experimental Psychology* 40: 439–51.

Galton, F. 1879. "Psychometric Experiments." *Brain* 2: 149–62.

———. 1883. *Enquiries into Human Faculty and Its Development.* London: Macmillan.

Garcia, J., and Ervin, F. R. 1968. "Gustatory-Visceral and Telereceptor-Cutaneous Condition—Adaptation in Internal and External Milieus." *Communications in Behavioral Biology* 1 (Pt. A): 389–415.

Garcia, J., and Koelling, R. A. 1966. "Relation of Cue to Consequence in Avoidance Learning." *Psychonomic Science* 4: 123–24.

Gardner, R. A., and Gardner, B. T. 1969. "Teaching Sign Language to a Chimpanzee." *Science* 165: 664–72.

Gates, A. I. 1917. "Recitation as a Factor in Memorizing." *Archives of Psychology* 6.

Gibson, E. J. 1940, "A Systematic Application of the Concepts of Generalization and Differentiation to Verbal Learning." *Psychological Review* 47: 196–229.

———. 1941. "Retroactive Inhibition as a Function of Degree of Generalization between Tasks." *Journal Experimental Psychology* 28: 93–115.

———. 1942. "Intralist Generalization as a Factor in Verbal Learning." *Journal Experimental Psychology* 30: 185–200.

———. 1969. *Principles of Perceptual Learning and Development.* New York: Appleton-Century-Crofts.

Gibson, E. J., and Levin, H. 1975. *The Psychology of Reading.* Cambridge, Mass.: MIT Press.

Gibson, E. J., and Walk, R. D. 1956. "The Effect of Prolonged Exposure to Visually Presented Patterns on Learning to Discriminate Them." *Journal Comparative and Physiological Psychology* 49: 239–42.

———. 1960. "The 'Visual Cliff'." *Scientific American* 202: 64–71.

Gibson, E. J.; Walk, R. D.; Pick, H. L., Jr.; and Tighe, T. J. 1958. "The Effect of Prolonged Exposure to Visual Patterns on Learning to Discriminate Similar and Different Patterns." *Journal of Comparative and Physiological Psychology* 51: 584–87.

Glanzer, M., and Cunitz, A. R. 1966. "Two Storage Mechanisms in Free Recall." *Journal of Verbal Learning and Verbal Behavior* 5: 351–60.

Glaze, J. A. 1928. "The Association Value of Non-sense Syllables." *Journal of Genetic Psychology* 35: 255–69.

Gormezano, I., and Kehoe, J. 1975. "Classical Conditioning: Some Methodological–Conceptual Issues." In *Handbook of Learning and Cognitive Processes*, edited by W. K. Estes. New York. Halsted Press.

Gormezano, I., and Moore, J. W. 1969. "Classical Conditioning." In *Learning: Processes*, edited by M. Marx. New York: MacMillan.

Goss, A. E. 1955. "A Stimulus-Response Analysis of the Interaction of Cue Producing and Instrumental Responses." *Psychological Review* 62: 20–31.

Grant, David. 1964. "Classical and Operant Conditioning." In *Categories of Human Learning*, edited by A. W. Melton. New York: Academic Press.

Greenwald, A. G. 1970. "Sensory Feedback Mechanisms in Performance Control." *Psychological Review* 77: 73–99.

Gross, M. L. 1978. *The Psychological Society*. New York: Random House.

Grube, G. M. A. 1976. *Plato's Meno*. Indianapolis, Ind.: Hackett.

Guthrie, E. R. 1935. *The Psychology of Learning*. New York: Harper.

———. 1946. "Psychological Facts and Psychological Theory." *Psychological Bulletin* 43: 1–20.

Guthrie, E. R., and Horton, G. P. 1946. *Cats in a Puzzle Box*. New York: Rinehart.

Guttman, N., and Kalish, H. I. 1956. "Discriminability and Stimulus Generalization." *Journal Experimental Psychology* 51: 79–88.

Hall, J. F. 1971. *Verbal Learning and Retention*. Philadelphia: J. B. Lippincott.

———. 1976. *Classical Conditioning and Instrumental Learning*. Philadelphia: J. B. Lippincott.

Hall, M. 1833. "On the Reflex Function of the Medulla Oblongata and the Medulla Spinalis." *Philosophical Transactions of the Royal Society* 123: 635–65.

Hamilton, W. 1861. *Lectures on Metaphysics*. Boston: Gould and Lincoln.

Harcum, E. R. 1975. *Serial Learning and Para-learning*. New York: Academic Press.

Harlow, H. F. 1949. "The Formation of Learning Sets." *Psychological Review* 56: 51–65.

Harlow, H. F.; Gluck, J. P.; and Suomi, S. J. 1972. "Generalization of Behavioral Data between Nonhuman and Human Animals." *American Psychologist* 27: 709–16.

Hartley, D. 1749. *Observations on Man, His Frame, His Duty and His Expectations.* London. (See any modern edition.)

Hayes, C. 1951. *The Ape in Our House.* New York: Harper & Bros.

Hayes, K. 1953. "The Backward Learning Curve: A Method for the Study of Learning." *Psychological Review* 60: 269–75.

Hebb, D. O. 1949. *The Organization of Behavior.* New York: Wiley.

———. "Distinctive Features of Learning in the Higher Animal." In *Brain Mechanisms and Learning,* edited by J. F. Delafresnaye. London and New York: Oxford University Press.

———. 1968. "Concerning Imagery." *Psychological Review* 75: 466–77.

———. 1972. *A Textbook of Psychology.* 3rd ed. Philadelphia: Saunders.

Herbart, J. F. 1891. *A Textbook of Psychology,* translated by M. K. Smith. New York: D. Appleton.

Herbert, M. J., and Harsch, C. M. 1944. "Observational Learning by Cats." *Journal Comparative Psychology* 37: 81–95.

Hernnstein, R. 1971. "I.Q." *Atlantic Monthly* 228: 44–64.

Hilgard, E. R. 1951. "Methods and Procedures in the Study of Learning." In *Handbook of Experimental Psychology,* edited by S. S. Stevens. New York: Wiley.

———. 1956. *Theories of Learning* 2d. ed. New York: Appleton-Century-Crofts.

Hilgard, E. R., and Bower, G. 1975. *Theories of Learning.* 4th ed. New York: Appleton-Century-Crofts.

Hilgard, E. R., and Marquis, D. G. 1935. "Acquisition, Extinction, and Retention of Conditioned Lid Responses to Light in Dogs." *Journal of Comparative and Physiological Psychology* 19: 29–58.

———. 1940. *Conditioning and Learning.* New York: Appleton-Century-Crofts.

Hintzman, D. L. 1978. *The Psychology of Learning and Memory.* San Francisco: W. H. Freeman.

Hobbes, T. 1650. *Human Nature.* See any modern edition.

———. 1651. *The Leviathan.* See any modern edition.

Hobhouse, L. T. 1901. *Mind in Evolution.* New York: MacMillan.

Hoffman, H. S., and De Paulo, P. 1977. "Behavioral Control by an Imprinting Stimulus." *American Scientist* 65: 58–66.

Horton, D. L., and Kjeldergaard, P. M. 1961. *An Experimental Analysis of Associative Factors in Mediated Generalization.* Psychological Monographs: General and Applied Series, whole no. 518.

Hovland, C. I. 1936. "Inhibition of Reinforcement and Phenomena of Experimental Extinction." *Proceedings of the National Academy of Science* 22: 430–33.

———. 1937. "The Generalization of Conditioned Responses. I, The Sensory Generalization of Conditioned Responses with Varying Sequences of Tone." *Journal General Psychology* 17: 125–48.

———. 1938. "Experimental Studies of Rote Learning: III, Distribution of Practice with Varying Speeds of Syllable Presentation." *Journal Experimental Psychology* 23: 172–90.

———. 1951. "Human Learning and Retention. *Handbook of Experimental Psychology*, edited by S. S. Stevens. New York: Wiley.

Hovland, C. I., and Kurtz, K. 1952. "Experimental Studies in Rote Learning: X, Prelearning Syllable Familiarization and the Length-Difficulty Relationship." *Journal Experimental Psychology* 44: 31–39.

Huey, E. B. 1908. *The Psychology and Pedagogy of Reading.* New York: MacMillan.

Hull, C. L. 1920. *Quantitative Aspects of the Evolution of Concepts.* Psychological Review Monographs no. 28: 85.

———. 1934. "The Rat's Speed-of-Locomotion Gradient in the Approach to Food." *Journal of Comparative Psychology* 17: 393–422.

———. 1943. *The Principles of Behavior.* New York: Appleton-Century-Crofts.

Hull, C. L.; Hovland, C. I.; Ross, R. T.; Hall, M.; Perkins, D. T.; and Fitch, F. G. 1940. *Mathematico-deductive Theory of Rote Learning.* New Haven, Conn.: Yale University Press.

Hume, D. 1739. *A Treatise of Human Nature.* See any modern edition.

Humphreys, L. 1939. "The Effect of Random Alternation of Reinforcement on the Acquisition and Extinction of Conditioned Eyelid Reactions." *Journal Experimental Psychology* 25: 141–58.

Ivanov-Smolensky, A. G. 1927. "On the Methods of Examining the Conditioned Food Reflexes in Children and in Mental Disorders." *Brain* 50: 138–41.

Izawa, C. 1971. "The Test Trial Potentiating Model." *Journal of Mathematical Psychology* 8: 200–24.

Jacobsen, E. 1932. "Electrophysiology of Mental Activities." *American Journal of Psychology* 44: 677–94.

———. 1938. *Progressive Relaxation.* Chicago: University of Chicago Press.

James, W. 1890. *The Principles of Psychology.* New York: Holt.

Jaynes, J. 1973. "The Problem of Animate Motion in the Seventeenth Century." In *Historical Conceptions of Psychology*, edited by M. Henle, J. Jaynes, and J. J. Sullivan. New York: Springer.

Jenkins, H. M., and Moore, B. 1973. "The Form of the Auto-shaped Response with Food or Water Reinforcers." *Journal of the Experimental Analysis of Behavior* 20: 163–81.

Jenkins, J. C., and Dallenbach, K. M. 1924. "Oblivescence during Sleep and Waking." *American Journal of Psychology* 35: 605–12.

Jenkins, J. J.; Foss, D. J.; and Odum, P. B. 1965. "Associative Mediating in Paired-Associate Learning with Multiple Controls." *Journal of Verbal Learning and Verbal Behavior* 4: 141–47.

Jenks, C.; Smith, M.; Ucland, H.; Bane, M. J.; Cohen, D.; Ginitis, H.; Heyns, B.; and Michelson, S. 1972. *Inequality: A Reassessment of the Effect of Family and Schooling in America.* New York: Basic Books.

Jensen, A. 1969. "How Much Can We Boost I.Q. and Scholastic Behavior." *Harvard Educational Review* 39.

Jones, M. C. 1924. "A Laboratory Study of Fear: The Cease of Peter." *Pedagogical Seminary* 31: 308–15.

Jung, C. G. 1910. "The Association Method." *American Journal of Psychology* 21: 219–69.

Kagan, J. S. 1969. "In Discussion: How Much Can We Boost I.Q. and Scholastic Achievement." *Harvard Educational Review* 39.

———. 1976. "Emergent Themes in Human Development." *American Scientist* 64: 186–96.

Kamin, L. 1974. *The Science and Politics of I.Q.* Potomac, Md.: Lawrence Erlbaum/New York: Wiley.

Kant, I. 1781. *The Critique of Pure Reason.* See any modern edition.

Kantor, J. R. 1947. *Problems of Physiological Psychology.* Bloomington, Ind. Principia Press.

Kanungo, R. 1967. "Meaning Mediation in Verbal Transfer." *British Journal of Psychology* 58: 205–12.

Katkin, E., and Murray, E. N. 1968. "Instrumental Conditioning of Autonomically Mediated Behavior." *Psychological Bulletin* 70: 52–68.

Katona, G. 1940. *Organizing and Memorizing.* New York: Columbia University Press.

Keller, F. 1958. "The Phantom Plateau." *Journal of Experimental Analysis of Behavior* 1: 1–14.

Kelly, E. L. 1934. "An Experimental Attempt to Produce Artificial Chromaesthesia by the Technique of the Conditioned Response." *Journal Experimental Psychology* 17: 315–41.

Kent, G. H., and Rosanoff, A. J. 1910. "A Study of Association in Insanity." *American Journal of Insanity* 67: 37–96.

Keppel, G., and Underwood, B. 1962. "Proactive Inhibition in Short-term Retention of Single Items." *Journal of Verbal Learning and Verbal Behavior* 1: 153–61.

Keppel, G.; Postman, L.; and Zawortink, B. 1968. "Studies of Learning to Learn: VII, the Influence of Massive Amounts of Training upon the Learning and Retention of Paired-Associate Lists." *Journal of Verbal Learning and Verbal Behavior* 7: 790–96.

Kimble, G. A. 1961. *Hilgard and Marquis' Conditioning and Learning.* 2d ed. New York: Appleton-Century-Crofts.

Kinkade, K. 1973. *A Walden Two Experiment: The First Five Years of Twin Oaks Community.* New York: W. Morrow.

Koffka, K. 1935. *Principles of Gestalt Psychology.* New York: Harcourt.

Köhler, W. 1925. *The Mentality of Apes*, translated by E. Winter. New York: Harcourt, Brace, and World.

Konorski, J. 1967. *Integrative Activity of the Brain: An Interdisciplinary Approach.* Chicago: University of Chicago Press.

———. 1970. "The Problem of the Peripheral Control of Skilled Movements." *International Journal of Neuroscience* 1: 39–50.

Konorski, J., and Miller, S. 1937. "On Two Types of Conditioned Reflex." *Journal of General Psychology* 16: 264–72.

Kosslyn, S. M., and Pomerantz, J. R. 1977. "Imagery, Propositions, and the Form of Internal Representation." *Cognitive Psychology* 9: 52–76.

Kotarbinski, T. 1966. *Gnosiology.* New York: Pergamon Press.

Krasner, L., and Krasner, M. 1973. "Token Economies and Other Planned Environments." In *Behavior Modification in Education*, edited by Carl E. Thoresen. Chicago: University of Chicago Press.

Krechevsky, I. 1932. "'Hypotheses' in Rats." *Psychological Review* 38: 516–32.

Kurtz, K. 1955. "Discrimination of Complex Stimuli: The Relationship of Training and Test Stimuli in Transfer of Discrimination." *Journal Experimental Psychology* 50: 283–91.

Landauer, T. K. 1975. "Memory without Organization: Properties of a Model with Random Storage and Undirected Retrieval." *Cognitive Psychology* 7: 495–531.

Lashley, K. 1924. "Studies of Cerebral Function in Learning: V, the Retention of Motor Habits after Destruction of the So-Called Motor Area in Primates." *Archives of Neurology and Psychiatry* 12: 249–76.

———. 1930. "Basic Neural Mechanisms in Behavior." *Psychological Review* 37: 1–24.

———. 1951. "The Problem of Serial Order in Behavior." In *Cerebral Mechanisms in Behavior*, edited by L. A. Jeffress. New York: Wiley.

Lester, O. P. 1932. Mental Set in Relation to Retroactive Inhibition.

Leuba, C. 1940. "Images as Conditioned Sensations." *Journal Experimental Psychology* 26: 345–51.

———. 1951. "Conditioning Imagery." *Journal Experimental Psychology* 42: 352–55.

Lick, J., and Unger, T. 1975, "External Validity of Laboratory Fear Assessment: Implications from Two Case Studies." *Journal of Consulting and Clinical Psychology* 43: 864–66.

Limber, J. 1977, "Language in Chimp and Child." *American Psychologist* 32: 280–95.

Lindley, R. H. 1963. "Association Value, Familiarity, and Pronounciability Ratings as Predictors of Serial Verbal Learning." *Journal Experimental Psychology* 4: 347–51.

Locke, J. 1690. *An Essay Concerning Human Understanding.* London: Oxford University Press.

Loftus, G. 1972. "Eye Fixations and Recognition Memory for Pictures." *Cognitive Psychology* 3: 525–51.

Logan, F. 1956. "A Micromolar Approach to Behavior Theory." *Psychological Review*, 63: 63–73.

Lorayne, H., and Lucas, J. 1974. *The Memory Book.* New York: Stein and Day.

Lorenz, K. 1965. *On Aggression.* New York: Harcourt, Brace, Jovanovich.

Luria, A. R. 1968. *The Mind of a Mnemonist.* New York: Basic Books.

Mandler, G., and Dean, P. J. 1969. "Seriation: Development of Serial Order in Free Recall." *Journal Experimental Psychology* 81: 207–15.

Marsten-Wilson, W., and Tyler, L. K. 1976, "Memory and Levels of Processing in a Psycholinguistic Context." *Journal of Experimental Psychology: Human Learning and Memory* 2: 112–19.

Martin, E. 1965. "Transfer of Verbal Paired Associates." *Psychological Review* 72: 327–43.

———. 1967. "Formation of Concepts." In *Concept Attainment and the Structure of Memory*, edited by B. Kleinmutz. New York: Wiley.

Marx, M. 1969. *Learning: Processes.* New York: Macmillan.

May, M. 1948. "Experimentally Acquired Drives." *Journal Experimental Psychology* 38: 66–77.

McDaniel, M. A., and Masson, M. E. 1977. "Long-Term Retention: When Incidental Semantic Processing Fails." *Journal of Experimental Psychology: Human Learning and Memory* 3: 270–81.

McDougall, W. 1908. *Social Psychology.* Boston: John W. Luce.

McGeoch, J. 1942. *The Psychology of Human Learning.* New York: Longmans.

McKeachie, W. 1976. "Psychology in America's Bicentennial Year." *American Psychologist* 31: 819–33.

McLaughlin, B. 1965, "'Intentional' and 'Incidental' Learning in Human Subjects: The Role of Instructions to Learn and Motivation." *Psychological Bulletin* 63: 359–76.

Mechanic, A. 1962. "The Distribution of Recalled Items in Simultaneous and Incidental Learning." *Journal Experimental Psychology* 63: 593–600.

Melton, A. 1963. "Implications of Short-Term Memory for a General Theory of Memory." *Journal of Verbal Learning and Verbal Behavior* 2: 1–21.

Melton, A., and Irwin, J. McQ. 1940. "The Influence of Degree of Interpolated Learning on Retroactive Inhibition and the Overt Transfer of Specific Responses." *The American Journal of Psychology* 53: 173–203.

Mill, J. 1829. *Analyses of the Phenomena of the Human Mind.* See any modern edition.

Mill, J. S. 1843. *A System of Logic, Ratiocinative and Inductive.* See any modern edition.

Miller, N. E. 1944. "Experimental Studies in Conflict." In *Personality and the Behavior Disorders*, edited by J. McV. Hunt. New York: Ronald Press.

———. 1969. "Learning of Visceral and Glandular Responses." Science 163: 434–45.

———. 1972. "Interactions between Learned and Physical Factors in Mental Illness." In *Biofeedback and Self-Control*, edited by D. Shapiro et al. Chicago: Aldine.

Miller, N. E., and Dollard, J. 1941. *Social Learning and Imitation.* New Haven, Conn.: Yale University Press.

Miller, G.; Galanter, E.; and Pribram, K. H. 1960. *Plans and the Structure of Behavior.* New York: Holt, Rinehart and Winston.

Minami, H., and Dallenbach, K. M. 1946. "The Effect of Activity upon Learning and Retention in the Cockroach." *American Journal of Psychology* 59: 1–58.

Montague, A. 1976. *The Nature of Human Aggression.* New York: Oxford University Press.

Montague, W. E., and Kiess, H. O. 1968. "*The associability of CVC Pairs.*" Journal Experimental Psychology Monograph, Series, no. 78, pt. 2 of no. 2.

Moore, B. 1973. "The Role of Directed Pavlovian Reactions in the Pigeon." In *Constraints on Learning: Limitations and Predispositions*, edited by R. A. Hinde and J. Stevenson-Hinde. London: Academic Press.

Mowrer, O. H. 1947. "On the Dual Nature of Learning—A Reinterpretation of 'Conditioning' and 'Problem Solving'." *Harvard Educational Review* 17: 102–48.

————. 1950. *Learning Theory and Personality Dynamics*. New York: The Ronald Press.

————. 1960a. *Learning Theory and Behavior*. New York: Wiley.

————. 1960b. *Learning Theory and the Symbolic Processes*. New York: Wiley.

————. 1964. *The New Group Therapy.* New York: D. Van Nostrand.

————. 1967. *Morality and Mental Life*. Chicago. Rand McNally.

Müller, G., and Pilzecker, A. 1900. In R. S. Woodworth, *Experimental Psychology*. New York: Holt, 1938.

————. 1900. In C. E. Osgood, *Method and Theory of Experimental Psychology*, p. 515. New York: Oxford University Press, 1953.

Murdock, B. 1960. "The Immediate Retention of Unrelated Words." *Journal Experimental Pschology* 60: 222–34.

————. 1968. "Modality Effects in Short-Term Memory: Storage or Retrieval." *Journal Experimental Psychology* 77: 79–86.

Neisser, U. 1967. *Cognitive Psychology*. New York: Appleton-Century-Crofts.

Neuringer, A. J. 1969. "Animals Respond for Food in the Presence of Free Food." *Science* 66: 399–401.

Noble, C. 1952. "An Analysis of Meaning." *Psychological Review* 59: 421–30.

Olds, J. 1956. "Pleasure Centers in the Brain." *Scientific American* 193: 105–16.

Olds, J., and Milner, P. 1954. "Positive Reinforcement Produced by Electrical Stimulation of Septal Area and Other Regions of the Rat Brain." *Journal of Comparative and Physiological Psychology* 47: 419–27.

Osgood, C. E. 1949. "The Similarity Paradox in Human Learning: A Resolution." *Psychological Review* 56: 132–43.

————. 1953. *Method and Theory of Experimental Psychology*. New York: Oxford University Press.

Osgood, C. E.; Souci, G. J.; and Tannenbaum, P. H. 1958. *The Measurement of Meaning*. Urbana: University of Illinois Press.

Paivio, A. 1967. "Learning of Adjective-Noun Paired-Associates as a Function of Adjective-Noun Word Order and Noun Abstractness." *Canadian Journal of Psychology* 17: 370–379.

——. 1971. *Imagery and Verbal Processes*. New York: Holt, Rinehart and Winston.

——. 1975. "Perceptual Comparisons through the Mind's Eye." *Memory and Cognition* 3: 635–47.

Paivio, A.; Yuille, J. C.; and Madigan, S. 1968. *Concreteness, Imagery, and Meaningfulness Values for 925 Nouns. Journal Experimental Psychology* Monograph Supplement Series, no. 76: 1, pt. 2.

Pavlov, I. P. 1927. *Conditioned Reflexes*. Anrep translation. London: Oxford University Press.

Peckstein, L. A., and Brown, F. D. 1939. "An Experimental Analysis of the Alleged Criteria of Insight Learning." *Journal of Educational Psychology* 30: 38–52.

Penfield, W. 1975. *The Mystery of the Mind*. Princeton, N.J.: Princeton University Press.

Penfield, W., and Rasmussen, T. 1950. *The Cerebral Cortex of Man*. New York: Macmillan.

Perky, C. W. 1910. "An Experimental Study of Imagination." *American Journal of Psychology* 21: 422–52.

Peterson, J. 1916. "The Effect of Attitude on Immediate and Delayed Reproduction: A Class Experiment." *Journal of Educational Psychology* 7: 523–33.

Peterson, L. R., and Peterson, M. J. 1959. "Short Term Retention of Individual Verbal Items." *Journal Experimental Psychology* 58: 193–98.

Piaget, J. 1954. *The Construction of Reality in the Child*. New York: Basic Books.

Plato. *Phaedo*. See any modern edition.

Posner, M. I., and Rossman, E. 1965. "Effect of Size and Location of Informational Transforms upon Short-Term Retention." *Journal Experimental Psychology* 70: 496–505.

Postman, L. 1975. "Verbal Learning and Memory." *Annual Review of Psychology* 26: 291–335.

Postman, L., and Adams, P. A. 1956. "Studies in Incidental Learning: III, Interserial Interference." *Journal Experimental Psychology* 51: 323–28.

———. 1957. "Studies in Incidental Learning: VI. *Journal Experimental Psychology* 54: 153–67.

———. 1960. "Studies in Incidental Learning: VIII, The Effects of Contextual Information." *Journal Experimental Psychology* 59: 153–64.

Postman, L., and Senders, V. L. 1946. "Incidental Learning and Generality of Set." *Journal Experimental Psychology* 36: 153–65.

Postman, L.; Adams, P. A.; and Phillips, L. W. 1955. "Studies in Incidental Learning: II, The Effects of Association Value and of the Method of Testing." *Journal Experimental Psychology* 49: 1–10.

Pratt, C. C. 1937. *The Logic of Modern Psychology*. New York: Macmillan.

Premack, D. 1970. "The Education of S*A*R*A*H." *Psychology Today* 4: 54–58.

Prewitt, E. P. 1967. "Number of Preconditioning Trials in Sensory Preconditioning Using CER Training." *Journal of Comparative and Physiological Psychology 64: 360–62.*

Putney, R. T.; Erwin, T. J.; and Smith, S. T., Jr. 1972. "The Facilitation of Conditioned Alpha Blocking with an Overt-Response." *Psychonomic Science* 26: 16–18.

Pylyshyn, Z. 1973. "What the Mind's Eye Tells the Mind's Brain." *Psychological Bulletin* 80: 1–22.

Reitman, J. S. 1971. "Mechanisms of Forgetting in Short-Term Memory." *Cognitive Psychology* 2: 185–95.

———. 1974. "Without Surreptitious Rehearsal, Information in Short-Term Memory Decays." *Journal of Verbal Learning and Verbal Behavior* 13: 365–77.

Rescorla, R. A. 1969. "Pavlovian Conditioned Inhibition." *Psychological Bulletin* 72: 77–94.

———. 1975. "Pavlovian Excitatory and Inhibitory Conditioning." In *Handbook of Learning and Cognitive Processes*, edited by W. K. Estes. New York: Halsted Press.

Richardson, A. 1969. *Mental Imagery*. London: Routledge & Kegan Paul.

Riesen, A. 1947. "The Development of Visual Perception in Man and Chimpanzee." *Science* 106: 107–8.

Robinson, E. S. 1932. *Association Theory Today.* New York: Century.

———. 1934. "Work of the Integrated Organism." In *Handbook of General Experimental Psychology*, edited by C. Murchison. Worcester, Mass.: Clark University Press.

Rock, I. 1957. "The Role of Repetition in Associative Learning." *American Journal of Psychology* 70: 186–93.

Roessler, R. L., and Brogden, W. J. 1943. "Conditioned Differentiation of Vasoconstriction to Subvocal Stimuli." *American Journal of Psychology* 41: 78–86.

Rogers, C. 1951. *Client-Centered Therapy.* Boston: Houghton Mifflin.

Romanes, G. J. 1882. *Animal Intelligence.* London: Kegan Paul, Trench.

Ross, J., and Lawrence, K. A. 1968. "Some Observations on Memory Artifice." *Psychonomic Science* 13: 107–8.

Rothkopf, E. I., and Bisbicos, E. E. 1967. "Selective Facilitative Effects of Interspersed Questions on Learning from Written Materials." *Journal of Educational Psychology* 58: 56–61.

Rousseau, J. J. 1762. *The Social Contract.* See any modern edition.

Russell, B. 1927. *Philosophy.* New York: W. W. Norton.

Russell, W. A., and Storms, L. H. 1955. "Implicit Verbal Chaining in Paired Associate Learning." *Journal Experimental Psychology* 49: 287–93.

Saltz, E. 1971. *The Cognitive Bases of Human Learning.* Homewood, Ill.: The Dorsey Press.

Saltzman, I. J. 1953. "The Orienting Task in Incidental and Intentional Learning." *American Journal of Psychology* 56: 593–97.

Schacter, S. 1977. "Nicotine Regulation in Heavy and Light Smokers." *Journal of Experimental Psychology: General* 106: 5–12.

Schlosberg, H. 1937. "The Relationship between Success and the Laws of Conditioning." *Psychological Review* 44: 37–394.

Schoenfeld, W. N.; Antonitis, J. J.; and Bersh, P. J. 1950. "A Preliminary Study of Training Conditions Necessary for Secondary Reinforcement." *Journal Experimental Psychology* 40: 40–45.

Sechenov, I. M. 1863. *Reflexes of the Brain.* Cambridge, Mass.: MIT Press, 1965.

Segal, E. 1964. "Demonstration of Acquired Distinctiveness of Cues Using a Paired-Associate Learning Task." *Journal Experimental Psychology* 67: 587–90.

Segal, S. 1970. "Processing of the Stimulus in Imagery and Perception." In *Imagery: Current Cognitive Approaches*, edited by S. Segal. New York: Academic Press.

Segal, S., and Fusella, V. 1970. "Influence of Imaged Pictures and Sounds on Detection of Visual and Auditory Signals." *Journal Experimental Psychology* 83: 458–64.

Seligman, M. E. P., and Hager, J. L. 1972. *Biological Boundaries of Learning.* New York: Appleton-Century-Crofts.

Senden, M. von. 1960. *Space and Sight: The Perception of Space and Shape in the Congenitally Blind Before and After Operation*, translated by P. Heath. London: Methuen.

Sheehan, P. W. 1967. "Reliability of a Short Test of Imagery." *Perceptual and Motor Skills* 25: 744.

Sheffield, F. D. 1961. "Theoretical Considerations in the Learning of Complex Sequential Tasks from Demonstration and Practice." In *Student Response in Programmed Instruction*, edited by A. A. Lumsdaine, pp. 13–32. Publication no. 943. Washington, D.C.: National Academy of Sciences, National Research Council.

Shepherd, R. N. and Meltzer, J. 1971. "Mental Rotation of Three-Dimensional Objects." *Science* 171: 701–3.

Sherrington, C. S. 1906. *Integrative Action of the Nervous System.* New York: Scribner.

Shipley, W. C. 1933. "An Apparent Transfer of Conditioning." *Journal of General Psychology* 8: 382–91.

Silver, C. A., and Meyer, D. R. 1954. "Temporal Factors in Sensory Preconditioning." *Journal Comparative and Physiological Psychology* 47: 57–59.

Simon, C. W., and Emmons, W. H. 1956. "Responses to Material Presented during Various Levels of Sleep." *Journal Experimental Psychology* 51: 89–97.

Skinner, B. F. 1938. *The Behavior of Organisms.* New York: Appleton-Century-Crofts.

———. 1947. *Verbal Behavior.* New York: Appleton-Century-Crofts.

———. 1948a. *Walden Two*. New York: Macmillan.

———. 1948b. "Superstition in the Pigeon." *Journal Experimental Psychology* 38: 168–72.

———. 1953. *Science and Human Behavior*. New York: Macmillan.

———. 1966. "The Philogeny and Ontology of Behavior." *Science* 153: 1205–13.

———. 1968. *The Technology of Teaching*. New York: Appleton-Century-Crofts.

———. 1971. *Beyond Freedom and Dignity*. New York: Alfred A. Knopf.

———. 1974. *About Behaviorism*. New York: Alfred A. Knopf.

Slamecka, N. 1964. "An Inquiry into the Doctrine of Remote Association." *Psychological Review* 71: 61–76.

Small, W. S. 1899. "Experimental Study of the Mental Processes of the Rat: II." *American Journal of Psychology* 11: 133–64.

Sokolov, E. N. 1957. "Higher Nervous Activity and the Problem of Perception." In *Psychology in the Soviet Union*, edited by B. Simon. Stanford, Calif.: Stanford University Press.

———. 1963. "Higher Nervous Functions: The Orienting Reflex." *Annual Review of Physiology* 25: 545–80.

Solomon, R. L. 1965. "Punishment." *American Psychologist* 19: 239–53.

Solomon, R. L., and Coles, M. R. 1954. "A Case of Failure of Generalization of Imitation across Drives and across Situations." *Journal of Abnormal and Social Psychology* 48: 291–302.

Spelt, D. K. 1948. "The Conditioning of the Human Fetus *in utero*." *Journal Experimental Psychology* 38: 338–46.

Spence, K. 1936. "The Nature of Discrimination Learning in Animals." *Psychological Review* 43: 427–49.

Spence, K. W. 1937. "The Differential Response in Animals to Stimuli Varying in a Single Dimension." *Psychological Review* 44: 430–44.

Spence, K. W. 1951. "Theoretical Interpretation of Learning." In *Handbook of Experimental Psychology*, edited by S. S. Stevens. New York: Wiley.

———. 1956. *Behavior Theory and Conditioning*. New Haven, Conn.: Yale University Press.

Spence, K. W., and Spence, J. A. 1953. "The Relation of Conditioned Response Strength to Anxiety in Normal, Neurotic, and Psychotic Subjects." *Journal Experimental Psychology* 45: 265–72.

Sperling, G. A. 1963. "A Model for Visual Memory Tasks." *Human Factors* 5: 19–31.

Spinoza, B. 1677. *The Ethics*. See any modern edition.

Staats, A. W. 1968. *Learning, Language, and Cognition*. New York: Holt, Rinehart and Winston.

Stout, G. F. 1899. *Manual of Psychology*. New York: Hinds and Noble.

Szasz, T. 1961. *The Myth of Mental Illness*. New York: Harper & Row.

Tait, R. W., and Suboski, M. D. 1972. "Stimulus Intensity of Sensory Preconditioning of Rats." *Canadian Journal of Psychology* 26: 374–81.

Thompson, R. F. 1976. "The Search for the Engram." *American Psychologist* 31: 209–27.

Thompson, W. R., and Heron, W. 1954. "The Effects of Restricting Early Experience on the Problem-Solving Capacity of Dogs." *Canadian Journal of Psychology* 8: 17–31.

Thorndike, E. L. 1898. *Animal Intelligence: An Experimental Study of the Associative Processes in Animals*. Psychological Review Monograph Supplement Series, 2, no. 8.

——— . 1913. *Educational Psychology: The Psychology of Learning*. Vol. 2. New York: Teachers College, Columbia University.

——— . 1932. *The Fundamentals of Learning*. New York: Teachers College, Columbia University.

Thorndike, E. L., and Lorge, I. 1944. *The Teacher's Word Book of 30,000 Words*. New York: Columbia University Press.

Thorndike, E. L., and Woodworth, R. S. 1901. "The Influence of Improvement in One Mental Function upon the Efficiency of Other Functions." *Psychological Review* 8: 247–61.

Thoreau, H. 1854. *Walden*. See any modern edition.

Thune, E. L. 1950. "The Effect of Different Types of Preliminary Activities on Subsequent Learning of Paired-Associate Material." *Journal of Experimental Psychology* 40: 423–38.

Titchener, E. B. 1909. *Lectures on the Experimental Psychology of the Thought Processes*. New York: Macmillan.

Tolman, E. C. 1932. *Purposive Behavior in Animals and Men*. New York: Appleton-Century-Crofts.

———. 1938. "The Determiners of Behavior at a Choice Point." *Psychological Review* 45: 1–41.

———. 1948. "Cognitive Maps in Rats and Men." *Psychological Review* 55: 189–208.

———. 1949. "There Is More Than One Kind of Learning." *Psychological Review* 56: 144–55.

Tolman, E. C., and Gleitman, H. 1949. "Studies in Learning and Motivation: I, Equal Reinforcements in Both End-Boxes, Followed by Shock in One End-Box." *Journal Experimental Psychology* 39: 810–19.

Tolman, E. C.; Hall, C. S.; and Bretnall, E. P. 1932. "A Disproof of the Law of Effect and a Substitution of the Laws of Emphasis Motivation, and Disruption." *Journal Experimental Psychology* 15: 601–14.

Tolman, E. C.; Ritchie, B. F.; and Kalish, D. 1946. "Studies in Spatial Learning: II, Place Learning versus Response Learning." *Journal Experimental Psychology* 36: 224–29.

Tulving, E. 1972. "Episodic and Semantic Memory." In *Organization of Memory*, edited by E. Tulving and W. Donaldson. New York: Academic Press.

———. 1974. "Cue Dependent Forgetting." *American Scientist* 62: 74–82.

Tulving, E., and Pearlstone, Z. 1966. "Availability versus Accessibility of Information in Memory for Words." *Journal of Verbal Learning and Verbal Behavior* 5: 381–91.

Twersky, B., and Sherman, T. 1975. "Picture Memory Improves with Longer On Time and Off Time." *Journal of Experimental Psychology: Human Learning and Memory* 1: 114–18.

Underwood, B. J., and Schultz, 1960. *Meaningfulness and Verbal Learning*. Chicago: J. B. Lippincott.

Voeks, V. 1948. "Postremity, Recency, and Frequency as Bases for Prediction in the Maze Situation." *Journal Experimental Psychology* 38: 495–510.

———. 1950. "Formalization and Clarification of a Theory of Learning." *Journal of Psychology* 30: 341–63.

———. 1954. "Acquisition of S——▶R Connections: A Test of Hull's and Guthrie's Theories." *Journal Experimental Psychology* 47: 137–47.

Walters, G., and Grusec, J. E. 1977. *Punishment*. San Francisco: W. H. Freeman.

Warden, C. J.; Fjeld, H. A.; and Koch, A. M. 1940. "Initiative Behavior in Cebus and Rhesus Monkeys." *The Journal of Genetic Psychology* 56: 311–22.

Washburn, M. 1916. *Movement and Mental Imagery*. Boston: Houghton Mifflin.

Watson, J. B. 1913. "Psychology as the Behaviorist Views It." *Psychological Review* 20: 158–77.

———. 1914. *Behavior*. New York: Henry Holt.

———. 1924. *Behaviorism*. New York: Norton.

Watson, J. B., and Raynor, R. 1920. "Conditioned Emotional Reactions." *Journal Experimental Psychology* 3: 1–14.

Weaver, G. E. 1974. "Effects of Post-Stimulus Study Time on Recognition of Pictures." *Journal Experimental Psychology* 103: 799–801.

Weaver, G. E., and Schultz, R. W. 1968. "Recall of A-B Following Varying Numbers of Trials of A-C Learning." *Journal Experimental Psychology* 78: 113–19.

Weisman, R. G. 1977. "On the Role of the Reinforcer in Associative Learning." In *Operant Pavlovian Interaction*, edited by H. Davis and H. Hurivitz. New York: Halsted Press.

Wendt, G. R. 1936. "An Interpretation of Inhibition of Conditioned Reflexes as Competition between Reaction Systems." *Psychological Review* 43: 258–81.

Wickens, D. D. 1940. "A Study of Conditioning in the Neonate." *Journal Experimental Psychology* 26: 94–102.

Wickens, D. D., and Briggs, G. E. 1951. "Mediated Stimulus Generalization as a Factor in Sensory Preconditioning." *Journal Experimental Psychology* 42: 197–200.

Wickens, D. D., and Cross, H. A. 1963. "Resistance to Extinction as a Function of Temporal Relations during Sensory Preconditioning." *Journal of Experimental Psychology* 65: 206–11.

Wickelgren, W. A. 1973. "The Long and Short of Memory." *Psychological Bulletin* 80: 425–38.

Williams, D. R., and Williams, H. 1969. "Auto-maintenance in the Pigeon; Sustained

Pecking Despite Contingent Non-reinforcement." *Journal of the Experimental Analysis of Behavior* 12: 511–20.

William, J. L. 1973. *Operant Learning: Procedures for Changing Behavior.* Monterey, Calif. Brooks/Cole.

Willis, J., and Giles, D. 1976. *Great Experiments in Behavior Modification.* Indianapolis, Ind.: Hackett.

Wilson, E. O. 1975. *Sociobiology: The New Synthesis.* Cambridge, Mass.: Belknap Press of Harvard University Press.

Woods, P. J. 1964. "A Taxonomy of Instrumental Conditioning." *American Psychologist* 29: 584–97.

Wolpe, J. 1958. *Psychotherapy as Reciprocal Inhibition.* Stanford, Calif.: Stanford University Press.

Woodworth, R. S. 1938. *Experimental Psychology.* New York: Holt.

Wundt, W. 1897. *Outlines of Psychology.* New York: Wilhelm Engleman.

Yates, F. A. 1966. *The Art of Memory.* Chicago: University of Chicago Press.

Zachs, R. T. 1969. "Invariance of Total Learning Time under Different Conditions of Practice." *Journal Experimental Psychology* 82: 441–47.

Name Index

Adams, P. A., 270, 271
Alberts, E., 215
Alger, Horatio, 107
Ammons, R. B., 304
Amsel, A., 126
Anderson, J. R., 201, 202
Aristotle, 31ff, 333
Aronfreed, J., 237
Asch, S., 217ff
Atkinson, R., 43, 249
Azrin, N. H., 350

Bahrick, H. P., 308, 314–15
Bahrick, P. O., 308, 314–15
Bain, A., 185
Baker, K. E., 227
Bandura, A., 236, 237
Barnes, J. M., 324
Bartlett, F. C., 289ff
Bass, M. J., 77–78
Battig, W. F., 138, 254, 255
Baumeister, A. A., 247
Beach, F., 56
Bekhterev, V., 101, 145
Berkeley, G., 33–34, 203
Bersh, P. J., 135
Betts, G. H., 190
Bilodeau, I. M., 323
Bisbicos, E. E., 288
Black, A. H., 339
Blodgett, H. C., 152ff
Boe, E. E., 77, 350
Boring, E. G., 186, 189
Bousfield, W. A., 254, 263
Bower, G., 29, 36, 111, 201, 286, 336
Brackett, H. R., 138, 255
Bransford, J. D., 291
Breland, K., 27
Breland, M., 27
Bretnall, E. P., 347
Briggs, G. E., 154
British empiricists, 33
Brogden, W. J., 154, 189, 193, 250, 259
Brown, F. D., 211

Brown, J. S., 170
Brown, P. L., 139
Brown, R., 261
Bugelski, B. R., 76, 115, 164, 170, 172, 190, 197, 201, 205, 247, 267–68, 272, 285, 299, 302, 342
Burt, H. E., 317
Bykov, K. M., 84

Cadwallader, T. C., 299
Cantor, G. N., 223
Capaldi, E. J., 97, 126
Carmichael, L., 65
Carrol, J., 261
Chomsky, N., 19, 26, 260ff
Church, R. N., 77, 350
Cohen, I., 21
Coles, M. R., 235
Conant, J. B., 331
Cook, J. O., 241
Cooper, E. H., 247
Craik, F. I. M., 279, 280–81, 337, 376
Cross, H. A., 154
Cunitz, A. R., 262

Dallenbach, K. M., 55, 295
Darwin, C., 60, 62ff, 106
Dean, P. J., 254
Deese, J., 263
DePaulo, P., 24
Descartes, R., 60ff, 258
Dewey, J., 92, 292
Dollard, J., 234, 235
Dooling, J. L., 256, 290
Dunlap, K., 365
Durant, A., 354
Durant, W., 354

Ebbinghaus, H., 37, 47, 49ff, 245, 254, 288, 291, 303, 308, 312–13, 317, 376
Ehrenfreund, D., 142, 215
Ellson, D., 154, 179, 189
Emmons, W. H., 380
Epstein, W., 255–56

Ervin, F. R., 26
Estes, W., 100, 251, 349

Farber, J. E., 250
Fechner, G. T., 47, 49
Finesmith, S., 174
Fitzgerald, R., 126
Fjeld, H. A., 235
Flanders, J. P., 235
Foss, D. J., 165
Franks, J. J., 291
Freud, S., 307, 354, 358
Fusella, V., 191

Gagne, R. M., 227
Galanter, E., 43, 189, 252
Galton, F., 36, 189, 201
Garcia, J., 26
Gardner, B. T., 26, 56, 258, 260
Gardner, R. A., 26, 56, 258, 260
Gates, A. J., 263, 269, 376
Gibson, E. J., 208, 225, 227, 228, 249–50,
    261, 297, 325
Giles, D., 363
Glanzer, M., 262
Glaze, J. A., 252
Gleitman, H., 152
Gluck, J. P., 24
Gormezano, I., 76, 140
Goss, A. E., 227
Grant, D., 105
Greenwald, A., 195, 196, 237
Gross, M. L., 366
Grube, G. M. A., 21
Grusec, J. E., 351
Guthrie, E. R., 64, 78, 89, 94, 97, 122,
    126, 134, 136, 139, 143, 145ff, 147,
    231, 237–38, 326, 333–34, 359, 364,
    365
Guttman, N., 78

Hall, C. S., 347
Hall, J. F., 100, 245
Hall, M., 62
Hamilton, W., 35, 47
Harcum, E. R., 246
Harlow, H. F., 24, 140–41, 220, 305
Harsch, C. M., 235

Hartley, D., 34, 73
Hayes, C., 260
Hayes, K., 246, 260
Hebb, D. O., 15, 55, 58ff, 66, 98, 99, 134,
    155ff, 157, 158, 189, 195, 205, 215,
    226, 237, 264, 283, 284, 310, 336,
    339
Herbart, J., 196
Herbert, M. J., 235
Hernnstein, R., 25
Heron, W., 66
Hilgard, E. R., 29, 36, 60, 81, 84, 102,
    103–4, 111, 121, 167, 253, 336
Hintzman, D. L., 139
Hobbes, T., 33, 73, 344
Hobhouse, L. T., 62
Hoffman, H. S., 24
Horton, D. L., 165
Horton, G. P., 147
Hovland, C. I., 78, 82, 219, 223, 248
Huey, E. B., 262
Hull, C. L., 15, 55, 59, 64, 82, 88, 89ff,
    113ff, 116, 118ff, 121, 135, 141, 144,
    152, 159, 162, 168, 190, 194, 203,
    248, 283, 325, 335, 339, 340
Hume, D., 186
Humphreys, L., 124, 126
Huxley, A., 16, 85

Irwin, J. McQ., 325
Ivanov-Smolensky, A. G., 259
Izawa, C., 255, 376

James, W., 97, 118, 185, 186, 194ff, 237,
    238, 283, 352
Jaynes, J., 61
Jenkins, H. M., 139
Jenkins, J., 165
Jenkins, J. C., 55, 295
Jenks, C., 25
Jensen, A., 25
Jones, M. C., 360
Jung, C., 37

Kagan, J. S., 24–25
Kalish, H. I., 78
Kamin, L., 25
Kant, I., 19

Kantor, J. R., 104
Kanungo, R., 299
Katkin, E., 368–69
Kehoe, J., 140
Keller, F., 246
Kelly, E. L., 154–55
Keppel, G., 306, 310
Kidd, E., 42, 285
Kiess, H. O., 253
Kimble, G., 121–22, 124, 126, 167, 367
Kinkade, K., 353
Kistler, D., 247
Kjeldergaard, P. M., 165
Koch, A. M., 235
Koffka, K., 47, 219
Köhler, W., 47, 211
Konorski, J., 101, 102, 105, 131, 366
Kotarbinski, T., 9–10
Krasner, L., 364
Krasner, M., 364
Kretchevsky, I., 142, 252
Kurtz, K., 219, 223

Lachman, R., 256, 290
Landauer, T. K., 323
Langfeld, H. S., 186
Lashley, K., 93, 97ff
Lawrence, D. H., 228
Lawrence, K. A., 42
Lester, O. P., 25, 320
Leuba, C., 149, 155, 179, 187, 189, 192
Levin, H., 228–29, 261
Lick, J., 361–62
Limberg, J., 258
Lindley, R. H., 254
Locke, J., 8, 18, 33
Lockhart, R. S., 279, 337, 376
Loftus, G., 248–49
Logan, F., 97
Lorayne, H., 41, 320
Lorenz, K., 23, 24
Lucas, J., 41, 320
Luria, A., 41

Madigan, S., 190, 253–54
Mandler, G., 254
Marquis, D., 81, 84, 102–3, 104, 127, 167
Marsten-Wilson, W., 283

Martin, E., 205, 299
Marx, M., 100
Masson, M. E., 272
May, M, 116
McDaniel, M. A., 272
McDougall, W., 22
McGeoch, J., 10, 111, 245, 296, 319–20,
    322, 325, 326
McKeachie, W., 371
McLaughlin, B., 269
Mechanic, A., 270, 271
Melton, A., 310, 325
Meltzer, J., 191
Meyer, D. R., 154
Mill, J., 36
Mill, J. S., 35
Miller, G., 43, 189, 252
Miller, N. E., 167, 170, 195, 234, 367ff
Miller, S., 101, 105, 131, 366
Milner, B., 368
Minami, H., 295
Montague, A., 23
Montague, W. E., 253, 254
Moore, B., 139
Moore, J. W., 76
Mowrer, O. H., 32, 85, 133, 134, 135,
    136, 139, 140, 166ff, 187, 189, 194,
    199, 236, 261, 283, 285, 340, 351,
    354ff, 367, 374
Müller, G., 54ff
Murdock, B., 247, 310, 326
Murray, N., 368–69

Neisser, U., 188
Neuringer, A. J., 118
Noble, C., 201, 253, 283
Norman, D. A., 375

Odum, P. B., 165
Olds, J., 368
Orwell, G., 19
Osgood, C. E., 200ff, 205, 226, 245, 252,
    283, 297ff, 303, 304

Paivio, A., 190, 199, 200, 201, 204, 205,
    252, 253–54, 255, 283, 285
Pantle, A. J., 247
Pavlov, I. P., 15, 47, 60, 69ff, 101, 110,

121, 122, 134, 139–40, 144, 204, 220, 259, 339, 341, 360
Pearlstone, Z., 323, 325
Peckstein, L. A., 211
Penfield, W., 188, 322, 325
Perky, C. W., 187, 189
Peterson, J., 254
Peterson, L. R., 310
Peterson, M. J., 310
Phillips, A. W., 270
Piaget, J., 21
Pilzecker, A., 54
Plato, 21, 31
Posner, M. I., 275, 310
Postman, L., 270, 271, 288, 306, 310–11
Pratt, C. C., 331
Premack, D., 26, 56, 258
Prewitt, E. P., 154
Pribram, K. H., 43, 189, 252
Pylyshyn, Z., 201–2

Rasmussen, T., 189
Raynor, R., 116, 169, 360
Reitman, J. S., 276
Rescorla, R. A., 81
Richardson, A., 186, 206
Riesen, A., 209–10
Robinson, E. S., 39, 82
Rock, I., 143, 246, 325
Roessler, 250, 259
Rogers, C., 340, 359
Romanes, G. J., 62, 235
Ross, D., 236
Ross, J., 42
Ross, S. A., 236
Rossman, E., 275, 310
Rothkopf, E. I., 288
Roussel, J., 126
Rousseau, J. J., 343
Russell, B., 332
Russell, W. A., 164–65

Saltz, E., 220, 223ff, 269, 271, 335
Saltzman, I. J., 271
Schacter, S., 365
Schlosberg, H., 84, 323
Schoenfeld, W. N., 135
Schultz, R. W., 165, 219

Sechenov, I. M., 70
Segal, E., 228
Segal, S., 188, 191, 192
Segmen, J., 42, 285
Seligman, M. E. P., 26, 27
Senders, V., 288
Sharlock, D., 164
Sheehan, P. W., 190
Sheffield, F. O., 149, 155, 158, 166, 179, 187
Shepherd, R. N., 191
Sherman, T., 309
Sherrington, C., 87
Shipley, W. C., 163
Silver, C. A., 154
Silver, D., 271
Simon, C. W., 380
Simonides, 41
Skinner, B. F., 15, 23, 59, 64, 97, 102, 104ff, 109, 111, 113, 114ff, 118ff, 121, 122, 127, 144, 159–60, 162, 175, 188, 196, 198–99, 228, 234, 236, 240, 241, 251, 259ff, 336, 340, 341, 344–45, 348, 349, 350ff, 362, 373
Slamecka, N., 53
Small, W. S., 57
Socrates, 8, 9, 19, 21
Sokolov, E. N., 71, 72, 220, 277
Solomon, R. L., 235, 350
Spelt, D. K., 65
Spence, J. T., 250
Spence, K., 89, 134, 142, 212ff, 250
Sperling, G. A., 275
Spinoza, B., 32, 319, 334–35
Staats, A. W., 251, 259, 261
Storms, L. H., 164–65
Stout, G. F., 185, 187
Suboski, M. D., 154
Suomi, S. J., 24
Szasz, T., 357

Tait, R. W., 154
Thompson, R. F., 87
Thompson, W. R., 66, 210
Thoreau, H., 117
Thorndike, E. L., 15, 47, 60, 62–63, 70, 102, 105ff, 115–16, 117, 118ff, 134, 144, 159, 162, 234, 235, 277,

299–300, 335–36, 343, 349, 350, 352
Thune, E. L., 305
Titchener, E. B., 185
Tolman, E. C., 14, 15, 64, 94ff, 105, 122, 134, 136, 158, 235, 283, 340, 349
Tulving, E., 143, 254, 263, 281, 308, 316, 323, 325, 326
Twersky, B., 309
Tyler, L. K., 283

Underwood, B., 219, 310, 324
Unger, T., 361

Voeks, V., 73, 149, 334–35
Von Restorff, H., 36
von Senden, M., 209, 220

Walk, R. D., 208, 225
Walters, G., 351
Walters, R. H., 236
Warden, C. J., 235
Washburn, M., 186
Watson, J. B., 15, 18ff, 65, 69, 85, 86, 101, 111, 116, 122, 144–45, 158, 169,

185, 234, 259, 360
Weaver, G. E., 165
Weber, E. H., 47
Weisman, R. G., 39–40
Weld, H. P., 186
Wendt, G. R., 81, 240
Wertheimer, M., 47, 210
Wickelgren, W. A., 310–11
Wickens, D. D., 65, 154
Wickens, T. D., 249
Williams, D. R., 139
Williams, J. L., 125, 135, 139
Willis, J., 363
Wilson, E. O., 23
Wittlinger, R. P., 308, 314–15
Wolpe, J., 360–61
Woods, P. J., 105
Woodworth, R. S., 245, 299–300
Wundt, W., 36, 185, 210, 283

Yates, F., 41
Yuille, J. C., 190, 253–54

Zachs, R. T., 247
Zavortink, B., 306, 310–11

Subject Index

abstract and concrete, 203–4
accessibility: and availability, 307
acquired distinctiveness of cues, 227
acquired drive, 116, 168–69
acquired equivalence of cues, 227
active avoidance, 170, 348
acts vs. movements, 143, 145–46
aggression, 23, 345–46
alpha wave cessation, 179
altruism, 23
animal research, 56, 66, 257–58
annoyers, 349, 352
antedating, 75, 312
anticipation method, 50, 138, 255
anti-intentional learning, 269
anxiety: as a drive, 250
approach: as a response, 97
association: basic postulate, 333; and conditioning, 158; laws of, 31–34, 38, 54; value, 54, 252
A/S (association area/sensory area) ratio, 58
associative shifting, law of, 109–10
attention, 109, 338, 342; and learning, 276–77, 277–78
autonomic nervous system: 84; and conditioning, 122 [to verbal cues, 250]
autoshaping, 139
aversive stimuli, 340, 347
avoidance learning, 96, 101, 103, 347

backward conditioning, 75
behavior, 15; control of, 9, 119, 138, 339–40, 364; disorders, 357–58; distinction from learning, 119
behavior modification, 359–60, 362ff
behavior therapy, 360–62
behavioral route, 151
behaviorism, 15, 63, 85, 150, 339–40
belongingness, 110
beta method, 365
biofeedback, 366–69

categories of learning, 103, 105, 167
cell assemblies, 156–58, 166, 226, 237
chaining, 128, 131ff, 341
chance responses, 106
Clever Hans, 67, 258
clustering, 110, 263–64
cognition, 151, 165
cognitive psychology, 183–84
computer language, 256
concepts, 203
conceptual nervous system, 156
concreteness-abstractness, 254
conditional stimulus, 72
conditioned emotional response, 83, 351
conditioned inhibition, 74, 80
conditioned response: difference from unconditioned response, 93
conditioned sensations, 155, 174
conditioning: as association, 39–40; [of images, 335]; classical, 69, 71, 73; and learning 102–3, 145; sensory-sensory, 153, 155; variety, 84
conditions for learning, 374
conflict behavior, 170–71, 352; neurotic, 354
connected discourse, 288
consolidation theory, 54
contiguity, 31, 148, 333
continuity, 114, 140–41, 249
copying behavior, 238
counter-conditioning, 360
cramming, 247–48, 382
crime, 353
cumulative curves, 124
curiosity reflex, 71, 276
cybernetics, 176

deduction, 233
delayed conditioning, 76, 163
deprivation, 118
depth perception, 208
determinism, 344–45
deterrence, 346

differential response, 226; stimuli, 335,
    379–80
disappointment, 175–76
discriminated stimulus, 119, 127–28, 228
discrimination, 28, 78–79, 221ff, 227,
    229, 284, 335, 379–80
disinhibition, 81
displacement theory of forgetting,
    321–22
disuse (decay theory of forgetting), 321
drive, 113; decrement, 176; increment,
    176
dual theory of learning, 169

early and late learning, 65–66, 219,
    284–85
education, 370, 371
effect, law of, 9, 103, 107–8, 110–11, 343
emotion: learning of, 65, 86–87, 171–72;
    and meaning, 200, 285, 340–41
empirical law of effect, 111
empiricism, 18
environment, role of, 66
episodic memory, 311
escape learning, 101, 103, 347
ethology, 22
exercise, law of, 108
expectancy, 150, 157, 284
experimental epistemology, 29
experimental neurosis, 360
external inhibition, 80
extinction, 73, 81; curves, 124; and
    forgetting, 324; and punishment,
    352; therapy, 365

faculty psychology, 20
familiarization: as first stage learning,
    219, 225
fear: as acquired drive, 116; in Mowrer's
    theory, 171; in punishment, 351
feedback, 176, 228, 369
first stage learning, 225
fixed interval schedules, 123
fixed ratio schedules, 123
forgetting: curves, 53, 313; and
    extinction, 324; theories, 320–22
fractional antedating goal response, 88ff,
    152, 232, 237, 283, 341; as a

mediator, 165, 194, 205; as a
    motivator, 341
Francini brothers, 61
free association, 30, 37
free recall, 110, 254
frequency, 54, 73, 334
functional disorders, 357

generalization, 77–78, 203, 232; and
    abstraction, 203; and
    discrimination, 221, 333, 364; of
    excitation, 213–14; of extinction,
    213–14
genetics (*see* heredity), 65
Gestalt approaches, 47, 210–11
goal gradient, 88

habit-family hierarcy, 90–91
habit strength, 114
hallucinations, 154
hedonism, 176
heredity, 65; and I.Q., 25
higher-order conditioning, 75
hope, 171, 173
how to study, 370
hypothetical constructs, 190, 191

iconic memory, 275
ideomotor action, 194, 237, 238, 239,
    341, 352, 353
imagery, 34, 150, 155, 158, 166, 174,
    185ff, 205, 206; and concepts, 203;
    cross-modal, 191; and imitation,
    237; in incidental learning, 267–68;
    as inner behavior, 188; and
    meaning, 198, 285, 291, 338, 304,
    342; as a response, 187, 192; in
    therapy, 361, 368, 376
imitation, 111, 153, 231ff, 233ff; and
    superstition, 242, 260, 374
imprinting, 24
incentive, 136, 341
incidental learning, 266–67;
    experimental designs of, 267, 276
individual differences, 293
information acquisition, 231
inhibition of delay, 76
initiation of behavior, 127, 194

insight, 22, 47, 211, 219
instinct, 22–23
instrumental associations, 158, 162; as unlearned responses, 170
instrumental learning, 101, 103, 105, 121–22
intellectual skills, 231
intent to learn, 266, 269, 272, 375
intent to remember, 319–20
interference theory of forgetting, 296, 322
intervening variable, 25, 191
intralist associations, 263
isolation, law of, 32, 335
invention in learning, 381

Kent-Rosanoff test, 37
kinesthetic feedback, 100, 102

language: in apes, 26, 257–58, 260–61; in babies (Mowrer theory), 177
Lashley jumping stand, 142
latent learning, 152–53, 339
learnability of materials, 252
learning: without action, 206; definition, 11, 64, 75; by doing, 111; early and late, 65–66; how to, 141, 305–6; as an inference, 10; and memory, 291; in neonates, 65–66; and performance, 15, 152; and practice, 10; sets, 141, 220–21, 305–6
lectures, 378–79
linguistics: and heredity, 26; and learning, 255
Little Albert, 169, 360
loci et res, 41
long term memory, 311

massed learning, 247–48
meaning: in cognitive psychology, 183–84, 199–200; of language, 199–200; in learning, 280–81, 283–85, 376
meaningfulness (m), 201
mediation, 163; unconscious, 283, 341; verbal, 164
memory: and computers, 256;

content related, 312; and retention, 308; time related, 309
mental illness, 357
Miller-Mowrer demonstration box, 116, 168
mind-body problem, 61
mnemonics, 40ff, 264, 382
modified free recall, 255
modified modified free recall, 255
morality, 353
motivation: and learning, 273, 336–37, 340; theory of, 179
motor equivalence, 87
movements, learning of, 149
movement-produced stimuli, 147, 163–64, 166, 171, 196, 238, 333, 341

nativism, 18, 19, 208
negative practice, 365
neonates: learning in, 65–66
nonintentional learning, 266
nonsense syllables: and conditioning, 249–50; as paired associates, 42, 302; rejection of, 252, 282; in serial order, 38, 50
nonspecific transfer, 304

observation: learning by (*see* imitation)
observing responses, 318, 220, 229
one kind of learning theory, 173, 367
one-trial learning, 143; and insight, 219, 334, 335
operant behavior, 104, 113, 194
operant rate, 362–63
orienting reflex, 71, 72, 220
orienting tasks, 265–66; kinds of, 267, 270–71, 274–75, 278, 376
overlearning, 318

paired associates: method of, 42, 302
partial reinforcement, 122; explanations of, 124
passive avoidance, 170, 347
past experience effects, 298–99
perceptual learning, 226–27
performance, 15, 119, 150, 339–40
periodic reinforcement, 122–23
perseveration theory, 54

phase sequence, 157
place versus response learning, 93
position habits, 142
postremity, 334
practice, 141
prediction (of behavior), 339
preparatory set, 278
preparedness, 27
primacy effect, 262
primary reinforcement, law of, 113–14
proactive facilitation, 294, 298
proactive inhibition, 294–95; and short-
    term memory, 310
proactive interference, 294, 301
probe technique, 326
problem solving, 105
processing: levels of, 274, 279, 280, 337,
    376
programmed learning, 336, 378
pronounceability, 254
propaganda, 243
propositional models of meaning, 201–2
proprioceptive stimuli (*see* movement-
    produced stimuli)
psychic reflexes, 70
psycholinguistics, 257
psychotherapy, 359
punishment, 110–11, 117, 340, 343ff;
    definitions of, 346–48; function of,
    349
pure stimulus act, 135 (*see* fractional
    antedating response)
"putting through," 131

rationalism, 8, 344
reactive inhibition, 64, 82, 248
readiness, law of, 275–76, 277
reading, 228, 261, 377
recall, 316
recency effect, 262
recency, law of, 148
recognition, 315, 325
redintegration, 35–36
reflex, 62; in conditioning, 85–86
rehabilitation, 346
rehearsal, 263
reinforcement, 113, 117, 118; learned,
    129; as motivation, 242–43; theory,

105; as an unconditioned stimulus,
    173, 340–41 (*see* reward)
reism, 9–10, 203
relationships: response to, 212
relaxation, in therapy, 361
relearning, 317, 381–82
relief, 175
remembering, 307
remote associations, 51
repetition, 246
respondent behavior, 104
response classes, 160
response features, 97; rapid serial, 97–98;
    sensory, 149
response substitution, 105
retaliation, 345
retention, 251, 293, 307ff; methods of
    measurement, 315–17
retrieval, 254, 322, 325, 382
retroactive inhibition, 32, 294, 295, 298
retroactive interference, 318
reward, 9, 113; and behavior control,
    340; and learning, 103, 146, 148, 171
rote learning, 246

satisfiers and annoyers, 108, 352
savings score, 53, 308, 317, 327
schedules of reinforcement, 122; fixed
    interval, 123; fixed ratio, 123;
    variable interval, 123; variable ratio,
    123
schemas, 289
secondary drives, 114, 116
secondary reinforcer, 115, 129; as
    incentive, 134
secondary reward: as a type of learning,
    103
second learning stage, 230
second signal system, 204, 259
semantic differential, 200
semantic memory, 311–12
sensory preconditioning, 154
sensory responses, 149
sensory-sensory conditioning, 153, 173,
    193, 235
serial order effects, 42, 50, 51
serial responses, 98, 133
set, 278, 288

shaping, 119, 128ff
short-term memory, 256, 275, 309–10
show and tell, 231ff
sign—significate, 134
similarity: in forgetting, 297
skills: learning of, 172–73
sleep: learning in, 55, 380
spaced versus massed learning, 247–48
species-specific factors, 26
split-brain, 339
spontaneous recovery, 74; of verbal
    material, 250, 324
stimulus complex, 147, 220
stimulus—response formula, 12, 145,
    157–58, 159, 165, 166, 183, 341
stimulus substitution (S—S), 72–73,
    150, 173
stimulus trace, 53, 76, 325
strategies in verbal learning, 251, 254,
    255, 262; imposed strategies, 265,
    375–76
structural disorders, 357
students as teachers, 380
study-test method, 138, 255, 376
subjective organization, 254, 265
subjects in learning experiments, 66;
    experimenter bias, 67; subject bias,
    67, 371
superstition, 240ff
suppression, 349, 351
symptoms: treatment of, 358
synesthesia, 154

tags for recall, 381–82
talking birds, 177, 236, 374
talking and thinking, 198
teachers: functions of, 372; as models,
    372, 374
teaching, 371
teaching machines, 336
temporal conditioning, 76
temporal factors in conditioning, 75, 76
temptation, 350, 353
time and learning, 246–47, 334, 374–75
token reinforcement, 363
total time principle, 247
trace conditioning, 76
transfer, 292; negative, 294, 298, 301;
    positive, 294, 298; and retroaction,
    297–98, 299; of training, 292, 293
trial and error, 107
two-stage learning, 219, 224

unconditioned stimulus, 72; as a
    reinforcer, 74
understanding, 281
unlearned knowledge, 232

variable interval schedules, 123
variable ratio schedules, 123
verbal learning, 160–61, 245ff
voluntary behavior, 102, 104, 194–95

warm-up, 304, 383
what is learned, 338
work (of learning), 280

About the Author

B. R. BUGELSKI is Distinguished Professor of Psychology at the State University of New York at Buffalo. He received his doctorate from Yale University and has taught at Antioch College, the University of Toledo, and the University of Buffalo. He chaired the Psychology Department at S.U.N.Y.A.B. and was President of the Eastern Psychological Association.

His research has been in the area of learning, animal and human, and he has published over 40 papers in professional journals dealing with learning and memory. Of late, his research has been primarily in the area of imagery, which is a rapidly developing field. The imagery studies and related topics of imitation and information processing have led to the development of a consolidated theory of learning, which is the subject of this book.

RELATED TITLES
Published by
Praeger Special Studies

THE ORIGINS OF THE NUMBER CONCEPT
Charles J. Brainerd

ORGANIZATION IN VISION: Essays on Gestalt Perception
Gaetano Kanizsa

THE NEUROPSYCHOLOGY OF DEVELOPMENTAL READING DISORDERS
Francis J. Pirozzolo